Connected Business

Oliver Gassmann • Fabrizio Ferrandina
Editors

Connected Business

Create Value in a Networked Economy

 Springer

Editors
Oliver Gassmann
ITEM-HSG
University of St. Gallen
St. Gallen, Switzerland

Fabrizio Ferrandina
Zühlke Engineering
Zühlke Group
Eschborn, Germany

ISBN 978-3-030-76896-6   ISBN 978-3-030-76897-3   (eBook)
https://doi.org/10.1007/978-3-030-76897-3

This Springer imprint is published by the registered company Springer Nature Switzerland AG.
The registered company address is: Gewerbestrasse 11, 6330 Cham, Switzerland

Preface

"Software is eating the world," this statement has become a matter of course, but is this still valid in a global networked business setting? Most valuable companies such as *Google, Amazon, Facebook, Apple, Microsoft, Alibaba,* and *Tencent* owe their success to connected rather than standalone software. These star companies are the ones that get the headlines but thousands of innovative companies in practically every industry have been busy making the transformation to smart and connected products and processes—from cars, machines, tools, and consumer products to digital pills. As part of the digitalization process, most innovative companies are jumping into the Internet of Things (IoT), which has emerged from smart products and is now evolving through the Artificial Intelligence (AI) revolution and new business models into the Economy of Things (EoT).

The potential of connected business based on IoT is huge. Currently, it is estimated that there are 25 billion connected devices worldwide; by 2030, this number is expected to rise to 50 billion. Today, everything creates enormous amounts of data—for example, a premium car generates up to 25 Gbytes/h. Of all the available data in today's world, 90% has been created within the last 2 years. Whether it is products, processes, things, humans, or companies, we are witnessing an exponential development in connectivity. Everybody wants to participate in the networked economy.

But success is not equally distributed. It is not enough to add IoT to your products, to digitalize your processes, or to create digital twins. Many companies fail and that includes several large technology companies. *GE Digital's* investment of billions of dollars in its IoT platform ended in a disaster; *Siemens's* Mindsphere platform did not deliver the expected results; *Ford's* new division, Smart Mobility, strayed too far away from the company's core business and consequently failed; *P&G* intended to become the "the most digitally enabled company in the world" but was let down by its unfocussed approach; *Daimler, Audi,* and *Volkswagen* have been catching up with *Tesla* in connected cars but still have major challenges ahead. The failure of hundreds of connected business initiatives has been obfuscated by business cases that have been grandiosely embellished. The truth of the matter is that companies fell for the hype of a new technology without understanding fundamental customer needs and the real essence of the business value they hoped to create.

Many years of research and experience in strategic projects for clients worldwide in dozens of industries have taught us one thing: the key to all connected business initiatives, without exception, is to create and capture business value. This is certainly true for every initiative, connectivity intrinsically allows a large amount of underlying business models, though. To avoid ineffectual investments, it is therefore all the more important to identify a priori those ones with a high-value potential.

This book is all about *how* to create and capture business value in the networked economy—for your customers, your partners in the ecosystem, and your own company. Many questions arise from its pursuit: What are the cornerstones of your new business model in terms of target customers, value proposition, supply chain architecture, and revenue model? How can you develop and orchestrate an ecosystem along the customer journey? How do you innovate business processes using end-to-end thinking? What are the success factors in developing multi-sided platforms? How can you use AI and machine learning for smart decision-making? How is it possible to create sustainable business models with a triple bottom-line impact for profit, people, and planet? How can companies use cybersecurity strategies to reduce the vulnerability of connected businesses? How should you tackle the digital transformer's dilemma and address the old and the new S-curves at the same time? What are the most critical success factors in setting up experiments for connected business initiatives? What are the network specialities for patent strategy, scale-up metrics, and business models? What can we learn about success and failure from projects undertaken by the hidden champions among manufacturing companies—both large multinationals and SMEs—beyond the triumphant stories of the glorious big five tech companies?

In order to address these questions, we asked leading authors from academia, consulting, and industry to share their knowledge and experience on how to create value in the networked economy. This book is divided into three parts:

Part I: "Exploring the Networked Economy" addresses the basic concepts and strategies of the networked economy, platform economics, ecosystems, sustainable AI, and IoT. Deep dives are taken into three essential industries such as health care, mobility, and industry 4.0.

Part II: "Management Strategies for Connected Business" focuses, at company level, on the digital transformer's dilemma concerning the two S-curves, the power of business experiments and their practical criteria, success factors in driving connected business initiatives, the potential that AI and machine learning has for decision making in the connected business arena, cybersecurity strategies in networked companies, and patent strategies for players in the networked economy.

Part III: "Case Studies on Connected Business" offers valuable lessons on various topics described by companies such as *4Players, ABB, AGL, AgriCircle, BASF, Bosch, Cambridge Analytica, Covestro, EnBW, Georg Fischer, Linde, Marquard Media, Siemens, Vontobel,* and *Zühlke.* All cases offer valuable lessons and advice that you can cherry-pick for your own journey. At the conclusion of each chapter, we have added a summary box with the success factors and lessons learned for hard-pressed readers.

The COVID-19 crisis has demonstrated that connected business is even more important than had first been envisioned. As research has shown, crises do not usually lead to trend reversal but rather to trend acceleration. Some industries have experienced real leapfrogging effects in achieving ubiquitous connectivity throughout their business networks. And so, the lesson to draw is that being connected is vitally important if business value is to be created. Given this ever more pressing need to create a superior journey for your customer, to integrate your partners, and to leverage your core competencies, the publication of this book would appear to be opportune.

We hope that you, our readers, will obtain interesting insights, and we wish you every success in implementing your connected business strategy and securing a sustainable competitive advantage. The bottom line remains: create and capture business value.

St. Gallen, Switzerland   Oliver Gassmann
Eschborn, Germany   Fabrizio Ferrandina
March 2021

Acknowledgement

This book has resulted from the efforts of many. First, we would like to thank our authors for giving their valuable time, their expertise, and their deep knowledge to write the chapters. We must also thank them for their patience throughout the extensive "revise and resubmit" process to achieve consistency as well as quality we have obtained in our final product.

We would like to thank Dr. Florian Huber and Hanna Bencseky for their steadfast dedication and support in editing this book, which we greatly appreciate. Our thanks goes to Dr. Prashanth Mahagaonkar and Ruth Milewski of Springer for their unstinting help throughout the entire publication process.

We are grateful to Philipp Sutter and many of our Zühlke colleagues for their encouragement, their constructive comments, and their invaluable insights, for which this book is all the better.

Contents

About the Editors

Oliver Gassmann, Prof. Dr., is Professor for Technology Management at the University of St. Gallen and Director of the Institute of Technology Management since 2002. His research focus lies on patterns and success factors of innovation. He has been visiting faculty at Berkeley (2007), Stanford (2012), and Harvard (2016). Prior to his academic career, Gassmann was the head of corporate research at Schindler. His more than 400 publications are highly cited, his book "The Business Model Navigator" became a global bestseller. He received the Scholarly Impact Award of the Journal of Management in 2014. He founded several spin-offs, is member of several boards of directors, like Zühlke, and an internationally recognized keynote speaker.

Fabrizio Ferrandina is Partner and CEO of the Zühlke Group, a global innovation service provider. Until 2018, he was CEO of the German subsidiary and member of the Zühlke Group Executive Board. His career has been dedicated to driving software and system projects for clients all over the world. Prior to his industry career, he worked as a researcher at the University of Frankfurt with a focus on software and data engineering where he published several scientific papers. He holds a degree in electronics engineering from the Università Politecnico di Milano, Italy and a postmaster MBA from CEFRIEL, Milan.

List of Figures

Digital Health Interventions

Mobility: From Autonomous Driving Towards Mobility-as-a-Service

Industry 4.0: Navigating Pathways Toward Smart Manufacturing and Services

Digital Transformer's Dilemma: Innovate Twice to Survive

Driving Connected Business Initiatives: Do's and Dont's

Patent Strategies in the Networked Economy

Bosch IoT Suite: Exploiting the Potential of Smart Connected Products

GF Machining Solutions: Real-Time Manufacturing Process in a Cloud Environment

Linde: Business Value with Connected Cylinders in Hospitals

Siemens: UK's First Fully Converted Electric Avenue "W9"

Groupon: Managing a Rapidly Growing Platform with Scale-Up Metrics

Cambridge Analytica: Magical Rise, Disastrous Fall

List of Tables

Part I

Exploring the Networked Economy

Connected Business: Creating Value in the Networked Economy

Oliver Gassmann and Fabrizio Ferrandina

The networked economy has become the main paradigm in today's business world; it is the emerging economic order within the information-based society. Products and services are created, produced, and distributed on networks, platforms, and ecosystems along the customer journey. The base of the networked economy on a company level consists of connected businesses where most products, processes, and services become smart and connected. It began with cars, machines, consumer electronics, and now embraces everything from connected oxygen cylinders in hospitals (e.g., *Linde*) and connected cows in agriculture (e.g., *Medria*) to connected, smart dust with sensor networks on the micrometer level to detect light, vibration, and chemicals (e.g., *IBM*). Technologically, the Internet of things (IoT) has built a bridge between these physical worlds and the world of bits and bytes. At its root, IoT analyzes products in real time while customers are using them. As a result, B2B can become B2B2C where the value chains come closer together. At the same time, however, they become more fragile and vulnerable as the COVID-19 crisis in 2020 has shown.

O. Gassmann (✉)
Institute of Technology Management, University of St. Gallen,
St. Gallen, Switzerland
e-mail: oliver.gassmann@unisg.ch

F. Ferrandina
Zühlke Group, Zürich, Switzerland
e-mail: Fabrizio.Ferrandina@zuehlke.com

O. Gassmann, F. Ferrandina (eds.), *Connected Business*,
https://doi.org/10.1007/978-3-030-76897-3_1

3

Connectivity is ubiquitous, from the connection of companies like *Amazon* with *Apple* to the connectivity of simple functions. *BMW*'s seat heating will allow owners to make a booking on a monthly basis with the touch of a button. The car manufacturer can now update not only the vehicle's infotainment system over the air but also every single line of code in the car's computer systems. Hardware features such as a seat heater, already installed, can be activated by customers at any time after purchase. Additional features will be offered on a monthly subscription basis. For example, customers could deactivate the seat heating system in summer and save money. The advantage for *BMW* is obvious: the production process is simplified because "everything" is built into every car. The activation of additional features will be only a matter of the business model applied.

Today's business leaders differ greatly in their response to the opportunities that the networked economy offers. And so it is extremely important that certain misunderstandings on connected business are set straight:

1. *Be afraid and freeze.* "Connected business is the digital storm of destruction which threatens the existence of our company. Companies are afraid and decide not to compete with the same weapons *Amazon* and *Google*, as an example, are using." Instead of exploring the opportunities of the networked economy and launching their own initiatives, these companies are frozen like rabbits in the headlights. Digitalization is seen as a competence belonging to others, as the CEO of a medium-sized manufacturing company intimated: "These digital players are threatening us, but software is not our core competence. We concentrate on our core business, which is non-digital." The result is that the opportunities to explore connected business are missed.

2. *Delegate to R&D.* Some managers believe, "Connected business is just 'innovation on the chip'." In other words, connectivity is viewed as falling naturally within the remit of R&D or the IT department. It's their job to create products that have sensors, are able to communicate, and provide connectivity for all processes. This purely technological view leads companies to develop over-engineered products that are generally too expensive. When customer perspectives are ignored and the full potential of connected business is downplayed, the business books tend to fill up with innovation flops. In particular, technologically oriented machinery companies are tempted to delegate digitalization to R&D, and the reason is obvious. That inside-out approach often worked in the past.

3. *Hire a chief digital officer.* There is also this belief that "we only need a chief digital officer where all digitalization is concentrated. He or she will digi-

talize our company and build up the connected business." This underestimates the efforts that business leaders need to make—as *Volkswagen* painfully experienced a few years ago. Establishing a chief digital officer's position is a perfectly sound starting point. However, a successful transformation requires business leaders to give their full commitment and buy into the company's journey of digital transformation. It has to be written in bold letters into the job description of every business leader. As happened with the creation of chief quality officers in the 1980s and 1990s, these chief digital officers will experience a first flush of enthusiasm and heightened awareness but will soon falter when confronted with the fundamental nature of the changes required. Often these positions degenerate into what can only be described as staff functionaries, who fail to exercise a sustainable impact on the business.

Those business leaders seeking to implement a successful connected business need to possess a fundamental understanding of the change drivers in the relevant industry and a deep insight into the way companies create and capture value.

> *IoT* is the technological base for the bridge between the physical and virtual world (technological view). It is based on five layers: (a) physical products and services, (b) integrated sensor technology, (c) connectivity between products and companies, (d) data analytics based on advanced algorithms and deep neural networks, and (e) digitally triggered product upgrades and services. The *networked economy* is the emerging economic order where products, processes, services, and value chains are connected via IoT within the information-based society (economic view). *Connected business* is concerned with the way companies exploit the potential of IoT in order to develop new business models aiming to create and capture more value (company view).

1   Game Changers in the Networked Economy

In the recent past, IoT has been used as a differentiating factor in creating competitive advantage, but, today, most technologies are mature, widely available, and relatively cheap. Connected products, per se, no longer provide a competitive advantage. In the future, the decisive factor will be the intelligent use of such technologies to create superior customer value and to build a sustainable business model. This will differentiate success from failure. What follows is a summary of twelve pivotal trends that have to be addressed when developing connected business for the networked economy:

1. *Ubiquitous connectivity has been increased.* The driving factor behind ubiquitous connectivity is the diminishing cost of computing due to Moore's law, miniaturization, and network effects. It is not only people who are "always on" but also things that are permanently connected, smart, and in communication with each other. People now find themselves firmly ensconced in the age of machines, as technology becomes ubiquitous and cheap. Connected products have been launched in the consumer market for professionals—for example, iPads that are used to service or even control heavy machinery or production facilities.

   IoT has become a big value driver as it bridges the physical and the digital world. The global IoT market amounted to over US$ 250 billion in 2019. It is projected to rise to nearly US$ 1500 billion by 2027 (Fortune Business Insights 2020). Today, most industries have been greatly affected by IoT: manufacturing 50%, energy 34%, mobility 32%, smart cities 31%, home 18%, and agriculture 13% (Statista 2019). Future applications can be observed in many industries such as health care—for example, remote diagnostics, wearables, and remote health interventions.

   Because IoT is being more widely used, information—specifically, vast amounts of environmental data, often unstructured—is collected and exchanged between machines and devices. These smart IoT products/ services and cyber-physical systems substantially reduce the amount of human interaction. Associated with the world of IoT is a huge bundle of enabling technologies such as RFID, near field communication (NFC), wireless sensor networks, cloud networking services, artificial intelligence (AI), and distributed ledger technologies (e.g., blockchain), as well as additive manufacturing technologies (3D printing). Indeed, the proliferation of APIs has further supported the connectivity of businesses and taken it across the borders of today's industry into new ecosystems that straddle the customer journey. As these systems become more vulnerable to hardware and operating systems that are widely trusted, the role of cybersecurity technologies becomes increasingly important.

2. *Digital technologies become commodities.* Despite all the talk about digitalization, these technologies are no longer differentiators. Standardization and application programming interfaces (APIs) drive modularity in technology development. As the speed of technology diffusion increases, any competitive advantage accruing from digital technologies is of very limited duration. For example, 10 years ago, there was only one major digital terrestrial commercial wide-range communication system to hand—the GSM cellular standard. Today's world offers several standards from which to select a smart connected solution (GSM LTE/5G, NB IoT, Sigfox,

LoRaWAN). The innovation cycles become shorter, while the available portfolio of applicable technologies increases significantly.

3. *Achieving mastery in orchestrating all necessary technologies in a single system becomes crucial.* Simply managing the technology is no longer enough. Selecting, mastering, and maintaining appropriate cutting-edge technologies is a necessary prerequisite for creating and delivering technically successful solutions for connected business, but it is no longer sufficient, judging by today's standards. Given the very interdisciplinary, widely distributed architecture and the broad diversity of technologies that must work seamlessly together to provide a reliable, scalable, end-to-end, connected business system, the interplay of technologies has to be clearly understood and fulsomely orchestrated if real customer value is to accrue. Only companies that have the required human and technical resources will excel in this market, or at the very least survive. In other words, a smattering of expertise in one or two technologies will no longer suffice.

4. *Transaction costs go down dramatically* with digitalization and standardized interfaces. A bank transaction costs US$ 4.00 through a branch, US$ 3.75 via a call center, US$ 0.85 using an ATM, and only US$ 0.08 by mobile online. The underlying trend is micropayment, realized by many initiatives such as *Apple Pay, Google Pay*, or national initiatives like *TWINT*. With transaction costs between companies decreasing due to standardized interfaces such as APIs (application programming interfaces), the cost of collaboration is decreasing in nearly all industries. This facilitates the creation of many new collaborative business models along the value chains. The rise of platform companies and ecosystem orchestrators could be merely enabled without low transaction costs.

   In future, secure, independent transactions between products and things are aimed at decentralized platforms via distributed ledger technology, such as blockchain and its most prominent application of digital currency, bitcoin. A necessary condition for these secure transactions is digital trust as well as digital identities. Both are promoted by the European *GaiaX* project to develop efficient and competitive, secure, and trustworthy data infrastructure in Europe, driven by *Bosch, BMW, Deutsche Telecom, SAP*, and *Siemens*.

5. *It is not about big data; it is about smart and relevant data.* Exponential data growth will continue, mainly driven by connected devices. In 2020, data was continuing to grow by 40% per year. By 2025, it is expected to reach 175 zettabyte—1 zetabyte equals 10^{21} bytes or 1 trillion gigabytes (Hagiu and Wright 2020). The fuel for a connected business is, in essence, data but data that has business relevance. The biggest challenge for a com-

pany is often how to identify the relevant data and transform it into useful information and business-relevant knowledge so that business models can create and capture value. Too often companies erect huge data cemeteries that are neither relevant nor usable.

In many regions of the world, the flow and use of data for connected business is largely unrestricted. However, in Europe, more strict regulations have been put in place to guide data usage and commercialization. Since 2018, Europe's General Data Protection Regulation (GDPR) introduced quite restrictive legislation on data protection and privacy, giving individuals greater control over their personal data. Nevertheless, it is fair to say that a mere click on "accept general terms and conditions" is enough to keep the data flowing (for an overview on compliance checks, see Chatzipoulidis et al. 2019, for instance).

6. *Data analytics increase the value of data.* Huge improvements in the development of algorithms have generated exponential advances in data analytics. Artificial intelligence (AI) and, in particular, machine learning have increased the value of data. While many companies spoke about their "data cemeteries" in the 1990s, the value of that data in today's world has been recognized in most industries. Data has become the new oil. But if data is the new oil, the trained model is the new refinery. A data strategy has, therefore, to include how to manage and protect the AI-based data model. Developing trust has become of vital concern to most companies, where explicit privacy principles are not only developed in consumer-oriented companies like *Apple* but also in B2B firms like *Bosch* and *Siemens*. In the age of ubiquitous connectivity, maintaining trust has been recognized as a source of competitive advantage.

7. *Shifting customer expectations drive user experience and convenience.* This trend has been triggered by technological feasibilities and represents a significant challenge for mature corporates. Technology combines greater convenience and user experience within one function, application, or industry with the result that it also raises expectations when undertaking other customer journeys. Customers expect a superior user experience in terms of convenience, one-stop shopping, provision of solutions, and ease of transactions in various areas (Leavy 2019). The experience of shopping at *Amazon* or booking a journey on *booking.com* leads to higher expectations in industries such as insurance and banking. As soon as pioneering FinTech companies like *Aladdin*, *PayPal*, and *Swissquote* entered the marketplace with superior convenience and simplicity—and additional lower transaction fees—they were quick to conquer the market.

8. *Points of sale are shifting in several product categories.* Insurance for consumer electronic products is sold by the retail company. Meta-portals like *Comparis* and *Check24* offer the cheapest prices for almost everything, whether it be property, cars and motorcycles, telecom services, credit cards, mortgages, health insurances, and many other products too numerous to mention. These price comparison platforms are financed by advertising or click redirection. Regardless of whether smartphone insurance is sold at the counter of a retailer or via a price-comparison platform, the margins for the insurance company are very much shrinking. Smartphone apps and the corresponding marketplaces have become the new points of sale. Not only has the point of sale relocated to your pocket via the smartphone app but the vendor has also changed. You pay *Uber* for the ride, not the local taxi driver; you pay *Netflix* or the ticket sales platform for the movie, not the local cinema owner.

9. *Platform companies with two-sided markets are winning in many industries.* Eight out of the ten most valuable companies worldwide such as *Amazon*, *Alibaba*, *Apple*, and *Google* are built on platforms based on the logic of the two-sided market. Due to direct and indirect network effects, a platform is able to scale very quickly once a critical mass has been reached. The winner-takes-all principle is a consequence of the network effects and is evidence that the platform is working effectively. After the success of the digital pioneers, asset-heavy companies also began to initiate platform activities. *Siemens* launched the IoT platform, Mindsphere, and *Daimler* unveiled its mobility platform, Moovel. *Trumpf* founded Axoom, a digital hub of the shop floor in manufacturing, which was later sold to GFT.

   Yet, most platforms of incumbents fail. In 2016, *GE* forecast that its IoT platform, Predix, would achieve a sales volume of nearly US$ 10 billion by 2020. But Predix did not take off as expected because it was trying to support too many verticals without the necessary domain expertise. Clearly addressing customer needs and creating perceived customer value remains no less important. In many cases, industry outsiders, because they are neutral players, have the best chance of securing wide market acceptance from all actors. Most companies do not want to jump on competitors' platforms.

10. *Value creation has shifted in the connected world.* Some players in the value chain gain more; others lose more. The music industry is a good illustration of this shift. In the unconnected age, the publishing label and the musician earned US$ 1 each per CD sold. In the connected Spotify world, music has become very cheap, and turnover has shifted to the music streaming service platform, *Spotify*. The label gets US$ 0.0016 per

song played; the musician only US$ 0.00029. The remainder of the sub-scription stays with Spotify as the intermediary. In 2020, *Spotify* had a turnover of nearly US$ 7 billion, the major proportion coming from premium subscribers. *Spotify's* huge increase in market share is undoubt-edly very promising, but it has yet to turn a profit.

There are similar examples in the B2B sector. The market for elevator maintenance used to be a fairly closed market, but it has undergone a major transformation due to connectivity. The typical business scenario was that an elevator got maintained, regularly inspected, and approved by the manufacturer's service team. But now, more and more companies have entered the market offering manufacturer-independent elevator ser-vices based on IoT using remote monitoring. These highly efficient remote diagnostics will only send out a service team when the condition of the elevator requires intervention—the service team can be in-house or third party. These new players have imposed themselves on the elevator maintenance market, rupturing the direct business relationship that had previously existed between the elevator manufacturer and the building owner or facility manager.

11. *The development of ecosystems along the customer journey requires multilat-eral partnerships.* Ecosystems are enabled by lower transaction costs com-bined with ubiquitous connectivity. The goal of such collaborative efforts is to develop a superior or new value proposition for the customer. This is enabled through data sharing in order to increase convenience and user experience and create positive spill-over effects from one service to the other. As a result, large ecosystems such as mobility, hospitability, educa-tion, housing, healthcare, and B2B marketplaces are being developed across today's industry boundaries. These ecosystems are expected to grow immeasurably in the decade to come. By 2025, *McKinsey* estimates that 30% of the world's expected turnover of US$ 190 trillion in revenue will be redistributed across today's industry boundaries. Hundreds of today's industries will reconstitute into 12–20 cross-industry ecosystems. Therefore, it will become imperative for companies to create dynamic partnering capabilities and a well-honed skillset for sensing, storing, and analyzing data. An important part of this dynamic will be to create strong emotional ties with customers and develop a powerful emotional connec-tion for their brand and company as a whole.

12. *Coopetition becomes more the norm than the exception.* A judicious mix of cooperation and competition finds expression in this new paradigm for ecosystems. *Amazon* and *Apple* cooperate when you buy your new iPhone via *Amazon*. But, at the same time, both companies are serious rivals

when offering competing digital media ecosystems: *Apple's* iTunes versus *Amazon* music. *Audi, BMW,* and *Daimler* are fierce competitors in the premium automotive sector but, at the same time, cooperate as joint owners of *HERE,* the location-based service company. *HERE* technologies capture location content such as road networks, buildings, parks, and traffic patterns and develop services to compete with the dominant competitor, *Google* Maps.

While traditional strategic management—taught, for example, by the famous academic, Michael Porter, in the 1980s and 1990s—aimed to create a comparative competitive advantage for a product or company, securing sustainable survival in today's global competition has become much more complex and challenging. Today's competition is no longer between individual companies or products but between entire value chains and business models. Given this hyper-competition, companies need to define with some degree of precision where they want to compete and where they aim to cooperate within the value chain. Cooperating with competitors is increasingly becoming the rule rather than the exception. The ultimate goal of all business activity is to achieve superior customer value.

Coopetition is by no means easy. How do you position your company and your products and services in the market against your competitors while cooperating at the same time? Even greater is the challenge of changing to a mindset that requires you to cooperate with a competitor in the non-competitive space. Small- and medium-sized companies (SMEs), in particular, seem to be highly reluctant to share relevant information with a competitor or even supplier. Nevertheless, coopetition is gaining in importance with the merger of industries, the rise of platform economies, and the trend toward one-stop offers.

To survive in the networked economy, companies need to consider such trends in relation not only to their overall competitive strategy but also for each individual product and service offering. Some industries such as retail and media have responded very quickly to these trends. Business leaders must constantly rethink how to create and capture value in a rapid and dynamically changing environment. Other industries such as mobility, energy, and health are in the process of change; an indicator of this trend is fast-growing pioneers entering the industry. Yet, some industries seem more resistant to these trends as shown by the higher degree of inertia among their players and customers. Overall, it is just a matter of timing and the pace of individual industries. Since business innovation is initiated primarily through industry outsiders, it is important to recognize the attractiveness that a particular industry may hold for new entrants.

Business leaders need to reflect on these change drivers in terms of their relevance to their own industry. They ought to ask themselves the following questions: *What are the implications of these new competition rules? What should companies strive for in these times of uncertainty? How can companies create comparative competitive advantages when superior technologies are no longer enough to win? How do companies keep their customers and win new ones when they shift their demands and the points of sale? How does a company position itself when industries merge into large ecosystems with new profit allocations?*

2   Getting More Out of It: Business Value

Answering these questions may appear straightforward, but they do present serious challenges for businesses. The first principle to recognize is that the purpose of a company is to create value. To survive in the long run, a company must create real value for its customers while capturing a share of the created value for itself. The "new economy" of the 1990s failed largely for two reasons: value creation for potential customers was never large enough, and value capture did not actually occur. Too much attention has been given to the clicks on a website and too little consideration to the conversion rates. At the end of the day, the crucial question is how many website visitors actually bought a product.

An important lesson to draw from the decade of enthusiasm for Internet-based business is: do not forget the real value of the company's activities. This is especially relevant to innovation in the early phase when the value is merely a number on a piece of paper, a concept study, or a business case but has yet to take a tangible form for real customers. When we speak of the value of products, services, and processes, we need to be more precise: It is not only about the objective value of products, services, and processes in terms of technical specifications, but it is also about the perceived value from the customer's point of view.

Business value is about creating and capturing value. This is relevant for all kinds of innovation, not just the networked economy. Developing the 72 generation of rear axles for *Volkswagen* is known terrain where customer insights and functions are clear. But starting a connected business initiative is much tougher. At the beginning of the innovation curve, several technologies are available, and multi-options on platforms, technologies, and functionalities produce uncertainty. Too often, implicit and untested assumptions on customer expectations lead to the neglect of business value considerations. Therefore, thinking in terms of business value is of particular importance in connected business initiatives.

Consider a simple definition of business value.

$$Business\ Value = Customer\ Value + Company\ Value \qquad (1)$$

Every product innovation, process innovation, and business innovation should follow this basic formula to create a core business value. Without business value, innovation makes no sense commercially.

This formula is valid and relevant for all kinds of business. Every innovation has to be checked for its potential to create value for the customer and for the individual company. A crucial lesson can be drawn from the IoT business domain: IoT per se has no value. There is no market for IoT as a technology on its own. There is only a market for the products, services, and processes of the company, developed through the deployment of its IoT capabilities. IoT requires sensors and connectivity, which make the product more expensive at first glance. Business value is based on value for its customers—for example, better user experience, greater convenience, lower costs, and/or value for the company itself through, for instance, lower maintenance costs, and higher employee satisfaction or safety.

2.1   Examples of Successful Business Value Are Much in Evidence

- The German high-tech company *Trumpf* enables their laser cutting machines through IoT to allow remote diagnostics, remote monitoring, and remote system parametrization. As a result, customers acquire value through higher performing machines, better process quality, and less unplanned downtimes. They gain an increase in efficiency and can focus on their core processes. *Trumpf* ultimately benefits as it can sell these intelligent and connected machines for higher prices. In addition, *Trumpf* captures valuable real-time insights for its R&D on how its machines are used on customer sites. Moreover, there is the benefit of increased customer loyalty.

- With its On!Track system, *Hilti* offers a robust system solution for managing all the assets of a construction company, anytime and anywhere. Customer value resides in lower tool stocks, lower costs, better preventive maintenance of the tools, fewer disruptive breakdowns, secure documentation, real-time location tracking of tools, and an increase in employee safety. The value proposition for customers can be summarized in the phrase: *greater efficiency through transparency.* The value for *Hilti* is also clear: it gets to know its customers much better, and it sees what tools the customer use and how often. On!Track customers are more profitable when compared to other customers, and they have the highest percentage of so-called truly loyal customers. These customers buy *Hilti* tools on all available channels as appropriate: from the *Hilti* salesmen on the construction side, to the physical *Hilti* store and the virtual *Hilti* store online.

The business value effect can be—for both customers and company—direct or indirect. Often direct effects such as realized cost reduction or higher margins per service are seen as more convincing, more tangible measures of a connected business project's success than indirect effects such as customer intimacy, customer loyalty, and smarter operations. However, it is also true that indirect effects are often overrated in project proposals and elevator pitches to investors while concurrently underestimated in terms of a company's long-term competitive advantage.

3   Creating Full Business Value for Multi-lateral Partnerships in Ecosystems

These basic business value considerations are a condition sine qua non for commercially successful innovation. However, in many areas of open ecosystems, it is not enough. *Amazon* on its own would never be as successful without dealers using its platform. In other words, if *Amazon*'s platform wasn't attractive enough for dealers to sell their products, there would be no value at all. It is crucial to create additional value for partners, especially when the platform is first launched. *Airbnb* and booking.com are only successful because they create value for their customers *and* their house landlords when they use the platform.

It is only when several partners come together to co-create new products and services that a whole value chain becomes competitive. This "full business value," as we call it, is essential in ecosystems where multi-lateral partnerships strive to create superior or new value for their customers. Every activity has to be focused on enhancing the customer journey. Shifting customer expectations toward convenience, superior user experience, and shifting points of sale demands collaboration among several partners. The orchestrator of an ecosystem has to consider the full business value. That is value creation for customers, company, and partners in the ecosystem.

Extended definition of business value in open ecosystems:

$$\text{Full Business Value} = \text{Customer Value} + \text{Company Value} + \text{Partner Value} \qquad (2)$$

The most impactful business value can be developed through win-win situations for the customer, the company, and its partners in the ecosystem.

Allocation of business value is not static; it changes dynamically. *Uber* became one of the most successful mobility providers without owning its own cars and without employing its own drivers. For the business to be successful, *Uber* needs its drivers as partners as much as it needs its customers. The appeal of the *Uber* platform should extend not only to customers but also to drivers. Numerous drivers in Boston use the *Uber* platform and also the *Lyft* platform, *Uber*'s toughest competitor. During peak hours after work, on Friday and Saturday nights, and during large events and festivals, the demand for mobility services exceeds the supply of drivers. In such circumstances, *Uber* responds by raising its fares to attract more drivers onto the road. In other words, *Uber* increases partner value. The same dynamic increase in partner value in the form of higher fares occurs at times when drivers' opportunity costs increase—for instance, at New Year's Eve or Christmas.

The dynamic pricing algorithm adjusts rates based on a number of variables, such as route time and distance, traffic, and prevailing rider-to-driver demand. Interestingly, *Uber* is aware of the customer's willingness to pay higher prices. When smartphone batteries are running low, people are more willing to pay for an *Uber* ride. When the *Uber* app switches to power-saving mode, it is showing its awareness of this fact. For the most part, dynamic pricing is based on machine learning; *Uber* creates a future-proof prediction of various independent conditions of the two-sided market: historical data, weather forecasts, holidays, global events, and traffic conditions are all factors that adjust pricing and, thus, the real-time sharing of business value between customers, partners, and *Uber* itself.

Thinking in terms of complex multilateral partnerships and stakeholders is becoming increasingly important for most ecosystems. Conceiving mechanisms to create value across the board for all stakeholders involved is more challenging than devising means to generate traditional business value, and it will become increasingly important in the future. This broad creation of value has been a demand of the stakeholder perspective for many years. A company should not only create value for its shareholders but also for its employees, customers, suppliers, and all partners including society as a whole (Harrison et al. 2010). In the modern ecosystem, this ethical stakeholder perspective has been reformulated into commercial thinking. Without at least long-term fair value creation and distribution to all relevant partners in an ecosystem, the innovation will not be sustainable.

4   Barriers to Creating Business Value

The trend toward connected business and ecosystems is a given. But how is it best to develop an ecosystem with multilateral partnerships that will generate new or superior customer value? Why do so many connected business projects fail? Why do only a small fraction of all platform projects succeed? Why is very little heard about the thousands of floundering initiatives? Why do most CEOs have too high expectations that are never met within the given time frame? Over the last decade, the digitalization of the world has created the basis for ecosystems, but, at the same time, some major barriers remain:

Technology for Technology's Sake. Companies often participate in the drive to digitalization because everyone else is doing it. This "bandwagon effect" is also known as the "hype cycle" of new technologies. Business value does not require the use of the most sophisticated, cutting-edge technology. Too often companies utilize innovation technologies because the attractiveness of solving customer pain points is seen as high. This so-called *hype cycle* or *fever curve* of new technologies can be observed in most industries at any time. Figure 1 illustrates a hype cycle of emerging technologies (Gartner 2020).

By the time a technology finds itself at the top of the hype curve, expectations have become inflated. Given the explosion of interest, individual projects can transform an entire industry. However, on average, failure rates have been very high when the new technology has been introduced. Bandwagon effects and the principle of hope lead to an overrated evaluation of the technology and, consequently, an overheated investment in it.

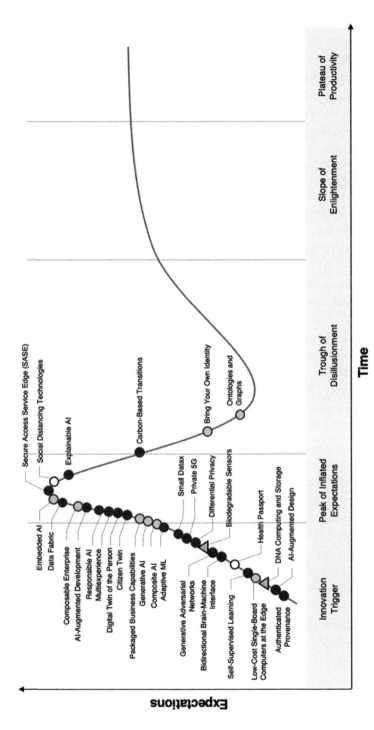

Fig. 1 Following the hype cycle for emerging technologies is often misleading, Gartner (2020)

In order to better judge the real value of a new technology, the potential for creating value and capturing value has to be analyzed. End-to-end thinking from customer gains and pains to technological solutions helps. *Tesla* did not use IoT as a fashionable gadget; instead, it was the first automotive company to fix cars over the air as they stood in the owners' garages, similar to smart phone software upgrades. In 2014, *Tesla* had already fixed broken charger plugs, increased the performance of its cars, and changed suspension settings to give the car greater clearance at high speeds. *Tesla* does not have the largest R&D center, nor does it have the longest experience in the automotive industry, but it is mostly able to place itself in its users' shoes.

Generalization from Failure. When the new economy bubble burst in 2000, everyone thought that the Internet was dead; but, today, the most valuable companies are Internet based. When the bitcoin market bubble burst and prices fell, this was widely perceived as a failure of the entire blockchain technology. But the underlying distributed ledger technology is independent of the commercial application of cryptocurrencies. When *Amazon*'s artificial intelligence (AI) based recruiting algorithm failed due to racial and gender biases, many HR managers responded with an across-the-board rejection of AI as a suitable technology for HR processes. But these managers failed to appreciate that AI is based solely on correlation and not causality. A more thorough training in AI would massively improve appreciation of its strengths. Otherwise, it should come as no surprise that "garbage-in" will inexorably deliver "garbage-out." To avoid the type of generalization that comes from failure, a deep root cause analysis should be conducted into failures. To go a step further, rather than speaking of failure, a real opportunity for learning should be welcomed. The best known example is *3M* with its Post-it sticker invention. The experiment to make a strong adhesive failed; the glue did not fully stick. Instead of giving up, one of the scientists, Art Fry, used the glue's "low-tack" properties to mark the hymns in his church choir's hymn book—he was a gospel singer in his freetime. After years of development in business discovery workshops, the success story of *3M* Post-it notes was finally born. This is not new. In the pharmaceutical industry, every active substance that has an effect also has a side effect. The business case defines what is effect and what is side effect. *Pfizer* developed Viagra as a drug for treating heart disease, which, in its clinical trials in the late 1990s, was shown not to work fully. But volunteers in the clinical trials had been reporting interesting side effects—*Pfizer* soon started with pilot studies on patients with erectile disfunction and went on to develop one of its most commercial drugs.

Privacy Restricts Data Usage. The digital world captures data on what we think: three million emails per second are sent; 660,000 new *Facebook* accounts are created per minute. It captures what we feel: 35,000 individual likes are given on *Facebook* per minute. It records our movements via GPS on our smart phones. It captures what we buy via retail companies; *PayPal* and credit card companies service our purchase transactions; 47,000 apps are downloaded per minute on *Apple*'s App Store alone. It tracks what we search; over two million search requests are placed per minute on *Google*. More and more, it tracks and captures how we use our products, machines, and processes as we use them. But, in Western countries and especially in Europe, people are becoming more and more sensitive to the way their data is used. The case of *Cambridge Analytica* with *Facebook* (see chapter "Cambridge Analytica: Magical Rise, Disastrous Fall") has raised alarm bells in our society. The smart city initiative in Toronto, *Alphabet*'s sidewalk labs, failed because of resistance on the part of data-sensitive citizens. Besides fulfilling the legal requirements, like the General Data Protection Regulation (GDPR) in Europe, many companies actively address the data privacy issue on several levels. Companies such as *Microsoft* and *Bosch* do have self-imposed data privacy principles that address transparency, control, and security issues. In addition, it is essential to obtain user consent and to do so without compromising the integrity of the process. Organizationally, several large companies have set up trust centers to further develop and enforce these privacy issues. This is especially important in ecosystems where data is shared across company borders.

Most Data Are Not Relevant to Business. "Always on" is not just a trend for teenagers with smart phones but for every human and physical thing. There are dozens of studies forecasting the number of IoT-enabled devices and the exponential growth of data. As early as 2014, an *Audi* A8 generated over 2000 data points. What data are relevant to *Audi*'s business? Who owns the driving data? Today a smart wind turbine of *Siemens* contains 300 sensors, which continuously transmit 200 gigabytes per day to *Siemens*, with an installed base of over 10,000 turbines worldwide. The challenge remains how to extract smart, business-relevant data out of the data universe and translate that data into business-relevant knowledge where real value for the customer can be developed. The biggest challenge is not the algorithm but the question: how to access business-relevant data. There are a few robust steps to take to prepare a dataset for machine learning: articulate the problem early, it all starts with the problem. Then, establish data collection mechanisms and format these data to make everything consistent. Finally, data reduction and rescaling are important. *Siemens* often collects data from its products, translates these data into business-relevant information, and tries to apply this information to relevant business models. Companies like *LinkedIn* or *Facebook* use their available data offered by users and the movements of eyeballs.

Customers Are Not Willing to Pay. The machinery industry creates plenty of value through smart connectivity of value chains, remote monitoring, remote diagnostics, remote system parametrization, and system optimization. The goal is clear: create recurrent revenues that will make the company resilient against economic downturns and build customer loyalty. But how do you convince customers to engage in new revenue models, such as subscription models, performance-based contracting, and pay-per-use models? If only sensors and SIM cards are added to the machines and tools without providing additional services, it just makes the product more expensive. If new services are created but the customer is not willing to pay for them, it only increases the overhead costs of the company. In such cases, often seen in product or machinery companies, neither customer value nor company value can be created. For those B2B firms that try to charge for services they have been giving free, three alternatives need to be evaluated: *Bill it, kill it, or keep it free.* Often, free lunches are not sustainable. It requires considerable effort and a mindset imbued with a service-dominant logic to convince customers that they receive a valuable service that they should now pay for. Companies should be recommended to evaluate pricing models that offer professional services of high quality, instead of delivering free, low-quality services.

Platforms Don't Scale. At this point *Bosch*'s Chief Technology and Chief Digital Officer Michael Bolle told us: "Nobody wants to be captured on another one's platform. Everybody wants to create his own platform. This is the reason why platforms do not scale and fail in most cases." Many successful business models are based on platform strategies with two-sided markets. Leading examples such as *Amazon, Facebook, Foursquare, Instagram, YouTube, eBay,* and *Uber* are known for their incredible success and market capitalization. The ubernization of the economy is a widely known phenomenon as platform companies capture more and more of the value while product companies are threatened with becoming commoditized. Due to increasing marginal returns, the winner often takes all. Most platform initiatives of imitators simply fail. *Siemens*'s Mindspere is doing just fine; *GE*'s Predix platform has been imploding in recent years. Most platform initiatives fail; it is a battle against the odds. The reason is not lack of attention on the customer side but mainly lack of traffic and—above all—lack of business. Manufacturing companies are often not successful in imitating platform players like *Alibaba* or *Amazon*. Instead, it is preferable to evaluate complementary roles in the ecosystem and use the power of these platforms to generate company growth. Since rising marginal returns and the winner-takes-all principle reduce the chance of blockbuster winnings, these companies would do well to evaluate their niche platforms and create the emotional and data-based stickiness that will bind existing customers to their platform.

Partnering Has to Be Learned. Lower transaction costs make cooperation between companies much easier: in particular, the costs of collaboration can be reduced by many factors. But companies are still not sufficiently well prepared to collaborate and conduct partnerships. Coopetition is particularly challenging when the mindset of cooperating with the competitor has to be developed from scratch. The efforts required to achieve a partnering mindset with competitors are often underestimated. If a competitor is growing faster and more profitably than the company in question, it can seem like an uphill struggle for business leaders to convince their teams to partner with this competitor and agree a proposition that will deliver superior value. Instead of concentrating on the customer journey and the joint superior value proposition, most companies want to become the orchestrator of the ecosystem rather than exercising a role committed to creating customer intimacy and stickiness. Roles Are Not Clearly Defined In connected business projects, the biggest challenge is often to get access to the right data in the right place. But unclear roles make this difficult. Data scientists love to solve complicated technical problems, delve single-mindedly into the algorithms, and leave IT and politics to the managers. IT managers want to run systems that are stable, maintainable, and secure; they often block new AI initiatives because of their perceived uncertainty. Business and sales think more in today's than in tomorrow's solutions; they want to sell the working system in the here and now. Top management is often too far away from a proper understanding of the cultural issues affecting teams. Overall, CIOs are often too focused on the pure technical side of the IoT solution. This is much too narrow a perspective, as Nick Jones, research vice president at *Gartner*, reiterates: "Successful deployment of an IoT solution demands that it's not just technically effective but also socially acceptable. CIOs must, therefore, educate themselves and their staff in this area, and consider forming groups, such as ethics councils, to review corporate strategy. CIOs should also consider having key algorithms and AI systems reviewed by external consultancies to identify potential bias."

The Wrong Key Performance Indicators (KPIs) Lead to the Wrong Activities. When IoT became popular, many companies set the goal of making all their products IoT enabled. According to an empirical study by Gebauer et al. (2020) from the *Bosch IoT lab*, this leads to high IoT investment and high operational costs. Due to a lack of service-oriented KPIs, companies are not able to recover these costs through corresponding returns from service offerings. There are a number of traps to be avoided:

- Companies often measure the customer acquisition costs necessary to convince customers to use and pay for services. But due to missing indicators on service quality, companies experience a high customer churn rate. As a result, customer acquisition costs become too high, leading the business case to fail.
- By aiming at recurrent revenues from services, companies often overlook the real value. *Microsoft* starts to measure (and incentivize) not only sales but real usage of all functionalities of the product. This creates higher customer satisfaction and emotional ties to the customers.

Management's attention should refocus on business value mainly for its customers, including setting KPIs that are more value based and less technology oriented. This is not an easy task to fulfill. It is easier to measure the share of IoT-enabled products in the overall portfolio than the real value created on the customer's balance sheet. But this is where the easy path can lead to—a commercial dead end.

5   End-to-End Thinking to Understand the Value Driver

Instead of simply jumping on a new technology trend, the emerging technology should be evaluated in a holistic *end-to-end view* to understand the complete solution. For early pioneers, it makes sense to completely rethink the entire business process, product and service, or business model. It is important to understand the pains and gains of customers and users or as Jobs said it "You've got to start with the customer experience and work backwards to the technology." Without deep customer insights and understanding of their likely pains and benefits, the risk of an electronic mouse trap is high. Over-engineering and technology for technology's sake are often R&D-driven responses.

For the innovation project, it's all about the perceived customer value. But in several cases, it is not even clear who the customer is, as a simple example shows: who is the customer in the elevator industry? There is no simple answer to this question. Is it the user who utilizes the vertical transportation in the building? Is it the investor who pays the bill for the elevator? Is it the owner who is interested in life-cycle costs? Is it the facility manager who maintains the building and is responsible for the service contracts? The service business is typically responsible for more than 60% of the total turnover of an elevator company and, therefore, highly business relevant. Is it the architects who design the building with its functionalities and thus strongly influence the choice of elevator, especially in complex high-rise buildings? Is it the elevator consultant who specifies the elevator and, therefore, strongly influences the buying decision? In the end, the pains and gains of all of the product's stakeholders must be considered from an end-to-end perspective. Every stakeholder gain created and every stakeholder pain alleviated contributes to the business value of the elevator company. The overall business value is maximized if the new offering represents real pain relief and gain for all stakeholders. In most cases, the stakeholders have conflicting interests: in our elevator case, the investor wants to minimize his investment; the facility manager wants ease of service handling; the owner of the building wants low life-cycle costs; the architect often wants the building to have a wow factor. And finally, the actual user of the elevator is interested in getting from A to B.

Moreover, often customers do not really know what they want. If you ask the users of an elevator, they will answer they would like to minimize waiting and travelling time. As a result, elevator companies have started a very costly race to increase elevator speed. The Taiwanese "Taipeh 101" building achieves speeds of 60 km/h, which requires a very costly internal air pressure control system to equalize pressure for users. While these races may be interesting to make it into the Guinness Book of World Records, the cost of such systems is exorbitantly high and, in the case of most buildings, offers limited benefits to users. Instead, research has shown that users actually do not like to stand around doing nothing, while waiting for the next elevator. They usually want to reduce *perceived* waiting time. But this is not the same as absolute time measured in minutes and seconds. Perceived waiting time reduction can be achieved more effectively and smarter by offering entertainment and convenience during the process of waiting, boarding, and travelling. Hence, the user experience can be enhanced through other means. Steve Jobs has been quoted as saying: "Why ask customers for their requests, it's our job to know what they want." From an end-to-end perspective, it is crucial to find the sweet spot where the user experience is optimized, and the user is delighted.

6   Thinking in Business Models: Overcoming Silos

Business value requires holistic thinking in business models. A business model is the story of how a company creates and captures value. Compared to product and process innovators, research has shown that business model innovators are more profitable, harder to imitate, and therefore create sustainable competitive advantages. However, it is very difficult to disrupt an industry as radical new ways beyond the dominant industry logic have to be considered. It is difficult for mature and experienced players in an industry to overcome this dominant logic and forget everything they have learned thus far. This is why disruptive innovations often come from outsiders. The disruption from landline phones to mobile phones took the input of the outsider, *Nokia*. But when mobile phones became smart, neither *Nokia* nor *Erickson*, *Motorola*, nor *Siemens* managed to make the breakthrough. Only when *Apple* entered the mobile phone market with the iPhone in 2007 did the disruption succeed. The reaction of the established companies at the time was typical: "The iPhone is just a niche market," commented *Nokia*'s CEO in *Forbes* magazine. Ironically, this was the start of *Nokia*'s rapid descent from dominant market leader to bankruptcy.

Industry outsiders can more easily ignore the dominant logic of an industry. They do not have to unlearn what others have learned over decades. They do not have to work against their corporate DNA. The reality should not be glorified, however. Start-ups and outsiders are much more likely to fail with their disruptive innovation. The higher the innovative step, the higher the probability of failing. But, if these business model innovators survive and succeed, the impact of change on the whole industry can be radical and sweeping, as the well-known examples of *Amazon, Apple, Ebay, PayPal, Uber, Alibaba*, and *TenCent* have shown.

It becomes more important to think of business models from the perspective of the customer journey. To fulfill the customer's desire for greater convenience and better user experience, many industries need to transcend company borders and think in terms of holistic solutions. *Daimler* does not just want to sell cars: it offers mobility. The insurance company, *Helvetia*, does not only want to sell household insurance; it intends to offer its customers comprehensive solutions in the home sector. *Roche* regards collaboration between healthcare and technology companies as the key driving forces for the future of healthcare (Huber 2021). In ecosystems, multilateral actors collaboratively develop joint value propositions, based on complementary modules. Often ecosystems are developed by an orchestrator who adopts the role of the hub firm.

The question is how to innovate the business model and disrupt an industry. How can a company get out of the low margin red ocean and create an uncontested market space? How can a company create a blue ocean and outcompete its competitors by ignoring them? How is it possible to create and capture value in a radical, new way? This requires strict thinking in business-model terms. A business model provides answers to four questions (see Fig. 3):

- WHO? Who is the target customer?
- WHAT? What is the value proposition?
- HOW? How is the value proposition being implemented?
- VALUE? How is it profitable?

In other words, a business model must address the target market, the value proposition, the supply chain architecture, and the revenue model. Business model innovation is finally reached when two or more of these dimensions are simultaneously changed. Every new product, process, and service should be assessed on its potential for business model innovation. Clearly, the creation of a new business cannot remain within R&D or product management. It is a task for the entire company deploying all its functions. Thinking in terms of business model structures has an important side effect for companies: it overcomes silos in a company, as several functions have to work closely together.

But how best to innovate business models? Following the business model navigator helps to overcome the dominant industry logic. It unfolds in four steps: initiation, ideation, integration, and implementation (Fig. 2).

Step 1: Initiation As a first step, a company has to analyze its ecosystem as it applies to today's world to understand today's business model in terms of the four questions: *Who is the target customer? What is the value proposition? How is the value proposition being implemented? How is it profitable?* It helps to get a much better understanding of today's business model when the actors in the industry are analyzed—that includes customers, suppliers, partners, competitors, and new entrants. Moreover, the change drivers for this industry have to be analyzed. This can be consumer shifts (e.g., hybrid customers in banking), market integration (e.g., *Apple* entered the mobile phone business), technological trends (e.g., digitalization), sustainability awareness (e.g., plastic-free packaging), or regulations (e.g., the last mile in telecommunications).

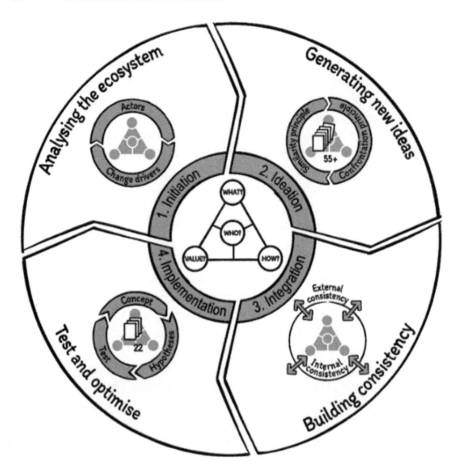

Fig. 2 Four steps toward a new business model, Gassmann et al. (2020)

Step 2: Ideation During the ideation phase, new business models are ide-
ated. Here, our research has shown that 90% of all business model revolutions
are based on 55+ business model patterns, which can be recombined like Lego
bricks. This principle, which has its origins in computer science and is also
used in mechanical engineering (the TRIZ methodology of Altschuller), has
proven very effective.[1] Popular business model patterns in connected business
are add-on, orchestrator, layer player, performance-based contracting, equipment as a service, integrator, guaranteed availability, hidden revenue, lock-in,
razor and blade, solution provider, subscription, and two-sided markets. These
patterns have to be recombined creatively for criteria and process (see
Gassmann et al. 2020).

---

[1] For more details on business model patterns and examples, see www.businessmodelnavigator.com.

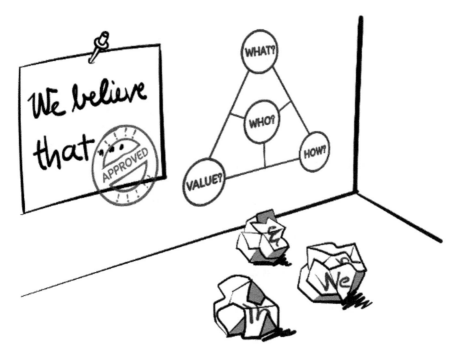

Fig. 3 Make your underlying assumptions explicit and testable, Gassmann et al. (2020)

Step 3: Integration This is a critical phase where the consistency of the new business model is evaluated. There are two major directions. First of all, the business model has to be internally consistent in terms of how the four questions are answered and how the business model fits into the internal competencies of the company. Secondly, the business model has to be checked for external consistency—for example, its fit with the other stakeholder's interests and the competitors' landscape as well as its fit with the change drivers of the industry. Often the devil is in the detail. *Hilti*'s fleet management, which today is a big success story responsible for 50% of the company's turnover, was close to failure due to complex contracts, adverse selection of customers, and salesman lacking the ability to sell the complex fleet concept—to name only a few. Every single factor can be a killer for the new business model.

Step 4: Implementation In the implementation phase, it is important to make the underlying assumptions of the business model explicit, develop hypotheses, and test them lean and fast. Connected business is much more about speed, scalability, and disruption than other innovation areas. This makes business model initiatives more attractive but also more fragile and riskier. It helps if the initiatives are launched with big visions but small steps to manage the risk. It is essential to speed up the learning process in terms of build, measure, and learn cycles. Building a minimum viable product (MVP) is important to learn about the latent requirements of the users, to understand the value drivers, and to validate the underlying assumptions of the product, the strategy, and the growth engine of the connected business. R&D engineers with a scientific background, PhDs in chemistry or engineering, perform their technological work very solidly. But, surprisingly, when it comes to business, pure trial and error replaces their scientific thinking. Not to be misunderstood, action is called for. But it helps when the team develops specific hypotheses on the product, the customer preferences, and the business model, and then validates those hypotheses. Thinking in lean start-up terms accelerates validated learning as a rigorous method for demonstrating progress. This is different to old school business cases on Excel sheets.

This is often misunderstood as proof of concept (PoC). But while technological feasibility needs PoC, understanding customer requirements is in greater need of proof of value (PoV). The most unknown factor consists more often in customer preferences and behavior or partner acceptance than in technological feasibility.

Speed remains crucial; flexibility and pivots are important. A dead end in terms of a false hypothesis should not be considered as a failure but as part of a learning process. As with experiments in natural science, lessons need to be learned from business experiments, to pivot the company's value propositions, partnering model, or revenue model. Experiments are opportunities to learn (see also chapter "Experimenting: What Makes a Good Business Experiment?") (Fig. 3).

7   Data Analytics Are Great, but Data Access Is Key

AI has revolutionized data analytics and reduced the cost of prediction. With the development of Alex Net in 2012, the first scientific breakthrough in deep neural networks was achieved, followed by a wave of deep learning applications in many product fields and industries. Importance is attached to the value created and captured, ranging from superior customer service, chatbots, preventive maintenance, health diagnostics to robots, and autonomous driving. The impact of neural networks on connected business value creation is enormous. And this is just the beginning, as innovation research has demonstrated in the past.

Most important are applications to better gain customer insights:

- The German construction product company, *Einhell*, uses AI, especially natural language processing, in order to evaluate product features from social media comments. While *Amazon* uses evaluations of a product in the round, *Einhell* uses product feature evaluations of products—for instance, "I like the battery of the *Einhell* PXC." *Einhell* uses these social media comments to identify and evaluate product features from a customer perspective. They identify the features and their perceived customer value.
- Many insure-techs have started to use chatbots in customer interaction. Experiments have shown that these chatbots can not only interact but also sell products. The performance of bots in sales can match the top 20% of human salesmen, if the situation is conducive (e.g., same gender of bot and customer; customer does not know that the "salesperson" is a bot). Research on marketing tech sees huge potential here, limited only by ethical considerations.

It is important to reiterate that AI is only based on statistical correlation and not causality. In order to train the algorithm, the quality of the data must be high. The biggest challenge facing most AI projects is how to obtain access to the right data in the right place. Hurdles are manyfold, from legal barriers like GDPR, non-standardized interfaces, and media breaks, to conflicting interests between participating companies and stakeholders.

Once a new technology fails to fulfill its expectations, the disappointment is huge, sparking immediate discussion in the press and media:

- *Starbucks's* AI designed a super-efficient duty roster that allowed baristas only five hours of a break between shifts.
- *Amazon* developed an HR algorithm that automatically weeds out women from job applications.
- *Google's* image recognition algorithm categorized black people as gorillas until 2015.

The algorithms were trained with non-representative data. Sample bias during the training phase is often the cause of weak models and thus weak prediction. AI is just based on statistical programs that have no values, no emotions, no reflection, and no morality.

Two things are crucial for AI and neural networks but often are forgotten: (a) AI has to drive business value; it must be supported by business models in order to create and capture value; (b) access to the right, business-relevant data has to be ensured.

8   Success Factors in Leading Connected Business Initiatives

Connected business has to create business value for its customers, partners, and company. In order to start a connected business project, the following cockpit or checklist has proven to be very helpful (see Fig. 4).

Develop the business model and answer the questions: Who is the customer? What do you offer to the customer? How is this offering implemented? Why is the business model profitable? In other words, address the target market, the value proposition, the supply chain architecture, and the revenue model. This is the core of the business model cockpit.

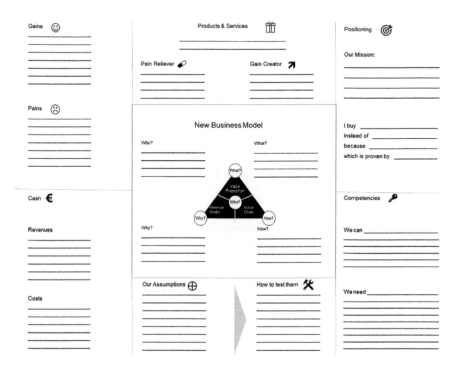

Fig. 4 Cockpit chart for disruptive business innovations as a checklist, author's own illustration

What are the gains and pains of customers? What are the gain creators and pain relievers, and how are they translated into the intended products and services? Then, what is the positioning of the product? In other words, how is it possible to create a comparative competitive advantage? It helps to write down the mission of the intended business—for example, "we want to facilitate our customers' success by providing… services." Then, stand in your customers' shoes and check: "I buy [this product] instead of [a competitor's product] because [the comparative advantage of our product] which is proven by [facts no arguments]."

The revenue model has to be explicit in terms of revenue streams and costs along the life cycle of the product. Often forgotten is the clear definition of the company's core competencies ["we can…"] and the definition of the required partnering competencies ["we need…"]. In most cases, the need for external knowledge and competencies is underestimated. This is particularly relevant in ecosystem and business model projects where own industry knowledge is no longer enough. Moreover, partnering is underestimated in the area of software development when the company itself has no software DNA.

It is essential for the cockpit chart to make the business's implicit, underlying assumptions explicit as a testable hypothesis and show how to test it. Learning from *Google* moonshot projects, try to kill your own project or, in other words, validate the most critical assumption first. It is important to fail earlier in order to learn faster and at less cost.

From the research and hundreds of connected business projects, it is important to summarize the lessons learned on how to lead such initiatives successfully.

1. Key to all connected business initiatives is the ability to create and capture business value. Be careful not to overemphasize technology. Instead, develop end-to-end solutions with customer value. For this, a deep understanding of the value driver of the applications is necessary.
2. Thinking in business models is not only about value creation and capture. It helps also to overcome company internal silos. The answer required of a business model is the integrated answer to four questions: Who is our customer? What do we offer to the customer? How do we implement our offering? Why is it profitable?
3. Carefully evaluate platform initiatives regarding direct and indirect network effects. If not feasible, than take complementary roles in the ecosystem.
4. AI is important but access to the right data is key. Since AI is only about statistical correlation and not about causality, it is important to train the

model with relevant data. If data is the new oil, the model is the new refinery.

5. Concentrate on your core competencies and collaborate with partners in ecosystems in order to create a superior value proposition for your customer along the customer journey. Be open to coopetition, even if this requires a major shift in mindset.

6. You only can manage what you can measure. KPIs need to focus on business value drivers where connectivity addresses the sweet spot between the effort expended and the impact on business value.

7. Get top management support; connected business is a strategic transformation journey that is often underestimated.

8. Set up a diverse team from different backgrounds and functions. Include outsiders to challenge your company logic and embrace ideas from outside. Think in terms of customer journeys and business models, and less in terms of company hierarchies and processes.

9. Make the underlying assumptions of the business model explicit. For each assumption, there should be a clear testing strategy: a picture is more than 1000 words but a prototype is more than 1000 pictures. Engage prototypes with customers and partners.

10. Develop the skills within the organization to walk the transformation journey. Develop a culture of openness and experimentation; there should be no sacred cow in the room. Be persistent and keep on trying. Aim to strike a balance between long-term benefits and short-term results. It is a long journey but it starts with small steps.

And finally, to summarize the lessons learned from being over 25 years in the innovation sector: "Think big, start small, fail cheap, and learn fast."

References

Chatzipoulidis A, Tsiakis T, Kargidis T (2019) A readiness assessment tool for GDPR compliance certification. Comput Fraud Secur 2019(8):14–19

Fortune Business Insights (2020) Market research report. https://www.fortunebusinessinsights.com/industry-reports/internet-of-things-iot-market-100307. Accessed 8 Jan 2021

Gartner (2020) Hype cycle for emerging technologies. https://www.gartner.com/en/research/methodologies/gartner-hype-cycle. Accessed 20 July 2020

Gassmann O, Frankenberger K, Choudury M (2020) The business model navigator: the strategies behind the most successful companies. FT Pearson, Upper Saddle River, NJ

Gebauer H, Lamprecht C, Wortmann F (2020) Working paper. Institute of Technology Management, University of St. Gallen

Hagiu A, Wright J (2020) When data creates competitive advantage. Harv Bus Rev, Jan-Feb

Harrison JS, Wicks AC, Parmar BL, de Colle S (2010) Stakeholder theory, state of the art. Cambridge University Press, Cambridge

Huber F (2021) Towards ecosystems: a qualitative analysis on the early stage of inter-firm collaboration. PhD thesis at University of St. Gallen

Leavy B (2019) Thriving in the era of the "connected customer". Strat Leadersh 47(5):3–9

Statista (2019) Internet of things (IoT) in Europe. https://www.statista.com/study/42750/internet-of-things-iot-in-europe/. Accessed 6 Jan 2021

Oliver Gassmann, Prof. Dr., is Professor for Technology Management at the University of St. Gallen and Director of the Institute of Technology Management since 2002. His research focus lies on patterns and success factors of innovation. He has been visiting faculty at Berkeley (2007), Stanford (2012), and Harvard (2016). Prior to his academic career, Gassmann was the head of corporate research at Schindler. His more than 400 publications are highly cited; his book *The Business Model Navigator* became a global bestseller. He received the Scholarly Impact Award of the Journal of Management in 2014. He founded several spin-offs, is member of several boards of directors, like Zühlke, and is an internationally recognized keynote speaker.

Fabrizio Ferrandina is Partner and CEO of the Zühlke Group, a global innovation service provider. Until 2018 he was CEO of the German subsidiary and member of the Zühlke Group Executive Board. His career has been dedicated to driving software and system projects for clients all over the world. Prior to his industry career, he worked as a researcher at the University of Frankfurt with focus on software and data engineering where he published several scientific papers. Fabrizio Ferrandina holds a degree in electronics engineering from the Università Politecnico di Milano, Italy, and a postmaster MBA from CEFRIEL, Milan.

Platform Economy: Converging IoT Platforms and Ecosystems

Sven Jung, Felix Wortmann, Wolfgang Bronner, and Oliver Gassmann

1 The Power of Platforms

Over the last two decades, many platform businesses have outperformed traditional businesses. In fact, as of today eight out of the ten most valuable companies globally are platform companies (e.g., *Apple*, *Amazon*, *Alibaba*), and many more are on the rise to disrupt entire industries (Price Waterhouse Coopers 2020). Some of the most famous examples that have disrupted entire industries are *Facebook* and *Instagram* in social media, *Amazon* and *eBay* in retail, *booking.com* and *Airbnb* in travelling, as well as *Uber* and *Lyft* in transportation.

S. Jung (✉)
University of St. Gallen, St. Gallen, Switzerland
e-mail: sven.jung@unisg.ch

F. Wortmann • O. Gassmann
Institute of Technology Management, University of St. Gallen,
St. Gallen, Switzerland
e-mail: felix.wortmann@unisg.ch; oliver.gassmann@unisg.ch

W. Bronner
Bosch IoT Lab, University of St. Gallen & ETH Zürich, St. Gallen, Switzerland
e-mail: wolfgang.bronner@bosch.com

© The Author(s), under exclusive license to Springer Nature Switzerland AG 2021
O. Gassmann, F. Ferrandina (eds.), *Connected Business*,
https://doi.org/10.1007/978-3-030-76897-3_2

The success of these companies is heavily based on network effects, i.e., an increased number of users leading to a higher value of the platform (Rochet and Tirole 2003). Compared to traditional businesses, platforms can scale much faster and more easily. This is because platforms often do not build or own any assets (e.g., apartments in the case of *Airbnb*) but instead provide the infrastructure that enables value-creating interactions between users (interactions between apartment owners and travellers in the case of *Airbnb*) (Parker et al. 2016). The success of platforms makes it almost inevitable for a manager to engage in the platform economy or as an entrepreneur to think about building a platform venture from scratch. But how do their underlying mechanisms work? How do the concepts of ecosystem and platform relate? And are platforms only for digital players? What is the impact of platforms on the physical world and the Internet of Things (IoT)?

While the digitalization made many platforms possible, early traits of platform thinking have already existed before. For example, car manufacturers like *Volkswagen* or camera manufacturers like *Nikon* have utilized platform thinking in their product development. While each camera model consists of a few unique features, most components are based on an underlying technology platform that is shared among all models. This type of platform is referred to as an "internal platform" (Gawer and Cusumano 2014) with the primary goal to make production more efficient.

However, when we talk about today's leading platforms—the *Amazons*, *Apples*, or *Airbnbs*—we usually have a different platform concept in mind. Tech companies like *Microsoft* or *Intel* were one of the first to utilize platform thinking for their business model. But what was so different compared to a traditional, pipeline business model? With *Microsoft* Windows, *Microsoft* developed an operating system and a platform that was open for external software companies to build complementary applications on top of Windows (ibid.). In comparison to a pipeline business where companies seek to optimize their internal value chain, *Microsoft* optimized its offering so that other companies, i.e., third-party software companies, could complement its own offering. Shifting value creation from the inside to the outside gave *Microsoft* Windows a competitive advantage in the years to follow, as numerous complementary software solutions were developed. The Windows platform was able to scale faster because *Microsoft* did not have to create all the competitive assets, such as complementary applications, but instead drew value from external resources (van Alstyne et al. 2016). This, in turn, benefited the adoption of Windows in the early years, making it the leading operating system—in turn, *Apple*'s operating system was left behind in the beginning, as they only opened up to external developers much later (Zhu and Iansiti 2019).

Although there are different perspectives on platforms, there are three characteristics that are fundamental to a platform business (Parker et al. 2016):

1. Platforms are intermediaries that bring two or more sides of a market (customer groups) together.
2. Platforms provide infrastructure and rules that facilitate transactions between the sides (transaction platforms like *eBay*) and/or enable innovation (innovation platforms like *Microsoft* Windows).
3. Platforms are based on network effects.

The value-adding interactions between two or more sides of a market could be of almost any sort. *Airbnb* is bringing hosts and travellers together to facilitate stays, *Amazon* is connecting sellers and buyers together to exchange products, and *Kickstarter* is linking investors and entrepreneurs together to exchange money and bring ideas to live. *WhatsApp* is bringing people together to exchange messages and photos, and *Apple* is bringing app developers and smartphone users together through their App Store.

While platforms can take many forms, network effects are core to platforms. They refer to the dynamic that "the more users who adopt the platform, the more valuable the platform becomes to the owner and to the users because of growing access to the network of users and often to a growing set of complementary innovations" (Gawer and Cusumano 2014). Due to a lack of network effects, many online stores, such as simple fashion online stores, are often incorrectly portrayed as platform businesses. Similarly, *Amazon* started as an online merchandiser selling books via an online shop and not as a platform business. It was only by transforming the online store to an open marketplace with third-party vendors joining that *Amazon* became the thriving platform we know of today.

Network effects are not only a distinguishing feature of any platform business but one of the features that make platform companies so successful (Rochet and Tirole 2003). However, there can also be negative network effects that should not be neglected. In general, network effects can be divided into direct and indirect effects (see Fig. 1).

Indirect network effects (1) refer to network effects between the different sides of the platform. The value for one side increases/decreases if an additional user from the other side joins the platform. For instance, in the case of *Amazon*, additional sellers lead to a larger product offering which attracts more buyers on the other side. Vice versa, more buyers lead to an increased demand which attracts additional sellers to join the platform. This re-enforcing dynamic is essential for all successful platform businesses. The example of

Fig. 1 Platform network effects, Parker et al. (2016)

Amazon also shows how positive network effects can turn into negative ones if the platform is not well managed. If too many sellers join the platform, at some point, buyers become overwhelmed by the unstructured offering leading to negative, indirect network effects.

In comparison, direct network effects (2) refer to the same side of the platform. The value for one user increases/decreases if an additional user from the same side joins the platform. For instance, in the case of *Amazon*, additional buyers lead to more reviews which, in turn, attract additional buyers onto the platform (positive, direct network effects). If you look at the other side of the platform, additional sellers intensify the competition in the long run, making it less attractive for new sellers to join the platform (negative, direct network effects).

Depending on the platform type as well as the competitive situation, network effects can generate so-called "winner-takes-it-all" platforms. Once the network has exceeded a certain threshold, it becomes enormously difficult for competitors to build a platform in the same segment. Due to the strength of the network, none of the sides would have an incentive to move from the existing to the new platform with the same offering but a weaker network. However, companies systematically overestimate their chances of creating a "winner-takes-it-all" platform. In fact, the platform economy can be characterized through a paradox: Everyone wants to create their own platform. However, network effects often do not unfold. This in turn is the reason why only a few platforms are highly successful and thousands of platform initiatives from corporates and start-ups fail.

2   Toward Platform Ecosystems

Platforms and ecosystems are closely related. But how do the concepts really relate to each other? Does a successful ecosystem need a platform or vice versa? While the term ecosystem has its origins in biology, the term was first coined in a business context by large corporations such as *Apple, Ford,* and *Walmart,* which began to build partnerships beyond industry boundaries. This ecosystem strategy gave them a competitive advantage in comparison to the "lone wolves" in the same market. *Apple* in its early days has been building an ecosystem with at least four industries: personal computers, consumer electronics, information, and communications. However, the early concept of the ecosystem was very broad and included various types of organizations, from suppliers to competitors to generic stakeholders (Iansiti and Levien 2004). The concept has since evolved, particularly in the context of digitization. An ecosystem can be characterized through the following three elements (Adner 2017):

1. **Common goal:** An ecosystem comprises multiple organizations working toward a common goal.
2. **Multi-lateral collaboration:** In an ecosystem, organizations collaborate and complement each other to achieve this common goal.
3. **Alignment:** The members of an ecosystem are independent but are being aligned by an orchestrator.
4. **Value proposition:** An ecosystem creates a superior or new value proposition for the customer through the aligned efforts.

An ecosystem distinguishes fundamentally from traditional business structures like hierarchical and market-based structures (Jacobides et al. 2018). In a hierarchical structure such as a traditional value network, the final product is determined by the central company. The central company can determine the suppliers and freely choose how their products are aggregated. This directly affects what and how the customer consumes. In comparison, an ecosystem allows suppliers to become complementors that equally face the end-customers. The consumer gets empowered and gets to choose what product(s) to combine and how to consume them. For instance, as an Android user, you can choose which complementary apps to install and combine on your smartphone—compared to the situation where *Google* would pre-define your smartphone with apps giving you no options. In a market-based structure, there is no alignment (complementarity) between the suppliers and customers can directly consume products from competing suppliers without any type of intermediary (Jacobides et al. 2018). In comparison, in an ecosystem, an orchestrator aligns the different offerings through common standards or interfaces. Here the concepts "ecosystem" and "platform" are often used interchangeably. Platforms also offer means to establish a standard as a basis for complementary innovations.

1. ***Nespresso's*** **ecosystem:** *Nespresso* was able to create an ecosystem including coffee, capsule producers, and coffee machine manufacturers. These products are naturally complementary and can only be consumed together (unique consumption). In addition, the manufacturers of the complementary products, for example, *Krups* coffee machine and *Dallmayr* coffee capsules, need to develop a special machine and comply with the *Nespresso* capsule standard. This alignment among the producers (unique production) makes *Nespresso* an ecosystem. In contrast, traditional coffee machine and coffee powder manufacturers do not constitute an ecosystem as they are so standardized that they can be produced without any coordination among producers. Other examples of ecosystems are the photovoltaic solar panel industry including panel producers, installation providers, racking producers, or the RunFlat technology for tires including car manufacturers, tire manufacturers, and garages.

2. ***Apple's*** **platform ecosystem:** *Apple's* smartphone operation system (iOS) and third-party applications is a platform ecosystem as it relies on network effects. The users' utility increases, the more applications are specifically developed for iOS (supermodular consumption). At the same time, it requires an alignment among the complementary producers (unique production). To align, *Apple* provides interfaces in form of software development kits (SDKs) upon which external developer can develop complementary applications. While *Apple* is in control, the app developers have some degree of autonomy. Another example is *Sony PlayStation* including third-party games.

3. ***Uber*** **and** ***eBay*** **are pure platforms:** Some platforms do not rely on an ecosystem and distinguish themselves from platform ecosystems. Although they rely on supermodular consumption and therefore gain network effects, production on platforms like *eBay* or *Uber* is very generic. This means there is almost no interdependency among the complementary products and the platform itself. Ultimately, for example, there is no need for coordination between different *eBay* sellers and the *eBay* platform itself. Sellers can just upload their products on *eBay* without the need to adjust specifically to the platform *eBay*. Furthermore, there is no need for sellers to coordinate with each other.

The above examples clearly illustrate how the concept of platforms and ecosystem overlap in practice. Nevertheless, the strategic priorities differ: In an ecosystem, the individual partners and the quality of their relationships play an important role. Platforms that are based on an ecosystem need to keep this in mind. They must also invest in the quality of individual partnerships. Transitioning from a platform ecosystem toward a pure platform, the individual partners and its complementary products become less important. Individual complementary products become interchangeable as the number of complementors is growing. Focusing on quantity instead of quality, the objective for a platform owner is to "grow the relevant sides of the market in order to increase value through direct and indirect network externalities" (Adner 2017). Here, the focus is on managing network effects instead of partnerships.

3   Toward Industrial IoT Platforms

To date, most of the leading platforms are consumer platforms that focus on digital value exchange. However, the platform economy is becoming increasingly important for the B2B segment and companies with a manufacturing background. One of the key enablers of this development is the Internet of Things.

The IoT does not refer to a product or a solution but can be seen as a phenomenon that depicts how technology makes it possible to connect physical products to the Internet. In essence, the IoT aims to connect the physical and digital world. It starts at the product level, where physical devices are equipped with software, sensors, and communication technology that allow products to connect to the Internet. Such smart, connected products enable different capabilities, from controlling and monitoring to product optimization and autonomy (Porter and Heppelmann 2014). However, the added value of IoT does not result from connectivity alone but from the many business opportunities that result from smart, connected products. Typically, the value add for the consumer or business is digital and a result of the analysis of data generated by the connected products and/or additional digital services (Fleisch et al. 2014).

Smart, connected products also enable companies to shift their focus from internal to external value creation. For instance, manufacturers who connect their products to the Internet can give external companies access to their product data to enable third-party analysis or digital services. Ultimately, smart, connected products open up possibilities for companies from adjacent industries to collaborate (Iansiti and Lakhani 2014). This is also where platform, ecosystem, and the IoT converge (see Fig. 2).

In the agricultural segment, for instance, physical products like tractors are being exceedingly connected with the Internet. These smart, connected products allow farmers to better manage and monitor their fleet. Typically, this often starts as a rather closed system (stage 1). There is no extensive platform thinking involved at this stage as this is typically a single initiative by the original equipment manufacturer (OEM) of the tractor. However, as soon as other devices, for example, connected harvesters or fields, are included in this system, an ecosystem is emerging (stage 2). For instance, a farm equipment system is bringing data of different systems together. As a user, you only benefit if you use the products together. At the same time, the manufacturers of the different machines have to align to enable standardized data exchange. Once external companies are allowed to be integrated into this system to provide value-adding services, such as yield optimization analytics, an IoT platform ecosystem is emerging (stage 3). For instance, a farm management platform brings machine manufacturers with external service providers and farmers together. The more value-added services are on the platform, the more attractive it is for farmers to join the platform and vice versa.

The ability to connect devices to the Internet has created many opportunities for businesses to participate in the platform economy. The example of smart agriculture has already briefly illustrated how platform, ecosystem, and IoT are converging. In fact, many different IoT-based platforms are currently emerging. To illustrate the diversity of IoT platforms in practice, it makes sense to distinguish them on the basis of their intended aim: transaction platform, innovation platform, and integration platform (Cusumano et al. 2019).

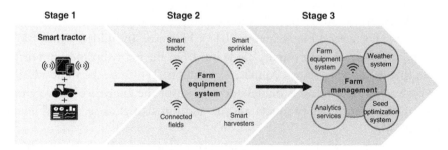

Fig. 2 The IoT shifting industry boundaries through platform thinking, Porter and Heppelmann (2014)

4   IoT Transaction Platforms like *Caruso*

Transaction platforms bring demand and supply sides together to exchange units of value. Many also refer to them as marketplaces (Cusumano et al. 2020). The unit of value can vary widely, ranging from physical to digital products and physical to digital services. One of the leading transaction platforms is Airbnb, where "stays" are exchanged as a core value unit. It brings apartment owners (supply side) together with people looking for temporary accommodation (demand side). By orchestrating external resources, i.e., empty apartments, *Airbnb* scaled very quickly. Although not owning any real estate, it has now become one of the leading companies in the travel industry with over seven million accommodations on its platform (Airbnb 2020). A common success factor for all transaction platforms—including *Airbnb*—is the ability to reduce transaction costs and offer consumers greater choice (Cusumano et al. 2020). But *Airbnb* also started small. Their strategy was to start in San Francisco and expand further once they had reached a critical mass in this local market. Other examples of leading transaction platforms are the *Amazon* marketplace, *eBay*, *Uber*, *WhatsApp*, and *Snapchat*.

In many industries, data is becoming a core resource for value creation in the future (Chen et al. 2014). IoT also contributes to this development by increasing the number of connected products and, thereby, producing valuable data. The transaction platform *Caruso* takes advantage of this development. Founded in 2017 as an industry-wide initiative, *Caruso* has become a marketplace for IoT-based mobility data (Caruso 2020a). It primarily connects automotive OEMs such as *BMW* or *Mercedes* with companies that want to utilize mobility data. This data can range from basic car information, e.g., battery and engine status, user-based data, e.g., mileage and location, to very specific data, e.g., crash data (Caruso 2020b).

This type of IoT marketplace can enable many new business opportunities (see Fig. 3). Traditionally, to offer driving-based insurances, insurance companies had to make bilateral agreements with all car OEMs to access their mobility data. Alternatively, they could install a retrofit solution in the insuree's cars to collect the data themselves. Both options are very costly and inefficient making driving-based insurance in many cases unprofitable. A marketplace like *Caruso* can reduce these transaction costs significantly and enable use cases that rely on data from various sources. Instead of making bilateral agreements, the insurance providers can directly access mobility data of all major OEMs through the marketplace.

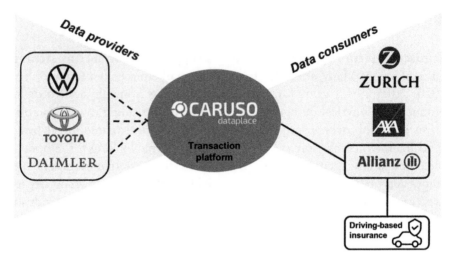

Fig. 3 Illustration of a potential use case for *Caruso*, a marketplace for IoT mobility data, author's own illustration

However, network effects are necessary for *Caruso*'s business model to work. Similar to *Airbnb*, the value for data consumers, e.g., insurance company, increases with the number of data providers, e.g., car OEMs. Hence, *Caruso* needs to provide strong incentives for OEMs to join its platform as data providers and to share their (sensitive) mobility data. On the other side of the platform, *Caruso* tries to attract companies that need data for providing value-adding analyses and services. To realize these positive, indirect network effects, *Caruso* relies heavily on standardization and scaling. *Caruso*'s strategy is to focus initially on flagship data providers, such as large OEMs, who, in turn, encourage data consumers to join the platform. Data consumers are additionally incentivized by free offers, e.g., free access for 3 months during the prototyping phase. Afterwards—borrowed from the consumer segment—*Caruso* tries to sell "data subscriptions" (Caruso 2020c).

Although *Caruso* is (so far) limited to mobility data, this type of marketplace for IoT data will play an increasingly important role in the future. In a world where data is becoming a key asset, such a marketplace can facilitate new business models. It can make this valuable and sensitive resource available to smaller actors and share it between producers, complementors, and end-consumers. Nevertheless, one must not forget how difficult it is to coordinate the various parties involved to exchange and use (each other's) data. This also illustrates the relevance of ecosystem thinking in the *Caruso* context, i.e., aligning and coordinating the producers of complementary products. It is, therefore, no wonder that *Caruso* is not a stand-alone company, but a consortium that began as an industry-wide initiative. Moreover, *Caruso* is still in its infancy, and its future success cannot be taken for granted.

5 IoT Innovation Platforms like *Bosch* IoT Suite

Innovation platforms are "products, services, or technologies developed by one or more firms, and which serve as foundations upon which a larger number of firms can build further complementary innovations" (Gawer and Cusumano 2014). One of the leading innovation platforms is the *Apple* operating system for computers (macOS). The operating system forms the basis on which external companies can develop complementary applications. *Apple* tries to orchestrate this innovation by offering standardized interfaces such as SDKs that support external companies in developing these complementary applications such as *Microsoft* Office. The value and network effect on an innovation platform result from the complementary innovation. The more applications there are, the higher the quality and benefit for the users. This increases the willingness for new users to join the platform, i.e., to buy a notebook with the Macintosh operating system. Vice versa, if more consumers are joining the platform, more software developers are attracted to develop complementary software. Typically, most innovation platforms converge with ecosystems. It is no wonder that further examples of innovation platforms are *Apple* iOS, *Firefox*, *Microsoft* Windows, and *Sony PlayStation*.

In the IoT, platforms cannot only serve as transaction intermediaries, as in the *Caruso* example. They can also offer manufacturers of devices the technology, in form of an innovation platform, to connect their devices to the Internet (see Fig. 4). With the connectivity of the devices, complementary applications, similar to the *Apple* operating system, can be developed. The *Bosch* IoT Suite is a good example for such a case. In its core, it provides software for manufacturers of devices to connect their physical devices with the Internet, collect data, and run analyses (Bosch.IO 2020a). This enables them to monitor and improve their products and services as well as build complementary innovation on top of the IoT platform.

The *Bosch* IoT Suite is based on open source software (Eclipse Foundation 2020) and provides, just like macOS, a basis for external developers to efficiently implement IoT applications. Similar to *Apple*, the more developers join the platform, the more applications are created. This, in turn, increases the benefits for the manufacturers of devices and their motivation to join the innovation platform, i.e., to purchase and integrate the IoT Suite. Vice versa,

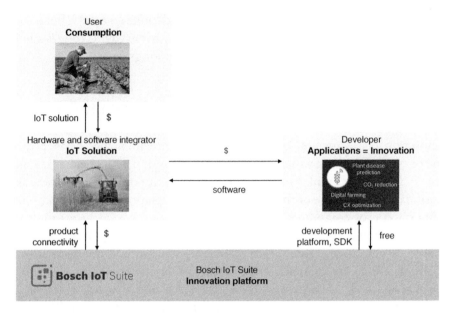

Fig. 4 Illustration of the *Bosch* IoT Suite, an IoT innovation platform, author's own illustration

the more IoT Suite users there are, the more developers are attracted. Also, data can be considered an additional driver of network effects in this cycle (Falk and Riemensperger 2019). The more data is generated via products connected through the *Bosch* IoT Suite, the more attractive it is for the developer to join this platform to develop complementary applications on the basis of existing data assets instead of joining a competitive IoT platform (see also chapter "Bosch IoT Suite: Exploiting the Potential of Smart Connected Products" for the *Bosch* IoT Suite).

Often, network effects known from consumer-based platforms like *Apple* iOS are not as strong in the case of B2B. Reasons are the heterogeneity of the user side, i.e., B2B companies, and the increased complexity for external developers to create complementary applications. Therefore, IoT innovation platforms like the *Bosch* IoT Suite try to provide an additional value with stand-alone applications. Instead of fully relying on complementary applications from the outside, *Bosch*, for instance, offers IoT solutions for different industries itself (Bosch.IO 2020b). This approach is also known in the consumer domain. *Apple*, for example, also providers its own macOS office suite with Keynote, Pages, and Numbers.

6   IoT Integration Platforms like *SAST*

Integration platforms combine a transaction and innovation platform. Thus, they are often referred to as a hybrid platform (Cusumano et al. 2020). *Apple* with its iPhone operating system (iOS) and the App Store can be regarded as one of the most successful integration platforms. On the one hand, *Apple* offers companies and individuals free SDKs to develop complementary applications (innovation platform). In fact, the iOS operating system has become the foundation for over four million complementary applications (Statista 2020). On the other hand, *Apple* brings app developers and users together via the App Store (transaction platform) to exchange apps. This has led to very strong indirect network effects between the two sides of developers and users. Other examples of successful integration platforms are *Salesforce, Google Play,* and *Facebook* with its SDKs.

While integration platforms have not yet become mainstream in IoT, there are promising ventures that bring innovation and transaction platform together. One example is *Security and Safety Things (SAST)*—a German-based start-up that has gone live at the beginning of 2020 (SAST 2020b). Its vision is—similar to *Google*—to create an app-store but for IoT-based security camera systems in the B2B segment. Based on the Android Open Source Project (AOSP), they have developed an operating system (see Fig. 5). Manufacturers of security cameras can integrate this OS into their smart, connected devices. *SAST* provides SDKs for its operating system so that external developers can create complementary applications for security systems (innovation platform). Furthermore, *SAST* provides a marketplace (transaction platform) for the developed security camera apps. Users or integrators of security cameras running *SAST* OS can easily download applications from this marketplace—in an *Apple* App Store kind of way—and add functionality to their surveillance camera. An exemplary B2B customer with a particularly high need for security is an airport. By purchasing hardware that runs on *SAST* OS, an airport could continuously improve the functionalities of its security cameras and adapt to changing legal requirements. A concrete application example could be AI-based baggage tracking of the owner in case of misplaced baggage on the airport premise or adding ad hoc functions like video-tracking of proper mask protection in the context of the Corona crisis (SAST 2020a).

However, for its vision to work, *SAST* must convince three sides: (1) the hardware manufacturers to implement their OS, (2) the application developers to use their SDKs, and (3) the customers to purchase *SAST* supported hardware. The current strategy is to bring many key market players on board

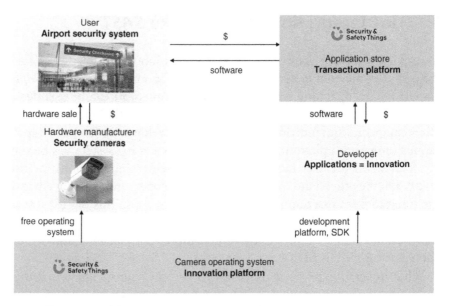

Fig. 5 Illustration of *SAST*, an IoT innovation platform and app store for security cameras, author's own illustration

to attract application developers to join as well. The offer of free SDKs and an initial demand will help to motivate application developers to participate. Recently—similar to the Android developer challenge in 2008—*SAST* launched a challenge with a 3× EUR 10,000 prize money for the best application (Bartlett 2020). To not inhibit the growth of network effects, *SAST* only charges a transaction fee for the purchase of applications—similar to the Apple App Store.

The indirect network effects of *SAST* can become quite strong as there are three sides. Essentially, if there are more manufactures (1) on the platform, more hardware runs on *SAST* OS which will attract more app developers and more users will potentially buy the hardware. If there are more developers (2), more complementary applications are built which, in turn, will attract more users and manufactures; if the user base is increasing (3), it becomes more attractive for additional manufacturers and app developers to join. However, having launched in 2020, the success of the platform has yet to be demonstrated. Nevertheless, the *SAST* application store already features—a couple of months after launching—72 applications for various use cases in different domains (SAST 2020a). The applications range from AI-based intrusion detection for commercial buildings, customer tracking for retail, privacy filters for airports, or livestock counting in agriculture.

7   Learnings from Building Platforms

The three examples illustrate that platforms in the IoT are particularly useful for making use of data and for enabling value-adding services. In fact, across the three platform types (transaction, innovation, and integration), IoT platforms (ecosystems) are becoming increasingly important. However, they also face unique challenges, in particular, compared to pure digital platforms in B2C, for instance.

Due to the nature of IoT, there is always hardware involved. Hence, platform owners have to understand the underlying physical products and their characteristics very well. For instance, *Caruso* has to deal with the "car" as the main source of shared mobility data. The *Bosch* IoT Suite has to deal with a variety of physical devices with different characteristics, from home appliances to special vehicle manufactures, and *SAST* has to understand security cameras and systems. Only in rare cases are platform owners also hardware manufacturers and can therefore already rely on their domain knowledge.

Due to the hardware component and heterogeneity of users, IoT platforms also do not scale as quickly, and network effects on IoT platforms tend to be weaker, especially compared to purely digital platforms like *Airbnb* or *WhatsApp*. On the other hand, data is given a very high priority. It is not just a unit of value exchanged over a platform, such as in the case of *Caruso*. It can also create opportunities for building new platforms, e.g., *Bosch* IoT Suite and *SAST*. In addition, data is becoming a major driver for network effects. In fact, network effects on IoT platforms depend not only on the growth of the two sides of the market but also on the data, as a result of the devices connected, to which the platform has access.

As platforms, ecosystems, and the IoT are converging, one has to think about the implications for their own business. A deeper look at the topic also shows that platforms oftentimes fail. Instead of joining forces with an existing platform to accelerate its network effects and to become the dominating platform, many companies try to establish their own platform leading to a situation where no platform can become successful. We, therefore, want to highlight ten success factors for developing platforms:

1. **Understand the fundamentals of (your) platform business:** Is it really a platform business you are aiming for? What are the network effects and how can you manage them? Or is it an internal technology platform? Regardless of your decision, it is important to fully understand the dynamics and consequences of the transformation from a pipeline to a platform business—even if you are not a platform owner but "only" a complementor.

2. **Do not reinvent the wheel but learn from existing platforms:** Many successful platform businesses have evolved. Utilize existing business model patterns to imitate or adjust them for the sake of your own business model. In particular, brainstorm about what the "core value" and "core transaction" should look like and how each platform participant could benefit from the platform.

3. **Consider all strategic paths in the platform economy:** Start with an initial analysis of your industry: Are there platforms in your industry—or in adjacent industries—with the potential to disrupt your business? Are there chances to develop an own platform for your business? Depending on the industry and competitive situation, think about participating as a complementor or as a co-owner. Keep in mind that it does not necessarily always make sense for a company to build its own platform and to become the orchestrator.

4. **Strictly focus on the customer journey:** What are the gains and pains of the customer? What are the explicit and hidden requirements of customers and participating partners to join the platform? Users only lock in on a platform if they can expect a superior value proposition. If there is no such promise or if it is not fulfilled, the platform will become a zombie: not enough alive to grow and flower.

5. **Differentiate between the purpose of a platform:** Platforms are not just platforms. It is often oversimplified when success factors for platforms are summarized. Instead, it makes sense to distinguish according to the different platform function: Is it a transaction, innovation, or integration platform? Transaction platforms should be easy and convenient; innovation platforms should offer an attractive development environment and carefully design their openness, e.g., through APIs and SDKs.

6. **Think early about how you can address common challenges of platforms:** Although most challenges are well recognized in theory, history shows that platforms often fail for obvious reasons. It is important to early think about how to address common challenges. In particular, a strategy is needed on how to build network effects, i.e., how to overcome the chicken-and-egg problem, and how your platform can be successfully monetized in the long run.

7. **Monitor and manage your platform growth closely:** To establish a sustainable platform business, it is not enough to simply track traditional financial KPIs such as revenue. Especially at the beginning it is important to closely track network effects as a key growth driver, e.g., via interaction quality or number of users. The most successful platform companies go even further and carefully monitor and manage negative network effects. They should not be neglected, as they can potentially lead to a negative

vicious circle, e.g., if fraud or an information overload makes the platform increasingly unattractive.

8. **Think big but prove yourself in a micro-market:** Since all platforms depend on network effects, a platform idea must have the potential to generate strong network effects. At the same time, a business idea should prove itself already as a prototype or in a small market. Most successful platforms took advantage of this thinking and started in micro-markets, with a geographical and/or product focus, and continued to expand from there once a critical mass had been reached.

9. **Think both ecosystem and platform—especially for IoT:** At some point in time, to innovate, most of the successful platforms have expanded into adjacent industries, e.g., Apple moving into the health segment or Tencent moving into the payment segment. To achieve this mission, they are aiming to build strong ecosystems. Since IoT has become very diverse and complex, specific domain knowledge is often needed. It is therefore important to also align with other companies in order to realize one common value proposition in your IoT platform ecosystem.

10. **Know the underlying dynamics when dealing with IoT platforms:** Compared to digital platforms, IoT platforms always rely on devices. To create a successful platform in the IoT, one must, therefore, fully understand the underlying product(s)—especially if one is not a manufacturer of the same devices. They also do not rely as much on network effects. IoT platforms, therefore, bring more stand-alone value to the platform. In addition, the role of data in IoT platforms, as a resource and a driver for network effects, needs to be clearly understood. This comes with both challenges, such as privacy and security concerns, but also many opportunities for building novel platform business.

Success Factors for Developing Platforms

- Understand the fundamentals of (your) platform business.
- Do not reinvent the wheel but learn from existing platforms.
- Consider all strategic paths in the platform economy.
- Strictly focus on the customer journey.
- Differentiate between the purpose of a platform: transaction, innovation, and integration.
- Think early about how you can address common challenges of platforms.
- Monitor and manage your platform growth closely.
- Think big but prove yourself in a micro-market.
- Think both ecosystem and platform—especially for industrial IoT.
- Learn about the underlying dynamics when dealing with IoT platforms.

References

Adner R (2017) Ecosystem as structure. J Manag 43(1):39–58

Airbnb (2020) About us. https://news.airbnb.com/about-us/. Accessed 1 Sept 2020

Bartlett, J (2020) Security and Safety things opens app challenge for developers. Security.World. https://security.world/security-and-safety-things-opens-app-challenge-for-developers/. Accessed 18 Apr 2020

Bosch.IO (2020a) Bosch IoT Suite service catalog. https://developer.bosch-iot-suite.com/service-catalog/. Accessed 1 Sept 2020

Bosch.IO (2020b) IoT use cases powered by AI. https://bosch.io/use-cases/. Accessed 1 Sept 2020

Caruso (2020a) Discover who we are and what we stand for. https://www.caruso-dataplace.com/about/#shareholder. Accessed 1 Sept 2020

Caruso (2020b) Success stories. https://www.caruso-dataplace.com/success-stories/. Accessed 1 Sept 2020

Caruso (2020c) Tailored pricing. https://www.caruso-dataplace.com/pricing/. Accessed 1 Sept 2020

Chen M, Mao S, Liu Y (2014) Big data: a survey. Mobile Netw Appl 19(2):171–209

Cusumano MA, Gawer A, Yoffie DB (2019) The business of platforms: strategy in the age of digital competition, innovation, and power. Harper Business

Cusumano MA, Yoffie DB, Gawer A (2020) The future of platforms. Sloan Manag Rev 61(3):46–54

Eclipse Foundation (2020) Eclipse Hono. https://projects.eclipse.org/projects/iot.hono. Accessed 1 Sept 2020

Falk S, Riemensperger F (2019) Three lessons from Germany's platform economy. MIT Sloan Manag Front. https://sloanreview.mit.edu/article/three-lessons-from-germanys-platform-economy/. Accessed 1 Sept 2020

Fleisch E, Weinberger M, Wortmann F (2014) Geschäftsmodelle im Internet der Dinge. HMD Praxis Der Wirtschaftsinformatik 51:812–826

Gawer A, Cusumano MA (2014) Industry platforms and ecosystem innovation. J Prod Innov Manag 31(3):417–433

Iansiti M, Lakhani KR (2014) Digital ubiquity How connections, sensors, and data are revolutionizing business. Harv Bus Rev 92(11)

Iansiti M, Levien R (2004) Strategy as ecology. Harv Bus Rev 82(3):68–72

Jacobides MG, Cennamo C, Gawer A (2018) Towards a theory of ecosystems. Strateg Manag J 39(8):2255–2276

Parker G, Van Alstyne M, Choudary SP (2016) Platform revolution. W.W. Norton, New York

Porter ME, Heppelmann JE (2014) Smart, connected products are transforming competition. Harv Bus Rev 92(11):64–88

Price Waterhouse Coopers (2020) Global top 100 companies by market capitalisation. https://www.pwc.com/gx/en/audit-services/publications/assets/global-top-100-companies-june-2020-update.pdf. Accessed 8 Sept 2020

Rochet JC, Tirole J (2003) Platform competition in two-sided markets. J Eur Econ Assoc 1(4):990–1029

SAST (2020a) Application store. https://store.securityandsafetythings.com/shop/catalog/c/main. Accessed 1 Sept 2020

SAST (2020b) Security and safety things brings growing IoT platform for security cameras to CES 2020. https://www.securityandsafetythings.com/news/press-release-january-2020. Accessed 7 Jan 2020

Statista (2020) Number of active apps from the Apple App Store 2008-2020. https://www.statista.com/statistics/268251/number-of-apps-in-the-itunes-app-store-since-2008/. Accessed 1 Sept 2020

van Alstyne MW, Parker G, Choudary SP (2016) Pipelines, platforms, and the new rules of strategy. Harv Bus Rev 94(4):54–62

Zhu F, Iansiti M (2019) Why some platforms thrive and others don't. Harv Bus Rev 97(1):118–125

Sven Jung is a PhD candidate at the Institute of Technology Management at the University of St. Gallen. He is part of the Bosch IoT Lab, a cooperation between the Bosch Group, University of St. Gallen and ETH Zurich, where he investigates (IoT) platform strategies and platform business models. Sven holds a Master's degree in Finance and Strategic Management from Copenhagen Business School and a Bachelor's degree in Business Administration from the University of St. Gallen. During his studies, he worked for a leading management consultancy, a biotech start-up and an investment bank advising technology start-ups.

Felix Wortmann, Prof. Dr., is Assistant Professor of Technology Management at the University of St. Gallen. He is also the Scientific Director of the Bosch IoT Lab, a cooperation between the Bosch Group, University of St. Gallen, and ETH Zurich. Felix Wortmann has published more than 100 publications and is among the top 5% of all scientists in business administration in the German-speaking countries (Wirtschaftswoche 2019). His research interests include the Internet of Things, machine learning, blockchain, and business model innovation in manufacturing, mobility, healthcare, and energy. From 2006 to 2009 he worked as an assistant to the executive board of SAP. After studying information systems, Felix Wortmann received his PhD in Management from the University of St. Gallen in 2006.

Wolfgang Bronner, Dr., is managing director of the Bosch IoT Lab, a cooperation between the Bosch Group, University of St. Gallen, and ETH Zurich. This lab is particularly dedicated on the Internet of Things, Data Science, and Business Model Innovation. Wolfgang Bronner had his first insight into the high-tech industry as a student at IBM in Silicon Valley. He has been working as an expert and manager in various industries and functions at Bosch in Germany and the USA since 2002. In his last position, he analyzed the impact of the most significant future technologies such as AI on Bosch, derived strategic recommendations, and discussed them with the executive management. He received his PhD in physics from the University of Stuttgart in 2003.

Oliver Gassmann, Prof. Dr., is Professor for Technology Management at the University of St. Gallen and Director of the Institute of Technology Management since 2002. His research focus lies on patterns and success factors of innovation. He has been visiting faculty at Berkeley (2007), Stanford (2012), and Harvard (2016). Prior to his academic career, Gassmann was the head of corporate research at Schindler. His more than 400 publications are highly cited; his book *The Business Model Navigator* became a global bestseller. He received the Scholarly Impact Award of the Journal of Management in 2014. He founded several spin-offs, is member of several boards of directors, like Zühlke, and is an internationally recognized keynote speaker.

Ecosystems: Unlocking the Potentials of Innovation Beyond Borders

Bernhard Lingens

1   The Good, the Bad and the Buzzword: Four Types of Ecosystems

The term "ecosystem" is spreading like a pandemic. Everyone refers to it, but few people know exactly what it means. This is particularly problematic in practice as implementation requires strategy. And strategy requires a sound analysis and educated discussion. How is that possible if the people in the boardroom are not sharing the same terminology and understanding of a concept? To make things worse, in the case of ecosystems, we can observe even four different concepts with all of them being characterized by very different goals and meanings, as shown in Fig. 1.

Industry ecosystem is nothing new. For instance, "the start-up ecosystem in the Silicon Valley" refers to all organizations being active in the start-up world in this region. Beyond that, there is no underlying concept nor meaning. Likewise, knowledge ecosystems are neither an emerging concept nor a very complex one. Their core idea is to facilitate knowledge exchange amongst different organizations, usually firms as well as universities. We all know industry clusters, co-working spaces, innovation hubs and similar examples for that type of ecosystems. The platform ecosystem, whilst heavily being promoted

B. Lingens (✉)
Institute of Marketing and Analytics, University of Lucerne,
St. Gallen, Switzerland
e-mail: bernhard.lingens@unilu.ch

© The Author(s), under exclusive license to Springer Nature Switzerland AG 2021
O. Gassmann, F. Ferrandina (eds.), *Connected Business*,
https://doi.org/10.1007/978-3-030-76897-3_3

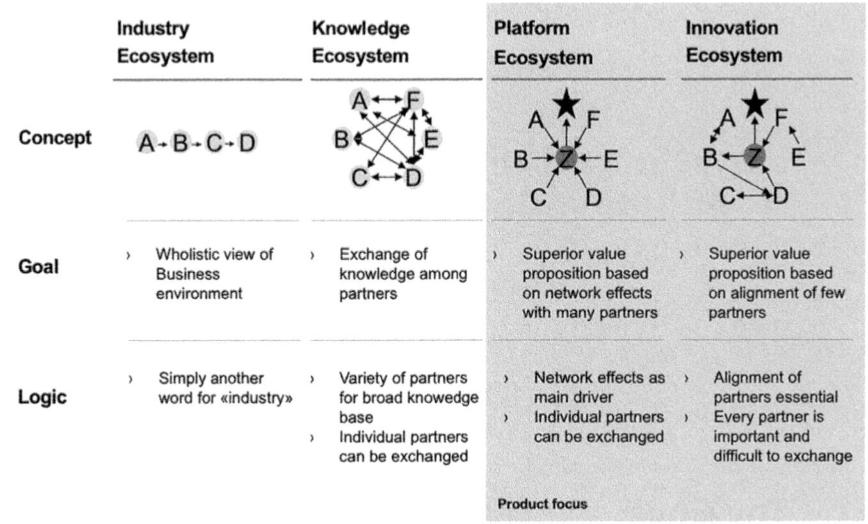
Industry Ecosystem
Knowledge Ecosystem
Platform Ecosystem
Innovation Ecosystem
Concept
A-B-C-D
Goal
Wholistic view of Business environment
Exchange of knowledge among partners
Superior value proposition based on network effects with many partners
Superior value proposition based on alignment of few partners
Logic
Simply another word for «industry»
Variety of partners for broad knowedge base
Individual partners can be exchanged
Network effects as main driver
Individual partners can be exchanged
Alignment of partners essential
Every partner is important and difficult to exchange
Product focus

Fig. 1 Overview on different types of ecosystems, author's own illustration

by consulting firms and business executives alike, is a widely established concept. Platform ecosystems such as the *Apple* iTunes store, *Facebook*, *WhatsApp* and *Amazon* can be viewed as (electronic) marketplaces, in which exchange between demand and supply takes place. The underlying idea is that of a quantitative network effect, as perfectly shown by *Amazon*: The more traders are using *Amazon*, the broader the offer and the more attractive the platform becomes from a buyer's perspective. The more attractive it is for the buyers, the more individuals are using *Amazon*, which makes the marketplace more attractive for the sellers, and so on. Eventually the network effect as a vicious cycle between offer and demand comes into place. This leads to two key implications. First, platform ecosystems need a critical mass on both sides of the platform in order for the network effect to successfully evolve. This makes scaling to the one of the most essential goals during the early stages of establishing an ecosystem. Second, once the network effect has developed, it is often driving the platform to a winner-takes-it-all logic. *Amazon* as the dominating online marketplace and *Facebook* as the most powerful social network in the western world are examples for that. In any case, a platform ecosystem is driven through a quantitative logic. Thus, scaling and growing are the existential paradigms.

2   The Innovation Ecosystem as a New Driver for Innovation

As suggested by its name, the ultimate purpose of an innovation ecosystem is the creation of an innovation a company could not create on its own. The Swiss start-up *Tailored Fits* serves as a great example for such setting. Within 1.5 years, with an investment of approximately CHF 300,000 and with just 1.5 employees, the firm managed to launch one of the first 3D-printed inlay soles for running shoes on the market. What seems to be a simple product is actually the holy grail of the sports industry. Leading players have been trying to do the same but usually needed around ten times the manpower and financial investment as well as three times the time *Tailored Fits* had at their disposal. This difference resulted out of the following approach: *Tailored Fits*, opposed to the large corporates of the sports industry, used an innovation ecosystem to bring their product to the market. They did not create all modules needed for this innovation to come true by themselves, namely, a dense network of stores serving as the customer interface, knowledge in biomechanics as well as 3D printing, production/printing facilities and so forth. Instead, each module was provided through a specialized partner—The network of stores by a sports retailer, the knowledge in biomechanics by a clinic, the 3D-printing facilities and knowledge by one of the largest 3D-printing companies in the world. All of these partners were coordinated by *Tailored Fits*. This example nicely shows the three key elements of an innovation ecosystem:

1. An innovation ecosystem is always aiming at a joint value proposition, in this case the customized sole.
2. The value proposition consists of complementary modules, provided by partners (here: 3D printing facilities, stores, etc.).
3. The partners are aligned and coordinated towards the joint value proposition by the orchestrator (here: *Tailored Fits*).

However, not all settings with these three elements are necessarily an innovation ecosystem. Even a traditional supply chain could be described like that. Thus, an innovation ecosystem approach is only necessary if one additional component comes into place: The modules do either not exist at all (unlikely in practice) or, at least, require a significant effort for development or adjustment. As a consequence, all partners become dependent on each other since the joint value proposition requires a successful development of all modules by all partners involved. If one partner does not deliver as promised, the ecosystem fails as a whole. And, as a second consequence, the orchestration of this collaborative innovation endeavour causes significant coordination efforts for the orchestrator as well as the partners involved. These two key challenges of innovation ecosystems are driven through the novelty of the modules. The more the modules need to be adapted or developed, i.e. the higher the associated development risks, the greater the mutual dependency amongst the actors as well as the coordination effort and the more an innovation ecosystem approach is needed. If none or only a small development is necessary, both key challenges are less significant, and the setting could more appropriately be described as a supply chain. Accordingly, if less development and development risk are involved, partners can be managed with strict contracts, which they are unlikely to agree to if they are aware of a major development risk and strong mutual dependencies in fulfilment to other partners. Beyond these challenges, innovation ecosystems create an overarching need for coordination and related questions: What is my role within the ecosystem? Am I the orchestrator or rather one of the partners? How to fulfil the role of an orchestrator?

Likewise, the two key advantages of innovation ecosystems are further driven through the novelty of the modules. First, innovation ecosystems allow firms to step into recent fields of business they could not approach in isolation due to a lack of resources or knowledge. Second, they make it possible to do so without significantly investing into building up these resources or competencies. Coming back to the example of *Tailored Fits*, using an innovation ecosystem approach enabled a small start-up from Switzerland to compete against the leading firms in the sports industry—with a fraction of their financial investment, manpower, and time for the very same product (Fig. 2).

3   Four Pathways of Unfolding the Strategic Potentials of Innovation Ecosystems

Based on the understanding of ecosystems and their key challenges as well as advantages, we can draw upon examples of leading corporates that show us how to use ecosystems in practice. In general, four pathways can be observed: (1) innovate the core offering, (2) extend the core offering, (3) grow along the customer journey and (4) step into novel fields of business (Fig. 3).

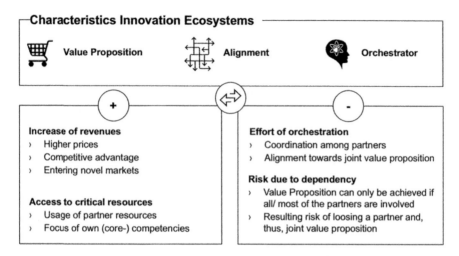

Fig. 2 Characteristics of innovation ecosystems, author's own illustration

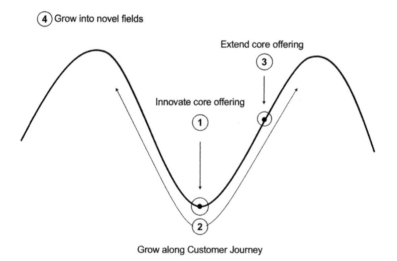

Fig. 3 Different ways of applying ecosystem strategies, author's own illustration

1. **Innovate the core offering: drones at *Swiss Post*.** *Swiss Post* is breaking new ground in Zurich and Lugano: completely autonomously flying drones deliver goods automatically from A to B. Even if this is currently only done in one specific application in the hospital sector, it does not require much imagination to assess the relevance for the way in which *Swiss Post* will organize delivery in the future. And whilst Swiss Post is still doing what they have always done, namely, delivering goods, they are doing so in an innovative and technologically advanced way.

Does *Swiss Post* have extensive expertise in the field of aviation and drones? No, but thanks to an innovation ecosystem consisting of the Swiss Air Traffic Control Authority (responsible for creating the regulation), a start-up from Silicon Valley (development of the drone) and the customer of the innovation (a hospital that had to adapt its internal logistics), this step into the future became possible. This example illustrates several points: It shows that innovation ecosystems can be used to implement an existing customer need in a new, technologically better or more sustainable way—even if the relevant fields of competence are not mastered. Also, whilst many people believe ecosystems are a means to build up large value propositions or offerings, *Swiss Post* and other firms using a similar approach demonstrate the value of innovation ecosystems by implementing a very specific product for a very specific need. And it shows that ecosystems are an opportunity for established companies to modernize and to carry out the digital transformation without having to build up expensive capabilities themselves.

2. **Extend the core offering: *Tradeplus24* and *Credit Suisse*.** *Credit Suisse* is not just one of the leading banks in Switzerland, it is also a major provider of financial services for small and medium-sized enterprises (SMEs). Lately, stepping into the innovation ecosystem of *Tradeplus24* allowed *Credit Suisse* to extend their core offering by an innovative product: *Tradeplus24* offers an innovative factoring solution, specifically relevant for SMEs doing business abroad. Many of these firms are confronted with long payment periods or delays, which makes factoring (a financial transaction in which a business sells its invoices to a third party at a discount) an interesting option for them to meet their cash needs. However, current factoring approaches are not suitable for all companies and are particularly difficult to get for SMEs being in an economically weak position. This is when Tradeplus24 comes into place: Their value proposition, the innovative factoring solution, is based on several modules: an automatic scan of the SMEs' invoices to standardize risks, an insurance taking over these risks and investors providing funding. *Tradeplus24* is the orchestrator of this innovation ecosystem. At a later stage, *Credit Suisse* became an ecosystem partner and created a win-win situation. They provide access to their clients, which offers an attractive potential for *Tradeplus24* to scale its business. And *Credit Suisse* can extend its core offering by integrating an innovative solution. Beyond that, the example shows that corporates do not necessarily have to be the orchestrator of an innovation ecosystem. Instead, they can be a complementor, which allows them to profit from the advantages provided by the ecosystem whilst not taking over the effort and

responsibility that come with maintaining the role of the orchestrator. Thinking one step further, corporates can establish a portfolio of solutions provided by different ecosystems in order to extend their product offering with innovative solutions. Also, this allows them to reduce the dependencies from a single ecosystem.

3. **Grow along the customer journey: ecosystem "HOME" by *Helvetia*.** *Helvetia* is a large, traditional insurance company in Switzerland and is very well positioned. However, differentiation on the basis of traditional insurance and financial solutions is difficult to achieve, the market is stagnating, and growth potentials beyond M&A are often hardly realizable.

   The solution: *Helvetia* no longer intends to be solely a provider of insurance and financial products in the residential segment but aims to be active along the customer journey "HOME" by offering a bundle of services. These services reach from searching for an apartment or a house towards financing and renovation to modernization and even smart living. This provides access to additional offers and sources of income and differentiation. However, *Helvetia* is not able to provide such an offer on its own. This is why *Helvetia* enters into ecosystem partnerships to design the new service package—whether it be start-ups such as the *Flatfox* brokerage platform, which creates innovative insurance products, or the *MoneyPark* mortgage comparison platform, around which services for the purchase of real estate are designed.

   The *Helvetia* case shows that ecosystems are not just a means of improving existing solutions or initiating new ones for the customer. They are also able to satisfy needs outside the core service or on the complete customer journey. They are creating new growth and differentiation potentials and a solution-oriented corporate strategy for their future market position.

4. **Step into novel fields of business: the case of *BMW* Switzerland.** This strategic pathway constitutes not only the bravest but also the most risky step that can be approached by using innovation ecosystems: to grow into novel fields of business. An example is *BMW* Switzerland. Confronted with adverse trends in the automotive market, such as car sharing, autonomous driving and the social megatrend of youngsters losing fondness for owning their own car, manufacturers need to transform their business model, from producing cars to offering mobility solutions. In the case of *BMW* Switzerland, the company decided to step into the field of smart mobility by providing inter-modal mobility solutions for business customers. This allows firms, for instance, the Swiss firm *V-ZUG*, to offer their employees smart mobility solutions and, thereby, to reduce needs for parking space or an extensive business car fleet. For *BMW*, this is not just a step towards a

novel business model, it is also one into a new field of business and technology. Producing and selling cars is only one part of the puzzle. The rest is mostly about software and IT as well as understanding the mechanisms of smart city and smart mobility. These aspects point towards an innovation ecosystem in order to get access to the competencies needed for that endeavour. As a consequence, *BMW* partnered with, among others, *SAP* and *Deloitte* to bring in the missing competencies.

The case of *BMW* shows several implications. First, innovation ecosystems allow firms to not only extend or innovate their core offering. They can be a means to even grow into very novel fields of business and embark towards new business models. Second, it shows that innovation ecosystems are not necessarily led by just one orchestrator. If the targeted business area requires a mix of competencies, network and knowledge stemming from different fields, several firms can orchestrate an ecosystem together. Finally, with every major step away from the boundaries of the traditional business, the associated innovation risk is growing as well. Thus, taking such massive steps into unknown land requires strong top-management backing and the awareness that such endeavours might take a long time before a return on investment can be achieved.

4   The Ten Ecosystem Commandments

As posed within the last section, innovation ecosystems open up very different pathways for achieving strategic value for the company. What they all have in common are some basic implications on how to build up ecosystems. In the following, we would like to discuss those:

1. Ecosystems are a means, not an end.

How many times have we heard sentences such as "we need an ecosystem" and "we see ecosystems as a key strategic priority"? As much as they might be positive signs for the respective firms innovative mindset, they are inherently wrong. The ultimate purpose of an innovation ecosystem is the establishment of an innovative value proposition. If such value proposition can be achieved in isolation, no ecosystem approach should be aimed for. It causes extra coordination effort and risks by dependencies from partners. Also, if the value proposition is based on exiting modules that just need to be assembled, there is no need for an ecosystem approach. Such setting would lead to a classic supply-chain approach. And whilst this might not sound as fancy as the magic term ecosystem, it is much easier to coordinate and comes with less dependencies and risks. As an implication, firms should not start with the preconception of building up an ecosystem. Instead, they should have the intention to achieve an innovation. If that requires an ecosystem setting, the firm can build up one. If it can be achieved with a classical open innovation or even supply chain setting, the firm does not need an innovation ecosystem.

2. Different types of ecosystems need to be applied for different purposes.

As described above, there are at least four different types of ecosystems. And all of them have different purposes and underlying mechanisms. Thus, ecosystems are tools that need to be used according to the purpose at hand. Is that purpose the exchange of knowledge? The creation of a digital marketplace? Or the creation of an innovation? Even though all of the associated concepts are called "ecosystems", they are very different means for very different ends. And this is more than just an academic exercise: Without an understanding of the values and purposes of these different concepts and their respective meanings, it might be difficult to have a structured discussion and decision-making in the boardroom.

3. Earning potentials are the natural barriers for innovation ecosystems.

Currently, we can observe the emergence of innovation ecosystems in some industries, whilst others might not yet being equally hit by that trend. Amongst the industries being seemingly prone to the emergence of innovation ecosystems are insurance, telecommunications, mobility, logistics and, more recently, banking. But why is that? And why are some industries less attracted by this novel concept? First, as stated above, ecosystems are a means, not an end. And this end is usually either growth or differentiation. Given the disadvantages of ecosystems, namely, coordination effort and dependencies, firms would usually try to grow and differentiate by innovating with the existing competencies and resources before trying to involve external parties. Thus, we can usually observe the emergence of ecosystems in those industries, in which the more traditional growth and differentiation levers are exhausted already. Also, stagnating market growths and homogenous product offerings within the industry are typical drivers for the emergence of ecosystems. And, finally, one important aspect is often forgotten: Ecosystems need to focus on offerings customers are willing and able to pay a premium for. This is since, on the one hand, the extra efforts and risks that come with ecosystems need to be covered. And, on the other hand, the remaining earnings need to be divided amongst the partners involved. Industries suffering from low margins due to decreased willingness to pay are not the best environment for the emergence of innovation ecosystems even though these industries might particularly profit from further innovation potentials.

4. Innovation ecosystems are not agile but increase long-term agility.

What seems to be contradictory is a direct result of the fundamentals of innovation ecosystems: The coordination of several, mutually dependent, partners at the same time makes it very inefficient to iterate the value proposition according to customer needs. Thus, firms usually come up with an initial value proposition, test it with customers and freeze the offering before involving partners for its instantiation. Hence, once the partners are on board, orchestrators usually avoid further iterations of the value proposition, even though these would have improved the value offered to the customer. This seems to be a throwback to the times of the "happy engineering" but is an inevitable approach to reduce transaction costs and time-consuming negotiations with partners or even exchange of those having been involved based on the initial value proposition and resulting business case. Whilst innovation ecosystems are not very compatible with agile thinking in terms of product development, they do help firms to become more agile structurally and in the long term. This is an effect of their characteristics too: Ecosystems allow firms to utilize new technologies without building up the required competencies and knowledge in-house. The resulting focus on existing or even core competencies reduces footprint and investments, which leads to greater structural agility in the long term.

5. As a corporate, always start with the assumption of NOT being the orchestrator.

"What will be your role in a future ecosystem? We will be the orchestrator since we are one of the biggest companies in our field." Does that conversation sound familiar? It has surely happened before and will happen again many times in the future. It shows that most firms confuse the position of the orchestrator with a position of power. However, this position only implies a role as a servant for the ecosystems, aligning the interests of all firms involved, coordinating the efforts in achieving the joint value proposition and ensuring long-term stability and, if needed, renewal of the ecosystem.

What makes a firm suitable to do so? First, it requires speed of product development. Since all firms involved knowing about their mutual dependencies, they are likely to lose trust in the orchestrator if things are not going as fast and as well as expected. Thus, most successful orchestrators manage to come up with an MVP within approximately 6 months and a more evolved prototype within a year. Most ecosystems we studied managed to bring their respective product to the market within 1–1.5 years. Whilst the initial business case is what makes firms to commit to the ecosystem, it is the progress in developing that value proposition that holds them on board.

Second, flexibility is key. If an ecosystem consists of several players, some of them being large corporates with well-established internal processes, long hierarchies and slow decision-making, it is the orchestrator that needs to adapt to them. Imagine the opposite: an orchestrator being as slow and inflexible as the partners—this usually leads to more discussions about contracts, legal issues and delays than those about the product development. Third, neutrality should not be forgotten. The partners expect the orchestrator to be the neutral conductor of the ecosystem. And, fourth, the establishment of ecosystem requires knowledge and network related to the targeted field of business. On the one hand, since knowledge is needed to define the value proposition, iterate it with customers, and understand the modules and contributions needed for its implementation. On the other hand, network and knowledge are essential to not just define relevant partners but also to understand their needs and agendas and create knowledge overlapping as a foundation for collaboration.

Are these characteristics typical for corporates? The last two eventually, but most likely not the first two. And even the third, neutrality, might be an issue for corporates with a long-standing history of doing business with certain companies. Accordingly, most successful innovation ecosystems are actually orchestrated by start-ups. But does that mean that corporates should not even consider to be the orchestrator? Not necessarily. Instead, they can think about spinning out the department responsible for ecosystem orchestration, thus creating the start-up-like structures they need to achieve the above-mentioned requirements. As another approach, they can initiate the ecosystem as a so-called strategic orchestrator and delegate the operational orchestration, i.e. product development and day-to-day management, to a smaller and more suitable player in a later stage of ecosystem development. Or they can follow the example of *Credit Suisse* and profit from ecosystems by being a complementor firm.

6. Ecosystem initiatives need top management backing.

Given their key challenges, namely, mutual dependency and coordination effort, innovation ecosystem initiatives are usually long-term projects that require significant resource input. On the one hand, there are costs associated with product development, IT and so forth, which come with any innovation project. On top of this, there are the efforts being ecosystem specific. To be more precise: Ecosystem establishment requires time and human as well as financial resources. Regarding the first, we can observe in practice that ecosystem initiatives usually take around 1.5 years (in case of single-orchestrator ecosystems) and up to 3 years (in case of corporate-led multi-orchestrator configurations) from the start to market introduction. Obviously, market penetration and scaling towards break-even might take even more time.

Second, the above-mentioned coordination costs require manpower. A rule of thumb, based on our experience: An ecosystem of approximately five partners requires 2–3 FTE for coordination over the time of the first 1–1.5 years. Once the value proposition is in place and the initial back-and-forth iterations with the partners are done, IT can help to reduce transaction costs. But until then, the human brain is needed to settle conflicts, built-up social interactions and a modus operandi that works for all partners involved. On top of this, the usual troubleshooting that comes with any innovation project, especially in the complex setting of a multi-corporate innovation, should not be forgotten. And this is time-consuming and requires skilled persons being in charge of it.

Taken together, building up ecosystems requires resources and, therefore, top management support over a longer period of time. This is particularly important given the mutual dependency of the partners involved: If the orchestrator or another player within the ecosystem cannot deliver as promised due to internal budget or resource discussions, the other partners might lose faith in the partner or even the ecosystem as a whole and start withholding their contributions as well. The resulting delay and loss of trust might be the nail in the coffin of the ecosystem. Thus, a clear business as well as implementation plan and regular reports to top management are crucial. This also involves a clear communication on how the ecosystem initiative is in line with and supports the corporate strategy. Plus, top management needs to have a clear understanding of the challenges and the required time and resources of the ecosystem initiative from the very beginning onwards.

7. **Innovation ecosystems are a people business and need people management.**
It is the human side of ecosystem establishment that makes things particularly complicated: The best methods and tools are useless if the people involved in or affected by the ecosystem initiative are not on board. And in an ecosystem context, this challenge is twofold: First, ecosystems create a new organizational setting being composed of members stemming from different organizations. They need to work together on a joint goal whilst still being members of their respective firms whose agendas they are requested to pursue. This collaboration might have an IT level, a contractual level or well-defined processes, but we should not

forget that the majority of what happens in our brains is merely unconscious and beyond the rational world of business. If the representatives of different firms are not connecting with each other on a personal level, things will be far more complicated than expected. Second, given their innovative character, ecosystems often require corporate change within the firm. Imagine a traditional insurance company, which intends to turn into a full-service provider in the context of home and living: What seems to be a straightforward idea is, in reality, a massive change of corporate identity. And it is likely to reduce the importance of the mighty sales executives of the firm if insurance solutions will be integrated in products or service instead of being sold as a stand-alone product. As a consequence, any ecosystem initiative should always be accompanied by a change project that aims to identify and overcome the main barriers on a cultural level.

8. **Choose your role in an innovation ecosystem—you do not need to take over all of them.**

Surprisingly, many people follow the misconception that being a member of an ecosystem implies to be everything at once: ecosystem leader, customer interface, module provider and so forth. In reality, three key roles in an ecosystem are to be characterized, and we can observe companies taking over all of them or just one or two. These roles are orchestrator, module provider and customer interface. As an example, *Tailored Fits* is the mere orchestrator of the ecosystem needed to create the 3D-printed inlay soles without taking over any further role. *BMW* serves as a co-orchestrator of its smart mobility ecosystem whilst also providing an essential mobility module to the joint value proposition. And *Helvetia* provides modules to the joint value proposition in its HOME ecosystem, serves as the orchestrator and is one of the customer interfaces.

Thus, firms need to assess their potential role and contribution by answering the following questions: (1) Do you fulfil the criteria of an orchestrator? (2) Are you able to contribute a module to the joint value proposition? If so, you might be a suitable module provider. And, (3) do you have a strong base within the targeted customers and a strong credibility amongst them to be the customer interface? Thus grounded, you can take over either one or all three roles within the ecosystem. In other words, firms need to choose their role not based on the faith of being orchestrator or customer interface by default but based on being the best possible partner for that respective task. Otherwise, potential ecosystem partners might not be willing to work in a setting of mutual dependency with firms that are not suitable to fulfil the roles they are assigned to.

9. Innovation ecosystems are small rather than huge.

Many so-called experts claim that ecosystems are huge and will take over whole industries. This might be true for platform ecosystems with their winner-takes-it-all logic, which is driven through network effects. Innovation ecosystems follow a different logic: Independent firms are collaborating in a setting of mutual dependency and coordination towards a joint value proposition. And the more firms are being involved in that setting, the more coordination costs occur and the higher the likelihood of one partner stepping out of the ecosystem, thus leading to its failure as a whole. As an implication, firms building up innovation ecosystems should rather start the initiative with a "minimum viable ecosystem" in mind than trying to achieve a huge and industry-dominating construct. The key question here is: How does a value proposition look like that is already useful for the customer and competitive on the market but can be achieved with a few partners in a setting as simple as possible? Once this value proposition has been implemented and the ecosystem partners are collaborating efficiently and effectively, it can be extended by adding additional modules and partners. The resulting principle is that of an onion: First, implement the minimum viable value proposition with the minimum viable ecosystem as the heart of the initiative. Subsequently, you can add further layers around to extend the customer value. Doing so allows for a step-by-step integration of additional partners and, thus, makes it possible to keep coordination efforts and risks of dependency as low as possible.

10. Build up a portfolio of ecosystems rather than one big ecosystem.

As a rule of thumb, around 90% of all innovation endeavours are deemed to fail. Even though the phenomenon of innovation ecosystems is too novel to allow for reliable statistics, the increased risks due to dependency and coordination are likely to lead to even higher failure rates. Thus, it might not be advisable to stake everything on one card. Rather think about a portfolio of value propositions and ecosystems. Given the associated (coordination) efforts, it might not be possible to be the orchestrator of or even the module provider in all of them. However, as explained above, firms do not need to take over all roles in an ecosystem at once. Thus, the portfolio of ecosystems might embrace those in which the firm acts as an orchestrator, some in which it is a mere module provider and some in which it occupies the customer interface. If the portfolio of ecosystems is well coordinated and addresses a joint field of business, knowledge and learning spillovers from one ecosystem to the other are likely to occur, and the individual value propositions are complementary to each other. The *Helvetia* Ecosystem HOME serves as a nice example for this logic. *Helvetia* is driving several innovation initiatives along the customer journey HOME, which are creating an overarching offer of complementary services and products. Some of them can be seen as small ecosystems, some are in-house developments, and some are even integrations of value propositions being provided by partners but offered to the customers by *Helvetia*. Such a portfolio helps to decrease dependency from a single innovation endeavour and create added value by complementarity between products and services along the customer journey.

Success Factors for Setting Up an Ecosystem

Relevance/feasibility of ecosystem concept?
- Complementary and innovative modules needed.
- Modules are being provided by several partners.
- Intended value proposition yields sufficient margins.

Fit between ecosystem and firm strategy?
- Ecosystem supports firm strategy.
- Attractive long-term business plan exists.
- KPIs and reporting to top management defined.

Ability to take over orchestrator role?
- Organizational flexibility in place.
- Fast product development possible.
- Neutrality given.
- Network and knowledge exist.

Definition of sound ecosystem strategy?
- Suitable type of ecosystem chosen.
- Portfolio of complementary ecosystems defined.
- Ecosystem managers exhibit necessary skills.
- Management of cultural change defined.
- Role within ecosystems defined.
- Minimum viable ecosystems defined.
- Potentials for extension of ecosystem envisioned.

Dr. Bernhard Lingens is a member of the board of directors and Head Area Innovation at the Institute of Marketing and Analytics, University of Lucerne, Switzerland. He is also a visiting professor at Aalborg Business School, Denmark, and a research fellow at the University of St. Gallen, Switzerland. Prior to his current occupation, he was heading the Helvetia Innovation Lab at the University of St. Gallen and had been working as a strategy consultant at Roland Berger and a postdoc at Imperial College London. He holds a PhD in Innovation Management and a M. Sc. in Business and Engineering. His main focus is the question of how firms can innovate in ecosystems.

Digital Health Interventions

Tobias Kowatsch and Elgar Fleisch

1 Non-communicable Diseases as Health and Economic Challenge

With 73%, non-communicable diseases (NCDs) such as cardiovascular diseases, chronic respiratory diseases, cancer, and neurological or mental disorders were the leading cause of death in 2017 (Roth et al. 2018).[1] Equally alarming is that deaths caused by NCDs increased by circa 23% from 2007 to 7.6 million in 2017 (ibid.). Even worse, one out of three adults suffers from multiple NCDs (Marengoni et al. 2011) with disproportionally serious consequences for mortality, cognitive and physical functioning, as well as quality of life (Newman et al. 2020).[2]

NCDs also lead to a significant economic burden. Data from 18 high-, middle- and low-income countries indicate that NCD-households spent on average a significantly higher percentage of their effective income on health care than non-NCD households, for example, 16% vs. 6% in China (Murphy et al. 2020). Moreover, NCDs led to 90% of health-care spending in the

---

[1] A non-communicable disease (NCD) is a disease that is not transmissible directly from one person to another.

[2] Several passages of this chapter were taken from the habilitation thesis of Tobias Kowatsch submitted to the School of Management, University of St. Gallen, Switzerland, in January 2021.

T. Kowatsch (✉) • E. Fleisch
University of St. Gallen, St. Gallen, Switzerland
e-mail: tobias.kowatsch@unisg.ch; elgar.fleisch@unisg.ch

© The Author(s), under exclusive license to Springer Nature Switzerland AG 2021
O. Gassmann, F. Ferrandina (eds.), *Connected Business*,
https://doi.org/10.1007/978-3-030-76897-3_4

United States in 2014 (Buttorff et al. 2017), and recent findings show that four major NCDs (cardiovascular and chronic respiratory diseases, cancer, and diabetes) are responsible for a GDP loss of circa 2% in Europe (Vandenberghe and Albrecht 2020). Projections are alarming, too. For example, the total economic burden of NCDs in 2015–2050 in the United States is estimated to sum up to circa US$ 250,000 per capita with mental disorders and cardiovascular diseases being the two most contributing NCDs (Chen et al. 2018). With the increasing number of elderlies suffering from multiple NCDs, health expenditures sometimes increase exponentially with each additional condition (Hajat and Stein 2018) as the management gets more complex and requires health resources and specialists from various disciplines (Newman et al. 2020). So are 12% of Americans affected by five or more NCDs but contribute 41% of total health-care spending (Buttorff et al. 2017).

To address this problem, health interventions must target behavioral risk factors, for example, poor nutrition, physical inactivity, tobacco use, alcohol consumption, and metabolic risks such as obesity, high cholesterol, high blood pressure, or high blood glucose levels (WHO 2020). The prevention and management of NCDs require therefore an intervention paradigm that focuses on health-promoting behavior in our everyday lives (Katz et al. 2018; Kvedar et al. 2016). However, a corresponding change in lifestyle is only implemented by a fraction of those affected (Katz et al. 2018; Renders et al. 2000), and health coaching delivered by human experts is neither scalable nor financially sustainable.

To this end, the question arises whether digital health interventions are appropriate means to address the health and economic burden of NCDs. Digital health interventions rely on information and communication technologies and allow medical doctors and other caregivers to scale and tailor long-term treatments to individuals in need at sustainable costs (Fleisch et al. 2021; Kowatsch et al. 2019). Examples include interventions delivered via chatbots (Kramer et al. 2020), voice assistants (Bérubé et al. 2021), cars (Koch et al. 2020), smartphones (Shih et al. 2019), smartwatches (Maritsch et al. 2020), holographic digital coaches (Kowatsch et al. 2021), or health-care robots (Papadopoulos et al. 2020).

An increasing amount of technology-based digital health innovations led to investments in digital health startups that were almost continuously growing since 2011 (RH 2020; see Fig. 1). The global telehealth market size is projected to increase from US$ 61 billion in 2018 to US$ 560 billion in 2027 (FBI 2020) with companies such as *American Well, Babylon Health, Kry, Lyra Health, Ping An Medical and Healthcare Management*, or *Teladoc Health*. The global mobile and digital health market is estimated to increase from US$ 43.1

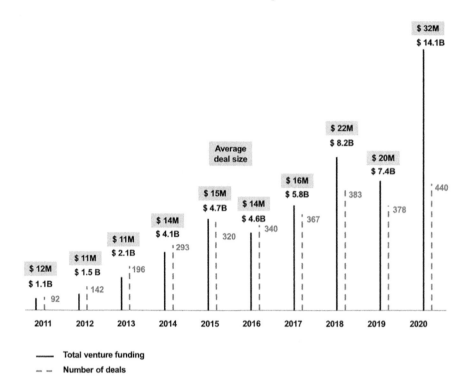

Fig. 1 US-based investments in digital health startups, Rock Health's 2020 market update, author's own illustration

billion in 2019 to US$ 174 billion by 2024 (PB 2020) with companies like *Curefit, Headspace, Keep, Omada, Virta Health, Welltok,* or *Zhangshang Tangyi.* And in a third relevant market for digital health interventions, biometric wearables and devices are offered, for example, by *Eight Sleep, iFit, Oura Health, Peloton, Supermonkey,* or *Whoop.* This market is also projected to grow from US$ 22.8 billion in 2019 to US$ 70.9 billion in 2024 (ibid.). For the development, licensing, and commercialization of their interventions, many digital health companies, for example, *Pear Therapeutics, Akili Interactive, Nightware, Propeller Health, Applied VR,* or *Happify Health,* also partner with large companies from the pharmaceutical industry like *Amgen, Astellas, AstraZeneca, Boehringer Ingelheim, Merck, Novartis, Roche, Sandoz, Sanofi,* or *Shionogi* (Patel and Butte 2020).

Against this background, we will provide an overview of digital health interventions and how they are linked to a connected ecosystem of various health-care actors. Key opportunities for these actors and digital health interventions are outlined in the next section. Afterward, we introduce the anatomy of digital health interventions with three key building blocks that focus on the prediction of vulnerable and receptive states as well as tailored support. Four digital health interventions are reviewed afterward to show their value for health-care systems. We then discuss specific challenges related to the design and delivery of digital health interventions and conclude with a summary and outlook.

2 Opportunities for Health-Care Actors and Digital Health Interventions

A health-care system involves actors that are connected to each other in various ways. Patients and healthy individuals consume health interventions while their family members and friends may act as emotional or physical supporting actors. Providers such as physicians, nurses, pharmacists, and private or public health organizations offer or prescribe health interventions, which are then reimbursed by payers, for example, health insurance companies, employers, or individuals. When it comes to individuals with multiple NCDs, a network and close collaboration of health care providers from different disciplines are required. Other actors develop and offer digital health interventions, for example, the pharmaceutical industry, MedTech and digital therapeutic companies, and research or patient organizations. And finally, regulatory and public health bodies oversee health interventions according to their effectiveness, costs, and safety. Against this background, digital health interventions offer various opportunities for these actors, as depicted in Fig. 2. Examples of these opportunities are provided in the following listing:

1. For **patients** to better manage their NCDs and advance digital health interventions: for example, digital health interventions may improve health literacy and self-management capabilities, reduce distress, or prevent life-threatening events such as heart attacks, exacerbations in chronic obstructive pulmonary disease, or very low blood glucose levels. Moreover, patients may donate their health-related self-report and behavioral and biometric data to help improve the effectiveness of digital health interventions by learning optimal features over time.

2. For **healthy individuals** to prevent the onset of NCDs and enhance digital health interventions: for example, digital health interventions may improve the physical constitution with high-intensity interval training and offering support to follow a sleep hygiene regime, to reduce alcohol con-

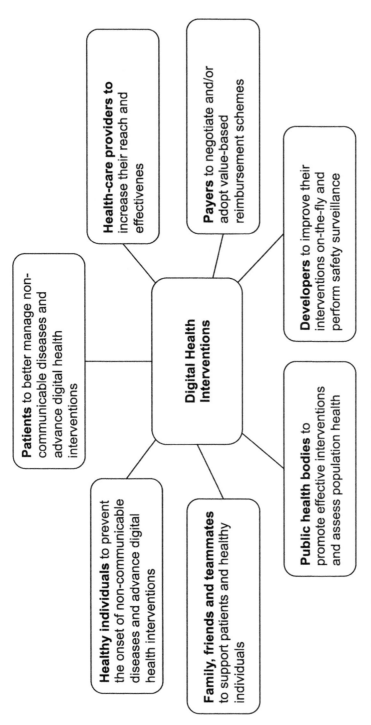

Fig. 2 Opportunities for various health-care actors and digital health interventions, author's own illustration

sumption and binge drinking, to stop smoking, to implement a nutrient-rich diet, or to strengthen mental health with the help of slow-paced breathing and mindfulness exercises. Moreover, healthy individuals may donate their health-related self-report and behavioral and biometric data, too as digital health algorithms and statistical tests also require data from healthy control groups (e.g., to draw the line between benign and malignant skin cancer).

3. For **family and friends and team mates** to support patients and healthy individuals: for example, digital health interventions may explicitly incorporate family members and friends of a target person in the prevention or management of chronic and mental illness by prompting social activities that promote health behavior (e.g., cooking nutrient-rich meals or having hikes together) or prevent life-threatening events (e.g., co-monitoring the health condition and providing support with medication adherence).

4. For **health-care providers** (e.g., physicians, nurses, pharmacists, health coaches, patient organizations, digital health companies, public health organizations) to increase their reach and effectiveness: for example, chatbots, voice assistants, or health-care robots may take over the role of scalable digital assistants of health-care providers that reach out to their clients in their everyday lives. Health-related data unobtrusively collected by these digital assistants can be used to provide just-in-time feedback to those affected and make on-site consultations more efficient (e.g., by better understanding adverse health behavior of patients) or even obsolete (e.g., in case optimal health promoting behavior is observed). The latter case may open up time for clients that need more face-to-face support by human experts in addition to a digital coach only.

5. For **payers** (e.g., health insurance companies, employers offering health plans to their employees, healthy individuals, patients, or public bodies) to negotiate and/or adopt value-based reimbursement schemes: for example, the focus on the prevention, management, or treatment of specific NCDs, the degree of evidence available through representative randomized controlled trials, the cost of an intervention, an individuals' health plan, or treatment success measured continuously in the field may trigger the most appropriate reimbursement scheme. Due to objective measurements and patient-reported outcomes in real-time, digital health interventions also enable reimbursement mechanisms that foster a healthy lifestyle.

6. For **developers** (e.g., digital health, MedTech, pharmaceutical, or insurance companies, health-care experts, hospitals, research and public health organizations) to improve their interventions on-the-fly and perform safety surveillance: for example, digital health interventions may incorporate self-

learning mechanisms into their digital health interventions based on data collected on-the-fly to improve the accuracy of predicting life-threatening events (e.g., COPD exacerbations or very low blood glucose levels) or to better predict the moment an individual is more likely to receive, process, and react to health-promoting messages; the sensing capabilities of digital health interventions may be used to better understand any unintended side effects (e.g., smartphone addiction), too. This, in turn, enables direct market surveillance of both the effectiveness and drawbacks of digital health interventions.

7. For **public health bodies** (e.g., public centers for disease controls, public health promotion bodies) to promote effective interventions and assess population health: for example, public health bodies may offer an infra-structure that allows patients, healthy individuals, health-care providers, developers, and payers to efficiently identify effective digital health inter-ventions for the prevention and management of chronic and mental illness that comply to various quality criteria. Moreover, anonymized data gath-ered through digital health interventions and donated by patients and healthy individuals may be used by public bodies to assess population health and identify shortcomings of health care. This population-wide data will then help the health-care industry and funding bodies in steering their resource allocation more efficiently.

3   Anatomy of Digital Health Interventions

Digital health interventions may continuously use data sources to predict vul-nerable states of patients or healthy individuals, select the most appropriate intervention option and dose, and deliver it at an opportune moment when the target person is in a receptive state (Nahum-Shani et al. 2018). A feedback loop informs whether and to which degree the intervention had a positive impact on the vulnerable state and, thus, may trigger optimization algorithms that learn—with every iteration of intervention delivery—which intervention option and dose works best for a particular individual and context (Hekler et al. 2018). For all of this to work seamlessly, digital health interventions require various Internet of Things services that provide health-related and contextual data and appropriate, easy-to-use user interfaces to unfold their full potential.

An overview of this closed-loop system, we call it the anatomy of digital health interventions, is depicted in Fig. 3. The three key building blocks of the

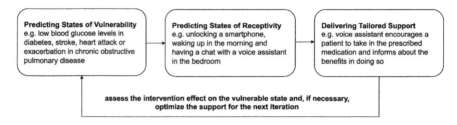

Fig. 3 Anatomy of digital health interventions, author's own illustration

anatomy, i.e., predicting states of vulnerability, predicting states of receptivity, and delivering tailored support, are described in more detail in the following sections.

3.1   Predicting States of Vulnerability

A vulnerable state is a "person's transient tendency to experience adverse health outcomes or to engage in maladaptive behaviors" (Nahum-Shani et al. 2015). A very first step in the development of effective digital health interventions must be, therefore, to predict adverse health outcomes or maladaptive behaviors by using relevant sensor and/or self-report data. For example, it has been shown that stress at the workplace can be predicted via computer mouse movements (Banholzer et al. 2021) or that the breathing frequency of individuals can be measured with a smartphone's microphone (Shih et al. 2019). Also, nocturnal cough frequency and sleep quality measured with a smartphone's sensor data has the potential as a prognostic marker for asthma control and attacks to avoid painful and costly hospitalizations in patients with asthma (Barata et al. 2020; Rassouli et al. 2020; Tinschert et al. 2020). In another investigation, smartphone data was used to predict health-related and potentially modifiable personality states such as conscientiousness and neuroticism (Rüegger et al. 2020). Moreover, voice was used to predict emotions in individuals (Boateng and Kowatsch 2020; Boateng et al. 2020), and both driving behavior derived from a vehicle's data bus (Kraus et al. 2018) and physiological data from wearables (Maritsch et al. 2020) were used to predict very low blood glucose levels in type-1 diabetes patients. And it was also shown how tapping patterns derived from smartphone interactions could indicate Parkinson's disease severity (Zhan et al. 2018).

Digitally and objectively measured indicators that reflect either an organic process occurring as a consequence of disease (e.g., decrease in blood oxygen saturation during the onset of an asthma attack) or an organic response to tailored support (e.g., increase in blood oxygen saturation after inhalation of asthma medication) are defined as digital biomarkers (Coravos et al. 2019). Digital biomarkers are, therefore, an essential building block of digital health interventions and depending on their purpose can be categorized into risk, diagnostic, monitoring, prognostic, predictive, or response biomarkers (ibid.).

With the increasing amount and quality of sensor data derived from wearables, smartphones, smart speakers, TVs, and even cars (Koch et al. 2020; Sim 2019), which are pre-processed and fed into state-of-the-art machine learning algorithms (Kakarmath et al. 2020; Rajkomar et al. 2019), there is a huge potential for innovators of digital health interventions to develop scalable and personalized markers that indicate states of vulnerability.

3.2   Predicting States of Receptivity

States of receptivity are "conditions in which the person can receive, process, and use the support provided" (Nahum-Shani et al. 2015). Not only have digital health interventions to predict states of vulnerability but also states of receptivity to make the delivery of tailored support useful at all and more efficient. For example, a smartwatch-based digital health intervention may not be able to reach the vulnerable person with tailored support if that person does not wear the smartwatch.

Similar to predicting states of vulnerability, various data sources such as geographic location (being at work vs at home), acoustic samples (e.g., talking to someone else or not), Bluetooth or WIFI signals (e.g., being close to others or in specific locations), interactions with the user interface (e.g., unlocking a smartphone), communication patterns (e.g., having phone calls), user-defined events (e.g., reminder for medication intake), time (e.g., every evening at 10 pm), or accelerometer data from smartphones (e.g., walking or running) can be used for this purpose.

Indeed, there is first evidence that predicting states of receptivity is feasible (Künzler et al. 2017) and investigations are ongoing to collect various sensor data streams in multiple studies to understand better and predict states of receptivity (Kramer et al. 2019; Mishra et al. 2021). Results show that age, personality traits, day/time, physical activity, geographic location, a smartphone's battery status, or physiological signals indicating a state of relaxation may be useful indicators for the prediction of receptive states (Chan et al. 2020; Choi et al. 2019; Künzler et al. 2019). Recently, a dynamic state of receptivity module was developed for smartphone-based and chatbot-delivered digital health interventions. This module learns over time and optimizes the prediction with incoming data to successfully predict states of receptivity in a several-week longitudinal field study (Mishra et al. 2021). However, more studies are required to improve the prediction models for different (patient) populations.

3.3   Delivering Tailored Support

If states of vulnerability and states of receptivity are predicted, the last important step of a digital health intervention concerns the delivery of tailored support. Examples of support include motivational messages (e.g., to reach a daily physical activity goal), reminders (e.g., for medication intake), self-monitoring prompts (e.g., to take blood glucose readings), educational content (e.g., health literacy video clips about asthma), or biofeedback (e.g., breathing training with heart rate variability feedback).

Support is often informed by behavioral change techniques (Knittle et al. 2020) and underlying theories about human behavior such as Social Cognitive Theory (Bandura 1991), Self-determination Theory (Ryan and Deci 2017), or the Health Action Process Approach (Zhang et al. 2019). Tailoring of support can depend on various static and time-varying characteristics of the target person, for example, gender, age, self-efficacy or mood, and the current context, for example, time of the day or the weather condition (Hekler et al. 2018; Nahum-Shani et al. 2018).

A novel way to deliver tailored support, and analog to how human health coaching, is the use of text- or voice-based conversational agents such as chatbots on smartphones, voice assistants via smart speakers, smart TVs or in cars, holographic digital coaches via virtual or augmented reality glasses, or healthcare robots. Conversational agents are computer programs that imitate the conversation with a human being and have been applied in various healthcare settings so far (Bérubé et al. 2021; Schachner et al. 2020; Tudor Car et al. 2020). Conversational agents are perceived as social actors, and it has been shown that individuals can build a working alliance with them (Kowatsch et al. 2021a, b). Working alliance is an important relationship quality in both face-to-face and technology-mediated health-care settings and robustly linked to treatment success (Flückiger et al. 2018).

4   Examples of Digital Health Interventions

This chapter will introduce four digital health interventions to better understand their anatomy and potential to address NCDs. First, we will introduce the digital public health intervention Ally that aims to support individuals in reaching dynamic daily physical activity goals. Second, we will provide an overview of Max, a conversational agent working together with health-care experts to support young patients with asthma and their family members. Third, we oversee Alex, a smartphone-based and holographic physiotherapy coach with the overall objective to increase treatment adherence in home exercises. And finally, we will describe Breeze, a scalable and playful biofeedback breathing training that aims to support individuals in strengthening their cardiac system and stress management capabilities.

4.1   Ally, a Digital Physical Activity Coach

Ally, the assistant to lift your level of activity, is a smartphone-based conversational agent that uses the step count of the smartphone or smartwatch sensor of an individual to infer states of vulnerability, defined in this case as physical activity levels below 10,000 steps a day. With the help of these vulnerable states, Ally motivates individuals to reach a personalized daily step goal. This motivational and tailored support involved setting up specific daily step goals, constrained to an upper limit of 10,000 steps, which were dynamically calculated based on the historic step count of an individual. This coaching approach was adopted to guide individuals step-by-step to an optimal daily step count of 10,000 steps. In addition to motivational messages delivered by Ally, individuals could win small cash or charity incentives in case a daily step goal was achieved. The goal achievement dashboard of the mobile app and an exemplary motivational conversational turn with Ally is shown in Fig. 4.

An 8-week experiment was carried out with 274 customers of a Swiss health insurer to assess the impact of incentives on step goal achievement. This experiment showed that cash incentives boosted the achievement of the daily step goal by circa 8% compared to a non-incentive control group (Kramer et al. 2020). Moreover, the experiment was also used to collect a vast amount of state of receptivity data with the overall goal to incorporate a state of receptivity module in a future version of Ally and other smartphone-based and conversational agent-delivered health interventions (Künzler et al. 2019; Mishra et al. 2021).

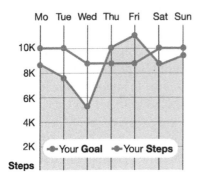 

Fig. 4 Goal achievement dashboard (left) and motivational conversational turn with Ally (right), author's own illustration

4.2 Max, a Digital Coach for Health-Care Experts, Patients, and Family Members

Successful management of chronic and mental illness requires teamwork among healthcare experts, patients, as well as supporting family members and friends. Conversational agents in the role of a team player may support this collaborative effort. With asthma being an example of a severe chronic condition, the conversational agent Max was developed to extend the reach of asthma experts into the everyday lives of young patients and their family members. Particularly, Max delivered a collaborative and gamified health literacy intervention with various educational video clips and exercises via a mobile application that was used by patients. In addition, Max sent text messages to family members and motivated them to support the patients in experiential learning activities. Moreover, Max collected relevant states of vulnerability data, such as knowledge about asthma via a quiz and video data indicating potential shortcomings in the inhalation technique of young patients. Asthma experts received an email from Max when a new video recording was available. With a web-based cockpit, the asthma experts could then assess the correctness of the inhalation technique and send their feedback directly to the mobile application. The interplay between the asthma experts, Max, the young patients, and their family members and a screenshot of the mobile application are depicted in Fig. 5.

A feasibility study was conducted in 2019 to assess Max in four Swiss hospitals and two outpatient offices of the Swiss lung association (Kowatsch et al. 2021a). The results of this study show that cognitive and behavioral skills of the young patients could be improved and that 75.5% of the 49 participating

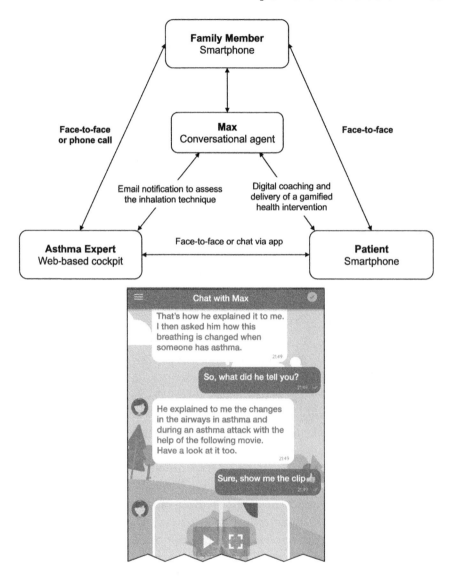

Fig. 5 Teamwork in the Max intervention (above) and a screenshot of the mobile application (below), author's own illustration

patients successfully completed the intervention. Moreover, family members worked closely together with the young patients in 97.8% out of 275 coaching sessions. The vast majority of interactions, i.e., 99.5% out of 15.152 conversational turns, took place among the young patients and Max. This clearly shows the scalability of this digital health intervention. To further improve the prediction of vulnerable states, future work may investigate the utility of smartphone-recorded nocturnal cough and sleep quality data to predict asthma control and attacks, which showed promising results in adults with asthma (Barata et al. 2020; Rassouli et al. 2020; Tinschert et al. 2020).

4.3   Alex, a Smartphone-Based and Holographic Physiotherapy Coach

Various activities related to the prevention and management of chronic and mental illness require home exercises. Non-adherence to these exercises is still an important problem for health-care systems because very often, it leads to prolonged treatments and, with it, increased treatment costs. The digital physiotherapy coach Alex was developed to increase adherence to home exercises in physiotherapy. Alex is a smartphone-based conversational agent and holographic digital coach. Consistent with the approach of Max described above, Alex supports health-care experts, here, physiotherapists, by extending their reach into the everyday lives of patients with chronic back pain. Delivering psychoeducation, personalized motivational messages, and reminders via a smartphone were some of the various jobs of Alex. Also, health-related outcomes such as quality of life instruments can be gathered and monitored through smartphone-based interactions with Alex. Additionally, and in the form of a holographic digital coach, Alex provides real-time exercise instructions, monitoring, and feedback with the help of augmented reality glasses. Vulnerable states, for example, an inaccurate execution of specific movements, can be measured in real-time with sensor data streams of the augmented reality glasses and can be fed back instantly to the patient through voice and augmented visual guides via the glasses. Patient-reported health outcomes and the exercises' performance data can also be sent back to the physiotherapist for upcoming on-site or remote coaching sessions. An overview of the interplay between the physiotherapist, Alex, and the patient and a view through the augmented reality glasses are provided in Fig. 6.

Alex was assessed in three lab experiments with a total of 50 physiotherapy patients and 11 physiotherapists. Alex was also evaluated in a 4-week field experiment with one patient. The study participants rated Alex quite positive with respect to his utility, ease of use, and they also enjoyed the interaction with Alex. The findings also indicate that the participants were able to build a working alliance with Alex. Moreover, interviews indicated that the real-time feedback and interactions with the holographic Alex resulted in a better understanding of performing exercises correctly. Physiotherapists also indicated that Alex would improve the treatment process. The experiment in the

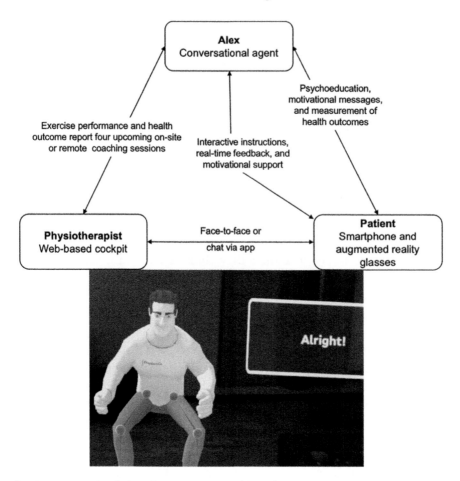

Fig. 6 Teamwork of the Alex intervention (above) and a view with the augmented reality glasses (below), author's own illustration

field led to an adherence rate of 92%, i.e., 11 out of 12 coaching sessions were completed by the patient with the augmented reality glasses. In addition, the accuracy of the exercises increased substantially over the course of those 4 weeks, indicating the utility of real-time monitoring and feedback. With only one specific squat training session supported by Alex as of today, future implementations must offer a variety of additional exercises to chronic care patients at home or in rehabilitation facilities.

4.4   Breeze, a Playful, Biofeedback-Guided Breathing Training

It has been shown that slow-paced and diaphragmatic breathing has a positive impact on both cardiac functioning and psychological well-being. Slow-paced breathing training can be supported by biofeedback that allows individuals to better control their breathing with the help of adequate physiological signals. Moreover, biofeedback can improve self-efficacy, an important factor one should consider in the design of health interventions (Zhang et al. 2019). Unfortunately, biofeedback is still not scalable because it requires instructions by human experts and dedicated hardware for sensing the physiological signals. In addition, slow-paced breathing training is less attractive to males and lower-educated individuals (Shih et al. 2019).

Breeze was developed to address these limitations (ibid.). Breeze delivers a smartphone-based, scalable, playful, and biofeedback-guided breathing training. For this purpose, Breeze uses the microphone of a smartphone to detect sounds of inhalation, exhalation, and silence and to derive the underlying breathing rate as a vulnerable state. The recorded sounds are then used to deliver a playful visualization. That is, a sailing boat is displayed on the smartphone screen and reaches its destination in the shortest amount of time if an individual's breathing follows a slow-paced pattern. The breathing detection relies on approximately 2.76 million breathing sounds that were recorded by 43 individuals. Furthermore, various control sounds were used, too, to improve the accuracy of the detection algorithm. A conceptual overview and the biofeedback-triggered visualization of Breeze is depicted in Fig. 7.

First empirical results show that Breeze was able to reduce the breathing rate in 16 individuals to a pre-defined target rate, i.e., six breathing cycles per minute. Moreover, Breeze significantly increased the high-frequency heart rate variability, an indicator of cardiac functioning (Shih et al. 2019). In another study with 170 participants, perceived relaxation scores for Breeze, and a validated breathing training were comparable, too (Lukic et al. 2021). These results suggest that Breeze could be employed in both clinical and self-management activities for the prevention and management of chronic and mental illness.

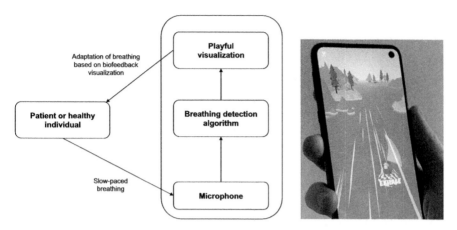

Fig. 7 A conceptual overview (left) and biofeedback-triggered visualization of Breeze (right), author's own illustration

5   Challenges of Effective Digital Health Intervention

The design and delivery of effective digital health interventions come not without challenges. This section will overview challenges with regard to behavioral, regulatory, reimbursement, safety, ethical, cybersecurity, privacy, and infrastructure-related aspects.

One of the biggest challenges related to the design of effective digital health interventions lies in the human nature itself, i.e., to help individuals in bringing up the effort and discipline required to adopt and maintain health-promoting behavior. Developers of digital health interventions must be therefore well aware of various aspects like the law of least effort (i.e., individuals will likely adopt a behavior that requires the least amount of cognitive or physical resistance) (Kahneman 2012), delay discounting (i.e., preferring smaller but immediate rewards over larger future rewards) (Leahey et al. 2020), and various other theories of human behavior (e.g., Bandura 1991; Zhang et al. 2019) and behavior change techniques (Knittle et al. 2020). And although the primary target behavior of digital health interventions is a health-promoting behavior (e.g., an elevated physical activity), developers must, of course, also consider factors that promote both reach and intended use of a digital health intervention. Besides, developers must be aware that digital health interventions should offer a minimum of technology-related interactions not only to reduce any side effects such as smartphone addiction (Haug et al. 2015) but first and foremost to let individuals live their lives without (too much) being dependent on technology. Reaching out to vulnerable populations, for example, those with a lower socioeconomic status, lack of motivation, or simply those that are unaware of their adverse health behavior, especially for the prevention of NCDs, represents another major challenge. Lessons learnt from epidemiology, technology marketing, and information systems research may therefore guide additional design considerations. And finally, effective interventions lead inevitably to sustained health-promoting behavior which, in turn, makes them obsolete. This "die-after-success" design must also be considered in business models underlying digital health interventions.

Another challenge with digital health interventions is the fact that regulatory frameworks and reimbursement schemes for digital health interventions are still "work-in-progress" in many countries. Although the US Food and Drug Administration cleared and approved multiple digital health interventions under regulatory pathways for medical devices (e.g. Welldoc's Blue Star for type-2 diabetes patients in 2010 or Pear Therapeutics' reSET for substance use disorder in 2017), and, due to COVID-19, has even relaxed access to digital health interventions, a dedicated framework for software-as-medical-device is still missing (Patel and Butte 2020). A promising example in this regard is Germany that recently implemented a dedicated regulatory framework (FIDMD 2020). Accordingly, first digital health interventions are cleared and can be prescribed by physicians, for example, Elevida by GAIA for individuals with multiple sclerosis (US$ 900, 90 days) or somnio by mementor for insomnia patients (US$ 560, 90 days). With the introduction of a public list of cleared digital health interventions and codes for reimbursement, Germany's approach addresses a related challenge, i.e., how to find evidence-based digital health interventions.

A further challenge concerns the safety of digital health interventions, especially, when it comes to the native and promising characteristics of digital health interventions such as their connectivity to other devices and services (e.g., blood glucose pumps and other wearables or medical devices), their updateability, or self-learning capabilities via artificial intelligence (Patel and Butte 2020). With the help of automated tests, developers and regulatory bodies can continuously assess the safety of digital health interventions, in particular, when they rely on third-party software and hardware, which is usually the case when they require or run on millions of smartphones, smart speakers, or smart watches (Kowatsch et al. 2019; Shezan et al. 2020). Moreover, mobile devices differ in price and sensor quality which may not only harm patients due to wrong predictions of vulnerable states (Shih et al. 2019) but also and inevitably to an increase of the digital divide and ethical questions about the quality of care and who will benefit most from digital health interventions around the globe (Sim 2019).

Data-driven digital health interventions as we have seen with Ally, Max, Alex, and Breeze above, must also offer easy to understand end-user license agreements, terms of service, and privacy policies (Patel and Butte 2020). Only a transparent collection, monitoring, use, and distribution of data governed by ethical considerations and regular audits by independent third parties will likely lead to broad adoption of and trust into digital health interventions.

A final challenge concerns the infrastructure required for the delivery of digital health interventions. Although COVID-19 has accelerated the digitization of health care in many countries (e.g., Agrawal 2020), there are still many people around the globe that have no or only limited access to digital health interventions (Holst et al. 2020). Even in high-income countries, technical barriers exist, for example, limited interoperability of existing healthcare infrastructures and availability of Internet access in clinics or rural areas (Kowatsch et al. 2021a). To this end, novel communication infrastructures may help overcome this challenge (Khaturia et al. 2020) flanked by a strong commitment of decision-makers.

6   Conclusion

In this work, we have shown that digital health interventions have the potential to improve the prevention, management, and treatment of NCDs, the topmost global health burden of the twenty-first century. Digital health interventions offer several opportunities for various health-care actors with the overall but challenging goal to help individuals bringing up the effort and discipline to adopt and maintain a healthy lifestyle. Digital health interventions that predict vulnerable states and deliver tailored support with the most appropriate intervention option and dose in opportune moments are likely to enable precision health. And although there exist still many challenges that limit the full potential of digital health interventions today, we see a significant and increasing number of investments in digital health companies and promising research that will push the borders of our traditional health-care arena.

The ongoing socio-demographic shift toward an aging population results inevitably to more and more individuals suffering from multiple NCDs. And although many countries have already started to deal with these complex and expensive integrated care scenarios, future digital health interventions must be able to orchestrate and offer services from different health disciplines while still being accessible and easy to use. All in all, we envision a future in which digital health interventions democratize health care so that everybody in need benefits from the best knowledge available.

Success Factors for Setting Up Digital Health Interventions

- Build up a strong interdisciplinary team consisting of experts in NCDs, health psychology and behavioral medicine, machine learning, software engineering, as well as health economics and business models.
- Co-design digital health interventions with end users and players from the very beginning on.
- Start with one NCD but think early about relevant comorbidities.
- Frame digital health interventions as digital social actors so that end users can build up a working alliance with them, i.e., attachment bond and a shared agreement about treatment goals and tasks.
- Measure vulnerable and receptive states as unobtrusive as possible based on self-reported, biometric or behavioral data.
- Design your interventions with on-going data-based improvement and assessment cycles to improve the prediction of vulnerable and receptive states as well as intervention options and their dose.
- Provide tailored support in a way that digital health interventions are as easy as possible to use.
- Reduce the number of interactions with your digital health intervention to a bare minimum; this will also reduce the burden of individuals using your interventions.
- Collect field data and provide real-world evidence for the effectiveness of your digital health interventions.
- Open up your digital health interventions for integrated care scenarios.

References

Agrawal A (2020) Bridging digital health divides. Science 369(6507):1050–1052

Bandura A (1991) Social cognitive theory of self-regulation. Organ Behav Hum Decis Process 50(2):248–287

Banholzer N, Feuerriegel S, Fleisch E, Bauer G, Kowatsch T Computer mouse movements as an indicator of work stress: longitudinal observational field study. J Med Internet Res 23(4):e27121, 10.2196/27121

Barata F, Tinschert P, Rassouli F, Steurer-Stey C, Fleisch E, Puhan MA, Brutsche M, Kotz D, Kowatsch T (2020) Automatic recognition, segmentation, and sex assignment of nocturnal asthmatic coughs and cough epochs in smartphone audio recordings: observational field study. J Med Internet Res 22(7)

Bérubé C, Schachner T, Keller R, Fleisch E, Wangenheim F, Barata F, Kowatsch T (2021) Voice-based conversational agents for the prevention and management of chronic and mental conditions: a systematic literature review. JMIR 23(3):e25933

Boateng G, Kowatsch T (2020) Speech emotion recognition among elderly individuals using multimodal fusion and transfer learning. In: International conference on multimodal interaction (ICMI '20). Virtual event, October 25–29. ACM, New York

Boateng G, Sels L, Kuppens P, Hilpert P, Kowatsch T (2020) Speech emotion recognition among couples using the peak-end rule and transfer learning. In: International conference on multimodal interaction (ICMI '20). Virtual event, October 25–29. ACM, New York

Buttorff C, Ruder T, Bauman M (2017) Multiple chronic conditions in the United States. https://www.rand.org/pubs/tools/TL221.html. Accessed 6 Sept 2020

Chan SWT, Sapkota S, Mathews R, Zhang H, Nanayakkara S (2020) Prompto: investigating receptivity to prompts based on cognitive load from memory training conversational agent. In: Proceedings of the ACM on interactive, mobile, wearable and ubiquitous technologies, vol 4, no 4, article 121

Chen S, Kuhn M, Prettner K, Bloom DE (2018) The macroeconomic burden of noncommunicable diseases in the United States: estimates and projections. PLoS One 13(11):e0206702.

Choi W, Park S, Kim D, Lim Y-k, Lee U (2019) Multi-stage receptivity model for mobile just-in-time health intervention. In: Proceedings of the ACM on interactive, mobile, wearable and ubiquitous technologies, vol 3, no 2, article 39

Coravos A, Khozin S, Mandl KD (2019) Developing and adopting safe and effective digital biomarkers to improve patient outcomes. Nat Digit Med 2:14

FBI (2020) Telehealth: global market analysis, insights, and forecast, 2019-2027 by Fortune Business Insights. Fortune Business Insights

FIDMD (2020) The fast-track process for digital health applications (Diga) according to section 139e Sgb V: a guide for manufacturers, service providers and users

Fleisch E, Franz C, Herrmann A (2021) The digital Pill: what everyone should know about the future of our healthcare system. Emerald, Bingley

Flückiger C, Del Re AC, Wampold BE, Horvath AO (2018) The alliance in adult psychotherapy: a meta-analytic synthesis. Psychotherapy 55(4):316–340

Hajat C, Stein E (2018) The global burden of multiple chronic conditions: a narrative review. Prev Med Rep 12:284–293

Haug S, Castro RP, Kwon M, Filler A, Kowatsch T, Schaub MP (2015) Smartphone use and smartphone addiction among young people in Switzerland. J Behav Addict 4(4):299–307

Hekler EB, Rivera DE, Martin CA, Phatak SS, Freigoun MT, Korinek E, Klasnja P, Adams MA, Buman MP (2018) Tutorial for using control systems engineering to optimize adaptive mobile health interventions. J Med Internet Res 20(6):e214

Holst C, Sukums F, Radovanovic D, Ngowi B, Noll J, Winkler AS (2020) Sub-Saharan Africa—the new breeding ground for global digital health. Lancet Digit Health 2(4):e160–e162

Kahneman D (2012) Thinking, fast and slow. Penguin, London

Kakarmath S, Esteva A, Arnaout R, Harvey H, Kumar S, Muse E, Dong F, Wedlund L, Kvedar J (2020) Best practices for authors of healthcare-related artificial intelligence manuscripts. NPJ Digit Med 3(1):134

Katz DL, Frates EP, Bonnet JP, Gupta SK, Vartiainen E, Carmona RH (2018) Lifestyle as medicine: the case for a true health initiative. Am J Health Promot 32(6):1452–1458

Khaturia M, Jha P, Karandikar A (2020) Connecting the unconnected: toward frugal 5g network architecture and standardization. IEEE Commun Stand Mag 4(2):64–71

Knittle K, Heino M, Marques MM, Stenius M, Beattie M, Ehbrecht F, Hagger MS, Hardeman W, Hankonen N (2020) The compendium of self-enactable techniques to change and self-manage motivation and behaviour V.1.0. Nat Hum Behav 4(2):215–223

Koch K, Liu S, Berger T, Wortmann F (2020) Towards the healing car: investigating the potential of psychotherapeutic in-vehicle interventions. In: European conference on information systems (ECIS). Virtual

Kowatsch T, Otto L, Harperink S, Cotti A, Schlieter H (2019) A design and evaluation framework for digital health interventions. IT Inf Technol 61(5–6):253–263

Kowatsch T, Schachner T, Harperink S, Dittler U, Xiao G, Stanger C, Oswald H, Fleisch E, von Wangenheim F, Möller A (2021a) Conversational agents as mediating social actors in chronic disease management involving healthcare professionals, patients, and family members: intervention design and results from a multi-site, single-arm feasibility study. J Med Internet Res 23(2):e25060

Kowatsch T, Lohse K-M, Erb V, Schittenhelm L, Galliker H, Lehner R, Huang EM (2021b) Hybrid ubiquitous coaching: a novel combination of mobile and holographic conversational agents targeting adherence to home exercises. J Med Internet Res (JMIR) 23(2):e23612

Kramer J-N, Künzler F, Mishra V, Presset B, Kotz D, Smith S, Scholz U, Kowatsch T (2019) Investigating Intervention components and exploring states of receptivity for a smartphone app to promote physical activity: study protocol of the Ally Micro-Randomized Trial. JMIR Res Protoc 8(1)

Kramer J, Künzler F, Mishra V, Smith SN, Kotz DF, Scholz U, Fleisch E, Kowatsch T (2020) Which components of a smartphone walking app help users to reach personalized step goals? Results from an optimization trial. Ann Behav Med 54(7):518–528

Kraus M, Feuerriegel S, Fleisch E, Kowatsch T, Laimer M, Stettler C, Wortmann F, Züger T (2018) Machine learning based hypoglycemia recognition from driving patterns in individuals with diabetes mellitus. In: 2018 INFORMS annual meeting phoenix. INFORMS, Phoenix, AZ

Künzler F, Kramer J, Kowatsch T (2017) Efficacy of mobile context-aware notification management systems: a systematic literature review and meta-analysis. In: IEEE 13th international conference on wireless and mobile computing, networking and communications (WiMob). IEEE, Rome, Italy, pp 131–138

Künzler F, Mishra V, Kramer J-N, Kotz D, Fleisch E, Kowatsch T (2019) Exploring the state-of-receptivity for Mhealth interventions. In: The proceedings of the ACM on interactive, mobile, wearable and ubiquitous technologies, vol 3, no 4, article 140

Kvedar JC, Fogel AL, Elenko E, Zohar D (2016) Digital medicine's march on chronic disease. Nat Biotechnol 34(3):239–246

Leahey TM, Gorin AA, Wyckoff E, Denmat Z, O'Connor K, Field C, Dunton GF, Gunstad J, Huedo-Medina TB, Gilder C (2020) Episodic future thinking, delay discounting, and exercise during weight loss maintenance: the pace trial. Health Psychol 39(9):796–805

Lukic Y, Klein S, Brügger V, Keller O, Fleisch E, Kowatsch T (2021) The impact of a gameful breathing training visualization on intrinsic experiential value, perceived effectiveness, and engagement intentions: between-subject online experiment. J Med Internet Res. Preprints. doi:10.2196/preprints.22803

Marengoni A, Angleman S, Melis R, Mangialasche F, Karp A, Garmen A, Meinow B, Fratiglioni L (2011) Aging with multimorbidity: a systematic review of the literature. Ageing Res Rev 10(4):430–439

Maritsch M, Föll S, Lehmann V, Bérubé C, Kraus M, Feuerriegel S, Kowatsch T, Züger T, Stettler C, Fleisch E, Wortmann F (2020) Towards wearable-based hypoglycemia detection and warning in diabetes. In: Extended abstracts of the 2020 CHI conference on human factors in computing systems. Association for Computing Machinery, Honolulu, HI, pp 1–8

Mishra V, Künzler F, Kramer J, Fleisch E, Kowatsch T, Kotz DF (2021) Detecting receptivity for mhealth interventions in the natural environment. The proceedings of the ACM on interactive, mobile, wearable and ubiquitous technologies (IMWUT), vol 5, no 2, article 74. doi:10.1145/3463492

Murphy A, Palafox B, Walli-Attaei M, Powell-Jackson T, Rangarajan S, Alhabib KF, Avezum AJ, Calik KBT, Chifamba J, Choudhury T, Dagenais G, Dans AL, Gupta R, Iqbal R, Kaur M, Kelishadi R, Khatib R, Kruger IM, Kutty VR, Lear SA, Li W, Lopez-Jaramillo P, Mohan V, Mony PK, Orlandini A, Rosengren A, Rosnah I, Seron P, Teo K, Tse LA, Tsolekile L, Wang Y, Wielgosz A, Yan R, Yeates KE, Yusoff K, Zatonska K, Hanson K, Yusuf S, McKee M (2020) The household economic burden of non-communicable diseases in 18 countries. BMJ Global Health 5(2):e002040

Nahum-Shani I, Hekler EB, Spruijt-Metz D (2015) Building health behavior models to guide the development of just-in-time adaptive interventions: a pragmatic framework. Health Psychol 34(suppl):1209–1219

Nahum-Shani I, Smith SN, Spring BJ, Collins LM, Witkiewitz K, Tewari A, Murphy SA (2018) Just-in-time adaptive interventions (JITAIs) in mobile health: key components and design principles for ongoing health behavior support. Ann Behav Med 52(6):446–462

Newman D, Tong M, Levine E, Kishore S (2020) Prevalence of multiple chronic conditions by U.S. State and Territory, 2017. PLoS One 15(5):e0232346

Papadopoulos I, Koulouglioti C, Lazzarino R, Ali S (2020) Enablers and barriers to the implementation of socially assistive humanoid robots in health and social care: a systematic review. BMJ Open 10(1):e033096

Patel NA, Butte AJ (2020) Characteristics and challenges of the clinical pipeline of digital therapeutics. NPJ Digit Med 3(1):159

PB (2020) Emerging tech research report Q2 2020: Retail health and wellness teach by pitchbook. Pitchbook

Rajkomar A, Dean J, Kohane I (2019) Machine learning in medicine. N Engl J Med 380(14):1347–1358

Rassouli F, Tinschert P, Barata F, Steurer-Stey C, Fleisch E, Puhan M, Baty F, Kowatsch T, Brutsche M (2020) Characteristics of asthma-related nocturnal cough: a potential new digital biomarker. J Asthma Allergy 13:649–657

Renders CM, Valk GD, Griffin SJ, Wagner E, van Eijk JT, Assendelft WJJ (2000) Interventions to improve the management of diabetes mellitus in primary care, outpatient and community settings. Cochrane Database Syst Rev 4:1–140. CD001481

RH (2020) Rocket health 2020 market insights report: chasing a new equilibrium

Roth GA, Abate D, Abate KH, Abay SM, Abbafati C, Abbasi N, Abbastabar H, Abd-Allah F, Abdela J, Abdelalim A, Abdollahpour I, Abdulkader RS, Abebe HT, Abebe M, Abebe Z, Abejie AN, Abera SF, Abil OZ, Abraha HN, Abrham AR et al (2018) Global, regional, and national age-sex-specific mortality for 282 causes of death in 195 countries and territories, 1980-2017: a systematic analysis for the global burden of disease study 2017. Lancet 392(10159):1736–1788

Rüegger D, Stieger M, Nißen MK, Allemand M, Fleisch E, Kowatsch T (2020) How are personality states associated with smartphone data? Eur J Pers 34(5):687–713

Ryan RM, Deci EL (2017) Self-determination theory—basic psychological needs in motivation, development, and wellness. Guilford, New York

Schachner T, Keller R, Wangenheim F (2020) Artificial intelligence-based conversational agents for chronic conditions: systematic literature review. J Med Internet Res 22(9):e20701

Shezan FH, Hu H, Wang G, Tian Y (2020) Verhealth: vetting medical voice applications through policy enforcement. In: Proceedings of the ACM on interactive, mobile, wearable and ubiquitous technologies, vol 4, no 4, article 153

Shih C-H, Tomita N, Lukic YX, Reguera ÁH, Fleisch E, Kowatsch T (2019) Breeze: smartphone-based acoustic real-time detection of breathing phases for a gamified biofeedback breathing training. In: Proceedings of the ACM on interactive, mobile, wearable and ubiquitous technologies, vol 3, no 4, article 152

Sim I (2019) Mobile devices and health. N Engl J Med 381(10):956–968

Tinschert P, Rassouli F, Barata F, Steurer-Stey C, Fleisch E, Puhan M, Kowatsch T, Brutsche M (2020) Nocturnal cough and sleep quality to assess asthma control and predict attacks. J Asthma Allergy 13:669–678

Tudor Car L, Ardhithy Dhinagaran D, Kyaw BM, Kowatsch T, Joty SR, Theng YL, Atun R (2020) Conversational agents in health care: a scoping review and conceptual analysis. J Med Internet Res 22(8):e17158

Vandenberghe D, Albrecht J (2020) The financial burden of non-communicable diseases in the European Union: a systematic review. Eur J Public Health 30(4):833–839

WHO (2020) Global action plan for the prevention and control of noncommunicable diseases 2013–2020. World Health Organization, Geneva

Zhan A, Mohan S, Tarolli C, Schneider RB, Adams JL, Sharma S, Elson MJ, Spear KL, Glidden AM, Little MA, Terzis A, Dorsey ER, Saria S (2018) Using smartphones and machine learning to quantify Parkinson disease severity: the mobile Parkinson disease score. JAMA Neurol 75(7):876–880

Zhang CQ, Zhang R, Schwarzer R, Hagger MS (2019) A meta-analysis of the health action process approach. Health Psychol 38(7):623–637

Tobias Kowatsch, is the Scientific Director of the Centre for Digital Health Interventions, a joint initiative of the Department of Management, Technology and Economics at ETH Zurich and the Institute of Technology Management at the University of St.Gallen (HSG). He is also Assistant Professor for Digital Health at HSG, Adjunct Assistant Professor, Saw Swee Hock School of Public Health at the National University of Singapore, and partner of Dartmouth's Center for Technology and Behavioral Health. In close collaboration with his interdisciplinary team and research partners, Dr. Kowatsch designs digital health interventions at the intersection of computer science, information systems research, and behavioral medicine. He also helped to initiate MobileCoach, an open-source software platform for digital biomarker and chatbot research.

Elgar Fleisch, Prof. Dr., is Professor of Information and Technology Management at the ETH Zurich and the University of St. Gallen and Director of the Institute of Technology Management. Dr. Fleisch was born in 1968 in Bregenz, Austria. He graduated from the HTL Bregenz in mechanical engineering, then studied business informatics in Vienna, and completed his doctoral thesis in the field of artificial intelligence in 1993. His research interests focus on the current fusion of the physical and digital world into an Internet of Things. With his transdisciplinary team, his goal is to understand this fusion in the dimensions of technology, applications, and social implications.

Mobility: From Autonomous Driving Towards Mobility-as-a-Service

Andreas Herrmann

1 What Is Mobility-as-a-Service?

Not associating mobility to personally owning a vehicle but rather providing it as a service is far from being a new invention. There have always been companies that made business through transporting customers via a diverse range of transportation means, such as horses, carriages/wagons in the old days, and cars and buses in modern times. However, the contemporary understanding of mobility-as-a-service has been shaped just recently within the year of 2014 at a conference in Helsinki. There, for the first time, it was called for a mobility service that consisted of coordinated modes of transportation. The aim was to form a mobility chain amongst bicycles, cars, buses, trains, scooters, and even the march on foot—hence expanding the connecting range to really all types of transportation. Thus, these means of transport are no longer owned by the customer but ought to be provided through public and private companies (UITP 2019).

However, mobility-as-a-service will only be able to establish itself if the various means of transportation will be coordinated through automation processes rather than by the customer itself. This is where mobility platforms come into play; they contain all available information on schedules, routes,

A. Herrmann (✉)
Institute for Mobility, University of St. Gallen, St. Gallen, Switzerland
e-mail: andreas.herrmann@unisg.ch

© The Author(s), under exclusive license to Springer Nature Switzerland AG 2021
O. Gassmann, F. Ferrandina (eds.), *Connected Business*,
https://doi.org/10.1007/978-3-030-76897-3_5

97

and availability of the means of transportation which fall under consideration. A corresponding app forms the interface with the customer, whose functions could be described as follows: The user enters the departure point and destination, adds the desired travel times, and specifies any special features wished for the trip. Immediately, the algorithm combines all means of transport using timetables, routes, availability, and the traffic situation. Based thereupon, the app offers travel suggestions to the customer in real time (Catapult 2016).

In that respect, mobility-as-a-service encompasses a variety of services that could not be offered through one provider on its own. Hence, if this service is to succeed, numerous companies, such as the rail, cab, rental car, and bus companies, must collectively cooperate with each other. This creates an ecosystem in which each company seizes its specific role—Indicating that the days where one dominant player was capable to control one entire value chain are over.

2   What Are the Advantages of Mobility-as-a-Service?

In particular, mobility-as-a-service in combination with autonomous, electric vehicles is helping to improve safety on the roads. Alcohol, drugs, medication, and smartphone distraction remain to be the most common causes of accidents on the road. More than 90% of crashes can be traced back to human error. It is not the machine, but rather the flaws of the driver itself are to be recognized as a threat (Herrmann and Jungwirth 2022; World Economic Forum 2018).

A number of projects with self-driving vehicles, whether in Singapore, Israel, or the USA, impressively indicate that there is a good chance of reducing the number and length of traffic jams as well as noise and exhaust fumes through relying on self-driving vehicles. It also opens up the possibility of deconstructing roads and parking lots and using the space gained for playgrounds, restaurants, cafés, stores, or apartments. In this area, there has been tremendous progress. A great example is the fleet of *Mobileye's* autonomous cars, which are even able to cope with the hectic traffic of Tel Aviv and Jerusalem, or *Waymo*, which has successfully set up a cab service with self-driving shuttles in Phoenix.

3   Sharing Is Crucial

The idea of sharing instead of having and using rather than owning is not only a growing trend within our society but also plays a crucial role in reducing the social costs of mobility. As a reminder, a vehicle today only transports 1.5 people on average. If we would succeed, for example, in getting from 1.5 to 1.8 or even to 2.0 passengers, the volume of traffic and environmental pollution could be significantly reduced. Let us depict this claim through a calculation. There are currently around 4.6 million cars registered in Switzerland, carrying an average of 1.5 passengers. Mathematically speaking, with an average of 2.0 travelers, only 3.5 million vehicles would be needed. About one million cars could be dispensed with, fewer roads and parking spaces would be necessary, and the freed-up space could be used for other purposes. Ride-sharing, ride-pooling, ride-hailing, and car-sharing are important steps towards this path. However, suitable incentives and, if necessary, financial, fiscal, or even legal interventions are needed so that sharing has a positive and not a negative impact on traffic.

An interesting company fitting this matter is *BlaBlaCar*, founded in Paris in 2006 by Frédéric Mazzella, Nicolas Brusson, and Francis Nappez. *BlaBlaCar* pursues the vision of setting up a Europe-wide network consisting of car-sharing agencies. The idea is that members offer a ride in their car or search for one themselves. One can even specify preferences about the rideshare drivers and also about the drivers themselves. Up until now, the company has its locations in 22 countries and has over 70 million members worldwide.

BlaBlaCar consists of a travel search engine connected to a social network. Registration is required to use the service. Drivers planning a car trip can offer their free seats to other members, specifying the route and price. Interested passengers reach out to one another. If their travel intentions match, they take the journey together. As the passenger must contribute to the cost of the trip, the costs are suggested for each journey, which can be changed by the drivers. However, the prices per trip are capped through *BlaBlaCar* so that the drivers do not make a profit.

4   Nothing Works Without Apps

Repeatedly, the argument comes up that the fare systems, especially in public transport, are too complicated and not well coordinated with one another. In addition, the critics indicate that multimodal transport, i.e., the interaction of different means of transport such as car, train, and bicycle, would not work anyway. If anything, travelers argue the offer should come from a single source, and an app should show the best, cheapest, or fastest connection. And most importantly, once the connection has been selected, the payment process must run automatically in the background to make it as convenient as possible for the customers to use.

In Helsinki, the idea of such mobility services, alternatively to private vehicle ownership, could be already successfully implemented. People are enthusiastic about it. With the app *Whim*, users can plan their routes across different modes of transportation. Thus, the app takes into account buses, streetcars, subways, car-sharing, rental cars, rental bikes, as well as cabs. The pricing system is based on a flat rate: For 49 euros a month, you can use Helsinki's public transport without limits, and for 499 euros a month, you can add rental bikes, rental cars, and cabs without paying any extra fee. Despite initial skepticism, the app has since established itself and is considered today as a worldwide exemplary showcase.

For this app to work, the availability of large amounts of datasets is required. In Finland, this has been enabled through a governmental regulation obliging all transport companies in Finland to disclose their data. Public transport companies transmit their timetables and stops and, like cab and car-sharing companies, share real-time data on the position of their trains, buses, and cars. This data is stored in the cloud. Therethrough, it can be accessed by the app to optimize travel time and thus travel costs for each passenger. Individual trip planning at the touch of a button is in turn a central concern of mobility-as-a-service.

In recent years, numerous comparable apps have emerged, all of which aim to connect multiple modes of transportation for users and enable quick and easy traveling. Some of these initiatives, such as *Shift2MaaS, IoMob, UbiGo, iMove, MaaS4EU, Citymapper, MyCorridor, NaviGogo,* and *MobilityX*, focus on individual cities or regions. With the *Jelbi* app, the Berlin transport company wants to motivate drivers to use alternative means of transportation, such as e-bikes, e-scooters, buses, and trains. Other apps, such as *Via, ReachNow, SkedGo, Justride, HERE Mobility, eMaaS, TimesUpp, myCicero,* and *GoogleMaps*, for example, are designed to cover at least individual countries or even the entire world. Each app has its own particular story, including *Grab*, which was launched to improve the disastrous traffic situations in Thailand. Millions of people across Southeast Asia now use *Grab* to plan their daily trips.

5   App or Steering Wheel

Cars fulfill a fundamental human need: they allow the freedom of mobility. And the easier, faster, more comfortable, more exciting this mobility gets, the more attractive do cars become. In addition, a vehicle can be recognized as a mirror reflecting an owner's self-worth. It is about attention, admiration, and even envy. The car on a psychological basis can be recognized as means of communicating with other people telling the outside world "I made it; otherwise, I wouldn't drive this car." Hence, vehicles grace us on the stage of social life. For this reason alone, replacing the mere ownership of a car through the concept of mobility-as-a-service will not be easy, and thus, vehicle ownership will continue to play an important role in the upcoming years.

The downside, however, is the everyday traffic jams on the way to work and back home in the evenings. The entire city planning is built around cars, and with the congestion of cars, noise, exhaust fumes, and accidents are all by-products affecting our daily lives. Metropolises are suffocating in traffic, and most ironically a great number of people are no longer mobile despite the large number of cars. When questioning people from all around the world, you often discern the deep desire for a different kind of mobility. Mobility-as-a-service can be a solution through organizing the shortest and the fastest route for each traveler, hence better utilization of transportation. Each means of transport is deployed where it performs particularly well in terms of emissions, transport performance, space consumption, travel comfort, and, of course, costs. And, not to be forgotten, a traffic control center that coordinates and optimizes the use of the types of transport.

6   Mobility Concepts

Autonomous vehicles can be integrated into a broad urban or regional transportation network that aims to achieve an interplay between public and private means of transportation. These vehicles can be used in particular to cover the first and last mile, for example, between our homes and the train station or workplace. Numerous studies simulating the use of such vehicles come to the conclusion that each shuttle can replace a considerable number of traditional cars. This is true not only for metropolitan areas but also in agglomerations. There, in particular, lies the possibility of combining the various means of transport in such a way that traditional car traffic can be at least partially replaced.

Such vehicles represent the real mobility revolution because they radically change not only the technology of driving but also the cost of transporting people and freight. Because these vehicles operate 24 hours a day, do not make empty runs, and can be maintained with foresight, there is a good chance that the cost per kilometer driven can be significantly reduced. Currently, about 60–80% of the cost of a trip in a cab can be traced back to personnel costs. These costs would be eliminated by using such vehicles. Using these cars throughout the day also leads to significantly reduced costs for maintenance and repair, financing and depreciation, and insurance coverage (Capgemini Research Institute 2019).

Self-driving cars are likely to differ in terms of size and range: Two-, four- or eight-seaters as well as buses for 16, 20, or 40 passengers could soon make up the fleet. In any case, completely new payment models can be expected, as the price per kilometer driven is likely to be well below ten cents. Cities and municipalities could assume the transport costs in order to solve the traffic problems caused by congestion and emissions in this way. Or companies could step in as sponsors to present their products and services on the screens in the vehicles. The vision of free transportation seems achievable, at least in some regions. However, free transportation also pays back by giving people access to jobs, education, health, entertainment, and more. Seen from this angle, free use of these vehicles could significantly improve not only the attractiveness but also the economic power of a region.

However, mobility-as-a-service can only succeed if the business model is designed as a system that involves numerous players. Operators must cooperate with cities and municipalities, integrate the vehicles into traffic, set up charging stations and traffic control centers, and perhaps even define traffic regulations. In addition, modalities around billing concepts need to be clarified. Furthermore, an intuitively usable app is needed; the routes of the vehicles must be coordinated with the routes of other means of transportation, especially buses and trains; and also micro mobility should be included (Forrester 2019).

As was indicated earlier, mobility-as-a-service is based on the idea of combining car, train, bus, bicycle, and scooter and possibly even including walking. Of course, you can get almost anywhere by car. However, the economic and ecological costs are far too great to remain in this status quo and cover every distance via car. It would be just senseless to connect every residential area to the streetcar network. There are more efficient ways to cover the first and last mile in the transport of people and goods. Therefore, mobility-as-a-service always aims at designing a transport chain by stringing together train, bus, car, and the other means of transport in the best possible way. When we talk about the best possible chain, we are always talking about mobility that is both ecologically and economically oriented (World Economic Forum 2020a).

Here is an example: Alessandro and Francesca live in Muratello, Italy, not far from Lake Garda. Today, they want to travel to Chambly, a small town located about 30 kilometers outside of Paris, and visit their relatives. To attempt their journey, they will first use e-bikes to get from their home to Brescia, where they will transfer to a train. One of the bikes has a trailer to carry the suitcases. The train takes a direct route to the main station in Milan, with no need to change trains en route. There Alessandro and Francesca change to a bus that takes them to Malpensa airport. By plane, they go to Paris, landing at Charles de Gaulle Airport. Finally, they will pick up the rental car and travel on the highway to arrive at their relatives home in Chambly just in time.

Another example: A commuter is on his way to work and wants to take advantage of the multimodal transportation options offered through his city. The associated app combines the means of transport so that he can get to the business park as quickly as possible. So far, so good. But since the app displays the fastest connection for all users, some parts of the city could be particularly affected by rush-hour traffic. All commuters have to pass through these residential areas in order to arrive at their workplace as quickly as possible. Therefore, one could also imagine a traffic control system that distributes traffic evenly across the city districts in order to relieve some residential neighborhoods of noise and pollutants. In short, does the app optimize an individual's commute or traffic throughout the city? A nice example of route planning via such an app, taking into account the traffic situation in the city, is the offers of "Transport for London."

Another aspect of designing multimodal travel chains concerns the role of the city government. Does it allow private players, such as providers of e-scooters or e-bikes, to operate at all? Are these companies allowed to develop new routes on their own? For example, in Singapore, it is primarily the city government that shapes the multimodal transport offer. In Tel Aviv, on the other hand, many novel technology companies are driving development—and both scenarios are working! Both approaches deliver outstanding mobility for people.

7   Pods and Shuttles

While for some, autonomous pods and shuttles represent the dawn of a new age of mobility, others are still skeptical about these mobility concepts and prefer to wait and further observe. The technology of autonomous driving has yet to prove itself. Still already numerous self-driving mini-buses are in use all over the world. Airports are a great example where they are increasingly used to transport passengers between terminals. Further, driverless vehicles are taking over the transportation of people and freight in industrial areas, between hospital and university buildings, in shopping centers, at trade fairs, and even in some city centers (EU-Cordis 2016).

Through expanding one's viewpoint toward researchers and developers, it becomes clear that autonomous driving technology is currently being advanced in many directions. Since there are only occupants and no driver anymore, novel interior designs are considered. Here, concept vehicles are being created that resemble rolling living, working, play, and conference rooms and are equipped with the best information and communication technology. Other ideas focus on inner-city transportation, especially connecting pods and shuttles to public bus and train services. Autonomous mobility offers the possibility of intelligently linking the various means of transportation. In this context, self-driving vehicles have the task of taking over the transportation of travelers, especially in the first and last mile, i.e., from home or work to the train station and back again. In order to actually implement the idea of mobility-as-a-service, two types of autonomous vehicles in particular are needed (Fig. 1).

Driverless pods are not a modification of existing vehicle models; they are rather designed from the outset as autonomous cars. These vehicles operate in

Pod   Shuttle

Fig. 1 Examples of a pod and a shuttle, Herrmann et al. (2018)

inner cities in a defined catchment area with previously measured routes. They belong to a fleet operated, for example, by a company, a rail or bus company, or a municipal utility. The customer does not own the pod but pays depending on usage or through a "flat rate." These vehicles can be reserved and requested using an app, and a traffic control center navigates them, taking into account traffic conditions and destinations. Pods are small and maneuverable and therefore suitable for urban traffic; they also offer the few passengers a degree of privacy.

It can be assumed that self-driving shuttles will be increasingly used in the next few years. Not large coaches, but small city buses with space for eight to twenty passengers. Some cities are already using these shuttles, but only on predefined routes and with few stops. "On-demand" stops with variable route selection should be possible in the next few years. The "CityMobil" project funded by the European Union was the first step in this direction. This project was intended to demonstrate the possibilities for automated passenger transportation in selected cities. The focus was not just on technological aspects but on what needs to be done to make passengers feel comfortable in these vehicles.

Whether you consider pods or shuttles, the variety of vehicles is considerable: Some are designed to transport passengers alone, whereas others carry cargo in addition to passengers. Still others have been developed to transport food and medicines to remote areas without a driver. It is noticeable that the previously common distinction between passenger and freight transport is blurring. Some applications even envisage a vehicle being used for passenger transport during the day and delivering goods from a central warehouse to individual stores at night.

8   Conclusion

We are all familiar with the fascination of the car. The vehicle embodies what is technically feasible and simultaneously what is socially desirable. The excitement about cars stems from the enthusiasm for engines, design, and materials. It is about the achievements of electronics, computer science, mechanical engineering, and further disciplines. The car, with all its functions, grace, and aesthetics, reflects many people's idea of what a society is capable of achieving. But the fascination with this marvel also stems from the possibilities it offers to people—mobility, freedom, independence, self-determination, and also social advancement as well as social recognition. No wonder people want to own cars so badly.

Nevertheless, the transport sector must also make a contribution to ensuring that the world changes for the better. People all over the world should have opportunities. They should have access to jobs, medical care, and education. Cities should develop into places worth living in. The focus must be on people and not on cars. We often forget that the sick, the disabled, and the elderly also want to be on the move. The way mobility is currently organized does not always work. Finally, most crucially, the mobility industry must make its contribution to the European Union's "green deal" and the Paris climate agreement. All of this is close to our hearts. And for that, it is worth making the ownership of manually operated vehicles obsolete in our everyday life (World Economic Forum 2020b).

Success Factors for Mobility-as-a-Service

– Self-driving vehicles will reduce accidents, traffic jams, noise, and exhaust fumes through connectivity.
– Individual trip planning via an app at the touch of a button is the central concern of mobility-as-a-service.
– Intelligent sharing instead of owning is a megatrend and will reduce the social costs of mobility.
– Mobility-as-a-service is based on the network effects of platform business models; hence, it is important to reach a critical momentum.

References

Capgemini Research Institute (2019) The last-mile delivery challenge. New York
Catapult (2016) Mobility as a service. Milton Keynes.
EU-Cordis (2016) Final report summary—CityMobil. Brussels
Forrester (2019) Forrester analytics: online retail forecast. New York
Herrmann A, Jungwirth J (2022) Mobility for all. Emerald, London
Herrmann A, Brenner W, Stadler R (2018) Die autonome Revolution. Frankfurt
UITP (2019) Mobility as a service. Brussels
World Economic Forum (2018) Designing a seamless integrated mobility system. Geneva
World Economic Forum (2020a) The future of the last-mile ecosystem. Geneva
World Economic Forum (2020b) Activating a seamless integrated mobility system: insights into leading global practices. Geneva

Prof. Dr. Andreas Herrmann is one of the leaders of the Institute for Customer Insight at the University of St. Gallen (ICI-HSG). Since September 2019, he has been a visiting professor at the London School of Political Science (LSE). His research mainly focuses on behavioral economics as well as brand management. Further, he has published 15 books and over 250 scientific papers, which have been published in leading international journals such as *Journal of Marketing* and *Journal of Marketing Research*. Andreas Herrmann is known for his close contacts to the business community and his practice-oriented research. For years, he has been involved in numerous cooperation projects with well-known companies such as Audi, Porsche, Roche, Sonova, and others. He completed his doctorate at the Otto Beisheim School of Management (WHU).

Industry 4.0: Navigating Pathways Toward Smart Manufacturing and Services

Thomas Friedli, Moritz Classen, and Lukas Budde

1 Eroding Margins in Manufacturing Industries

The struggle of manufacturers in developed economies is real. The rise of global competitors operating at a lower cost, trade restrictions caused by the US-China dispute and local content requirements, and eroding margins in many product businesses all exert downward pressure on industrial firms' profitability. This is further exacerbated by the short- and long-term economic consequences of the COVID-19 pandemic. Many industries have seen equipment sales collapse, plants temporarily closing, and global value chains coming to a halt. Subsequently, some manufacturers are facing severe liquidity issues that endanger business continuity in the short term. The long-term consequences are substantial too. One lesson manufacturers learned is that value chains need to become more resilient to external shocks. For this to happen, global footprints need to be reevaluated. This need for change trickles down to operations. Production processes need to become more flexible to adjust for short-term changes in demand, and customer support has to be ensured even when travel restrictions apply.

These recent developments point toward the increased use of digital technologies in operations. This trend is not entirely new. Since 2010, political

T. Friedli • M. Classen • L. Budde (✉)
University of St. Gallen, St. Gallen, Switzerland
e-mail: thomas.friedli@unisg.ch; Moritz.Classen@unisg.ch; lukas.budde@unisg.ch

© The Author(s), under exclusive license to Springer Nature Switzerland AG 2021
O. Gassmann, F. Ferrandina (eds.), *Connected Business*,
https://doi.org/10.1007/978-3-030-76897-3_6

109

programs to drive digitalization in manufacturing have flourished under different names, such as "Industry 4.0" in Germany or "Smart Manufacturing" in the USA (Osterrieder et al. 2020). Amidst the abundance of interpretations (Benninghaus and Richard 2016), this chapter builds on the initial definition of Industry 4.0 as the "technical integration of cyber-physical systems in manufacturing and logistics, as well as the application of the Internet of Things (IoT) and Services in industrial processes" (Kagermann et al. 2013, 18, own translation). What has changed, however, is the urgency and speed of implementation. The COVID-19 pandemic has additionally served as a catalyst for digital transformation, where 3D printing, big data and artificial intelligence (AI), drones, robotics, and IoT were swiftly deployed to respond to the health and economic crisis, thereby spurring the mainstreaming of Industry 4.0 technologies in consumer and business contexts (United Nations Industrial Development Organisation 2020).

Figure 1 provides an overview of the diversity of application fields, technologies, and objectives related to Industry 4.0. Industry 4.0 implementation patterns can be distinguished in front-end application fields and base technologies. The front-end encompasses the fields of manufacturing, smart connected products, the new way of working, and the digitalized up- and downstream supply chain.

Although there are differences in the exact scope and focus, all concepts promote modern IT technologies and the usage of data in manufacturing

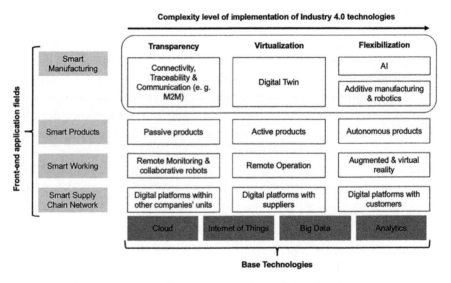

Fig. 1   General Industry 4.0 implementation framework, Frank et al. (2019)

(Thoben et al. 2017). Four key technologies for Industry 4.0 or smart manufacturing have been identified: cloud, big data, Internet of Things, and analytics. These are also understood as "base technologies" (Frank et al. 2019) because they serve as a foundation for different front-end application fields. The further the manufacturing company moves toward automation, flexibilization, and autonomy, the higher the complexity of implementation the company will face. Uncertainties about the success of implementation, in terms of innovation and profitability, determine the characteristics of the complexity of this transformation. To navigate through this jungle of opportunities, different dominant implementation patterns have been identified. We analyzed 27 generic smart manufacturing use cases in depth to develop the framework for the transformation journey toward smart manufacturing.

Digital technologies fuel two growth engines of manufacturing firms. First and foremost comes the stabilization and improvement of the core business along the iron triangle of cost, quality, and flexibility. For instance, in high-volume production, a sensor-based in-line quality inspection may close control loops, reducing the need for manual labor without compromising quality (Schmitz et al. 2019). Similarly, remote service operations can harness augmented reality and advanced analytics to assist customers in a faster, more targeted, and cost-efficient way.

Second, digital technologies allow manufacturers to exit their comfort zone and venture into new business opportunities. Consider *KUKA*'s "SmartFactory as a Service" business model. The robot manufacturer has teamed up with IT consultancy *MHP* and reinsurer *Munich Re* to offer production capacities "as-a-service," leveraging their respective core competencies of software integration, automation technology, and risk management (KUKA 2018). This is a bold move for *KUKA*, as their domain of activity shifts from selling equipment to taking over manufacturing operations for third parties and managing revenue and operational risks.

However, to realize such potential, firms need to navigate the labyrinth of digitalization, which boils down to three main questions. First, *why start?* Executives may feel a sense of urgency to "digitalize," putting pressure on the organization to launch digitalization projects but neglecting the need for strategic alignment. Digitalization for its own sake is unlikely to yield sustainable returns. Instead, top management needs to define a set of quantified objectives guiding all digitalization initiatives. Second, *where to start?* The number of digital technologies and potential applications within and beyond the firm can be overwhelming. Decision-makers need a compass directing them to potential use cases tailored to the firm-specific situation. Third, *how to proceed?* Regardless of the number of use cases selected for implementation, the right timing and sequencing of digitalization initiatives are essential. Focusing on a few promising opportunities avoids spreading organizational resources on too many digitalization fronts, which is likely to be costly and ineffective.

This chapter advances six steps to successfully navigate the transformation toward smart manufacturing and services:

1. Modernize core operational processes.
2. Clarify digitalization objectives.
3. Identify and select use cases.
4. Exploit efficiency potentials.
5. Adapt the organization.
6. Build new business models.

The pathways will be unfolded within the next section.

2   Pathways Toward Smart Manufacturing and Services

2.1   Modernize Core Operational Processes

Some basic homework needs to be done before going full throttle on digitalization. Catching up on state-of-the-art lean practices is fundamental to ensure transparency, robustness, and standardization of manufacturing processes. Survey data shows that industrial managers expect lean and digitalization to co-exist and mutually reinforce each other going forward (Benninghaus and Richard 2016). The complementarity of both is evident: high-quality data facilitates the identification of waste, while streamlined processes facilitate the integration of digital solutions in manufacturing (Lorenz et al. 2019).

Moreover, the eternal search for continuous improvement should be ingrained in the DNA of any organization embarking on the digitalization journey. Our work with companies suggests that digitalization initiatives often reveal archaic and inefficient operational processes that require serious revamp *before* introducing additional digital tools. Such routines often exist for historical reasons so that nobody in the active workforce questions them. They are difficult to break and thus reveal a lack of continuous improvement in an organization's culture, which is essential to build.

Consider the case of a global pharmaceutical company. After duplicating the syringe-filling process to a second site, quality problems emerged. An unusually high rate of cracked syringes led to costly product returns.

Subsequent in-depth analysis revealed similar problems that had occurred in the production ramp-up in the first site. However, because no "lessons learned" session was conducted when transferring the product to the second site, similar mistakes were repeated. Integrating systematic knowledge exchange in transfer projects was, therefore, imperative. Such measures can be effective before committing additional resources to digitalization.

2.2   Clarify Digitalization Objectives

Digitalization can change industry rules. Most notably, new entrants may be able to capture a growing share of profit pools. Think about *Microsoft*, who becomes increasingly interlocked in the value chain of manufacturing. The Azure Internet-of-Things cloud stores data from production processes to customer interaction. The augmented reality glasses HoloLens can be used to guide assembly but also remote repair operations. While tech companies can assist manufacturers in ramping up digitalization, they also pose a significant competitive threat, as they have the potential to substitute highly profitable activities, particularly in field interventions.

Consequently, some advisers promote a digitalization strategy at the corporate level. We view it in a slightly more nuanced way. Certainly, digitalization needs to be at the top of the executives' agenda. A critical assessment of how digitalization might change a firm's competitive environment and operating model is crucial. To us, however, digitalization is not an objective in itself. Instead, we see digitalization as an enabler for the corporate strategy, as a tool to achieve a set of superordinate objectives.

At the highest level of abstraction, executives are faced with the choice between exploration and exploitation. Digitalization can address both fundamental profit levers.

First, digitalization permits an increase in efficiency for current operations, thereby unlocking cost-saving opportunities. Second, manufacturers may tap on new revenue streams enabled by digital technologies, either by selling more of the same or by introducing entirely new offerings. Both tracks of exploitation and exploration can be explored simultaneously or subsequently, as we will discuss in more detail later.

Picking between either revenue or cost objectives of digitalization is not easy. In our work with industrial firms, we have requested executives to choose a side. While companies will often attempt to reach both objectives, an initial choice of direction is essential to prioritize between the plentitude of potential digital activities in a typical mid-sized manufacturer. The same applies when the starting point for digitalization is still unclear, as the next section argues.

2.3   Identify and Select Use Cases

The implementation is not straightforward because of diverse uncertainties, different circumstances, and diverse initial starting points (e.g. different automation levels). The questions where to start and on which use cases to focus on should be linked to the strategic and operational targets the company wants to address. This is why the first step should be the specification of the competitive priorities (quality, costs, speed, etc.) and the definition of their relative importance. Next comes the identification of application fields where the identified competitive priorities can be best supported. Based on that, the relevant use cases can be derived.

The selection of relevant use cases can be oriented along with the typical tasks to perform in a factory (planning, execution, and support). The framework (see Fig. 2) of existing generic smart factory use cases supports this selection process. The generic use case patterns in this framework are built upon a database of more than 500 use cases from practice. It helps companies reflect their own position and identify potential white spots for implementation to achieve higher efficiency levels.

2.4   Exploit Efficiency Potentials

Based on the selected use cases, the process of implementation and testing needs to begin. Many of the use cases, especially use cases that address higher autonomy levels in the factory and are based and depend on data (such as autonomous job scheduling, self-regulating material flows, and predictive maintenance), encompass a higher complexity. It is not foreseeable when and whether at all there will finally come the breakeven. Thus, there is no guarantee for the use case's success and, consequently, no guarantee for any return on investment. The "valley of tears" companies need to go through that considerably longer than in earlier technology investments. This is also why the implementation should not start with the modernization of the IT infrastructure and new sensors for the machine, for instance. This captures too many resources and efforts that do not directly create additional value for the company or customer. The focus in the early stages should be on feasibility testing and impact evaluation.

The procedure in such projects emphasizes a sound process understanding as a critical enabler for achieving sustainable improvements in machine availability and quality. Creating a common process understanding of all involved persons, such as operators, process engineers, and data analysts, is the pivotal

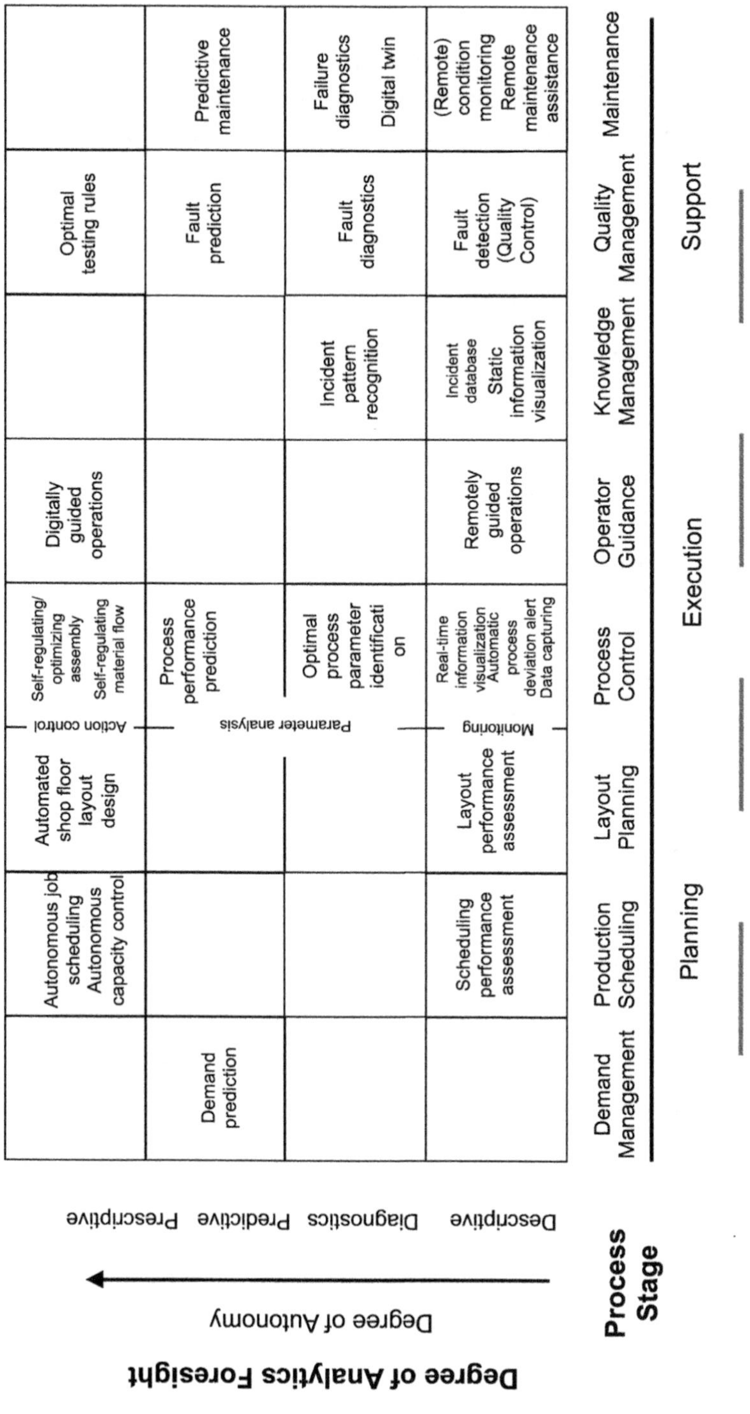

Degree of Analytics Foresight

Degree of Autonomy →

Degree of Autonomy / Foresight	Demand Management	Production Scheduling	Layout Planning	Process Control	Operator Guidance	Knowledge Management	Quality Management	Maintenance
Prescriptive		Autonomous job scheduling; Autonomous capacity control	Automated shop floor layout design	Self-regulating/optimizing assembly; Self-regulating material flow *(Action control)*	Digitally guided operations		Optimal testing rules	Predictive maintenance
Predictive	Demand prediction			Process performance prediction			Fault prediction	Failure diagnostics; Digital twin
Diagnostics		Scheduling performance assessment	Layout performance assessment	Optimal process parameter identification *(Parameter analysis)*		Incident pattern recognition	Fault diagnostics	
Descriptive				Real-time information visualization; Automatic process deviation alert; Data capturing *(Monitoring)*	Remotely guided operations	Incident database; Static information visualization	Fault detection (Quality Control)	(Remote) condition monitoring; Remote maintenance assistance
Process Stage	Planning	Planning	Planning	Execution	Execution	Execution	Support	Support

Fig. 2 Use case framework 27 generic use cases, Classen et al. (2018)

starting point in the journey of data-based predictive maintenance. Furthermore, stakeholders of the initiative need to assess the capability of the machine and supporting IT infrastructure to measure, collect, and make available relevant data. Only by thoroughly understanding the process and the kind of available data, plausible and well-founded hypotheses on quality issues and breakdowns can be derived and tested statistically. Without establishing process understanding first, people tend to jump to premature conclusions and derive solutions that do not address the real problem. Deriving irrelevant assumptions based on an inadequate perception of the process leads to a waste of resources, especially as the data-gathering process is a highly time-consuming and, therefore, expensive activity. Consequently, one needs to ensure to ask the right questions before deciding which data should be collected.

Furthermore, digital technologies help to tap in on significant improvement potential in service operations backstage, at the line of visibility, and frontstage. Foremost, there is ample room for improving support processes using digital means. In the last years, manufacturers have undertaken substantial efforts to introduce CRM systems for storing data from customer touchpoints. Still, more often than not, data collection is spotty or limited by technical constraints. With knowledge about customers and interventions on their installed base fragmented across the organization, loops from one service mission to another are not closed. Long repair times spent on identifying knowledge sources on a specific incident are rather the norm than the exception in our work with companies.

Moreover, the efficiency potential of digitalizing customer touchpoints seen in consumer markets can also be reaped in business-to-business services. While in their private life, professional buyers increasingly shop for everything from electronics to groceries online, the purchasing experience in their daily work dramatically lags. We worked with an equipment manufacturer on the introduction of a remote service. An online spare parts catalog was already in place. It consisted of a rudimentary directory of hundred-plus-page PDF files that listed spare parts numbers, pictures, and specifications. Unsurprisingly, any spare part sold, while yielding a substantial gross margin, also entailed high process costs. The company then developed a webshop that would significantly enhance customer experience and dramatically reduce process costs from handling orders.

Typically, webshops open the door for more comprehensive digitalization of customer touchpoints. Again, players in consumer markets have paved the way for reaching cost-effective service excellence by using self-service technology (Wirtz and Zeithaml 2018). Manufacturers leading in digitalization are following a similar path. German industrial conglomerate *Voith* positions "MyVoith" as a one-stop digital platform. MyVoith is the gateway to Voith's digital service world, offering over 20 applications, from webshops to asset management. In a similar vein, as of 2020, over 6000 customers of Swiss process equipment manufacturer *Bühler* use the "myBühler" portal to manage their installed base and order spare parts conveniently.

Consumer markets show that there is more to come. For instance, chatbots powered by artificial intelligence have earned their place in the financial services industry. *Capital One*, a US bank, has virtual assistant Eno to help prospective customers find the right credit card and provides active customers with financial information. Industrial service providers we worked with are also moving in the same direction to standardize customer support.

Arguably, the most discussed efficiency lever of digitalization can be pulled at the frontstage. There are many ways of digitalizing service missions. Swiss elevator manufacturer *Schindler* has been at the forefront of innovation on this matter, leveraging three digitally enabled tools to increasing service efficiency (Schindler 2020). New elevator installations are equipped with the "CUBE," an *edge device* continuously transmitting equipment status data, such as door movements and component wear. This data is monitored from *technical operation centers* and fed to field operation. If any issue is detected in the installed base, the center is responsible for coordinating reactions and deploying technicians. Finally, FieldLink—an iPhone *application* used in China—guides the field force during troubleshooting and helps find the right spare parts.

Still, for many manufacturers, the cost-saving potential in field missions remains substantial. A Swiss manufacturer of textile machinery was struggling with rising service costs in Asia. While China, India, and Pakistan were the largest markets in terms of new product sales, service revenues were negligible. Equipment sales generated sufficient gross margins to finance the relatively low labor cost of local service technicians. Therefore, providing free maintenance during the warranty period and beyond was still a viable option in most cases. Some breakdown incidents, however, required specialist advice from the second-level support in the Swiss headquarters. Due to the noisy working environment and language barriers, some incidents could not be solved over the phone, requiring a technician from the headquarters to be flown in. To reduce repair time and service costs, a digitally enabled remote service was needed.

2.5   Adapt Your Organization

Digitalization initiatives require top management commitment to drive visibility and perseverance. While use cases should be implemented at a small scale first, their success needs to be disseminated across the entire organization. We have seen tier-1 automotive suppliers appointing seasoned executives to lead specific task forces to coordinate digitalization activities across the firm. Given the firm size, the risk of losing sight of parallel activities was all too real.

Moreover, top management commitment cannot be just a fad. Our benchmarking data suggests that investments in digital technologies are typically expected to pay off after 2–5 years (Friedli et al. 2018). The reality can be slightly more complicated, though. Digitalization profit curves tend to be left-skewed because substantial initial cash outlays for hard- and software investments are required, with returns materializing only after a certain period of time. Against this backdrop, representatives from family-owned successful practice companies highlighted a favorable impact of their ownership structure. In the cases under study, top management proved to embrace a long-term perspective, encouraging digitalization initiatives despite them not breaking even in a short time period (Friedli et al. 2019).

Manufacturers need to develop a range of new capabilities to succeed in the long run. For many niche players, capabilities in the domain of large-scale data analytics are virtually nonexistent. At this point, the decision to buy or build analytical capabilities is of strategic importance. For some manufacturers, partnering with big tech companies is a way to kick-start digitalization. *Bühler*, for instance, leverages proprietary algorithms from *Microsoft* Azure to run its MoisturePro moisture control solution. Given their size and finite amount of resources, small and medium enterprises are especially more likely to buy plug-and-play solutions from established players instead of building these capabilities themselves.

But trying to simply buy analytic capabilities can also backfire, as the example of a German industrial solutions provider shows. In a pilot project, asset data was transferred to an IT start-up with the hope of extracting insights about failure patterns. However, the start-up lacked the domain know-how to feed the artificial neural network with relevant configuration parameters, leading to faulty conclusions drawn from the model.

Other firms may choose to build these capabilities for data privacy reasons. For instance, a Swiss watchmaker categorically refused the idea of tapping on external resources and tools for data analytics. As one of their managers said,

"Such [analytic] tool—we will buy it and put it to work ourselves." While this allows them to operate largely independently from technology vendors, it also requires some larger initial investments with uncertain payoffs. In short, the decision to buy or build analytical capabilities depends on firm-specific factors.

Customer-oriented capabilities are required too. Our industry work points toward the predominant "box-mover mentality" as a major organizational barrier to digitalization. While firms have routinely developed goods and shipped them as is to customers, digitalization changes the rules of the game. Developing capabilities to pierce through the fog of emerging customer needs for digitalization is imperative. This encompasses agile innovation capabilities, where first pilots are co-created with customers and then iteratively improved based on early feedback loops. Embracing such uncertainty can be new to some manufacturers and requires management to embrace risk to a somewhat higher extent.

2.6   Build New Business Models

The moment of launching the second growth engine needs to be timed meticulously. If the core business is still underdeveloped in terms of digital capabilities, attempts to drive growth through new business models are compromised. This was essential learning for an industrial equipment manufacturer in the automotive industry. The service department had come up with the idea of a consignment stock for spare and wear parts embodied in a vending machine installed on the customer's shop floor. The customer value proposition seemed promising: the offering would cut machine downtimes and spare parts lead times while freeing up cash by reducing inventory. However, the manufacturer's logistics processes were not up to speed. Transparency about the availability of spare parts scattered around the globally dispersed warehouses was inexistent. Rolling out the consignment stock too quickly posed a risk of over-accumulating spare parts on a global scale. Opposition from the firm's subsidiaries managing the warehouses ensued. As a consequence, a much-needed initiative to improve the transparency of spare parts availability was launched, causing a delay in the consignment stock rollout, but eventually helping to catch up on long-time neglected improvement potentials.

Once the digitalization homework is done, manufacturers can switch to a higher gear. There are two strategic moves to innovate business models using digital technologies: leveraging the core and blazing a new trail. Both are introduced in Table 1 and unpacked subsequently.

Table 1 Two moves for business model innovation in industrial firms, author's own illustration

Move	Leverage the core	Blaze a new trail
Profit lever addressed	Revenue and cost	Revenue
Synergies with core business	High	Low
Industries served	Predominantly existing	Predominantly new or adjacent
Setup	– Existing brand and legal entity – New business unit within parent company	– New brand and legal entity – Spin-off
Examples	– Equipment-as-a-service (*Rolls-Royce, Hilti, Michelin*) – Logistics management (*SFS e-logistics*)	– Manufacturing-as-a-service (*KUKA*) – Platform-as-a-service (*BuildingMinds, Axoom*)

3   Leverage the Core

The first move consists of enriching the firm's core capabilities with value-adding activities that create revenue or cost synergies. Typical capabilities leveraged include product and service know-how, operations and supply chain capacity, and sales channels. Value is created for customers by reducing their working capital, transaction, or overhead costs. Usually, customers within already served industries are targeted, albeit from different segments. Because the overlap with the core business is significant, these business models are typically provided by the existing firm. Existing brand names and corporate structures are used to foster trust, while new sub-brands or business units may be formed for stronger separation from existing business models.

Construction equipment manufacturer *Hilti* has made such a move with their fleet management service. Customers pay monthly fees for tool usage, including an all-inclusive service package. This business model, initiated in 2001, rests on three core capabilities of *Hilti*:

(a) First, an industry-leading product quality in terms of reliability and performance, endorsed by the *Hilti* brand name.
(b) Second, service excellence. In their regular product business, *Hilti* promises product repair in "3 days or free." This is ensured by around 100 wholly owned repair shops subject to rigorous continuous improvement initiatives. The fleet management service leverages these operational capabilities.

(c) Third, their direct sales force. *Hilti* relies exclusively on direct channels, thereby drastically cutting time to market for new offerings. To provide sufficient leeway to scale service business models, a separate "Tool Services" business unit was spun off in 2018.

Digital technologies are a critical enabler for innovative business models. Take the example of Swiss component manufacturer *SFS*. Their core product portfolio encompasses fastening and building components. Product differentiation is difficult for many of these products, given their low price and interchangeability. To counter eroding margins and integrate deeper into customer processes, *SFS* has launched "e-logistics," a c-parts-management solution enabled by smart containers. Built-in sensors and data transmission technology allow customers to order spare parts by simply turning or pushing a button on the container. These containers trigger replenishment of c-parts manufactured by *SFS* or any other third-party supplier integrated into the e-logistics supply chain. Hence, e-logistics is a new business model building on two elements: (1) core capabilities in manufacturing and distributing c-parts and (2) additional activities providing incremental customer value and in this case, reducing overhead costs.

4   Blaze a New Trail

The second move is even bolder. When answering the question *In what business am I in?* manufacturers may choose to look for revenue opportunities outside the core. When synergies with existing core competencies are low, building up a new business under another brand name can help gain a foothold in entirely new industries, while limiting risks of brand damage if the new venture goes south.

A number of manufacturers have leaped forward by getting into the platform business. *Schindler* has recently formed *BuildingMinds*, a Berlin-based start-up offering a platform for real estate management. While Schindler elevators and escalators can be integrated into *BuildingMinds*, they are just one of the many building-related assets managed from the platform. Arguably, the overlaps between, on the one hand, manufacturing and servicing elevators, and, on the other hand, operating a building Platform-as-a-Service (PaaS) are limited. Given the low synergies between both businesses, operating the platform as a separate venture seems like a sensible choice.

In a similar vein, there is an ongoing race for the dominant platform in manufacturing. Industry heavyweights *GE* and *Siemens* appear to be slightly ahead with their Predix and MindSphere platforms, respectively. However, unlike their counterparts in consumer markets (think of *Amazon*, *Facebook*, and *Google*), no manufacturing platform has yet reached the critical mass to "take it all," as the adage goes. Smaller companies are active too. *ADAMOS* incorporates the attempt of industrial firms from German-speaking countries, including *DMG MORI*, *Dürr*, and *Zeiss*, to build a vendor-agnostic manufacturing platform. Thus, *ADAMOS* was built from scratch as a neutral venture. This has allowed other companies to buy shares from the *ADAMOS* consortium, as the professional service firm *PwC* did in April 2020 (PwC 2020).

Conversely, the bold move of going into the platform business may be reversed at any point in time. Two years after its inception, *KUKA* sold the PaaS offering "Connyun" to technology holding *Körber* in 2018 (Weinzierl 2018). About a year later, manufacturer *Trumpf* sold its "AXOOM" platform to an IT firm, while development activities pertaining to the connectivity of *Trumpf* machines were reintegrated into the headquarters (Pankow 2019). While *Trumpf* remained silent about the specific reasons for divesting from PaaS, it seems as if the stretch from the rest of the firm's activities was too large to justify further investments, such that the executive board decided to focus resources on activities nearer to the core business.

5   Conclusion

Six pathways toward smart manufacturing and services were introduced in this chapter. The first consists of the modernization of operational processes, which is imperative for manufacturers to stay in business, regardless of further digitalization initiatives. Second, the clarification of digitalization objectives is a necessity that has to be done before any further digitalization initiative is launched. Third, a use-case-based selection of activities is appropriate when starting on a clean slate. It gets digitalization moving without committing too many resources upfront. Fourth, there are clear cases for exploiting efficiency potentials through digitalization across manufacturing and service operations. Fifth, organizational adaptation is necessary to get digitalization activities off the ground in the first stage and succeed against the competition in the long run. Sixth, to profit from the potential of Industry 4.0, manufacturers can make bold moves by introducing new business models that either leverage their core business or blaze an entire trail in the ways of creating and capturing value.

The future will reveal whether manufacturers will sustain the pace of adoption of digital technologies witnessed in 2020. Now that many are up to speed in terms of connecting assets and operators and serving customers digitally, the real race for competitive advantage begins. Industrial firms that leapfrog the competition by digitalizing their operations *and* business models will be able to appropriate economic rents and stay on top of their game if they continuously innovate products, processes, and services.

Success Factors for Industry 4.0

- Robust processes: Leverage established techniques to standardize and streamline and fail-proof processes before digitalizing at scale.
- Relentless prioritization: Focus managerial attention and marshal resources to a limited set of key digitalization initiatives.
- Inexpensive pilots: Zero in on the use-case appropriate for your firm's situation, test and learn iteratively, and then scale across functions and sites.
- Customer orientation: Empathize with customers to pinpoint improvement opportunities along the customer journey.
- Long-term orientation: Consider the substantial time required for minds to change, capabilities to build, savings to materialize, and revenues to take off.

References

Benninghaus C, Richard L (2016) Industrie 4.0—from a management perspective. Final report. https://www.alexandria.unisg.ch/252971/. Accessed 6 Sept 2020

Classen M, Blum C, Budde L, Hänggi R, Friedli T (2018) Digitalisierung À La Carte. ZWF 113(12):850–854

Frank AG, Dalenogare LS, Ayala NF (2019) Industry 4.0 technologies: implementation patterns in manufacturing companies. Int J Prod Econ 210:15–26

Friedli T, Budde L, Benninghaus C, Elbe C, Pejić T (2018) Benchmarking digital technologies. Evolution of production in high-wage countries: general report. https://www.alexandria.unisg.ch/257625/. Arbeitsbericht

Friedli T, Classen M, Osterrieder P, Stähle L (2019) Smart services—transformation of the service organization. Benchmarking report. https://www.alexandria.unisg. ch/257104/

Kagermann H, Wahlster W, Helbig J, Hellinger A (2013) Umsetzungsempfehlungen Für Das Zukunftsprojekt Industrie 4.0: Deutschlands Zukunft Als Produktionsstandort Sichern ; Abschlussbericht Des Arbeitskreises Industrie 4.0; Deutschlands Zukunft Als Produktionsstandort Sichern. Forschungsunion, Berlin, 112 S. http://gateway-bayern.de/BV041628328

KUKA (2018) SmartFactory as a service. https://www.kuka.com/de-de/future-production/industrie-4-0/smartfactory-as-a-service-home. Accessed 18 Aug 2020

Lorenz R, Buess P, Macuvele J, Friedli T, Netland TH (2019) Lean and digitaliza-tion—contradictions or complements? In: Ameri F, Stecke KE, von Cieminski G, Kiritsis D (eds) Advances in production management systems. production man-agement for the factory of the future, IFIP advances in information and commu-nication technology, vol 566. Springer, Cham, pp 77–84

Osterrieder P, Budde L, Friedli T (2020) The smart factory as a key construct of industry 4.0: a systematic literature review. Int J Prod Econ 221:107476. https://doi.org/10.1016/j.ijpe.2019.08.011

Pankow G (2019) GFT Übernimmt Geschäftsaktivitäten Und Mitarbeiter Von Axoom. https://www.produktion.de/wirtschaft/gft-uebernimmt-geschaeftsaktivitaeten-und-mitarbeiter-von-axoom-113.html. Accessed 31 Aug 2020

PwC (2020) Industrie 4.0-plattform: PwC Deutschland Beteiligt Sich an ADAMOS GmbH. https://www.pwc.de/de/pressemitteilungen/2020/industrie-4-0-plattform-pwc-deutschland-beteiligt-sich-an-adamos-gmbh.html. Accessed 31 Aug 2020

Schindler (2020) Full year results presentation 2019. https://www.schindler.com/com/internet/en/investor-relations/reports/_jcr_content/contentPar/download listcontent_7804229/downloadList/359_1581655255063.download.asset.359_ 1581655255063/schindler-fy-2019-presentation.pdf. Accessed 21 Aug 2020

Schmitz C, Tschiesner A, Jansen C, Hallerstede S, Garms F (2019) Industry 4.0: capturing value at scale in discrete manufacturing. https://www.mckinsey.com/~/media/McKinsey/Industries/Advanced%20Electronics/Our%20Insights/Capturing%20value%20at%20scale%20in%20discrete%20manufacturing%20 with%20Industry%204%200/Industry-4-0-Capturing-value-at-scale-in-discrete-manufacturing-vF.pdf. Accessed 18 Aug 2020

Thoben K, Wiesner S, Wuest T, BIBA—Bremer Institut für Produktion und Logistik GmbH, the University of Bremen, Faculty of Production Engineering, University of Bremen, Bremen, Germany, Industrial, and Management Systems Engineering (2017) "Industrie 4.0" and smart manufacturing—a review of research issues and application examples. Int J Autom Technol 11(1):4–16. https://doi.org/10.20965/ijat.2017.p0004

United Nations Industrial Development Organisation (2020) COVID-19 implica-tions & responses: digital transformation & industrial recovery. https://www.unido.org/sites/default/files/files/2020-07/UNIDO_COVID_Digital_Transformation_0.pdf. Accessed 18 Aug 2020

Weinzierl S (2018) Körber Übernimmt IIoT-Spezialist Connyun Von Kuka. https://www.produktion.de/wirtschaft/koerber-uebernimmt-iiot-spezialist-connyun-von-kuka-125.html. Accessed 27 Aug 2020

Wirtz J, Zeithaml V (2018) Cost-effective service excellence. J Acad Mark Sci 46(1):59–80. https://doi.org/10.1007/s11747-017-0560-7

Prof. Dr. Thomas Friedli is a professor of production management at the University of St. Gallen in Switzerland. His main research interests are in the field of managing operational excellence, global production management, and management of industrial services. He is a lecturer in the (E)MBA programs in St. Gallen, Fribourg, and Salzburg. He spent several weeks as adjunct associate professor at Purdue University in West Lafayette, USA. Prof. Friedli leads a team of 15 researchers who develop new management solutions for manufacturing companies in today's business landscape. He is also the editor, author, or co-author of 14 books and various articles.

Dr. Moritz Classen graduated in industrial engineering and management at the Karlsruhe Institute of Technology. He gained professional experience within the automotive and power generation industry. Moritz Classen is with Prof. Friedli's Division of Production Management at the University of St. Gallen, where he leads the competence center *Smart Manufacturing and Services*. He pursues a PhD in management with a focus on smart service strategy, marketing, and sales.

Dr. Lukas Budde studied mechanical engineering at the Technical University of Darmstadt and received his PhD from the University of St. Gallen. Since 2015, Lukas Budde has been a post-doc and project manager in the field of production management at the Institute for Technology Management at the University of St. Gallen. His research focus lies on patterns for smart manufacturing and digital platform ecosystems in manufacturing companies. He is a lecturer for Operations Management courses and in custom programs of the Executive School of the University of St. Gallen.

Decentralized Platform Ecosystems for Data and Digital Trust in Industrial Environments

Kilian Schmück, Monika Sturm, and Oliver Gassmann

1 Creating Value with Industrial Data?

Many manufacturing companies and traditional service providers are trying to keep up with the digital age and connected business era. The core of connected business is about gaining access to data and generating information to monetize acquired knowledge. Platform companies have already secured an international competitive advantage concerning private user data. The strong GAFA quartet (*Google, Apple, Facebook, Amazon*) dominates the American and European markets, while *Tencent* and *Alibaba* dominate the Chinese market. The cornerstone of connected business is the digitalization of business which began with the advent of the Internet protocol TCP/IP. When Tim Berners-Lee invented the World Wide Web in 1989 at *CERN* to enable simplified data exchange between Swiss and French laboratories, the enormous economic implications were not imaginable. However, the European economy did not take up the Internet; there was a lack of imagination and

K. Schmück (✉) • O. Gassmann
Institute of Technology Management, University of St. Gallen,
St. Gallen, Switzerland
e-mail: kilian.schmueck@unisg.ch; oliver.gassmann@unisg.ch

M. Sturm
Siemens, Vienna, Austria
e-mail: monika.sturm@siemens-energy.com

O. Gassmann, F. Ferrandina (eds.), *Connected Business*,
https://doi.org/10.1007/978-3-030-76897-3_7

127

willingness to take risks. Why should they? The automobile industry was buzzing, and there was no end in sight. Today, we know what a dramatic development this convenience has taken for the digitalization to end user.

However, there is still the opportunity to get a foot in the door when it comes to industrial data. However, these business rules are different from those of the platform economy. The mistake of copy-pasting should be avoided in this case. The opportunity in the industrial B2B sector is decentralized platform ecosystems. Decentralized platform ecosystems are not owned by a single party but are coordinated and operated by an entire network. The technological basis is distributed ledger technologies (DLTs) like blockchain and the ideology of data sovereignty, data portability, and data interoperability. Essential for such democratization are governance models that regulate coordination and the incentives to unify the network. Similar to politics: to turn a dictatorship into a democracy, a constitution is needed to enable society's unity. A prime example of a European initiative for data sovereignty in the industrial sector is *GAIA-X: A Federated Data Infrastructure for Europe*. Initiated by the German Federal Ministry of Economics led by its minister, Peter Altmaier, and now supported, coordinated, and developed by European companies such as *Bosch, Siemens, BMW, SAP, Deutsche Telekom, Amadeus, Atos, Électricité de France*, and *Orange* (more members to follow). In the following chapters, we will go into more detail about the platform economy and decentralized platforms, as well as coopetition (cooperate to compete) and governance models.

2   The Benefits and Disadvantages of Digital Platforms

The platform economy is primarily based on digital, two-sided marketplaces, where supply and demand are transparently aligned. *Uber*, as an intermediary, connects drivers and passengers. *Airbnb* connects homeowners with travelers. The platform companies charge a transaction fee for matching.

The growing marginal utility is central to the success of transaction platforms: more providers of apartments on *Airbnb* result in a higher attractiveness of the platform for travelers. More travelers attract more housing providers. These self-reinforcing effects lead to dependencies, as participants no longer switch to alternative marketplaces. If one platform succeeds, it becomes more and more dominant. *Amazon* has already conquered between 42 and 49% of all internet trade in Europe. These so-called network and lock-in effects provide the primary explanation for the high company valuations of global tech giants like *Facebook, Google, Amazon, Alibaba, Uber*, and *Tencent*. Even with initially limited resources, enormous growth rates could be achieved, and entire markets orchestrated and dominated.

This dominance causes quasi-monopolistic market situations and leads to the often-excessive transaction fees for the marketplace participants, resulting in extremely high revenues per employee for the platform company. For example, *Uber* continuously receives up to 28.5% of the travel costs for the pure provision of its platform in Berlin. While the *Uber* driver is confronted with fuel costs and his time on the cost side for each trip, *Uber* has no direct costs and low risk. The more journeys are made, the more *Uber* benefits.

3   The Core of Platform Democratization Lies in Distributed Ledger Technologies

These disproportionalities, data security concerns, and excessive transaction fees are addressed by distributed ledger technologies (DLTs) such as blockchain. The primary purposes of central platforms—securing a transaction (e.g., trip or product purchase), the accounting of the transaction in progress, and the maintenance and further development of the platform—can be handled decentrally and automatically by DLTs. The consequences are revolutionary: the central platform company becomes obsolete; the current astronomically evaluated digital business models of platform companies are being stripped of their ground. The added value is once again more in the hands of the companies that provide it.

How would a decentralized superstructure work? A decentralized app (DApp) would link drivers and passengers directly with each other. The passenger orders and also pays (again) the driver directly, but the positive marketplace effects are still leveraged—this time, however, without a central platform owner. Such a decentralized platform is often set up and managed by a consortium of companies or a foundation. This is where new business models emerge, based on reorganizing the former central platform company's activities and incentives. The high transaction fees, which previously went to a single intermediary, are now shared between providers, demanders, and other value-adding network participants. However, this requires a change of mindset within the companies. Traditional platform business models are becoming obsolete or are being redefined. On the other hand, direct networking between companies and customers creates a much closer customer relationship. Not surprisingly, companies are increasingly concerned with the implications of decentralization. The key to success is the openness to multilateral partnerships and concentration on the respective core competencies.

4   Decentralized Mobility Platforms

Particularly new emerging or reorganizing industrial ecosystems can benefit from these developments. Opportunities exist primarily for the continuously value-adding companies with non-digital core business. The desired effect of this would be to leverage the core business digitally on the common decentralized platform, but without integrating a new intermediary or creating lock-in effects. One segment currently undergoing major reorganization is mobility. Up to now, public transport companies, cab companies, and private vehicles have dominated the mobility market. Today, more than 14 mobility providers offer their services in Berlin. From e-scooters (*Tier, Circ, Lime, Voi*), e-scooters (*Emmy, Tier*), bicycle-sharing (*Uber JUMP*) to bicycle subscriptions like *Swapfiets*. In addition, there are mobility offers such as car sharing (*WeShare, MILES, ShareNow*), ride-hailing (*Uber, FreeNow*), and ridesharing (*Berlkönig, CleverShuttle*), which supplement individual mobility offers with regular bus and train services. Privatization is leading to competition between these providers. Forcing promising margins or rapid growth, each of these companies offers its services via central transaction platforms. Here, there is a new trend toward "mobility-as-a-service" (MaaS; see also chapter "Mobility: From Autonomous Driving Towards Mobility-as-a-Service"): all participating service providers are directly involved in the mobility process and correspond digitally on a marketplace. The decisive question is on what technical basis this MaaS concept will be developed in the future.

One option is the central platform. Here, a central platform company orchestrates the MaaS marketplace, similar to *Amazon Marketplace*—with the disadvantage of the information asymmetry that arises. In the long run, this leads to dependencies for the mobility providers from the platform companies. The other option would be to implement a decentralized platform operated by a platform network. On the one hand, this allows mobility providers to participate. On the other hand, complementary, additional partners, such as *HERE*, have access too. The map provider—once a joint acquisition by *Audi, Daimler,* and *BMW*—now integrates other companies such as *Intel, Bosch,* and *Continental* under one umbrella. As a consortium, the various core competencies could now be combined, and a decentralized platform operated, which avoids dependencies and thus strengthens each individual's core business. *Daimler Mobility* is currently developing a decentralized mobility platform. The aim is to create an intermodal platform where all heterogeneous mobility service providers can connect in an interoperable manner.

At the moment it is not clear whether the relevant actors can agree toward a decentralized platform strategy. The seduction to develop an own platform and become an *Amazon* of its business is attractive—every company tries to build up own platforms and therefore cannot realize the important direct and indirect network effects of a platform economy.

5   The Platform Economy Is Decentralizing for Further Market Growth

Existing examples for the development of decentralized platform ecosystems initiated by current platform companies are manifold: *Facebook* published in 2019 its plans for *Diem* (in Italian), a global digital currency for cashless payments, especially in emerging market. The basis for this initiative is a private blockchain, which would be coordinated by the *Diem Association*. Current members of the *Diem Association* include *Andreessen Horowitz, Lyft, Shopify, Spotify,* and *Uber. PayPal, Visa, Mastercard, Stripe,* and *Vodafone* have left the association due to regulatory uncertainties. *Facebook* is developing a wallet access solution called *Novi* (formerly *Calibra*). *IBM* and *Maersk* have been cooperating since 2018 to form the blockchain-based shipping platform *TradeLens*. The goal is a smooth and integrated process for international transport across national borders. It is based on the blockchain *Hyperledger Fabric,* which *IBM* once developed and made available to the *Hyperledger* project (*Cisco, Fujitsu, IBM, Intel, NEC, Red Hat,* etc.) through the *Linux Foundation. AWS, Microsoft,* and *Google* offer blockchain-as-a-service for enabling similar projects. The platform economy, especially the *Hyperscaler,* is already at the technological front, and they are participating in the European *GAIA-X* project.

6   DLTs: A Short History of the Most Relevant Protocols

The technological groundwork for such applications is available; the crux of the matter is the ecosystem building on top of the DLT protocols. The origins of the DLT protocols lie in *Bitcoin,* which appeared in 2008—just one year after the financial crisis of 2007. While *Bitcoin* pushes purely monetary transactions without an intermediary, it quickly became apparent that decentralized systems could also apply in an industrial context. For this purpose, *Ethereum* was launched in 2015, developed by Vitalik Buterin, Gavin Wood, and Jeffrey Wilcke. The decisive difference was that the protocol could trigger smart contracts in addition to financial transactions. Smart contracts are programmed if-then relationships, which are automatically executed on the DLT protocol when all required conditions are fulfilled. For example, mobility services could be automated if the conditions "customer has a valid driver's license," "customer has the necessary amount of money," and "car is cleared for usage" are fulfilled. With the increasing popularity of Ethereum also among nontechnical user groups, the challenges of a non-consistently formalized governance model became bigger with *Ethereum*. For instance, crypto exchanges had different interests than *Ethereum*'s core developers. Decision-making on a not exclusively technical direction led to disputes. Gavin Wood, one of *Ethereum*'s founders, therefore founded the *Web3 Foundation*, which launched *Polkadot* in 2020. *Polkadot* combines technological advancements such as interoperability with other DLT protocols and higher scalability with formalized on-chain governance mechanisms designed to streamline the decision-making processes.

The technological basis for decentralized platform ecosystems is nowadays feasible. What is required is a mindset of concurrent cooperation and competition between companies to exploit the technological advantages in the business environment.

7   Toward the European Vision of Economy of Things (EoT)

There are already projects being developed in Europe: the project *LISSI* (Let's Initiate Self-Sovereign Identity) of *Commerzbank*'s *Main Incubator* has turned into the *IDunion* test network, which is now operated by the *IDunion* consortium. The project is supported by the German Federal Ministry of Economics, and the consortium currently includes the *Bundesdruckerei, esatus, Main Incubator, Bosch,* and the *Technical University of Berlin.* Associated partners include *Commerzbank, Creditreform Boniversum, BMW, Deutsche Börse, Telekom Innovation Laboratories, Deutsche Bahn, Festo, ING-DiBa, Ministry of Economic Affairs, Innovation, Digitalization and Energy of the State of North Rhine-Westphalia,* the *City of Cologne,* and *Siemens.* The goal is to create a digital login similar to *Gmail* or *Facebook* login, but with a decentralized structure, so that the identities themselves remain in the owner's sovereignty. The *European Central Bank (ECB)* is considering introducing a digital and programmable Euro (E-Euro), which would be based on decentralized technologies but would still be controlled by the *European Central Bank.* Combining all these initiatives on digital identities (*LISSI; IDunion*), digital payment (E-Euro), and a decentralized data infrastructure (*GAIA-X*) with the Internet of Things (IoT) brings us one step closer to the vision of the Economy of Things (EoT).

In the Economy of Things, things are no longer just connected but can also make decisions and perform actions independently. The electric car thus decides for itself when it needs to be charged. Electricity providers and the type of power generation are selected separately. Parking, loading, and payment of invoices are also operationally and economically autonomous. *Bosch*, *Siemens*, and *EnBW* have already implemented pilot projects. An electric car (*Bosch*) and a charging station (*EnBW*) negotiate a price independently so that the vehicle can head for this charging station. In a second step, a similar project between *Siemens* and *Bosch* operates the communication between the car and traffic lights or barriers. For example, if the car is allowed to access the parking lot where the selected charging station is located, the barrier opens. These transactions run independently through smart contracts on the *Ethereum* blockchain.

However, this requires the integration of various digital basic technologies, such as artificial intelligence. Moreover, such commerce requires that things have both identities and rights and that trust exists in the system even without an intermediary. Technologies that create this trust, for example, through automated step-by-step contracts and fraud-proof rules, are DLTs. This requires a decentralized, interoperable platform that integrates stakeholders and different technologies in a nondiscriminatory and equal way and implements these "rules of the game" in the programming code. Such a platform's central element is the governance model, which defines incentive mechanisms and rules for connecting, excluding, managing, or adapting these rules itself.

In summary, the EoT is about the synergetic combination of different digital basic technologies to create economic sovereignty. IoT provides connectivity. Artificial intelligence provides decision-making and the autonomy of the devices. DLTs create a trust layer and give room for maneuver; associated governance models ensure interoperability and incentive mechanisms. The potential of the EoT is enormous. A joint implementation by several initiators—without unilateral ownership—is therefore necessary.

8   How to Set Up Coopetition Models

The keyword of such visions is coopetition: cooperation in the development and operation of the common decentralized platform to increase the efficiency of the market processes as well as own service offering processes. A subsequent competition is based on this new efficiency level with its own business models by leveraging the new efficiency level and gathering a higher value capture. For example, in the field of MaaS: The new efficiency level would be to build and operate a common decentralized mobility platform. This would reduce transaction costs for the entire network by allocating all providers and users' supply and demand transparently and bundled. By this, the customer touchpoint is shared by the whole network, while a subsequent competition between companies and their business models is achieved by the actual mobility service quality and not because the one platform owner owns also the customer touchpoint and leverages this resource independently from the service quality.

Thereby, the whole platform network wins and the customer, due to higher competitiveness of services, which leads to higher service quality or a more varied spectrum of services. Through such further organic development of the services and the platform, a decentralized platform ecosystem is ultimately created. But how is money earned in the respective mode? A distinction between incentive mechanisms and business models is essential in this context. During the joint development of the platform, there should be cooperative work. Competitive behavior through business models would be counterproductive here. The governance model of the decentralized platform must accordingly provide for compensatory incentive mechanisms. For example, the decentralized platform-inherent tokens could serve as an incentive. In the beginning, a joint monetary investment is made in the token's value. In the further course of the project, the participating companies can work on the respective aspects of the platform development to add value and receive a share of tokens that is relative to the respective activity. Once the platform is built, those who have been particularly active in value-adding activities will also be credited with a corresponding share of the tokens.

Based on the platform that is now created, the respective business models compete with each other. In this mode, thinking in the logic of business models is again decisive. Coopetition models are particularly relevant if the goal is to build up network effects. By jointly initiating the decentralized platform by companies already active in the market, network effects can be quickly established once the platform is launched. *GAIA-X* is an excellent example of this.

At present, European companies and governments are investing in developing an independent data infrastructure, which will enable digital business later on in more efficient terms and with the long-term benefits of data sovereignty. However, it is vital to have goal-oriented governance, effectively enabling access rights, incentive mechanisms, and decision-making.

Success Factors of Decentralized Platforms

- Digital identities for products and actors are a necessity for business on decentralized platforms.
- Data sovereignty as a strong value driver for companies has been recognized by European players too.
- Openness to agree on common rules and delegate governance are required for a functioning decentralized platform system.
- Thinking beyond single use cases: Too often companies think too narrow in use cases, but infrastructures are often not build on single use cases. Thus, a broader strategic thinking in real options beyond a single use case is crucial.
- Mindset of coopetition: Distinguish between precompetitive collaborative governance of the decentralized platforms on the one side and competing business models and products on the other side.

Kilian Schmück is a research associate and a project manager at the Institute of Technology Management at the University of St. Gallen. His research areas cover decentralized platform ecosystems, governance models, distributed ledger technologies, and respective business models. He leads several cooperation projects with the industry and initiated the St. Gallen Blockchain Roundtable, where data sovereignty and democratization of the platform economy are dealt together with academia, economy, and politics. Previously, he worked for the Volkswagen Group in the Group Digitalization, where he was engaged in digital business models for automobile manufacturers. He received his bachelor's and master's degree in Mechanical Engineering from RWTH Aachen University.

Prof. Dr. Monika Sturm has over 20 years of experience in business operation, management, and research and development including IT and strategy positions within Siemens Energy Management. She worked as head of the Energy Distribution Services and Metering Service business and as senior manager for Sustainable Cities, and currently, she works as principal key expert for digitalization, with special focus on blockchain/distributed ledger technologies. Currently, she is heading the Blockchain Incubator at Siemens Energy. In addition to her professional responsibilities, she holds a professorship at the Leibniz University Hannover.

Prof. Dr. Oliver Gassmann is a professor of technology management at the University of St. Gallen and the director of the Institute of Technology Management since 2002. His research focus lies on patterns and success factors of innovation. He has been a visiting professor at Berkeley (2007), Stanford (2012), and Harvard (2016). Prior to his academic career, Gassmann was the head of corporate research at Schindler. His more than 400 publications are highly cited. His book *Business Model Navigator* became a global bestseller. He received the Scholarly Impact Award of the *Journal of Management* in 2014. He founded several spin-offs. He is a member of several boards of directors, like Zühlke, and is an internationally recognized keynote speaker.

Sustainable AIoT: How Artificial Intelligence and the Internet of Things Affect Profit, People, and Planet

Wolfgang Bronner, Heiko Gebauer, Claudio Lamprecht, and Felix Wortmann

1 Addressing the Triple Bottom Line

To achieve long-term business success, purpose for associates, and acceptance in today's societies, business leaders must keep a close eye on social and environmental dimensions in addition to the prerequisite of attaining adequate profits. This is especially true during times of major technological transformations. A fascinating breakthrough technology pushing such a transformation is artificial intelligence (AI). AI has great potential to make devices intelligent in the Internet of Things (IoT)—referred to as AIoT. In this chapter, we evaluate how a sustainable AIoT supports the three interrelated dimensions of profit, people, and planet.

Megatrends such as population growth, resource scarcity, and climate change drive and shape today's businesses and society, which is reflected by

W. Bronner (✉)
Bosch IoT Lab, University of St. Gallen & ETH Zurich, St. Gallen, Switzerland
e-mail: wolfgang.bronner@bosch.com

H. Gebauer • C. Lamprecht
University of St. Gallen, St. Gallen, Switzerland
e-mail: heiko.gebauer@unisg.ch; claudio.lamprecht@unisg.ch

F. Wortmann
Institute of Technology Management, University of St. Gallen,
St. Gallen, Switzerland
e-mail: felix.wortmann@unisg.ch

© The Author(s), under exclusive license to Springer Nature Switzerland AG 2021
O. Gassmann, F. Ferrandina (eds.), *Connected Business*,
https://doi.org/10.1007/978-3-030-76897-3_8

intensive discussions in the media and through activities of supranational organizations, such as the United Nations, e.g., Sustainability Development Goals (SDGs) and the Intergovernmental Panel on Climate Change (IPCC). Even the financial industry asset manager *BlackRock* has joined France, Germany, and other global foundations to establish the Climate Finance Partnership, a public-private effort to improve financing mechanisms for infrastructure investment. In his annual letter to investors, *BlackRock* CEO Larry Fink wrote in 2020: "[…] awareness is rapidly changing, and I believe we are on the edge of a fundamental reshaping of finance" (Fink 2020). *Bosch* with its approximately 245 manufacturing plants worldwide announced its intent to become carbon neutral (Scope 1 and 2 emissions) as the first global industrial enterprise from the year 2020 (Bosch 2019).

Another important trend is the social fragmentation of societies. The financial crisis of 2008, the US elections in 2016, and Brexit in 2020 sent shock waves through the political and financial elites within the EU and the USA. These events compelled global movements to engage leaders across business, government, and civil sectors and encourage them to practice and invest in ways that extend the opportunities and benefits of our economic system to everyone, e.g., non-governmental organization (NGO) Inclusive Capitalism, which is supported by E.L. *Rothschild LLC*, among others (NGO Inclusive Capitalism 2020).

Companies must consistently align themselves with these drivers by means of a modern accounting framework and performance reporting, which should transcend the important measures of profits, return on investments, and shareholder value to include environmental and social dimensions. During the mid-1990s, John Elkington developed such a sustainability framework called the triple bottom line (TBL), which included the interrelated dimensions of profit, people, and the planet (Elkington 1994; Slaper 2011).

The interesting and likely provocative question is whether the AIoT actually supports this TBL sustainability framework:

- **Profit**: Companies investing in digitalization do not achieve an acceptable return on investment and adequate profits similar to their traditional business, which is called the digitalization paradox (Gebauer 2020). According to a study conducted by *Cisco* in 2017, "[…] 60 percent of IoT initiatives stall at the proof of concept (PoC) stage and only 26 percent of companies have had an IoT initiative that they considered a complete success. Even worse: a third of all completed projects were not considered a success […]" (CISCO 2017).

- **People**: The impacts of AI and related automation on the future of work have been widely discussed since approx. 2011 (Arntz 2016; Frey 2017). These impacts even induced public discussions about the necessity to introduce an unconditional basic income (Die Zeit 2015).
- **Planet**: The billions of connected devices, communication infrastructures, and data centers require electricity in their usage and resources and energy for their production (Andrae 2017). The greenhouse gas emissions produced by these processes are comparable to those of air traffic today.

In the following, we reflect on the fundamental impact of the AIoT on profit, people, and planet.

2   The AIoT Profit Opportunity

The AIoT offers opportunities that arise from creating new business models, building deeper customer relationships, improving the value proposition, and therefore increasing revenues and profits. Adequate profits are a necessity for sustainable companies to finance growth, to make important investments, or to have the leeway to raise wages. Here, we emphasize service business and product-as-a-service (PaaS), which is the principal concept of selling the outcomes a product can provide rather than the product and related services itself. Generally speaking, customers no longer purchase products and services and maintain product ownership. Instead, customers avoid initial investments and only pay for the actual use and performance of a product. The AIoT is one key driver of PaaS. Intelligence and connectivity enable an entirely new set of product functions and capabilities (Porter and Heppelmann 2014): monitoring, control, optimization, including updates over-the-air, and autonomy. A company that offers connected products has transparency about how the customer uses the product and what the condition of the product is, e.g., operating hours, performance, and malfunctions.

2.1   Product-as-a-Service as a Business Model

Companies embracing PaaS indicate that it is the foundation for stable and more predictable revenues and hence for more sustainable and resilient business models (Tzuo 2018). Prominent examples in the B2C context are the very popular subscription-based business models introduced by *Spotify*, *Netflix*, and *Apple*. Rather than purchasing DVDs, approximately 2/3 of households in the

USA stream movies via the Internet (ibid.). For manufacturing companies, PaaS is thought to be the holy grail of monetizing IoT data, with a current market size of US\$ 21.6 billion (2019), which is expected to grow with a CAGR of 35% until 2025 (NGO Inclusive Capitalism 2020).

PaaS has been conceptualized through notions including pay-per-use, service-oriented business models, use-oriented and result-oriented product-service systems, outcome-based services, substituting services, and so on. The topic itself originated as early as 1920, when *Michelin* tires introduced the idea of being paid for every kilometer a tire accrued instead of selling tires. *Xerox* disrupted the entire plain-paper copier industry by charging per copy instead of selling the copier.

PaaS has recently gained a lot of momentum through digital technologies, given that product connectivity allows product providers to gain deep insights regarding customers' financial requests, the entire product life cycle, customers' daily operations, and risk mitigation requirements. Thus, an increasing number of PaaS approaches have been launched recently and are currently scaled up. Some examples include printing as a service, machine tools as a service, compressed air as a service, jet engine as a service, farming equipment as a service, commercial garage lift as a service, vacuum handling equipment as a service, robot uptime as a service, earth-moving equipment as a service, and compressor as a service.

2.2   Creating Sustainable Growth with Product-as-a-Service

PaaS not only offers various benefits for customers and product providers but also supports environmental sustainability:

- *Customers* can become financially flexible and relieve their balance sheet by having operational expenses (OPEX) instead of capital expenditures (CAPEX). Furthermore, customers benefit from aligned incentives between them and the manufacturer in addition to the possibility of minimized risks. For example, the risk of equipment breaking down and not running at the optimal performance level can be transferred to the manufacturer through a PaaS business model.
- For *product providers*, PaaS represents a recurring source of revenue that is less volatile than the economic and investment cycles of products. In the current COVID-19 crisis, business opportunities have opened up, as customers have had to stretch their financial budgets. PaaS will continue to

have strategic benefits for product providers even in a post-COVID-19 world. In addition to being a recurring source of revenue, PaaS allows a manufacturer to secure or win back service revenues from third-party providers.

- Furthermore, PaaS is assumed to improve *environmental sustainability* (the planet dimension). Some reasons for this are highlighted in Gebauer et al. (2017): PaaS encourages sensible consumption and leads to product designs, which maximize resource efficiency. PaaS also incentivizes resource-efficient product usage. In addition, PaaS leads to more preventative maintenance activities, resulting in longer lasting products and easier remanufacturing (e.g., a photocopier company lets customers pay per copy, later refurbishes a used copier, and then provides it to new customers to offer pay-per-copy). This last example shows that PaaS is an opportunity to reduce environmental impact by shifting away from the linear take-make-waste economy toward a circular system.

As a leading manufacturing company, *Bosch* established PaaS business models. In the following, two prominent examples are explained:

- Homeowners often hesitate to modernize or install a state-of-the-art heating system due to the high initial costs. The *Bosch Heating+* service eases this decision by allowing customers to benefit from a new heating system without a major initial investment.
- Coin-operated communal washing machines are the past. *WeWash* (WeWash 2021) offers everything from installation in lieu of maintenance and repairs to a cashless billing process, which reduces the costs associated with providing a laundry room in serviced apartments and hotels for the operator.

2.3 Implementing and Adopting Product-as-a-Service

In addition to these benefits, various requisite management actions make PaaS a success beyond a handful of PaaS pilots with a few selected customers. Managers often phrase this as "the PaaS pilot never fails, but PaaS never scales":

- Products for which PaaS has a provable positive effect on easy-to-measure performance metrics are particularly suitable. Management should be aware of this and target these products accordingly.

- To transfer PaaS from a few success pilots at the periphery of a company into their core offerings, companies have to ensure the commitment of top management to obtain the necessary human and financial resources.
- Top management needs to be aware that PaaS might challenge the existing product-dominated culture. Companies should therefore begin with lighthouse projects to validate the PaaS approach and obtain the necessary momentum.
- Once lighthouse projects have been proven successful, companies should invest in a broader PaaS enablement structure (small teams, use cases, competence development).
- Often, the switch to a PaaS business model leads to a revenue drop, as small recurring payments replace large initial revenue. Simultaneously, costs increase due to the necessarily large pre-investments. Management needs to be aware of this period in which costs exceed revenues to prepare stakeholders accordingly.

3   The AIoT People Opportunity

It is undeniable that digital technologies create fascinating benefits for individual people and societies. This has become particularly clear over the course of the COVID-19 crisis. The pandemic has demonstrated how online marketplaces have become part of society's critical infrastructure as the success of companies like *Amazon* has shown. Digital technologies also drive the AIoT. The result is a virtuous cycle of value improvement between both areas: Growing IoT—growing volume of data—improved AI algorithms—growing IoT. The benefits of this are that IoT devices with AI can even act autonomously, e.g., logistics robots that transport goods in complex environments, such as hospitals. *Bosch*, as a leading automotive supplier, is applying AI, e.g., in safety systems for cars and trucks pursuing the Vision Zero with the aim of achieving no fatalities or serious injuries involving road traffic. In healthcare, AI expert systems support medical professionals in making diagnoses that are more accurate and suggest better therapies. These examples prove that the AIoT improves the overall quality of life of people and thus has a positive impact on the people dimension.

Nevertheless, as the breakthroughs in AI were shared in recent years with the public (e.g. *AlphaGo, IBM Watson*), there has been a debate about its impact on employment: will the resulting automation destroy working capital and therefore the social performance of companies, e.g., will it lead to a massive reduction of the total number of associates or apprentices? The starting point was a study by Frey and Osborne from Oxford University published online in 2013. This study suggested that 47% of jobs in the USA were at a high risk of being automated (Frey and Osborne 2013) and triggered further examinations of the expected impact of AI-driven automation on the economy, e.g., the Whitehouse report of the executive office of the US president (2016) or the comprehensive study by the *McKinsey* Global Institute (McKinsey Global Institute 2017). The following subchapter is based on these studies.

3.1   Future of Work with AI

Historically, societies have already experienced significant transformations driven through technological and scientific progress, e.g., automation in agriculture and the industrial revolution in the nineteenth century based on the steam engine. Such technological progress drove complex adaptions within societies. From a long-term perspective, it created more jobs and prosperity. There are three primary reasons why productivity and job growth mainly complemented each other in the past:

- *Cost savings and higher wages*: Productivity gains reduce the prices of products and services (e.g. the telecommunication industry in the past). Companies can afford higher wages when their workers are more efficient. Both drive higher or new consumption. In addition, efficiency gains are a source of larger profits, which can be reinvested.
- *Increased value and quality of outputs boosts demand*: Productivity growth is also about increasing the value and quality of outputs for any given input. For example, the automotive industry has massively improved the value of cars for their customers by implementing new comfort and safety features. At the same time, supplier and car manufacturers have managed to maintain or even improve quality.
- *Sustaining global competitiveness requires ongoing productivity gains*: Innovations and the related productivity gains sustain or even increase local jobs.

An important question now arises: Will AI also create prosperity and jobs in the future? There is no simple answer because there are too many influencing factors in a complex modern economy. The following four questions support a balanced analysis of the impact of AI and the respective time horizon:

- *What are the limitations of AI systems and technological barriers?*
  AI systems are currently optimized for narrow-specific tasks. These systems are programmed with little innate knowledge and possess no common sense about the world or human psychology. Generalizing these systems to other tasks with different contexts is not possible at present. In addition, important AI systems are black boxes whose outputs cannot be explained, even if the algorithms are known. On the other hand, there is a great demand from customers to understand the decisions of AI systems, e.g., if a financial AI system of a bank declines a customer's mortgage application. Finally, verifying and validating AI systems for safety critical applications needs to be solved (e.g., for fully autonomous driving).
- *In which areas and markets are AI system cost competitive (lower marginal costs)?*
  AI-driven automation is implemented through economic reasoning. There are higher incentives to automate in advanced economies than in developing economies because of the higher wage rates in the former. Installed conventional systems are typically not replaced until they are depreciated. Investments in infrastructure typically have particularly long time horizons. Therefore, even if AI systems offer new functionalities and higher productivity, decision-makers may postpone their introduction.
- *How long is the adaption time for people and institutions?*
  The speed and extension of software-based innovations throughout the globalized world connected by the Internet far surpasses that of steam engines during the industrial revolution. AI-driven automation has a direct impact on repetitive and administrative tasks. Even highly paid academics are affected. For example, one repetitive task of a radiologist is to analyze MRI images. There is no clear answer as to whether entire occupations will go extinct or whether AI systems will only assist with certain tasks. In the example given, this would mean that an expert system detecting tumors in MRI images would not replace a radiologist but would rather increase their productivity and diagnostic quality.
- *What is the reaction of governments in a time with inequality in societies with populists forcing national shielding?*
  This new wave of automation comes at a time when we are already discussing other economic effects, such as globalization and the outsourcing of jobs. New governmental regulations could slow the penetration of AI-driven automation, especially if inequality in societies is expected to increase.

Hypothesis: A significant share of working activities have the potential to be automated. However, the proportion of work actually replaced will be much lower due to technical, economic, and social factors, and, as history demonstrates, completely new occupations will emerge. Investments in infrastructure, healthcare, and energy in response to megatrends also generate further demand for work. Many countries are also faced with the fact that their population is aging disproportionately, e.g., aging societies such as China and Germany. In the interim, there is a risk that frictional unemployment will increase as downward pressure lowers wages because of the fast technological evolution. Income polarization could continue in advanced economies, e.g., stagnating middle-class wages in the USA due to declining middle-wage occupations. In the long term, associates will need to adapt as their occupations evolve alongside increasingly capable AI systems. Processing data, collecting data, and other repetitive and predictable physical tasks will be increasingly automated, and a large proportion of associates are expected to switch occupational categories. There will continue to be a high demand for jobs that require social and emotional skills, creativity, and advanced cognitive skills. Educational institutions such as schools and universities should be prepared. Training and re-education of the existing workforce within companies will be necessary.

3.2   The Strategic Imperative of AI

AI is a strategic imperative for leaders. *Bosch*, for example, intends that all of its products either will contain AI or will be developed or manufactured with its help by 2025. To achieve this objective, *Bosch* founded the *Bosch* Center for AI in 2017 (Bosch 2021). Therefore, how can an enterprise become a robust AI company? The popular AI Transformation Playbook from Andrew Ng offers five steps as clear guidance (Ng 2018):

1. *Execute pilot projects to gain momentum*: The first AI projects chosen should succeed in increasing faith in the new capabilities of AI. This momentum is more important than choosing the most valuable project from a business perspective.
2. *Build an in-house AI team*: Such a centralized AI team should execute an initial sequence of cross-functional projects to support different product groups/divisions/business units with AI competence. An in-house AI team helps to build a unique competitive advantage, e.g., applying specific domain knowledge of the company.
3. *Provide broad AI training*: AI talent is hard to find. In addition, executives and leaders of the company need to understand what AI can do for their

enterprise. With the availability of digital content such as online courses (e.g., Coursera), training large numbers of associates in new AI skills is very cost-efficient today.

4. *Develop an AI strategy*: After obtaining momentum (see steps 1–3), identify the areas in which AI can create the largest impact and value. Focus restricted resources on those areas. A company will most likely not be able to develop a professional AI strategy without basic experience with AI. Create an advantage with AI specific to the companies' industry sector/s. Given that data function as a key asset for AI, develop a sophisticated data strategy.

5. *Develop internal and external communication*: The public debates the opportunities and risks of AI, e.g., artificial general intelligence has been overhyped in the media. In addition, AI has the potential to affect significantly an enterprise. Accordingly, communication should be developed to ensure alignment with the key stakeholders: investors (clear value creation thesis), the government (building trust and goodwill), customers (appropriate marketing of new benefits), external AI talent (employer branding to attract and retain talent), and associates (explain AI to address associates' concerns).

4   The AIoT Planet Opportunity

Digital technologies have the potential to support sustainability by reducing resource consumption, energy consumption, and emissions. For example, the AIoT is an imperative to manage energy supply and demand in a world with decentralized producers of renewable energy, such as photovoltaics (Meeuw et al. 2020). On the other hand, it is undeniable that digital devices and the Internet infrastructure require energy to operate. A public debate has emerged since Bitcoin mining and video streaming provoked controversy regarding the significant amount of electricity they consume. An important question is whether the economic growth induced by digital technologies is associated with an increase in energy consumption and greenhouse gas (GHG) emissions, as has been the case in the past.

There are no studies specific to the AIoT to date. Therefore, we present the results of an analysis aggregating the impact of all information and communication technologies (ICTs). It is important to note that ICTs affect the environment in two ways. *Direct effects* lead exclusively to an increase in energy consumption, GHG emissions and resource consumption caused by the production, and the use and disposal of ICT hardware (e.g., devices, data servers). *Indirect effects* arise from the fact that the use of ICTs leads to induced changes in consumption and production patterns.

4.1   Direct Effects: Information Processing Requires Energy

Each operation of a single bit in a computer needs an absolute minimum amount of energy of 2.75 zepto joules at room temperature, which is called the Landauer limit (Landauer 1961). Erasing a single bit creates waste heat. The physics behind this limit is the fundamental second law of thermodynamics. In addition, digital devices, communication networks, and data centers have to be produced, which also requires energy and resources. According to scenarios developed in 2015 from Andrae and Edler (2015), ICTs will expand from 8 to 21% of worldwide total electricity demand by 2030 (Jones 2018). Andrae takes into account the production and use of digital devices, communication networks, and data centers holistically. Regardless of the chosen scenario, power consumption in the usage phase decreases for digital devices over the next decade and increases for networks and data centers (Andrae and Edler 2015).

A meta-study by *bitkom* (see Table 1) shows the amount of greenhouse gas emissions caused by ICTs (Bitkom 2020). With 1.8–3.2% of global GHG emissions for 2020, the ICT sector is comparable to air traffic (Graver et al. 2019). The principal reason for the generation of these GHGs is the large number of digital devices. It can be assumed that GHG emissions will increase significantly over the next decade due to the continued growth of digital infrastructures and the increasing number of households and companies equipped with digital devices.

Table 1 Approximate energy demand and greenhouse gas emissions (GHG) for 2020, Bitkom (2020)

Category	Data centers		Communication networks		End devices incl. desktops, notebooks, tablets, smartphones, TVs	
	Best-case	Worst-case	Best-case	Worst-case	Best-case	Worst-case
Energy (TWh)	200	1000	200	500	–	–
GHG (Mt CO_{2e})	100	500	140	300	720	1200

4.2   Indirect Effects: Changing Consumption and Production Patterns

ICTs cause changes in consumption and production patterns and therefore affect greenhouse gas emissions and energy demand indirectly. The resulting effects can have positive or negative characteristics from an environmental point of view. For example, a modern video chat application, such as MS-Teams, can support working at home—eliminating daily commutes to a company's office building. On the other hand, by intensifying competition, flight booking platforms have contributed to the emergence of the low-cost flight sector and thus to an increase in air travel and the associated GHG emissions (Bitkom 2020).

Positive Characteristics

As discussed above, the AIoT enables PaaS, which is assumed to improve environmental sustainability. There are of course further opportunities of the AIoT to generate value in the dimension of the planet. Examples from four industry sectors are given below:

- *Energy and building*: Decarbonizing the energy sector by improving grid efficiency, integrating renewables, and enabling decentralized energy trading; making smart buildings; and avoiding unnecessary energy consumption through automated monitoring and control of heating systems and air conditioning.
- *Mobility and logistics*: Enabling the home-office by video chat apps, which reduces commuting to workspaces. Video conferencing helps to avoid business trips. Apps on smartphones enable intermodal travel and car sharing in a world with rapid growth in urbanization. Connected trucks and logistic platforms help to avoid empty runs and detours of trucks and will likely improve intermodal global supply chains (e.g., transfer of loads from trucks to trains).
- *Manufacturing*: Industry 4.0 supports the creation of high-performance plants that are fully optimized in their consumption of all the used resources, comprising productive components, such as raw materials, and basic resources, such as energy and water.
- *Agriculture*: Smart agriculture reduces the need for herbicides/pesticides/fertilizers and simultaneously increases the yields of agricultural land.

Negative Characteristics

As explained above, ICTs can cause changes in consumption and production patterns. Flight booking platforms have contributed to the emergence of the low-cost flight sector and thus to an increase in air travel and the associated greenhouse gas emissions. In the previous section, we also provided examples concerning efficiency-enhancing measures within four industry sectors. Implementing such measures can also cause unintended negative effects—called rebound effects. Rebound effects can lead to an increase in demand/consumption so that the absolute savings of an input factor such as energy demand or greenhouse gas emissions fall short of expectations. If, for example, energy-saving lamps replace conventional light bulbs and customers install more of them or leave them burning longer, then the saving effects of the new lamps are less than expected. Such rebound effects can even exceed 100%, in which case they are called backfire effects. In our example of bulbs, a backfire effect would occur if more energy is collectively used after the transition from conventional bulbs to energy-saving lamps.

4.3   Overall Impact on Environmental Sustainability

As shown, ICTs have high potential to support environmental sustainability (indirect effects with positive characteristics). At the same time, ICTs create a significant footprint (direct effects plus indirect effects with negative characteristics). Hence, the following question arises: will ICTs have an overall positive or negative impact on environmental sustainability and thus in the planet dimension by 2030?

Clearly, this question is difficult to assess across all concerns. However, there are useful estimates of greenhouse gas emissions in 2030. According to a meta-study from bitkom (Bitkom 2020) the enablement factor (EA) expresses the relationship between the potential to reduce greenhouse gas emissions and the GHG footprint of ICTs:

- *Best Case Scenario* (EA = 16.3): The potential to reduce GHG emissions is 16.3 times larger than the GHG footprint.
- *Worst Case Scenario* (EA = 0.3): The GHG footprint is three times larger than the potential to reduce GHG emissions.

4.4   Environmental Sustainability with the AIoT

This result clearly shows the uncertainty in such estimates. There is great potential but without certainty that everything will turn out well ("no free lunch"). Accordingly, it is recommended to consider the following measures when implementing new AIoT solutions:

- *Business models*: Develop AIoT solutions specifically improving sustainability. Instead of selling products (hardware) maintain ownership and offer customer pay-per-use.
- *Processes*: Implement footprint/lifecycle assessments. Enable circular economy with digital technologies.
- *Technology*: Follow the trend toward hyperscale data center and operate them with renewable energy. Minimize data bandwidth. Foster new computing and communication hardware with improved energy efficiency.

5   Conclusion

The sustainable IoT with artificial intelligence (AIoT) can strongly support the triple bottom line with the three interrelated dimensions of profit, people, and planet. Addressing all the dimensions simultaneously certainly creates complexity and tensions. However, entrepreneurial responsibility has to reconcile the three dimensions and has to take these tensions. According to the *Bosch* CEO Volkmar Denner "[…] it is not problem solving that is the primary management task, but increasingly the resolution of dilemmas" (Bosch 2021). Business leaders that successfully manage the three dimensions generate purpose inside companies, lend companies legitimacy in modern societies, and support business success. Generating value in all three dimensions is often straightforward.

A prerequisite to being profitable is an economically viable business model. Connected products can increase customer satisfaction and enable new service businesses. PaaS is one major option to increase revenues and margins while reducing the environmental footprint of a company and its customers. In addition, business models based on PaaS are typically more robust in economic crises, such as the financial crisis in 2008 or the current COVID-19 pandemic, which gives associates peace of mind.

Improving environmental sustainability often goes hand in hand with profit. For example, a reduction in electricity demand also means lower energy costs. Moreover, customers are willing to pay higher prices for environmentally friendly products, which increases margins.

The basis of a successful company is a loyal and highly motivated workforce. People are the key to success. High profits provide leeway for higher salaries. Investing in new apprenticeships and training for the existing workforce increases loyalty and strengthens the competencies within the company. Environmental sustainability also tends to be meaningful for associates. Overall, this supports employer branding and therefore attracts and retains talent, e.g., specialists who are in very high demand in the labor market. On the other hand, negative reviews of employers on social networks have a wide reach and discourage job applicants.

Well-known companies prove that it is possible to manage the triple bottom line successfully: *Apple* is powered by 100% renewable energy worldwide and is one of the most successful enterprises (Apple 2018). *BASF* has already adapted its balance sheet by addressing performance indicators in addition to classic economic KPI, such as social performance, e.g., numbers of associates and apprentices (BASF 2019). *Bühler* contributes to "[…] safely feeding the worlds and is doing its part to protect the climate [...]" (The Bühler Group 2021). *Bosch*, with its slogan "Invented for Life," is a privately owned company. Through the charitable foundation Robert Bosch Stiftung, profits are used to benefit society, the environment, and future generations (Bosch 2021). *Bosch* also has a dedicated sustainability strategy: "*Bosch* strongly believes that a social and ecological balance is needed to do business successfully in the long term. For this reason, the company aims to secure its business success in a way that preserves resources for current and future generations" (Bosch 2021).

Lessons Learned from the AIoT

- The convergence of the IoT and AI (AIoT), i.e., smart connected products and the AI-based exploitation of their data, offers great potential to improve the triple bottom line: profit, people, and planet.
- Profit: The AIoT is an enabler of product-as-a-service business models that foster stable, recurring, and thereby sustainable revenues.
- People: The AIoT will generate significant benefits for people, e.g., with respect to health, safety, and comfort. Therefore, it is an important driver of future prosperity.
- Planet: The AIoT and the continuous adoption of information and communication technologies (ICTs) lead to a direct increase in energy consumption (direct effects). However, the AIoT and ICTs have the potential to help massively to reduce green-house-gas emissions across multiple domains (indirect effects). As of today, most research is optimistic that ICTs, including the AIoT, will have a net positive impact on the environment.
- Companies have to manage the triple bottom line and carefully balance the trade-offs between profit, people, and planet. The AIoT is one means to push existing trade-offs beyond current boundaries.

References

Andrae ASG (2017) Total consumer power consumption forecast

Andrae ASG, Edler T (2015) On global electricity usage of communication technology: trends to 2030. Challenges 6:117–157

Apple (2018) Apple Newsroom 2018. https://www.apple.com/de/newsroom/2018/04/apple-now-globally-powered-by-100-percent-renewable-energy/. Accessed 8 Sept 2020

Arntz M (2016) The risk of automation for jobs in OECD countries: a comparative analysis. OECD, social, employment and migration working papers, no. 189

BASF (2019) https://report.basf.com/2019/en/. Accessed 5 Sept 2020

Bitkom (2020) Klimaschutz durch digitale Technologien—Chancen und Risiken. https://www.bitkom.org/klimaschutz-digital. Accessed 7 Jan 2020

Bosch (2019) https://www.bosch-presse.de/pressportal/de/en/climate-action-bosch-to-be-carbon-neutral-world-wide-by-2020-188800.html. Accessed Dec 2020

Bosch (2021) CEO Blog—Denner's view. https://www.bosch.com/stories/denners-view-values-and-technology/. Accessed 6 Jan 2020

CISCO (2017) Cisco survey reveals close to three-fourths of IoT projects are failing. https://newsroom.cisco.com/press-release-content?articleId=1847422. Accessed 7 Oct 2020

DeepMind, AlphaGo. https://deepmind.com/research/case-studies/alphago-the-story-so-far. Accessed 5 Oct 2020

Die Zeit (2015) Telekom-Chef Höttges für bedingungsloses Grundeinkommen. https://www.zeit.de/zustimmung?url=https%3A%2F%2Fwww.zeit.de%2Fwirtschaft%2F2015-12%2Fdigitale-revolution-telekom-timotheus-hoettges-interview. Accessed 5 Sept 2020

Elkington J (1994) Towards the sustainable corporation: win-win-win business strategies for sustainable development. Calif Manag Rev 36(2):90–100

Executive Office of the US President (2016) Artificial intelligence, automation, and the economy

Fink L (2020) Letter to the CEOs. https://www.blackrock.com/corporate/investor-relations/larry-fink-ceo-letter. Accessed 6 Dec 2020

Frey CB (2017) The future of employment: How susceptible are jobs to computerisation? Technol Forecast Social Change 114:254–280

Frey CB, Osborne MA (2013) The future of employment: how susceptible are jobs to computerisation? Oxford Martin Programme on Technology and Employment

Gebauer H (2020) Growth paths for overcoming the digitalization paradox. Bus Horiz 63:313–323

Gebauer H, Haldimann M, Saul CJ (2017) Competing in business-to-business sectors through pay-per-use services. J Serv Manag 28(5):914–935

Graver B, Zhang K, Rutherford D (2019) CO_2 emissions from commercial aviation, 2018. International Council on Clean Transportation

IBM, IBM Watson. https://www.ibm.com/watson. Accessed 5 Oct 2020

Jones N (2018) How to stop data centres from gobbling up the world's electricity.. https://www.nature.com/articles/d41586-018-06610-y. Accessed 6 Jan 2020

Landauer R (1961) Irreversibility and heat generation in the computing process. IBM J Res Dev 5:183–191

McKinsey Global Institute (2017) Jobs lost, jobs gained: workforce transitions in a time of automation. McKinsey

Meeuw A, Schopfer S, Woerner A, Ableitner L, Tiefenbeck V, Fleisch E, Wortmann F (2020) Implementing a blockchain-based local energy market: Insights on communication and scalability. Comput Commun 160:158–171

Ng A (2018) AI transformation playbook, landing AI

NGO Inclusive Capitalism (2020) https://www.coalitionforinclusivecapitalism.com/what-is-inclusive-capitalism/. Accessed 5 Sept 2020

Porter ME, Heppelmann JE (2014) Harvard Business Review. https://hbr.org/2014/11/how-smart-connected-products-are-transforming-competition. Accessed Sept 1 2020

Robert Bosch LLC. Bosch Center for Artificial Intelligence. www.bosch-ai.com. Accessed 6 Jan 2021

Slaper TS (2011) The triple bottom line: what is it and how does it work? Indiana Bus Rev 86(1)

The Bühler Group (2021) https://www.buhlergroup.com/content/buhlergroup/global/fr/about-us/organization.html. Accessed 10 Sept 2020

Tzuo T (2018) Subscribed, Penguin

WeWash (2021) https://we-wash.com/en/. Accessed 2 Sept 2020

Wolfgang Bronner, Dr., is managing director of the Bosch IoT Lab, a cooperation between the Bosch Group, University of St. Gallen, and ETH Zurich. This lab is particularly dedicated on the Internet of Things, Data Science, and Business Model Innovation. Wolfgang Bronner had his first insight into the high-tech industry as a student at IBM in Silicon Valley. He has been working as an expert and manager in various industries and functions at Bosch in Germany and the USA since 2002. In his last position, he analyzed the impact of the most significant future technologies such as AI on Bosch, derived strategic recommendations, and discussed them with the executive management. He received his PhD in physics from the University of Stuttgart in 2003.

Heiko Gebauer, Prof. Dr., is a visiting professor of international and strategic management at Linköping University, Sweden. He also heads the Data Mining and Value Creation project at the Fraunhofer IMW and works at the Bosch IoT Lab of the University of St. Gallen. He investigates three empirical phenomena—service, scaling, and digitization paradoxes—and has published various articles on these phenomena in academic and management journals. He also serves as an academic adviser to a variety of companies.

Claudio Lamprecht is a PhD candidate at the Bosch IoT Lab at the University of St. Gallen where he investigates Equipment-as-a-Service business models. Claudio holds an M.A. in Accounting and Finance from the University of St. Gallen, BSc in Business Administration—International Financial Services from the University of Liechtenstein—and an engineer (Ing.) in technical computer science. During his studies Claudio gained professional experience in several industries, e.g., surveying and engineering (Leica Geosystems), banking (VP Bank AG), and automotive (BMW).

Felix Wortmann, Prof. Dr., is Assistant Professor of Technology Management at the University of St. Gallen. He is also the Scientific Director of the Bosch IoT Lab, a cooperation between the Bosch Group, University of St. Gallen, and ETH Zurich. Felix Wortmann has published more than 100 publications and is among the top 5% of all scientists in business administration in the German-speaking countries (Wirtschaftswoche 2019). His research interests include the Internet of Things, machine learning, blockchain, and business model innovation in manufacturing, mobility, healthcare, and energy. From 2006 to 2009 he worked as an assistant to the executive board of SAP. After studying information systems, Felix Wortmann received his PhD in Management from the University of St. Gallen in 2006.

Part II

Management Strategies for Connected Business

Digital Transformer's Dilemma: Innovate Twice to Survive

Karolin Frankenberger, Hannah Mayer, Andreas Reiter, and Markus Schmidt

1   What the Dilemma Is About

At the end of 2018, executives at *Saubermacher*—a waste management company headquartered in the quaint Austrian town of Graz—has demonstrated how a digital transformation job can be most successfully managed. "Wastebox," an app-based waste disposal solution, connecting construction companies with waste disposal firms via a digital platform, had garnered a significant valuation only 2 years after inception, and *Saubermacher* was wooed by one of the global industry leaders, *Veolia of France*, to engage in a partnership with them. While waste management isn't the sexiest of

This chapter is based on Frankenberger, K., Mayer, H., Reiter, A., Schmidt, M. (2020) The Digital Transformer's Dilemma: How to Energize Your Core Business While Building Disruptive Products and Services. Hoboken, NJ: Wiley.

K. Frankenberger • A. Reiter (✉)
University of St. Gallen, Institute of Management & Strategy,
St. Gallen, Switzerland
e-mail: karolin.frankenberger@unisg.ch; andreas.reiter@student.unisg.ch

H. Mayer
Harvard Business School, Boston, USA

M. Schmidt
QSID - Digital Advisory, Stuttgart, Germany
e-mail: markus.schmidt@qsid.de

industries, there is still something to be learned about digital transformation from this particular case. The success Wastebox experienced was not a lucky strike; instead, they followed the textbook recipe for running a digital transformation. We have observed similar "recipe ingredients" across 100+ interviews with senior executives at globally leading companies from a variety of industries. In the context of digital transformation, they all face the same dilemma: how can they maintain profitability in their legacy-based, core business activities (the first S-curve) while reaping the full potential in a new, digital business (the second S-curve)?

Before approaching this question, we have to start with a bit of bad news and some good news. The bad news are that the legacy business can be compared to a dinosaur and is therefore threatened with the same fate: extinction. New start-ups, powerful tech companies, and other game changers are threatening the existence of almost every incumbent. The good news is that firms, unlike literal dinosaurs, are able to prepare for drastic changes. Our digital transformation framework is designed to help organizations prepare to meet the threat and succeed, by guiding them along the path of transformation. The lesson is one must transform twice: legacy firms need to transform their core, legacy-driven business, while in parallel setting up new, disruptive mostly digital businesses. That is, *all* firms. Irrespective of their industry, geography, or size, companies ought to strike that balance between two very different worlds. Large, well-known companies—like *Michelin, Volkswagen, AB InBev, Nestlé, Novartis,* and *BNP Paribas*—are just as much affected as smaller, hidden champions such as Ohio-based manufacturer of precision instruments *Mettler-Toledo,* Swiss-based diversified tech conglomerate *Bühler,* or Indonesian bank *BTPN.* All of these companies and many more have been interviewed to understand that there is no safe haven for any particular kind of organization. Why is that? Within the essence it can be recognized that it's wrong to distinguish based on size or geography when it comes to digital transformation. Though some differentiation based on industry is possible due to differing sector maturity and the resulting differences in urgency to transform, the most relevant distinguishing factor is the age of the organization in question, making this a "start-up versus legacy firm" competition. Start-ups can launch disruptive innovations more easily than legacy firms because they are not bogged down by past (infra-)structural or mindset baggage. Legacy firms, on the other hand, cannot act as quickly because the organizational realities they face are more complex and harder to overcome. For them to continue to be successful in the old world while at the same time succeeding in a new world remains to be a challenge.

The good news are the digital world order that organizations need to brave is not as dystopian as one might think. On the contrary disruptive innovations, including business model innovation, are paired with or based on the use of artificial intelligence (see Chapter "AI for Decision-Making in Connected Business"), platform-based businesses (see Chapter "Platform Economy: Converging IoT Platforms and Ecosystems"), product-as-a-service (see Chapter "Sustainable AIoT: How Artificial Intelligence and the Internet of Things Affects Profit, People and Planet"), and digitized customer journeys (see Chapter "Driving Connected Business Initiatives: Do's and Dont's"). We illustrate how organizations can not only understand but master the challenge of creating a radically new business which will rely on fundamentally different success factors than the core business. Avid management literature readers will know that some books and concepts have addressed the necessity for disruptive innovations already. Yet one thing is missing: a concrete guide to the differing success factors in the core business versus those in the new disruptive business, particularly as relates to the implementation of such a transformation, and to how the tension inherent in the coexistence of these two businesses can best be managed. This is where our framework can serve as a guide to digital transformation practitioners from all sorts of organizations and across all career levels along the implementation of a holistic, two-tier digital transformation.

2   Lacking Adaption to the Digitalization

Digitization is complicated, exciting, and perilous. The possibility of autonomous cars has led automotive players to make huge investments in radically rethinking mobility. *Daimler* and *BMW*, which have formed a joint venture covering new-generation services, are just good examples. Now a doctor's appointment can be scheduled via your phone while riding the subway to work. And don't we all value being able to search property listings online instead of having to drive to dozens of properties? On the more negative, perilous side of digitization, besides the much-covered collapse of *Nokia* and *Kodak*, you may remember *Nike* halving the size of its digital unit, *Lego* defunding its digital designer virtual building program, and *P&G* not being able to achieve its ambition of becoming "the most digital company on the planet" (Davenport and Westerman 2018). And, if nothing else, you have maybe wondered how jobs, including your own, will be affected by digitization—given that 60% of occupations have at least 30% of constituent work activities that could be automated and because significant skill shifts are expected as a result of automation and digitization (Manyika et al. 2017). It's understandable then that individuals and sometimes entire occupational groups fear digitization. We find that surprisingly few established firms have a clear view on how to best navigate the change brought about by digitization. All of them will, however, need to rethink their business if they want to ensure sustainable success. The bad news: sprinkling a bit of "digital glitter" over incumbents' core businesses does not suffice. Instead, a fundamental overhaul of the business is necessary: a *digital transformation*. From a fundamental economic and business perspective, the beauty and power of digitization comes from the fact that any digital representation can be perfectly replicated and transmitted at almost no marginal cost to a practically infinite number of globally dispersed customers. This implies that a real digital transformation is not simply the deployment of information technology to aid traditional business models. Instead, it fundamentally re-architects the way business is done and gives rise to new success factors. The changes are so radical that a digital transformation is more akin in impact on economy and society to the Industrial Revolution than to your run-of-the-mill cost-cutting transformation, which have become commonplace in many for firms and employees alike. Historically, digitization has had an important, yet somewhat restrained impact on firms because it was introduced almost as a kind of "window dressing" on top of existing organizational systems, still reflecting typical processes. Most organizations did not drastically rethink their business model. By contrast, a business whose operations are founded on digital assets, structured around the ubiquity of data and information flows, would have profoundly different processes and constraints; this is a fundamentally new and (digital) business. While the digitization of the core business is vital for any digital transformation, the future of the business lies in the latter, hence the disruptive new products and services (see Fig. 1).

3   Incumbents Need to Energize Their Core Business While Building Disruptive New Products and Services

However, the digital transformer's dilemma in the end only arises once companies have understood there is a necessity to act across two businesses. Once they have embarked on their digital transformation journey, the dilemma they are all bound to face is: how can they maintain profitability in their legacy-based, core business activities (which we call the first S-curve) while reaping

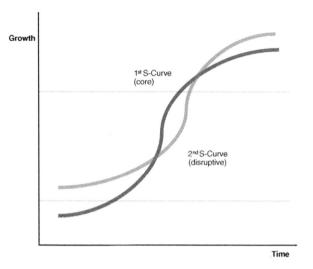

Fig. 1 Two S-curves, Tarde (1903)

the full potential in a radically new, disruptive (digital) business (which we refer to as the second S-curve)? In other words, how can the pursuit of the digitized first S-curve and the development of the innovative, digital second S-curve best be reconciled in one organization, ensuring adequate links between the two? Or, how can firms digitize their core while reinventing their future, hence not just at the senior strategy-setting level but on the operational level as well? That is the essence of the digital transformer's dilemma. The reality is that companies often struggle with striking that balance between first and second S-curve efforts, often leading to animosities between the two. Think about it: the first S-curve will continue to generate the majority of the top-line revenue for the time being and now also has to cover for the second S-curve which is bound to break even only later in the process. Still, however, the second S-curve will often be marketed to both the outside world and internally as a showpiece and token for visionary innovation. No wonder the first S-curve might feel undervalued and unjustly treated; similarly, no wonder that the second S-curve might feel superior. Managing the tensions between the two S-curves is indispensable for the success of the digital transformation as a whole. The key to achieving that is for management and staff to internalize that the success factors on both S-curves differ significantly and that only through a well-orchestrated interplay between the two can the maximum digital transformation potential be realized.

4   Success Is Not Success: The Rules Are Different in the Old and New Worlds

Many publications center around the "why" of digital transformation, convincing C-level executives of the role a digital overhaul plays for the continued success of a company and evangelizing there is a need to act to begin with. The "why" certainly is important because, arguably, knowledge is the first step to improvement. But we aspire something more. To date there has been very limited guidance on the "how" of running a digital transformation. While the *Alibaba*'s and *Amazon*'s of the world may be prime examples for navigating the digital world, they never had to deal with the requirements of transforming a legacy business. Instead, we focus on those companies with a long legacy to showcase how they can transition into the digital age while keeping their core intact and maintaining their traditional business activities on the first S-curve while reaping the full digital potential on the second S-curve. Thereby, it is explored how to best tackle the interaction between the two S-curves while making sure to strike a balance between maintaining profitability in the core and at the same time establishing the new, disruptive (digital) business. This holistic look at the two S-curves instead of just zeroing in on second S-curve champions is a departure from what others have written. It would be grossly negligent to disregard growth opportunities in the core business that can be taken advantage of when digitization is introduced. In many industries and business lines, it is imaginable that the second S-curve eventually becomes the first S-curve and the original first S-curve ceases to be a considerable top-line revenue contributor. But these are natural, longer-term developments. Even when that happens, though, a new second S-curve will be waiting around the corner. Striking a balance between two very different worlds will remain a central topic for organizations even in the future. To best illustrate how the differing the success principles on the first and second S-curve pan out holistically, we cast these insights into a four-part framework.

WHY to Act Companies need to internalize a necessity to act. Businesses and especially those with a long legacy may feel threatened to remain competitive in the face of newly emerging industry entrants competing with them in the digital space (e.g., tech players or start-ups). Organizations may also perceive shifting trends in customer preferences or industry trends that force them to transform. No matter their specific reasons, companies need to realize their continued economic performance will depend in large part on their ability to continue running their core business (first S-curve) while preparing their new digital business (second S-curve). Managing this transformation is not solely a change project. Instead, we are talking about a fundamental overhaul, complicated by its pervasiveness across first and second S-curves and, particularly, the complexities of having to ensure a link between the two to successfully run a dual business. When talking about the need to act, a multinational conglomerate we interviewed illustrates how internal and external forces played out to motivate the firm's move into industrial IoT. Before the firm started to invest in its industrial Internet of things platform, they realized digital transformation poses an immediate threat as well as a big opportunity for them. The management noticed that the firm was slowly being disintermediated by third-party firms that started to build on its products. These firms tried to pull out machine data and leverage it to create new insights that could then be used to make production processes and interactions with other machines more efficient. The increasing digitization of machines, customer interfaces, and communication steadily reduced the importance of the company's own service employees. Management became aware that they were at risk of losing their direct customer contact as new players were trying to occupy the customer interface and that their own efforts to digitize applications and communications with clients were cannibalizing their customer service efforts.

Luckily, the same development that put the firm at risk of disintermediation held some opportunities. At the time, consumer platforms such as iOS and Android already existed, but there was nothing similar for B2B markets. This was when the management realized that the wave of disruption that was hitting one B2C industry after the other was soon to affect B2B industries as well. The management diagnosed that these digital trends were likely to impact how industrial assets are built, maintained, and repaired. To proactively address this development, the firm tried to better understand the factors that were driving those B2C disruptions and how they might apply in an industrial context. This marked the birth of the firm's own industrial Internet of things platform that could connect streams of machine data to powerful analytics, create new valuable insights for the firm and its customers, and more efficiently manage assets and operations. Interesting to note that the point of departure was a consideration of how B2C trends could be transferred to a B2B setting.

WHAT to do Once organizations have realized the need for a dual business, they will have to define a digital strategy and the right business model to support it. A key challenge will be the discussion around financing decisions and priorities, since the core business will initially have to fund efforts on both

S-curves. This means companies need to conceive an overarching digital strategy covering three dimensions: First, organizations need a sound strategy for the core business, focusing on how digitization can help safeguard and increase the competitiveness of the core. Second, organizations need a strategy for the inception of a new digital business to complement the core and generate additional growth. Third, organizations need to consider and plan for possible interactions between the core and the new digital business. This will include both opportunities, such as planned synergies, and risks, such as potential cannibalization and/or disruption of the core business. The purpose is to reach clarity of the overarching digital strategy and how the two S-curves can complement each other. This whole effort needs to yield both a digital business model rooted in novel ways of value creation and a rethinking of the business model in the core.

HOW to do it While it's indispensable to go through this process, great thinking is only the beginning. The real challenge lies in the nuts and bolts of getting the transformation done. To make sure the implementation goes smoothly, companies need to set up the right infrastructure, such as organization, technology, and processes, and institute the right mindset and talent, thereunder fall aspects such as leadership, people, and culture.

- **Flexible organization**: A digital transformation typically requires fundamental changes to the organizational setup, and the buildup of a new separate and flexible unit with dedicated people. The key challenge lies in the coexistence and alignment of two differing organizational setups within a single company. One senior executive at a European consumer goods company told us that large organizations like theirs can never act like a start-up, so to be fast and agile, separation is indispensable. The ultimate structure of the new unit, i.e., digital lab vs. internal accelerator and so forth, depends on the overarching digital strategy and the scope for the second S-curve. Despite a clear separation, a solid integration of the two S-curves is essential to minimize silos and potential antipathies. Integration is also necessary to unleash potential synergies. The required balance between separation and integration will depend on factors such as similarity to core business and the digital maturity level of the organization.
- **Technology as enabler**: Newly emerging technologies, such as artificial intelligence, big data, and the Internet of things, are threat and opportunity alike. Incumbents need to leverage these technologies to support the digitization of the core business and exploit possibilities for new digital business. The challenge is to build up new competencies quickly, following

a balanced approach across both S-curves. Incumbents should also employ a mix of internal development of competencies and accessing of expertise from external sources, as, for example, through mergers and acquisitions. Many of the opportunities for the second S-curve have to do with the buildup of platforms or the participation therein. We find that the active shaping of Internet of things platforms is especially critical for suppliers of legacy equipment. If these suppliers don't find a way to play an active role in the emerging ecosystem and platform game, they risk becoming a "white-label back office" (Atluri et al. 2018) that's merely supplying components or products to the platform, without direct customer access and control over the relationships. A good example to illustrate how technology can be used wisely is *Schindler*, the Swiss producer of escalators and elevators. *Schindler* equipped all its machines with sensors that enable it to track and monitor the performance of its equipment 24/7. *Schindler* can engage in predictive maintenance and optimize servicing activities, for example, maintenance workers know in advance what parts they need to replace and bring to the client site.

- **Processual setup**: Compared with traditional approaches on the first S-curve, new processes on the second S-curve must allow for more freedom and flexibility—something that often feels unnatural to incumbents. The key challenge is to adjust the requirements and setup to the respective business development phase (i.e., seed—incubation—acceleration—scaling). This means that the decision-making body needs to define initial minimum process requirements, deviating from cumbersome standard requirements and to evaluate the projects along a number of stages, following a venture capital-like approach. This however is often a challenging task. As a member of the executive team at a multibillion-dollar business pointed out, saying that companies, once they've made a financial commitment to something that ends up not performing well, are often reluctant to kill the initiative. They end up staying in it for too long, when instead they shouldn't be afraid to get out.
- **Transformational leadership**: Reconciling the two differing leadership approaches of transactional and transformational in one organization is a challenge and finding leaders that can employ both authentically even more so. While some traditional leadership qualities will continue to be important in select areas of the first S-curve, as, for example, a zero-failure tolerance in production, it will become increasingly important not only on the second S-curve but also in the digitized first S-curve to employ a transformational leadership style rather than an authoritarian-directive one. Leaders will put more emphasis on empowering and incentivizing teams to

take the initiative rather than having them perform only their assigned core tasks. Their focus will be on leading people instead of on performing classic management tasks. In fact, the CEO of a pharma company's internal venture told us, "Classic leadership models are outdated. We see leaders as servants who create a safe space for employees to perform at their best."

- **"Right-skilled" people**: Configuring the right mix of people is the gauntlet companies are running to build the workforce of the future. Across both S-curves, the most important lever in this respect is training. Educational efforts will need to cover a variety of fields; most importantly, companies need to make sure their employees have the right competencies to thrive in a digital transformation environment. For instance, a steel company we spoke with built a dedicated digital academy to retrain and upskill employees in digital proficiency, thus investing hugely in their employees' long-term development. Besides investing in the existing employees' careers, other options to configure the workforce of the future include hiring new employees that already have the necessary skills and mindset; contracting freelancers to fill a short-term need or to outsource entire functions; redeploying people, geographically or task-wise; or releasing employees in roles no longer needed post-transformation.

- **Culture of change**: A fundamental shift toward a modern, change-embracing corporate culture is needed if the transformation is to succeed and yield reputational spillover effects. While there may be internal resistance to change, promoting a culture of encouragement to innovate, instituting a supportive work climate, and providing lifelong learning opportunities are must-dos. A change in ways of working will be necessary, including the departure from siloed bureaucratic hierarchies and long development cycles and instead toward a new collaboration model based on cross-functional teams embracing an agile "fail fast, fail cheap" approach. The company culture change needs to be driven by top management to stress the priority and sincerity of the transformation. FMCG and retail senior executives we spoke with stress that what is key is an open-door policy, whereby employees' doubts are addressed by the most senior leaders in everyday conversations. The biggest challenge, however, will be the evangelization of the middle management. By the end, the cultural change will have to pervade all levels to have a chance at establishing itself as the new norm.

WHERE to See Results Let's assume companies have tackled all the above. They are surely expecting bottom-line effects or else the whole transformation would be futile. Seeing that we define a digital transformation as spanning across the two S-curves, it is only natural that it will be reflected in the performance of both. Where and how exactly it has effects will differ across the two S-curves so KPIs need to be determined specific to the respective S-curve and the relevant stage, an example would be incubation vs. scaling. The KPIs should reflect a healthy mix of quantitative and qualitative measures, whereby qualitative KPIs can initially prevail on second S-curve and later be displaced by quantitative ones. Setting objectives, assigning accountability, and ensuring transparency vis-à-vis the relevant stakeholders are almost as important as the KPIs themselves. This stresses yet again the crucial role of measuring impact because even in a digital transformation the age-old saying holds: only what gets measured gets done. But then, luckily what goes around does come around.

A final piece in our framework-rollercoaster logic is the inexorable truth that even if you have mastered the four elements and survived the ride, this is not the end. Eventually your second S-curve might just become a first S-curve again as the original first S-curve ceases to represent any value to customers. And then the whole cycle starts anew. The conditions then may be different; the underlying technologies may have changed; your customers may have fundamentally new mindsets. But the reality of companies having to transform themselves yet again, and to do this in parallel to continuing to pursue what will have become their core business by then, remains unchanged. As Ginni Rometty, former CEO of *IBM*, correctly pointed out: "The only way to survive is to continuously transform" (Hempel 2013).

To go back to *Saubermacher*, following these steps paid off. Within months, *Wastebox* turned into Austria's offering construction waste disposal services. *Veolia* ended up acquiring a minority stake in the digital ecosystem business in 2018, which allowed *Wastebox* to expand to two more markets internationally, with more lined up to follow in the near future. This also boosted performance of the legacy business, with *Saubermacher* not only owning the platform but using it as a lighthouse example to speed up and digitize their core services. And the journey is not over: company executives told us that the goal is to expand the platform worldwide via a franchise system and use the gathered know-how to position *Saubermacher* as the leader in digital waste intelligence across a range of services. We subsequently show you two more cases should illustrate the framework (for more see Frankenberger et al. 2020).

5   The Case of *Heidelberger Druckmaschinen*

Heidelberg is the world's largest manufacturer of offset printing presses with a 40% share of the global market. Their traditional business model is based on selling offset printing presses and related supplies ("consumables") and providing maintenance services to B2B customers.

In the course of their strategy development, Heidelberg realized they could grow their business not by selling more printing presses but by taking a share of the utilization of the installed machine, following a subscription-based business model. To understand the mechanics behind this logic, one must understand the most important driver of profitability of the printing press industry: overall equipment effectiveness (OEE), which is a utilization degree of resources employed. The print industry today is transforming from typically small handcraft print shops to highly industrialized factories. The potential for productivity increases across the entire industry is thus enormous. Just so you get a feeling for the numbers, OEE in the printing industry is ~30%; in the automotive industry, it is ~70%. Meanwhile the print production volume of the total industry will not grow considerably, but the effect of having to distribute industry profits among fewer competitors will offset the limited growth. These will use fewer but much more productive and thus better utilized machines to produce the same outcome, which brings the machine sales model of Heidelberg under pressure. On the other hand, compared to a small handcraft print shop, a highly industrialized print shop consumes much more software, services, and higher volume of consumables, such as ink, per machine.

Despite this growth opportunity in service and consumables even with industrialized customers to compensate for the limited machine unit growth, Heidelberg's consumables business was also under threat. Heidelberg does not produce the consumables themselves, but is a leading authorized dealer. The larger the end print company is, the more likely they were to buy directly ex works from OEMs and not from an authorized dealer like Heidelberg. As a consequence of the industry's consolidation, Heidelberg's consumables business was at risk as well because buying ex works became more commonplace. As Heidelberg struggled to grow and compete on a product-by-product basis, the solution to counter such problems was to combine all such "products" required to print a sheet (machine, software, consumables, and performance services) into one single solution. Such a product system solution would generate more value to the customer than its single parts sold per unit. The "Smart Print Shop" was born. A key capability of Heidelberg was to manage such a product system to its optimum through its access to big data enabled by IoT connectivity of the machines. Such data allows Heidelberg to understand the performance of a print shop even better than its customers.

As a consequence, Heidelberg has started to transform its business model from a traditional "sell more units"-oriented business to an "outcome-oriented" business model. Revenue growth comes from higher utilization of machine units installed. In this new business model, customers basically pay for the printed sheet, including a monthly fee with a guaranteed outcome of printed sheets. Here Heidelberg provides the whole "Smart Print Shop" at its own cost and generates revenue when the system starts to print. The price per sheet for the customer assumes a relatively high level of productivity of the "Smart Print Shop," which is attractive for the customer who can focus more on marketing than production issues. It is also attractive to Heidelberg, of course. If Heidelberg manages to exceed such productivity levels, meaning, if more sheets are printed on top of the plan based on better utilization, the company receives a profit share from its customers as a premium. All products became an integral part of a single connected smart solution.

Heidelberg introduced the "Nespresso principle" to the printing industry. One kilo of *Nespresso* coffee costs 70 EUR but you are willing to pay that premium because of significantly less coffee waste and/or better utilization per cup, and more importantly because of the convenience it affords you—no more messy coffee filters that produce a liter of coffee when you only need a cup, no more being bound to the kitchen to do all that, and so forth. Thanks to the better utilization of the resources required to produce a printed sheet, Heidelberg is able to charge a lower price per sheet compared to the current cost per sheet of its customer. At the same time, the price per liter of ink may be much higher compared with what customers pay today, but better utilized. On top of that, customers don't have to worry about setting up the machine, maintaining it, and so forth which creates time to focus on product innovation and customer acquisition instead of spending time on production issues. In addition to this new model, Heidelberg continues to remain in business with its traditional transactional sales approach while driving the new model more and more to rely on a less cyclical, more recurring, thus more stable, more easily plannable, and more profitable business.

6   The Case of *Covestro*

Material sciences company *Covestro* made a conscious decision against establishing a separate digital unit, neither for the first nor for the second S-curve, for fear it would be hard to integrate and scale results and to keep them connected. Instead, the digitization of the traditional business happens directly in the core organization and new business models—at least during their incubation period—are developed in the corporate area, under Hermann Bach, Head of Innovation Management and Commercial Services. Once the corporate venture is ready to be spun off and if the business model necessitates a separation from the core, it is separated from *Covestro*. Case in point is *Asellion*, an e-commerce platform for the chemical industry. The idea for the business initiated in 2016 within *Covestro* and it is now a stand-alone subsidiary based out of the Netherlands.

Thorsten Lampe heads *Asellion* and talks about how it manages the interaction to the parent *Covestro* and how he orchestrates a leadership exchange:

> Once we spun off from *Covestro*, we were met with sentiments revolving around 'those guys no longer belong to us, they do their own thing, they even have their own name'. Then it didn't even matter anymore that we developed the name with *Covestro* trademark experts and that *Covestro* has a 100% stake in us. As soon as we were out, we felt a 'not invented here' backlash from the core— including leaders in the core—despite the fact that we were indeed invented there. What helped us overcome this is a lot of communication with leaders in the core organization. The communication didn't happen as a push whereby we provided transparency on what we do. Instead, we reached out in a maximum friendly, pleasant way to understand their pain points and how we can help them, how we can deliver value to them. Our platform actually does deliver a lot of value so convincing them with content was one way to build the trust needed to establish an ongoing dialog. In addition, we also made sure to institutionalize the exchange, where possible—for example, by setting up Slack channels to be able to easily converse with relevant decision makers on the *Covestro* side.

What helped *Asellion* leaders strengthen the connection to the core was an empathic, proactive dialog, clearing away any reservations vis-à-vis e-commerce and outlining the concrete value-add for the core business from the newly spun-off digital business.

7   Lessons Learned

Acting under pressure does not make things any easier. Incumbents should therefore get inspired by business models from other industries and consider how customer-centric trends from other industries might affect their own business. If the organizational setup is such that the digital venture is already fully separated and stand-alone, the not-invented-here syndrome can kick in. To overcome the divide, empathy and patience are key. Discussions between second S-curve leaders and their first S-curve counterparts may be necessary. It may be particularly helpful not to formalize these exchanges but to let them mature over time, with no pressure. The goal needs to be to de-alienate the first S-curve, which can be done outlining the value-adding aspects of the second S-curve to the first S-curve.

To succeed, incumbents need to make sure to feed learnings from the digital venture back into the core organization. While the core business can certainly benefit from the new processes and ways of working, the new digital business should consider the established ways of doing business during its scale-up phase. So not only can effects of the successful digital business become pervasive in the core but the new digital business can also start to rely on proven success factors from the core. The two S-curves thus do not live in isolation but cross-fertilize each other.

> **Success Factors for Managing the Digital Transformer's Dilemma**
>
> - Sprinkling some "digital glitter" does not suffice. Organizations need to upgrade their traditional business while exploring new digital ways of value capture.
> - Anticipate changes and get inspired from other industries. By anticipating trends that threatened traditional business models, the case firms were able to act proactively, ward off negative hits, and successfully transfer business models from other industries.
> - Orchestrate a regular exchange between first and second S-curve digital leaders. Ensure maximum transparency over what the respective other is doing and leverage learnings from both S-curves.

References

Atluri V, Dietz M, Henke N (2018) Competing in a world of sectors without borders [Online]. Available at: https://www.mckinsey.com/~/media/McKinsey/Business%20Functions/McKinsey%20Digital/Our%20Insights/Digital%20McKinsey%20Insights%20Number%203/Digital-McKinsey-Insights-Issue-3-revised.ashx. Accessed 7 Aug 2019

Davenport TH, Westerman G (2018) Why so many high-profile digital transformations fail. Harv Bus Rev March 09. Available at: https://hbr.org/2018/03/why-so-many-high-profile-digital-transformations-fail. Accessed 7 Aug 2019

Frankenberger K, Mayer H, Reiter A, Schmidt M (2020) The digital Transformer's dilemma: how to energize your Core business while building disruptive products and services. Wiley, Hoboken, NJ

Hempel J (2013) Ginni Rometty reveals the future of Watson. Fortune 17 May. Available at: https://fortune.com/2013/05/17/ginni-rometty-reveals-the-future-of-watson/. Accessed 7 Aug 2019

Manyika J, Lund S, Chui M, Bughin J, Woetzel J, Batra P, Ko R, Sanghvi S (2017) Jobs lost, jobs gained: what the future of work will mean for jobs, skills, and wages. https://www.mckinsey.com/featured-insights/future-of-work/jobs-lost-jobs-gained-what-the-future-of-work-will-mean-for-jobs-skills-and-wages. Accessed 7 Aug 2019

Tarde G (1903) The Laws of imitation. Henry Holt and Company, New York

Karolin Frankenberger, Prof. Dr., is a full professor in strategy and innovation at the University of St. Gallen, Switzerland, where she is also Director of the Institute of Management and Strategy and the Academic Director of the Executive MBA. Prior to her academic career, Karolin worked for 7 years at McKinsey & Company. Her award-winning research focuses on (digital) business transformation, business model innovation, ecosystems, and circular economy. Karolin is an internationally renowned keynote speaker and supports company leaders in their strategy and innovation challenges. She holds a PhD with highest distinction from the University of St. Gallen and was a visiting PhD student at Harvard Business School and the University of Connecticut.

Hannah Mayer is a PhD Fellow at Harvard Business School and part of the Laboratory for Innovation Science at Harvard. She does research on (digital) business ecosystems and platforms—an area she explored as part of her doctoral studies, which she completed at the University of St. Gallen (Switzerland). Prior to her academic career, Hannah was a consultant at an international management consultancy and spent 2 years at Google as a Digital Strategist. In addition to her PhD, Hannah holds Masters degrees from Queen's University (Canada) and the Vienna University of Economics and Business (Austria).

Andreas Reiter is a PhD student at Karolin Frankenberger's Chair at the University of St. Gallen, Switzerland, specializing in digital transformation and (digital) business ecosystems. His prior academic career saw him graduate with honors in business administration from the Vienna University of Economics and Business (Austria) and London Business School (UK). His professional experience includes 2 years at a globally leading management consulting firm, where he focused on digital transformation projects and the setup of digital business models for incumbents in the financial services industry.

Markus Schmidt is the CEO and founder of QSID Digital Advisory, a consulting boutique dedicated to supporting medium-sized and family-owned companies in their strategy, leadership, and digital transformation challenges. This role was preceded by a long experience leading globalization and digital transformation efforts at Valeo and Bosch, most recently as Executive Vice President at Bosch Automotive Electronics. He now draws on these as a coach and advisor to C-level executives in digital transformation implementation matters, as a keynote speaker at industry events, and as a lecturer at multiple universities. Markus also serves on the board of Fashion 3 of Mulliez Group and XTECH Invest/Clayens NP Group.

Experimenting: What Makes a Good Business Experiment?

Stefan Thomke

1   Learning from *Amazon*: Do More Experiments

In 2016, Jeff Bezos gave shareholders a rare insight into *Amazon*'s innovation engine. In his annual letter, he explained:

> One area where I think we are especially distinctive is failure. I believe we are the best place in the world to fail (we have plenty of practice!), and failure and invention are inseparable twins. To invent you have to experiment, and if you know in advance that it's going to work, it's not an experiment. Most large organizations embrace the idea of invention, but are not willing to suffer the string of failed experiments necessary to get there.[1]

---

[1] Reprinted by permission of Harvard Business Review Press. Excerpted from Experimentation Works: The Surprising Power of Business Experiments. Copyright 2020 Stefan Thomke. All rights reserved

---

Our success at Amazon is a function of how many experiments we do per year, per month, per week, per day.
—Jeff Bezos, CEO, Amazon

S. Thomke (✉)
Harvard Business School, Technology and Operations Management, Boston, USA
e-mail: sthomke@hbs.edu

© The Author(s), under exclusive license to Springer Nature Switzerland AG 2021
O. Gassmann, F. Ferrandina (eds.), *Connected Business*,
https://doi.org/10.1007/978-3-030-76897-3_10

175

Bezos didn't stop there. For him, the business logic for tolerating, even inviting, failure came from the outsized economic returns of winning. He explained why experiments have been so important to *Amazon*'s growth model:

> Outsized returns often come from betting against conventional wisdom, and conventional wisdom is usually right. Given a ten percent chance of a 100 times payoff, you should take that bet every time. But you're still going to be wrong nine times out of ten. We all know that if you swing for the fences, you're going to strike out a lot, but you're also going to hit some home runs. The difference between baseball and business, however, is that baseball has a truncated outcome distribution. When you swing, no matter how well you connect with the ball, the most runs you can get is four. In business, every once in a while, when you step up to the plate, you can score 1000 runs. This long-tailed distribution of returns is why it's important to be bold. (SEC archives 2016)

Business experimentation has become part and parcel of how *Amazon* makes decisions, through a process Bezos calls "the unnatural thing of trying to disconfirm our beliefs." After all, humans strongly prefer evidence that confirms their preexisting beliefs. But such confirmation bias gets in the way of making decisions about innovation, an arena in which most ideas don't work. So it should not have come as a surprise when, partially in an effort to kick its experiments up a notch, *Amazon* acquired *Whole Foods* about 14 months after Bezos wrote the letter. Industry observers felt that its physical supermarkets could become laboratories for radical experiments. Correspondingly, share prices of competing grocery chains plummeted after the announcement (Jesdanun 2017). *Amazon*'s reputation for fearless innovation was fueled by such radical business experiments—so-called big swings—and, equally important, the tens of thousands smaller and disciplined experiments that have led to a highly optimized user experience in its web store.

If the case for business experimentation is so compelling, then why don't more companies conduct rigorous tests of their risky overhauls and expensive innovation proposals in order to make better decisions? Why do executives rely on hierarchy, persuasion, or PowerPoints instead of demanding that teams present experimental evidence before making business decisions? Clearly, there are cultural obstacles that inhibit experimentation. It's also true that managers often misuse the term, saying "We experiment" in lieu of "We are trying something new," but without putting enough thought into the discipline and rigor needed to get useful test results. In the most egregious cases, projects or business initiatives become "experiments" after they are finished, in an effort to excuse poor execution.

But I've also found that many organizations are reluctant to fund good business experiments and have considerable difficulty executing them. Although the process of experimentation seems straightforward, it is surprisingly hard in practice, owing to myriad organizational, management, and technical challenges. Moreover, most tests of new business initiatives are too informal. They are not based on proven scientific and statistical methods, and so executives end up misinterpreting statistical noise as causation—and make bad decisions. In this chapter, we will see how companies can run good experiments by systematically following a clear set of principles (Thomke and Manzi 2014).

In an ideal experiment, testers separate an independent variable (the presumed cause) from a dependent variable (the observed effect) while holding all other potential causes constant. They then manipulate the former to study changes in the latter. The manipulation, followed by careful observation and analysis, yields insight into the relationships between cause and effect, which ideally can be applied and tested in other settings. To obtain that kind of learning—and ensure that each experiment yields better decisions—companies should ask themselves seven important questions: (1) Does the experiment have a testable hypothesis? (2) Have stakeholders made a commitment to abide by the results? (3) Is the experiment doable? (4) How can we ensure reliable results? (5) Do we understand cause and effect? (6) Have we gotten the most value out of the experiment? And finally, (7) are experiments really driving our decisions? Although some of the questions seem obvious, many companies conduct tests without fully addressing them.

2   Q1: Does the Experiment Have a Testable Hypothesis?

Companies should conduct experiments if they are the only practical way to answer specific questions about proposed management actions—and of course, if the answer isn't already obvious. Consider Kohl's, the large retailer, which in 2013 was looking for ways to decrease its operating costs. One suggestion was to open stores an hour later on Monday through Saturday. Company executives were split on the matter. Some argued that reducing the stores' hours would result in a significant drop in sales; others claimed that the impact on sales would be minimal. The only way to settle the debate with any certainty was to conduct a controlled experiment. A test involving 100 of the company's stores showed that the delayed opening would not result in any meaningful sales decline.

In determining whether an experiment is needed, managers must first figure out exactly what they want to learn and measure. Only then can they decide if testing is the best approach to achieve their answer and, if so, what the scope of the experiment should be. In the case of Kohl's, the hypothesis to be tested was straightforward: Opening stores an hour later to reduce operating costs will not lead to a significant drop in sales. This is referred to as the null hypothesis, which is the default statement when there is no measurable change. The null hypothesis is generally assumed to be reliable until empirical evidence suggests otherwise. And when the result of an experiment is statistically significant, it simply means that the observed (sample average) drop is unlikely to be the result of chance. Similarly, if the result is not statistically significant, it does not prove that a treatment had no impact; it simply means that either the observed change or the sample size is not large enough to support a finding (and the related decision) with sufficient confidence.

It's important here to note an important tenet of the scientific method—that experiments can refute, but not prove, a hypothesis. This important tenet of the scientific method is neatly worded by Albert Einstein: "No amount of experimentation can ever prove me right; a single experiment can prove me wrong" (Calaprice 2005). A new fact is thus established if repeated, rigorous experiments fail to refute the null hypothesis. For Kohl's, management's hypothesis "Opening one hour later has no impact on sales" was not proven by their experiment(s)—it simply wasn't rejected.

All too often, though, companies lack the discipline to hone their hypotheses, leading to tests that are inefficient, unnecessarily costly, or, worse, ineffective in answering the questions at hand. A weak hypothesis—for example, "We can extend our brand upmarket"—doesn't present a specific independent variable to test on a specific dependent variable and cannot yield measurable outcomes. Thus, it is difficult either to support or to reject it. A good hypothesis helps delineate those variables and suggests metrics. Consider what the physicist William Thomson, better known as Lord Kelvin and father of the first two laws of thermodynamics, observed about science and knowledge:

When you can measure what you are speaking about and express it in numbers you know something about it; but when you cannot measure it, when you cannot express it in numbers, your knowledge is of meager and unsatisfactory kind: it may be the beginning of knowledge, but you have scarcely, in your thoughts, advanced the stage of science, whatever the matter may be (Thomson 1891).

If the science of management is about building and organizing knowledge through testable explanations and predictions, then perhaps the debatable maxim "What gets measured, gets done" ought to be replaced by "What gets measured, gets explored (and hopefully understood)."

Good hypotheses often come from customer insights: qualitative research (e.g., focus groups, usability labs), analytics (e.g., patterns found in customer support data), or even serendipity. Consider what happened at the financial software company Intuit when an engineer noticed that about 50% of prospective customers tried the company's small business product 20 minutes before they had to make payroll (Cook 2018). The problem was that all payroll companies took hours or even days to approve new customers before the first employee could be paid. Wouldn't potential customers be very pleased if they could make payroll before the long approval process was done? To make sure that there was a genuine need, the engineer and product manager ran a usability study. The result: None of the 20 participants were interested in a fast payroll solution. But instead of shelving the idea, Intuit modified its webpage within 24 hours and ran a simple experiment that offered two versions of the software—one with the option to click on "Pay employees first" and another one with "Do set-up first." (When users clicked on the "Pay employees first" option, they got a message that the feature wasn't ready.) Contrary to the usability test results, the experiment revealed that 58% of new users picked the faster payroll option. Ultimately, the feature became hugely popular, lifted the software's conversion rate by 14%, and generated millions in additional revenue.

The team also discovered that testing customers' actual behavior is more important than trusting what they say they will do. It's not unusual to run into this saying-doing gap in customer focus groups. That's what the Dutch technology company *Philips* realized when it conducted a focus group of teenagers to assess their color preferences for a new boom box. During the session, most teenagers selected "yellow" as their preferred color. After the session, the teenagers received a boom box as a reward for their participation and were offered a choice of two colors: yellow and black. Most participants selected "black," even though they had chosen "yellow" when their preference was posed as a hypothetical question (Cross and Dixit 2005). When it comes to customer behavior, it's usually better to trust the experiment.

In many situations, executives need to go beyond the direct effects of an initiative and investigate its ancillary effects. For example, when Family Dollar wanted to determine whether to invest in refrigeration units so that it could sell eggs, milk, and other perishables, it discovered that a side effect—an increase in the sales of traditional dry goods to the additional customers drawn to the stores by the refrigerated items—would actually have a bigger impact on profits. Ancillary effects can also be negative. A few years ago, Wawa, the convenience store chain operating in the mid-Atlantic United States, wanted to introduce a flatbread breakfast item that had done well in spot tests. But the initiative was killed before the launch when a rigorous experiment—complete with test and control groups followed by regression analyses—showed that the new product would likely cannibalize other more profitable items (McCann 2010).

3   Q2: Have Stakeholders Made a Commitment to Abide by the Results?

Before conducting any test, stakeholders must agree how they'll proceed once the results are in. They should promise to weigh all the findings, rather than cherry-picking data that supports a particular point of view. Perhaps most importantly, they must be willing to walk away from a project if it's not supported by the data. But that's easier said than done.

When *Kohl's* was considering adding a new product category—furniture—many executives were tremendously enthusiastic, anticipating significant additional revenue. A test at 70 stores over 6 months, however, showed a net decrease in revenue. Products that now had less floor space (to make room for the furniture) experienced a drop in sales, and *Kohl's* was actually losing customers overall. Those negative results were a huge disappointment for those who had advocated for the initiative, but the program was nevertheless scrapped. The *Kohl's* example highlights the fact that experiments are often needed to perform objective assessments of initiatives backed by people with organizational clout. Of course, there might be good reasons for rolling out an initiative even when the anticipated benefits are not supported by the data—for example, a program that experiments have shown will not substantially boost sales might still be necessary to build customer loyalty. But if the proposed initiative is a done deal, why go through the time and expense of conducting a test? In such cases, it's best to call programs for what they are—a rollout, commitment, or implementation (a possible litmus test is reversibility: If a new program cannot be easily reversed, it certainly fails one of the most basic attributes of an experiment).

To ensure an organization abides by the results, there must be a process that ensures test results aren't ignored, even when they contradict the assumptions or intuition of top executives. At *Publix Super Markets*, a chain in the southeastern United States, virtually all large retail projects, especially those requiring considerable capital expenditures, must undergo formal experiments to receive a green light. Proposals go through a filtering process in which the first step is for finance to perform an analysis to determine if an experiment is worth conducting. For projects that make the cut, analytics professionals develop test designs and submit them to a committee that includes the vice president of finance. An internal test group then conducts and oversees the experiments approved by the committee. Finance will approve significant expenditures only for proposed initiatives that have adhered to this process and whose experiment results are positive. "Projects get reviewed and approved much more quickly—and with less scrutiny—when they have our test results to back them," according to Frank Maggio, the senior manager of business analysis at *Publix* (Thomke and Manzi 2014).

When constructing and implementing such a filtering process, it is important to remember that experiments should be part of a learning agenda that supports a firm's organizational priorities. At *Petco*, the pet supplies retailer, each test request must address how that particular experiment would contribute to the company's overall strategy to become more innovative. In the past, the company performed about 100 tests a year, but that number has since been trimmed to 75. Many test requests have been denied because the company has done a similar test in the past; others are rejected because the changes under consideration are not radical enough to justify the expense of testing (e.g., a price increase of a single item from US$ 2.79 to US$ 2.89). As John Rhoades, the company's former director of retail analytics, noted, "We want to test things that will grow the business. We want to try new concepts or new ideas" (Thomke and Manzi 2014).

4   Q3: Is the Experiment Doable?

Experiments must have testable predictions. But the causal density of the business environment—that is, the complexity of the variables and their interactions—can make it extremely difficult to determine cause-and-effect relationships. Learning from a business experiment is not necessarily as easy as isolating an independent variable, manipulating it, and observing changes in the dependent variable. Environments are constantly changing, and the potential causes of business outcomes are often uncertain or unknown; so linkages between them are frequently complex and poorly understood.

Consider a hypothetical retail chain that owns 10,000 convenience stores, 8,000 of which are named *QwikMart* and 2,000, *FastMart*. The *QwikMart* stores have been averaging US$ 1 million in annual sales and the *FastMart* stores US$ 1.1 million. A senior executive asks a seemingly simple question: Would changing the name of the *QwikMart* stores to *FastMart* lead to an increase in revenue of US$ 800 million? Obviously, numerous factors affect store sales, including the physical size of the store, the number of people who live within a certain radius and their average incomes, the number of hours the store is open per week, the experience of the store manager, the number of nearby competitors, and so on. But the executive is interested in just one variable: the stores' names (Manzi 2012).

The obvious solution is to conduct an experiment by changing the name of a handful of *QwikMart* stores (say, ten) to see what happens. But even determining the effect of the name change on those stores turns out to be tricky, because many other variables may have changed at the same time. For example, the weather was very bad at four of the locations, a manager was replaced in one, a large residential building opened near another, and a competitor started an aggressive advertising promotion near yet another. Unless the company can isolate the effect of the name change from those and other variables, the executive won't know for sure whether the name change has helped (or hurt) business.

To deal with environments of high causal density, companies need to consider whether it's feasible to use a sample large enough to average out the effects of all variables except those being studied. Unfortunately, that type of experiment is not always doable. The cost of a test involving an adequate sample size might be prohibitive, or the change in operations could be too disruptive. In such instances, as we'll see later, executives can sometimes employ sophisticated analytical techniques, some involving big data, to increase the statistical validity of their results. That said, it should be noted that managers often mistakenly assume that a larger sample will automatically lead to better data. Indeed, an experiment can involve a lot of observations, but if they are highly clustered, or correlated to one another, then the true sample size might actually be quite small. When a company uses a distributor instead of selling directly to customers, for example, that distribution point could easily lead to correlations between customer data.

The required sample size depends in large part on the magnitude of the expected effect. If a company expects the cause (e.g., a change in store name) to have a large effect (a substantial increase in sales), the sample can be smaller. If the expected effect is small, the sample must be larger. This might seem counterintuitive, but think of it this way: The smaller the expected effect, the greater the number of observations that are required to distinguish it from the surrounding noise with the desired statistical confidence. Selecting the right sample size does more than ensure that the results will be statistically valid; it can also enable a company to decrease testing costs and increase innovation. Readily available software tools can help companies choose the optimal sample size.

5   Question 4: How Can We Ensure Reliable Results?

The previous section described the basics for conducting an ideal experiment. However, the truth is that companies typically have to make trade-offs between reliability, cost, time, and other practical considerations. In cases where such trade-offs are warranted, the following methods can increase the reliability of the results.

6   Randomized Field Trials

The concept of randomization in medical research is simple: Take a large group of individuals with the same characteristics and medical affliction, and randomly divide them into two subgroups. Administer the treatment to just one subgroup and closely monitor everyone's health. If the treated (or test) group does statistically better than the untreated (or control) group and the results can be replicated, then the therapy is deemed to be effective. Similarly, randomized field trials can help companies determine whether specific changes will lead to improved performance. The financial services company *Capital One* has long used randomized experiments to test even the most seemingly trivial changes. For instance, it might test the color of envelopes used for product offers by sending out two batches (one in the test color and the other in white) to random recipients and determining any differences in responses. As *Capital One*'s cofounder and CEO Richard Fairbank explained, the same principle can be applied to more crucial issues, such as when customers call to cancel their credit cards due to a better interest rate offer from another bank:

> A classic test for *Capital One* is to randomize all the people who are calling the retention department saying: "I'm outta here." To respond appropriately requires some knowledge of who's bluffing and who's not, as well as some knowledge about which customers we'd like to keep. To get this information, we perform a test with, for the sake of simplicity, three different actions across three randomized groups of people. Group 1, we call their bluff and close their account.

Group 2, we match their (allegedly) better offer. And Group 3, we meet them halfway. Then, we collect lots of information on what the responses of these offers are, and build statistical models to link these results to the data we had on these people. So now, when somebody calls *Capital One*—instantaneously—we make an actuarial calculation of the customer's lifetime Net Present Value and assess the customer's likely response. Right on the screen, the customer service rep sees an instant recommendation, such as to negotiate the APR down to 12.9%. (Anand et al. 2000)

Randomization plays an important role, as it is virtually impossible to control all variables in a business experiment. It helps prevent systemic bias, introduced consciously or unconsciously, from affecting an experiment, and it evenly spreads any remaining (and possibly unknown) potential causes of the outcome between the test and control groups. But randomized field tests are not without challenges. For the results to be valid, the field trials must be conducted in a statistically rigorous fashion, and it's easy for managers to slip.

Instead of identifying a population of test subjects with the same characteristics and then randomly dividing that population into two groups, managers sometimes make the mistake of selecting a test group (say, a group of stores in a chain) and then assuming that everything else (the remainder of the stores) should be the control group. Or they select the test and control groups in ways that inadvertently introduce biases into the experiment. Petco used to select its 30 best stores to try out a new initiative (as a test group) and compare them with its 30 worst stores (as the control group). Initiatives tested in this way would often look very promising but fail when they were rolled out. Now *Petco* considers a wide range of parameters—store size, customer demographics, the presence of nearby competitors, and so on—to match the characteristics of the control and test groups (*Publix* does the same). The results from those experiments have been much more trustworthy.

7   Blind Tests

To minimize biases and increase reliability further, *Petco* and *Publix* have conducted "blind" tests, which help prevent the so-called Hawthorne effect: the tendency of study participants to modify their behavior, consciously or subconsciously, when they are aware that they are part of an experiment (named after Hawthorne Works, a factory outside Chicago that conducted experiments in the early twentieth century to see if better lighting increased productivity). At *Petco*, none of the test stores' staffers know when experiments are underway; at *Publix*, stores are continually rolling out new prices, so the tests are indistinguishable from normal operating practices. Blind procedures make sure that experimenters and participants don't change behaviors just because they are part of a test.

Blind procedures, however, are not always practical. For tests of new equipment or work practices, *Publix* typically informs the stores that have been selected for the test group. Otherwise, stores may be reluctant to participate or even confused why the changes are made. *Note:* A higher experimental standard is the use of "double-blind" tests, in which neither the experimenters nor the test subjects are aware of which participants are in the test group and which are in the control. Double-blind tests are widely used in medical research but are not commonplace in business experimentation.

8   Big Data

In online and other direct-channel environments, the math required to conduct a rigorous randomized experiment is well known by data scientists, who can employ sample sizes involving millions of customers. But many consumer transactions are still conducted through complex distribution systems such as store networks, sales territories, bank branches, fast-food franchises, and so on. In such environments, sample sizes are often smaller than 100, violating typical assumptions of many standard statistical methods. To minimize the effects of this limitation, companies can utilize specialized algorithms in combination with multiple sets of big data. Interestingly, the smallest sample sizes require the most sophisticated analytical processing and big data methods.

Consider the real example of a large retailer that was contemplating a store redesign that would cost a half-billion dollars to roll out to 1300 locations. To test the idea, the retailer redesigned 20 stores and tracked the results. The finance team analyzed the data and concluded that the upgrade would increase sales by a meager 0.5%, resulting in a negative return on investment. The marketing team conducted a separate analysis and forecast that the redesign would lead to a healthy 5% sales increase.

As it turned out, the finance team had compared the test sites with other stores in the chain that were of similar size, demographic income, and other variables but were not necessarily in the same geographic market. It had also used data 6 months before and after the redesign. In contrast, the marketing team had compared stores within the same geographic region and had considered data 12 months before and after the redesign. To determine which results to trust, the company employed big data, including transaction-level data (store items, the times of day when the sale occurred, prices), store attributes, and data on the environments around the stores (competition, demographics, weather). In this way, the company selected stores for the control group that were a closer match with those in which the redesign was tested, which made the small sample size statistically valid. It then used objective, statistical methods to review both analyses. The results: The marketing team's findings were the more accurate of the two, and the redesign was approved.

Even when a company can't follow a rigorous testing protocol, analysts can help identify and correct for certain biases, randomization failures, and other experimental imperfections. In one common situation, an organization's testing function is presented with nonrandomized natural experiments—the vice president of operations, for example, might want to know if the company's new employee training program, which was introduced in about 10% of the company's markets, is more effective than the old one. As it turns out, in such situations the same algorithms and big data sets that can be used to address the problem of small or correlated samples can also be deployed to tease out valuable insights and minimize uncertainty in the results. The analysis can then help experimenters design a true randomized field trial to confirm and refine the results, especially when they are somewhat counterintuitive or are needed to inform a decision with large economic stakes.

For any experiment, the gold standard is replication; that is, others conducting the same test should obtain similar results. Repeating an expensive test is usually impractical, but companies can verify results in other ways. *Petco* sometimes deploys a staged rollout for large initiatives to confirm the results before proceeding with a companywide implementation. And *Publix* has a process for tracking the results of a rollout and comparing them with the predicted benefit.

9   Q5: Do We Understand Cause and Effect?

Because of the excitement over big data, some executives may mistakenly believe that causality isn't important and experimental controls are optional. In their minds, all they need to do is establish correlation, and causality can be inferred. But it's not that simple. Sometimes two variables are correlated because they have a common cause, such as the relationship between drowning and ice cream consumption (outside temperature), or because the correlation is simply a coincidence. In one analysis, researchers found that the number of lawyers in California correlates very highly with money spent on pets in the United States (Tylervigen 2018). I leave plausible explanations to your imagination.

To categorize the different levels of understanding causality, Judea Pearl and Dana Mackenzie propose a three-tier ladder in *The Book of Why* (Pearl and Mackenzie 2018). The first and lowest causality tier, association, is about finding regularities in observations. One event is associated, or correlated, with another if observing one changes the likelihood of observing the other. The authors place modern-day analytics and big data in this tier. The second, intervention, requires changing one or more variables and observe changes in outcomes. Experiments are such interventions. The third and highest tier, counterfactuals, includes the strongest test of causality. Instead of just asking, "Did A cause B?" a higher standard includes the counterfactual, "Would B have occurred if not for A?" Here is an example from my teenage years: I had a friend who firmly believed that drinking a glass of salt water (A) after alcohol consumption prevented a hangover (B) the next day. But would his hangover (B) have occurred if he didn't drink salt water? The difficulty with counterfactuals is that you can't go back in time, repeat the experiment with a different or no intervention, and then compare two outcomes using the same person. Often, personal remedies are based on anecdotes or a handful of personal experiences that could have been explained by other factors; in my friend's case, I suspect that the thought of drinking nauseating salt water may have compelled him to consume less alcohol.

Notwithstanding these causality tiers, the excitement over big data led to the extraordinary claim that the scientific method is no longer needed. In 2008, *Wired* magazine published a provocative article, "The End of Theory: The Data Deluge Makes the Scientific Method Obsolete," using *Google* as an example of an organization that succeeded without any models of cause and effect (Anderson 2008). Similarly, books on big data cited anecdotes in which correlation was now sufficient to make important business decisions (Mayer-Schönberger and Cukier 2013). One popular company example was—once again—*Google* and how its Flu Trend algorithms simply mined 5 years of web logs containing hundreds of billions of searches and thus became better at predicting the incidence of flu than government statistics. But in 2014, a team of Harvard-affiliated researchers found that between August 21, 2001, and September 1, 2013, *Google*'s algorithms had overestimated flu prevalence in 100 out of 108 weeks (Lazer et al. 2014). Importantly, many publications overlooked the fact that *Google* isn't just a big data miner but also a ferocious experimenter. The company understands that correlations are excellent sources of hypotheses that need to be rigorously tested for causality. The Mark Twain adage comes to mind: "The rumors of [the scientific method's] death have been greatly exaggerated."

The following two examples further illustrate the difficulty of inferring causality from correlation—and also highlight the shortcomings of experiments that lack control groups (Kohavi and Thomke 2017). The first concerns two teams that conducted separate observational studies of two advanced features for *Microsoft* Office. Each concluded that the new feature it was assessing reduced attrition. In fact, almost any advanced feature will show such a correlation, because people who will try an advanced feature tend to be heavy users, and heavy users tend to have lower attrition. So while a new advanced feature might be correlated with lower attrition, it doesn't necessarily cause it. Office users who get error messages also have lower attrition because they too tend to be heavy users. But does that mean that showing users more error messages will reduce attrition? Hardly.

The second example concerns a study *Yahoo* did to assess whether display ads for a brand shown on *Yahoo* sites could increase searches for the brand name or related keywords. The observational part of the study estimated that the ads increased the number of searches by 871% to 1198%. But when *Yahoo* ran a controlled experiment, the increase was only 5.4%. If not for the control, the company might have concluded that the ads had a huge impact and wouldn't have realized that the increase in searches was due to other variables that changed during the observation period.

Clearly, observational studies cannot establish causality. This is well known in medicine, which is why the US Food and Drug Administration mandates that companies conduct randomized, controlled clinical trials to prove that their drugs are safe and effective. Of course, there are circumstances when controlled experiments are neither practical nor ethical. In such cases, great care must be taken to remove, investigate, and measure bias in observational studies. But it's important to remain skeptical when drawing conclusions from nonrandomized studies. In a famous study of 45 highly cited clinical research studies on the effectiveness of medical interventions (e.g., therapies, procedures, medicine), only 17% of nonrandomized studies stood up to replication by subsequent studies that had a stronger research design. By contrast, 77% of the findings of randomized studies were replicated (Ionnidis 2005).

Just understanding simple cause and effect isn't always enough. What if you are able to determine that one thing causes another, but you don't know why? Should you try to understand the causal mechanism? The short answer is yes, in particular when the stakes are high. Between 1500 and 1800, an estimated two million sailors died of scurvy groups (Kohavi and Thomke 2017). Today we know that scurvy was caused by lack of vitamin C in the diet of sailors, who didn't have adequate supplies of fruit on long voyages. In 1747, Dr. James Lind, a surgeon in the Royal Navy, decided to conduct an experiment to test six possible cures. On one voyage he gave some sailors oranges and lemons, and others alternative remedies like vinegar. The experiment showed that citrus fruits could prevent scurvy, although no one knew why. Lind mistakenly believed that the acidity of the fruit was the cure and tried to create a less perishable remedy by heating the citrus juice into a concentrate, which destroyed the vitamin C. It wasn't until 50 years later, when unheated lemon juice was added to sailors' daily rations, that the Royal Navy finally eliminated scurvy among its crews. Presumably, the cure could have come much earlier and saved many lives if Lind had run a controlled experiment with heated and unheated lemon juice. In the same way, companies may be better at implementing changes effectively if they know why the change has the effect they desire, so they aren't implementing the change in the wrong way or wasting resources on elements that don't matter.

That said, we don't always have to know the "why" or "how" to benefit from knowledge of the "what." This is particularly true when it comes to the behavior of users, whose motivations can be difficult to determine. At *Microsoft's Bing*, some of the biggest breakthroughs were made without an underlying theory. In 2013, for example, *Bing* ran a set of experiments with the colors of various texts that appeared on its search-results page, including titles, links, and captions groups (Kohavi and Thomke 2017). Though the color changes were subtle, the results were unexpectedly positive: They showed that users who saw the slightly darker shades in titles and slightly lighter shades in captions were successful in their searches a larger percentage of the time and found what they wanted in significantly less time. Even though *Bing* was able to improve the user experience with those subtle changes in type colors, the company had no well-established theories about color that could help it understand why. Here, the evidence and rigor of experimental protocols created trust in the results and took the place of theory.

A similar phenomenon happened at *Petco*. When executives investigated new pricing for a product sold by weight, the results were unequivocal. By far, the best price was for a quarter pound of the product, and that price was for an amount that ended in US$ 0.25. That result went sharply against the grain of conventional wisdom, which typically calls for prices ending in 9, such as US$ 4.99 or US$ 2.49. "This broke a rule in retailing that you can't have an 'ugly' price," notes Rhoades. At first, executives at Petco were skeptical of the results, but because the experiment had been conducted so rigorously, they eventually were willing to give the new pricing a try. A targeted rollout confirmed the results, leading to a sales jump of more than 24% after 6 months.

But without fully understanding causality, companies leave themselves open to making big mistakes. Remember the experiment *Kohl's* conducted to investigate the effects of delaying the opening of its stores? During that testing, the company suffered an initial drop in sales. At that point, executives could have pulled the plug on the initiative. But an analysis showed that the number of customer transactions had remained the same; the issue was a drop in units per transaction. Eventually, the units per transaction recovered and total sales returned to previous levels. *Kohl's* couldn't fully explain the initial decrease, but executives resisted the temptation to blame the reduced operating hours. They didn't rush to equate correlation with causation.

10   Q6: Have We Gotten the Most Value Out of the Experiment?

Many companies go through the expense of conducting experiments but then fail to make the most out of them. To avoid that mistake, executives should take into account a proposed initiative's effect on various customers, markets, and segments and concentrate investments in areas where the potential paybacks are highest. The best question is usually not, "What works?" but "What works where?" or "What is surprising?"

Petco frequently rolls out a program only in stores that are most similar to the test stores that had the best results. By doing so, it not only saves on implementation costs but also avoids involving stores where the new program might not deliver benefits or might even have negative consequences. Thanks to such targeted rollouts, *Petco* has consistently been able to double the predicted benefits of new initiatives.

Another useful tactic is value engineering. Most programs have some components that create benefits in excess of costs and others that do not. The trick, then, is to implement just the components with an attractive return on investment (ROI). As a simple example, let's say that a retailer's tests of a 20% off promotion show a 5% lift in sales. What portion of that increase was due to the offer itself, and what resulted from the accompanying advertising and training of store staff, both of which directed customers to those particular products? In such cases, companies can conduct experiments to investigate various combinations of components (for instance, the promotional offer with advertising but without additional staff training). An analysis of the results can disentangle the effects, allowing executives to drop the components (say, the additional staff training) that have a low or negative ROI.

Moreover, a careful analysis of data generated by experiments can enable companies to better understand their operations and test their assumptions of which variables cause which effects. With big data, the emphasis is on correlation—discovering, for instance, that sales of certain products tend to coincide with sales of others. But business experimentation can allow companies to look beyond correlation and investigate causality—uncovering, for instance, the factors causing the increase (or decrease) of purchases. Such fundamental knowledge of causality can be crucial. Without it, executives have only a fragmentary understanding of their businesses, and the decisions they make can easily backfire.

When *Cracker Barrel Old Country Store*, the Southern-themed restaurant chain, conducted an experiment to determine whether it should switch from incandescent to LED lights at its restaurants, executives were astonished to learn that customer traffic actually decreased in the locations that installed LED lights. The lighting initiative could have stopped there, but the company dug deeper to understand the underlying causes. As it turned out, the new lighting made the front porches of the restaurants look dimmer, and many customers mistakenly thought that the restaurants were closed. This was puzzling—the LEDs should have made the porches brighter. Upon further investigation, executives learned that the store managers hadn't previously been following the company's lighting standards; they had been making their own adjustments, often adding extra lighting on the front porches. Thus, the luminosity dropped when the stores adhered to the new LED policy. The point here is that correlation alone would have left the company with the wrong impression—that LEDs are bad for business. It took experimentation to uncover the actual causal relationship.

What's important here is that many companies are discovering that conducting an experiment is just the beginning. Value comes from analyzing and then exploiting the data. In the past, *Publix* spent 80% of its testing time gathering data and 20% analyzing it. The company's current goal is to reverse that ratio.

11   Q7: Are Experiments Really Driving Our Decisions?

Not all management decisions can or should be resolved by experiments. The decisions to acquire another company or to enter a new market segment are best left to judgment, observation, and analysis. Sometimes running an experiment can be very difficult, if not impossible, or imposes so many constraints on the experimenter that the results aren't useful. But if everything that can be tested is tested, experiments can become instrumental to management decision-making and fuel healthy debates. That's what happened at *Netflix*, which has built a sophisticated infrastructure for large-scale experimentation. According to the *Wall Street Journal*, the company's executives were torn when tests showed that a promotional image that included only Lily Tomlin, one of the stars of the comedy Grace and Frankie in 2016, resulted in more clicks by potential viewers than images showing both Tomlin and her costar Jane Fonda (Ramachandran and Flint 2018). The content team was concerned that excluding Fonda would alienate the actor and possibly violate her contract. After heated debates that pitted empirical evidence against "strategic considerations," *Netflix* chose to use images that also included Fonda, even though customer data didn't support the decision. However, the experimental evidence made the trade-offs and decision-making process more transparent.

When they do choose to make decisions according to test findings, companies should ensure the validity of their test results by paying attention to sample sizes, control groups, randomization, and other factors. The more valid and repeatable the results, the better they will hold up in the face of internal resistance, which can be especially strong when results challenge long-standing industry practices and assumptions. More importantly, hierarchy and PowerPoint presentations should not be accepted as a substitute for experimental evidence.

Consider how running business experiments changed decision-making at *Bank of America* when the company studied waiting time in bank branches (Thomke and Nimgade 2002a, b). Around the year 2000, the bank operated some 4,500 banking centers in 21 states, serving approximately 27 million households and 2 million businesses, and processing 3.8 million transactions each day. Internal researchers, who "intercepted" some thousand customers at bank lines, noted that after about 3 minutes, the gap between actual and perceived wait time rose exponentially. Two focus groups with sales associates and a formal analysis by the Gallup organization provided further corroboration—and the transaction zone media (TZM) experiment was born. The team speculated, based on published psychology literature, that "entertaining" clients through television monitors above the lobby tellers would reduce perceived wait times by at least 15%. The team chose two similar branches for the TZM experiment and its control so they could maximize their learning from the experiment. It installed monitors set to the Atlanta-based news station *CNN* over teller booths in the branch. The team then waited for a week's "washout" period to allow the novelty to wear off before measuring results for the subsequent 2 weeks.

Results from the TZM-equipped branch showed that the number of people who overestimated their actual wait times dropped from 32% to 15%. During the same period, none of the other branches reported drops of this magnitude. In fact, the branch used as a control saw an increase in overestimated wait times from 15% to 26%. Though these were encouraging results, the team still had to prove to senior management that the TZM could positively affect the corporate bottom line. To do so, the team relied on a model that used the easily measurable "Customer Satisfaction Index" (based on a 30-question survey) as a proxy for future revenue growth.

Prior studies indicated that every one-point improvement in the Customer Satisfaction Index corresponded to a US$ 1.40 in added annual revenue per household from increased customer purchases and retention. Thus, an increase in the index of just 2 points for a banking center (branch) with a customer base of 10,000 households would increase its annual revenues by US$ 28,000. Percentages generally ranged in the mid-80s in Atlanta, Bank of America's test market, and in the high 70s to low 80s nationally. The team measured an overall 1.7% increase after installation of the TZM monitors. Sufficiently encouraged, they entered a second phase to study and optimize the impact of more varied programming, advertising, and different sound speaker parameters.

While the benefits of the TZM program were laudable, the team now had to consider whether they outweighed the costs. Studies indicated that it would cost some US$ 22,000 to install the special TV monitors at each branch that was part of its experimentation portfolio. For a national rollout, the estimated economies of scale would bring costs down to about US$ 10,000 per site, which could be directly compared against the implied financial benefit for the bank. Based on this data, managers were hesitant to install TV monitors nationally.

The lesson from *Bank of America, Kohl's, Publix*, and the other examples in this chapter is not merely that business experimentation can lead to better ways of doing things if managers ask the right questions. Experimentation can also help overturn wrongheaded conventional wisdom and the faulty business intuition of even seasoned executives. And smarter decision-making will ultimately lead to improved performance. In general, better testing has helped save *Publix* tens of millions of dollars by doing two things: First, it provides the company with the confidence to proceed with innovative proposals that will improve performance. And second, it helps the company avoid making a change that could ultimately damage the bottom line.

Checklist for Good Business Experiments

Hypothesis
- Is the hypothesis rooted in observations, insights, or data?
- Does the experiment focus on a testable management action under consideration?
- Does it have measurable variables, and can it be shown to be false?
- What do people hope to learn from the experiments?

Buy-in
- What specific changes would be made on the basis of the results?
- How will the organization ensure that the results aren't ignored?
- How does the experiment fit into the organization's overall learning agenda and strategic priorities?

Feasibility
- Does the experiment have a testable prediction?
- What is the required sample size? Note: The sample size will depend on the expected effect (e.g., a 5% increase in sales).
- Can the organization feasibly conduct the experiment at the test locations for the required duration?

Reliability
- What measures will be used to account for systemic bias, whether it's conscious or unconscious?
- Do the characteristics of the control group match those of the test group?
- Can the experiment be conducted in either "blind" or "double-blind" fashion?
- Have any remaining biases been eliminated through statistical analyses or other techniques?
- Would others conducting the same test obtain similar results?

Causality
- Did we capture all variables that might influence our metrics?
- Can we link specific interventions to the observed effect?
- What is the strength of the evidence? Correlations are merely suggestive of causality.
- Are we comfortable taking action without evidence of causality?

Value
- Has the organization considered a targeted rollout—that is, one that takes into account a proposed initiative's effect on investments in areas when the potential payback is the highest?
- Has the organization implemented only the components of an initiative with the highest return on investment?
- Does the organization have a better understanding of what variables are causing what effects?
- Not all decisions can or should be resolved by experiments.
- Experimental evidence makes decision-making more transparent.

References

Anand B, Rukstad M, Page C (2000) "Capital one financial corporation," Harvard Business School case no. 700–124. Harvard Business School Publishing, Boston

Anderson C (2008) The end of theory: the data deluge makes the scientific method obsolete, Wired

Calaprice A (2005) The new quotable Einstein. Princeton University Press, Princeton, NJ

Cross R, Dixit A (2005) Customer-centric pricing: the surprising secret of profitability. Bus Horiz 48:483–491

http://www.tylervigen.com/view_correlation?id=2956 (Accessed April 4, 2018). For a list of more spurious (and fun) correlations, see http://www.tylervigen.com/spurious-correlations

Ionnidis JPA (2005 July) Contradicted and initially stronger effects in highly cited clinical research. J Am Med Assoc 294(2):218–228

Jesdanun J (2017) Amazon deal from whole foods could bring retails experiments. Washington Post, June 16

Kohavi R, Thomke S (2017) The surprising power of online experiments. Harvard Bus Rev, 95(5), 74–82

Lazer D et al (2014, March 14) The parable of Google Flu: traps in big data analysis. Science 343(6176):1203–1205

Manzi J (2012) Uncontrolled: the surprising payoff of trial-and-error for business, politics, and society. Basic Books, New York, pp 132–141

Mayer-Schönberger V, Cukier K (2013) Big data: a revolution that will transform how we live, work, and think. Houghton Mifflin Harcourt, Boston

McCann D (2010) Big retailers put testing to the test. CFOcom, November 8

Pearl J, Mackenzie D (2018) The book of why: the new science of cause and effect. Basic Books, New York

Personal interview with Scott Cook (2018) February 29

Ramachandran S, Flint J (2018) At Netflix, who wins when It's Hollywood vs. the algorithm? Wall Street J, November 10

SEC archives (2016) 2015 Letter to Amazon Shareholders from CEO Bezos

Thomke S, Manzi J (2014) The discipline of business experimentation. Harvard Business Review, December 2014. The chapter draws extensively from text, concepts, and examples presented in this article. Unless otherwise noted, the examples came from the authors' interviews with managers and were approved by company designates

Thomke S, Nimgade A (2002a) "Bank of America (A)," Harvard Business School Case No. 603–022. Harvard Business School Publishing, Boston

Thomke S, Nimgade A (2002b) "Bank of America (B)," Harvard Business School Case No. 603–023. Harvard Business School Publishing, Boston

Thomson W (1891) Popular lectures and addresses, vol 1. MacMillan, London, p 80

Stefan Thomke, Prof. Dr., a leading authority on the management of innovation, is the William Barclay Harding Professor of Business Administration at Harvard Business School. He is author of the books *Experimentation Works: The Surprising Power of Business Experiments* (HBR Press 2020) and *Experimentation Matters: Unlocking the Potential of New Technologies for Innovation* (Harvard Business Review Press 2003), as well as over one hundred articles, case studies, and notes in books and journals, such as *Harvard Business Review, Management Science,* and *MIT Sloan Management Review.* Thomke has taught in and chaired numerous executive education programs, both at Harvard Business School and in companies around the world. He is also a frequent conference speaker and advisor to global business leaders.

Driving Connected Business Initiatives: Do's and Dont's

Mario Schmuziger and Peter Guentzer

1   Value Drivers for Connected Business

For over 15 years, *Zühlke* has been helping companies to adapt emerging technologies in the field of IoT in order to carve out competitive advantages from smart connected solutions. During this time, thousands of initiatives have been launched globally to generate strategic gains from connecting remote sensors, devices, machines, and even the entire plants through the Internet. This is especially true in the industrial environment, where companies have been manufacturing and selling physical assets into business-to-business markets with direct or indirect sales channels. The presence of physical assets in the field and their maintainability is the most relevant starting point for such initiatives.

There are typically three key value drivers for connected business initiatives:

1. **Product and service innovation**: getting new products and services onto the market. The constant acquisition of data and its context-related exploitation also offers advantages for the customer and the organisation.

M. Schmuziger (✉) • P. Guentzer
Zühlke Group, Zürich, Schweiz
e-mail: Mario.Schmuziger@zuehlke.com; Peter.Guentzer@zuehlke.com

© The Author(s), under exclusive license to Springer Nature Switzerland AG 2021   **197**
O. Gassmann, F. Ferrandina (eds.), *Connected Business*,
https://doi.org/10.1007/978-3-030-76897-3_11

Example: High-precision machine manufacturer offers paid performance and process integrity guarantee of his machines to his customers, based on automated remote parameter surveillance and calibration of his connected machines.

2. **Greater customer proximity**: increasing the transactions between customer and company by offering novel ways of collaboration and knowledge-sharing and thereby also increasing lock-in effects.

Example: Consumer Kitchen Appliance Manufacturer offers automated consumables provisioning (e.g. coffee capsules) based on consumption, individual preferences, and response to highly targeted advertising of each customer.

3. **Improved process efficiency**: leveraging data analysis to reduce maintenance and service costs and ensure higher field service quality.

Example: The manufacturer of lift vehicles uses IoT data retrieved from defective vehicle in the field and AI to advise on the most relevant needed spare parts, increasing significantly the first-time fix rate of its service technicians sent out for repair. Or: The manufacturer of heavy construction vehicles supervises machine use and operating conditions remotely. If machine is frequently used far beyond optimal operating conditions (gear selection, engine torque and revolution speed, etc.), the manufacturer proposes shorter maintenance intervals and/or provides advice to machine operator.

Unsurprisingly, over 70% of these initiatives are situated in the third bucket of 'improved process efficiency' (MSM 2017). It is often much easier to calculate a return on investment by comparing investment costs with cost reduction on the bottom line than predicting newly introduced monetisation models in unknown markets. Nevertheless, there have been some successful initiatives aimed specifically at 'product and service innovation' and 'increased customer proximity', often resulting in more upwards potential to conquer new markets, ecosystems, and thus customers.

Within the underlying chapter, the emphasis lies on crucial success factors for connected business initiatives from all the value drivers, and on showing potential links between these. But first, let's have a look at the so-called proof-of-concept trap.

2 From PoC to PoV: Avoiding the 'Proof-of-Concept Trap'

Many companies have meanwhile carried out proof of concepts (PoCs) for IoT and smart connected products or solutions as a starting point of their journey into connected business. Despite the fact that most of these PoCs have been successful in terms of 'working according to specification', they end up in a show-case at a trade-show or are being put back in the drawer for later use, which usually never happens. Having triggered some initial internal enthusiasm, they caused no significant impact on used technology, did not lead to any strategic or business advantages, or make their way to the customer in the shape of a new product and new feature.

The worst case is the proof of concept, shown to you, the CEO, or a real customer on a trade show, creating a promise which cannot be kept ('That's interesting! How could I get this, I'm thinking of having 1000 of these kinds deployed in the field next month!'), because it was never meant to be used at scale. In other words: The PoC failed bitterly in terms of driving the business forward!

At *Zühlke*, we have customers that literally state 'We are really sick of PoCs!', or, more ironically 'We have created a nice proof of concept—it works, now we search for a matching problem that wants to be solved…!' We call this the 'proof-of-concept trap'.

Don't get this wrong: Applied correctly, a PoC is a perfect 'tool' *for engineers* to *proof technical feasibility*, but when it comes to entering uncharted territory in terms of new business opportunities and models—and that applies to the majority of companies in terms of connected business—it is just the wrong tool. This is where the proof of value (PoV) comes into play: Applied correctly, it is a remedy for this pattern.

3 The Proof of Value: Explained

The key question to be decided is: What do you want to proof? The technical feasibility of a new realisation concept, or the benefit or the value of a new solution, product, or service?

Nowadays, the basic feasibility of IoT technology as one foundation of connected business is generally assumed to work out, while the benefit, the business value created, are often based on assumptions and hypothesis. The customer interest is shifting from 'how do I get my data?' (= feasibility) to 'what further benefit do I get from my data, beyond just having it at hand in real time?' (=value). The gained business insights and even actionable items provided by a connected business solution shift into the focus, and the raw data is 'just' the foundation. To provide an example, vibration data is used to detect worn-out bearings of a machine. Acquiring the vibration data is just a means to achieve a more abstract target. So the question at an early stage is not more 'can it be done?' but 'should it be done (this way)? Will it provide the desired benefit when completed?'

This question is what the proof of value answers.

In a Nutshell: Proof of Value Versus Proof of Concept

- The proof of concept answers the question: Can it be built? Will it work?
- The proof of value answers the question: Why should it be built? Is it worth to be built? Will somebody be willing to pay for it?

Please note the PoV is not meant to be minimum viable product (MVP); because the MVP *provides* the intended value to the (end) customer, it is a product. The PoV just proves the intended value. Therefore, the PoV can be realised much faster and therefore earlier than an MVP, but just like the PoC, it is not meant to be a marketable product.

Let's check out an example: Develop a tractor with very narrow track width for steep vineyard harvests (Fig. 1).

Proof of concept	Proof of value
• Is it technically feasible?	• Will it deliver the desired value?
• Will it work?	• Is it worth the effort?
	• Will people be willing to pay for it?

Coming back to the connected business perspective, the differences between a PoC and a PoV can be shown looking at the existing *Zühlke* projects: A manufacturer of production machinery wants to connect his machines to be able to predict necessary maintenance. Based on this solution he wants to grant less downtime of his production, because an unscheduled downtime of a machine (machine fails suddenly) can be turned into scheduled, synchronised downtime of the whole production plant. This leads to increased overall equipment efficiency of his customers' production plant—a very important KPI for his customer. This is a unique new service he wants to charge as part of a new service contract. Together with *Zühlke* he has identified two mission critical issues: He needs to be able to retrieve data from the machines using cellular network, since he is not allowed to use the production IT network.

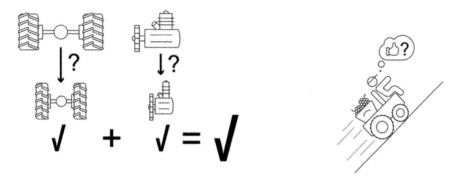

Fig. 1 Difference between proof of concept and proof of value, author's own illustration

Will this be possible? And he wants to make sure his customers are willing to conclude the new service contracts.

The first questions could be answered by a thin technical end-to-end prototype solution, deployed on a machine, acquiring and forwarding selected machine data, even test or simulated data, via cellular network. If the desired data acquired from the machine is accessible in the cloud for predictive maintenance calculation, the question is answered: The concept is proven to work. It can be built! The proof of concept was successful.

The second question will be answered through a different approach: Data from machines will still be needed but can be acquired simply by accessing a machine in regular intervals and copying logfiles manually. The data will be evaluated manually in a lab, predicting appropriate maintenance point in time. With this knowledge, the machine manufacturer approaches his customer and tells him: 'This machine will need a maintenance in 4–6 weeks, so we advise to carry out the maintenance when you have a scheduled downtime of your production in that timeframe anyway'. The absence of the unscheduled downtime, because the machine does not fail suddenly, clearly proves the value to the production plant owner. Looking at the achievable increase in overall equipment efficiency, the value can most likely even be expressed in an increase of productivity. This is clearly a proof of value.

4   Anatomy of Connected Business Initiatives

Key to connected business initiatives is developing a solid plan for how to capture value through them. Most of the initiatives that *Zühlke* has been involved in have been asset-driven. Assets with sensors and actors in the field

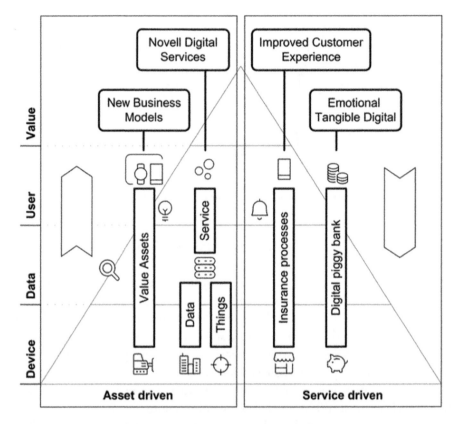

Fig. 2 Value capturing in connected business initiatives, author's own illustration

are a superb starting point for working your way up the value pyramid described in Fig. 2: value capturing in connected business initiatives.

Device integration, data collection, and analysis, as well as user-specific visualisations, have been the dominant, asset-driven approach for connected business initiatives. Recently, the same stack has been used top down to also work in a service-driven way (e.g. insurances, music provider, retail banks) and to add assets on the edge level. The capturing of sensor data has not been established at device level but offers fundamental advantages in the value chain of service-oriented businesses. A prominent example is fleet management and driver behaviour measurement in the field of insurance, or digital piggy banks from financial institutions to target young non-customers with their sales and marketing approach.

- **Value**: Drive business value through improved service offerings, service quality, and service speed and shape new businesses or capture value through quantum leaps in operational performance.
- **User**: Provide contextual value and close feedback loops to different stakeholders by visualising actual status, historical trends, future issues, and actionable items or by triggering business processes.
- **Data**: Analyse context-relevant data from different sources to gain insights and automate decision-making or further actions through continuous flow of data and long-term storage.
- **Device**: Steady real-time data acquisition from decentralised sensors, things, or industrial assets in order to manage them during their lifecycle and directly interact with customers.

To make full use of connected businesses, all levels have to be considered during development and successful solutions must touch all mentioned levels to generate a real return.

5   Digital Phases of Connected Business Initiatives

The anatomy of connected business initiatives is generally divided into three distinct phases (see Fig. 3) which are used to address fundamentally different questions during the journey. Most organisations have already started their digital journey and have achieved results in an early **exploration** phase. They have recognised that there is a strong need to make their customer experience more mature through an evolved digital value proposition, to strengthen their technological platform, to build future services, and to have a clear monetisation strategy. Sometimes, it's even a case of changing customer expectations and requirements. By mastering complexity through evaluating and

Fig. 3 Phases to drive successful connected business initiatives, author's own illustration

validating critical hypothesis, an evidence-based, informed managerial decision can be made before stepping into the **maturation** phase.

On the basis of this sound rationale, the digital service can be built up to act as a solid basis for all further services by providing a stable technical foundation, clear customer value, and a well-conceived business perspective. It has been found to be beneficial for organisations to prove that novel services offer a real return before moving on to the next phase.

In the **scale** phase, a scalable digital business model should be ready to be further exploited by scaling the number of customers and products, leading to successful realisation of the digital strategy. In this phase, a rapid adoption of customers and users is key to generating the expected return on investment.

6   Exploration Phase

In general, one should find a baseline for connected business initiatives which reflects an anticipated or forced change in customer or user expectation and behaviour. Increased transparency over daily operations, failure predictability, remote access for software maintenance, and other areas are often described in the form of use cases and reveal the foundations for rough planning in the first steps. Use cases or user stories are valuable tools for providing a clear scope for one of the value drivers. It has been found that, especially in the early stages, describing and assessing the cases in terms of 'benefits for connected business' and 'complexity in realisation' provides a first qualitative classification that can serve as the basis for prioritisation and further exploration.

By assessing, testing, and validating critical hypothesis (Bland and Osterwalder 2020) for the most important use cases, a sound recommendation and informed decision should be possible. When structuring the hypothesis, a three-dimensional practice has proved to be beneficial:

1. **Customer desirability**: what need do you fulfill or what problem do you solve? Does the use case's value proposition show outstanding user benefits or support the user with their tasks? Is a customer stakeholder willing to pay for this benefit? Is there a high product-market fit?
2. **Technical feasibility**: is the right technology or a set of tools available to implement the case? What critical functional and non-functional requirements must be assessed, tested, or treated as highest priorities? Is the technical solution a make or a buy approach? Where are the potential cost traps?

3. **Business viability**: who are you selling to? How will you reach your customer? How will you deliver the digital service? What is your monetisation method? Who is your competition (direct and indirect)? What is your USP and how will you differentiate your product or service? How big is the market and what is your customer adoption rate? What investments am I considering in the long run? What is the impact on my organisation in terms of skills, processes, and structure?

By answering these questions early on in the innovation process, not to the full extent but where the impact is critical, a solid basis for future success of the initiative can be established. Remember the words of Richard Feynman, an American theoretical physicist: 'It doesn't matter how beautiful your theory is, it doesn't matter how smart you are. If it doesn't agree with experiment, it's wrong'.

Exploration Phase Checklist: Transition Criteria to Maturation Phase

- A set of potential use cases has been developed, assessed, and prioritised.
- Critical hypotheses for most prominent use cases have been defined, tested, and validated.
- Conscious decision by senior management has been made, taking into account the most imminent strategic topics for moving on to the next phase.
- Use cases have been validated with real customers, making sure it brings value to the customers and triggers a direct or indirect willingness to pay (see PoV above).

There is a strong evidence in the market that roughly three quarters of IoT proof of concepts fail for different reasons. Reason number one is the limited view brought in to solve just a small number of use cases perceived primarily as technical challenge ('Can we build it?'), leaving out the business perspective ('Is it worth for us to build it?') and the failure to fully explore the organisation's as well as customers' own strategic directions and potential for radical innovation. Another prominent reason is not asking for help from the outside but, rather, giving internal R&D engineers the task of building something that is completely new to them. The innovator's dilemma described by Christensen (1997) becomes evident.

Still, among the main issues are underestimating cyber security threats, as well as inappropriate threat modelling and mitigation measures. This shortcoming usually pops up during the later phases and is hard to fix during operations.

Example: *Linde Healthcare*—a manufacturer and supplier of medical-grade gases for medical treatments—has found its market in a downwards price spiral of commodity. To escape this, the gas cylinder valve has been digitalised and newly designed with a display to improve data gathering and fill-level status accuracy and thereby increase confidence in the treatment by healthcare professionals. But cost versus additional value was not perceived by the buyer, so there was no customer desirability. By determining the exact needs of the stakeholder groups with regard to efficient and effective handling of the gas cylinder supply within a healthcare organisation, two more user groups were identified. By using the data provided by the newly designed valve and by building a comprehensive platform to close feedback loops to cylinder supply personnel and operations management, the perceived value for effective supply management has been increased significantly (see also Chapter "Linde: Business Value with Connected Cylinders in Hospitals" for Linde).

7   Maturation

Once the choice to invest further in connected business initiatives has been made (the innovation risk has been reduced appropriately and the potential return has been evaluated), the next phase can be started. During the maturation phase, the focus is on realising novel 'connected business' services throughout the full stack, from device integration to the user interface and back.

The emphasis is on 'building it right'. Ideally, from a top-level enterprise architecture viewpoint, a technical high-level architecture is developed. The different parts of the edge architecture, the backend architecture, and the frontend architecture are built according to actual use cases implemented. Commonly used services such as identity/access management or security should also be taken into account (technology is covered in more detail later on). This is also the time to really spread the digital mindset throughout the organisation by fostering learning and short feedback cycles with the customers. It has been found that close collaboration with selected customers during development (e.g. technical adoption programme or lead customer programme) offers substantial benefits due to early feedback.

Maturation Phase Checklist
  - Start building a scalable digital foundation for connected businesses.
  - Install a fast feedback cycle with different stakeholders, users, and customers.
  - Constantly evaluate your investments and pivot if feedback does not prove valuable.
  - Create the prerequisites for successful scaling.

On the other hand, during build-up and learning, the organisation may re-evaluate the influence of the initiative at strategic level, adapt the monetisation mechanisms, and adjust the business models or the organisational structure. After defining the services in the maturation phase, organisations must create three essential prerequisites for successful scaling of the business in the next step—in a technology, process-related, and organisational sense.

Example: An important phrase to bear in mind is 'IoT fails at scale'. In most instances, the initial backend architecture had to be redesigned after a while to address volume-related or changing non-functional requirements before the scaling phase. At a swiss security equipment manufacturer the first architectural design was very use-case-driven and more monolithic. During the further development, two important factors came into play: First, subsidiaries were working in the same direction of digital services but for themselves, and also with monolithic architectures, and second, the different services needed to be decoupled from each other to support the increasing volume and complexity of the solution. The approach of implementing a microservice-based architecture has helped not only to gain flexibility in release cycles for different digital services but also to gain an advantage by properly decoupling services and exposing them to distinctive users and other services. Through that, a future-proof architecture was designed and can be further developed as a digital platform.

8   Scale

When a digital service within a connected business initiative passes a certain level of maturity (customer desirability, technically, and from a business-mechanics perspective), the main goal is to increase customer adoption as fast as possible in order to cross the chasm between early adopters and early majority (Moor 1991). To do so, the marketing and sales organisations (as well as distribution channels) in particular must be ready (educated, incentivised, supported by technical sales) to impact the existing and potential new markets—by leveraging the right processes and personnel to onboard new customers seamlessly, helping them to explore the value of new digital services, and integrating them into their ecosystem and processes.

The scaling process can be properly planned and executed with a strict best practice or sense-categorise-respond approach.

Scale Phase Checklist

- Ensure proper planning and straight execution of a 'cross the chasm plan'.
- Install and train appropriate personnel to support a steep adoption curve and ensure a 'digital at scale' organisation.
- Monitor, operate, and maintain the digital service via service levels in a DevOps organisation.
- Build and manage a digital service portfolio in alignment with the product portfolio.

Constantly re-evaluate whether novel services make a positive contribution to the portfolio, and decide to boost them further if they show growth potential. If they are performing badly, they must be pivoted or even dumped.

9   Business Perspective

While, for most companies we have seen, going digital is a technology-driven journey, we constantly emphasise the impact that a connected business initiative will have on the whole organisation. In Fig. 4 the most important aspects to consider and evaluate if experts from different fields are to be involved in the preparation of decisions, or even in more impactful changes, are shown.

Example: At *Schaerer Coffee Machines*, at a certain market penetration with digital services (*Schaerer Coffee Link*) and the following volume in connected devices, a formerly well-equipped customer service organisation was not able to cope with the increasing customer demand for those services on a technical level. By building a DevOps organisation, all technical issues relating to the fast-evolving and changing digital services have been routed to them. As a result, a fast feedback cycle to development has been established to detect bugs and glitches, and operational issues are addressed much faster. Time to resolution dropped significantly, and service quality can be further increased.

Strategy & Innovation	Customer Experience	Process Automation	Culture & Organization	Technology, IT & Communications	Data, Analytics & Visualization
The digital strategy supports the strategic goals and objectives of the organization. technology programs are an integrated part of the organization's strategic roadmap, including the necessary prioritization, funding and governance.	Through technology, organizations can greatly impact the customer touchpoints and corresponding business models across each of the awareness, evaluation, purchase, support and loyalty stages.	Effective use of technologies through-out the lifecycle of an automation project. Data-driven insights help assess and determine requirements, design, development, factory and client site acceptance testing and client site deployment, use and service.	Just like many other strategic digital initiatives, technology greatly impacts the way a business operates and interacts with its competitors, suppliers, employees and clients. Culture and the organizational structure must reflect and support these changes.	In order to deploy a reliable, safe, secure and above-all successful digital strategy, the organization must put the necessary infrastructure and support in place, incl. connectivity and gateway solutions for the connected devices.	A successful digital strategy assures continuous and constant availability of user and process data. In order to derive value from these immense pools of data, the data needs to be integrated, aggregated, analysed and visualized for each stakeholder.
Security			**Legal, Regulatory & Compliance**		
By implementing a Security by Design approach towards the development of all hard- and software of the connected device, connectivity and use of the data, systems can run as free of vulnerabilities and become more resistant to attacks as possible, without compromising the user experience.			The digital strategy assures full compliance with all relevant legal and regulatory stipulations. The most prominent areas are (cross-border) privacy, data protection and security with respect to device connectivity and corresponding data transfer.		

Fig. 4 Relevant organisational elements to drive successful connected business initiatives, author's own illustration

10   Technology Perspective

In future, smart connected solutions will be the most complex systems to be conceptualised, built, and maintained and will give rise to a whole new technological complexity for organisations, due to their nature of multiple data sources, complex data flows, changing algorithms, numerous user interfaces, the involved hardware and software, release cycles, device lifecycles, and many other factors.

Thus, there are numerous important aspects to consider on the technology side of going connected. The most prominent questions, as indicated in Fig. 5, technology elements to drive successful connected business initiatives, are:

1. **Collect:** How can I generate a reliable, secure, and trustworthy collection of data from field devices and to send them towards a dedicated backend, and aggregate it with data from other systems and sources or even from outside the organisation?
2. **Investigate:** How can a context-relevant analysis of the received data be carried out? How can historical and real-time data be incorporated to generate real insights for different needs?
3. **Act:** How can user-specific applications and interaction channels be built to close the feedback loop between devices and humans and to make use of automated processes?
4. **Monetise:** How can value be captured for the organisation by constantly monetising the interactions with the user?

Experience shows that operational technology (OT, e.g. machines, assets, vehicles) on customer sites or on the road often loses connection with the company after delivery or installation. On the other hand, companies are using information technology (IT, CRM, PLM, ERP) and systems to support their standardised processes, as well as in product development, manufacturing distribution, and services. Both technologies (OT and IT) generate valuable data, and, when combined, substantial insights can be delivered to different stakeholders in an asset context. To handle the long implementation time for such complex systems, it has proven beneficial to start with a classification of potential use cases before determining the priorities and deciding on a digital platform archetype.

By implementing step by step according to a clear roadmap, obstacles can be anticipated early on and options for specific problems can be created without affecting the overall platform. It should not be a specify-build-done type

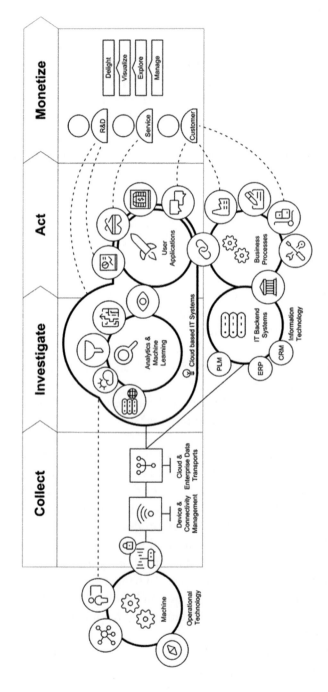

Fig. 5 Technology elements to drive successful connected business initiatives, author's own illustration

of solution. Organisations need to learn to work on an evolving technology stack and incorporate changes during full operation. To do this, the following points must be considered.

> **Technology Checklist**
>
> – Define a conceptual technology stack based on basic functions (e.g. device integration, edge logic, connectivity, etc.) and outline proper integration points to allow flexibility.
> – Outline an early architectural vision based on prominent use cases and the requirements including dependencies to other systems and data sources.
> – Search and select promising technologies, products, and engineering providers. Do not base the decision on price alone but also on experience, long-term perspective, and partnership.
> – Start to build the platform from the OT towards the user, step by step, case by case.

Depending on the use case, a strong make or buy decision must be made at every level of the technology stack. A pure use-case-driven platform decision may be fast at delivering one specific value, but it might also be an obstacle to further growth in more context-driven and individual use cases. With more than 200 platforms fighting for the customer's favour, the technology decision isn't an easy one.

The technology decision should ideally be built on a sound analysis of the functional requirements, non-functional requirements, supply chain and service processes, organisational circumstances, customer care systems, and lifecycle management of your devices.

11   Conclusion

During the time supporting connected business initiatives of different sizes in different industries, it has become clear that smart connected solutions have a positive influence on becoming a data-driven company and fostering the adaptability of emerging technologies to create value for organisations and their customers.

Our experience at *Zühlke* has shown that every customer, every organisation, and every business-driven ecosystem have its own specific context when it comes to fully exploiting the potential. There is no off-the-shelf solution. Important success factors for connected business initiatives are:

1. The initiative and all the efforts must follow a clear vision and a defined strategic objective.
2. An informed managerial decision on the use cases to pursue is needed to focus efforts and to set the scope for the architectural concepts.
3. A sound understanding of changing processes and organisational topics is crucial to ensuring later integration into daily operations.
4. A decision on partnerships to bring in missing skills and expertise and transfer this knowledge into the organisation to become core technologies is key for long-term success.

Success Factors

- Complexity matters: Hardware engineering is about mastering physics, software engineering about taming complexity. Adjust your teams to your maturity level and the questions to be answered. Pursue a probe-sense-respond approach to master complexity in the early stages.
- Ideas are cheap: Build, test, learn—again and again. If the result doesn't resonate with experiment, the idea is probably wrong. Try the next one and build up further expertise.
- Create to destroy: To prove the critical hypothesis right or wrong, one must invest time, money, and passion to create something which can be assessed. If there is no evidence of potential success, the idea has to be pivoted or dumped. Keep it cheap until you have reduced the innovation risk.
- Learning curve: Going connected for the first time means educating your engineers, marketers, salespeople, and service team. And your customer, too. Give them time to adapt and build a learning culture and develop the courage to innovate. Innovate from simple to more complex use cases, from local to global.
- Although it is tempting, do not start with 'what is technically feasible?'. Start with 'which non-technical (!) problem do I want to solve?' and 'what value does my solution provide?' when thinking about your new connected business, product, or service. Technology is never the target, it just provides the toolset to reach the target.

References

Bland DJ, Osterwalder A (2020) Testing business ideas. Willey, Hoboken, NJ

Christensen C (1997) The Innovator's dilemma: when new technologies cause great firms to fail. Harvard Business School Press, Boston, MA

Moor G (1991) Crossing the chasm. HarperCollins, New York

MSM (2017) Studie Industrie 4.0, MSM Research, Schaffhausen 2017

Mario Schmuziger is Director Solution Center and leading complex digital transformation and Innovation engagements for Zühlke customers. He has long-term experience in high-tech environments within the industrial, medical, and telecommunications sector and has founded a start-up. As consultant, Mario Schmuziger is helping customers on a strategic level and also in realizing innovation. He holds a master degree in mechanical engineering and a master in management, technology, and economics both from ETH Zurich.

Peter Guentzer has many years of implementation experience in the field of connected products. Prior to joining Zühlke, he was technical project manager at Siemens cellular phones, as well as cofounder and CTO of a development and product provider for IoT, telematics, and smart connected devices. His passion and responsibility at Zühlke lies in the successful combination of innovative technology with strategic and entrepreneurial goals, combined with a sense for what is technically feasible. Outside Zühlke, Peter Guentzer is involved pro bono in solar energy projects in Africa.

AI for Decision-Making in Connected Business

Naomi Haefner and Philipp Morf

1 Increasing Importance of AI

The number of connected devices is soaring: The installed base is expected to increase from 11 billion today to 125 billion in 2030 (Russo and Wang 2019). Accordingly, the volume of data generated by these devices is skyrocketing. Simultaneously, powerful technologies and methodologies for storing, processing, analyzing, and making intelligent use of these huge amounts of data are widely available. The scene is therefore set for a host of exciting developments enabled by the amalgamation of these technologies. For example, recent research has shown that artificial intelligence (AI) and machine learning (ML), respectively, are used in 60% of Internet of things (IoT) activities (Lamarre and May 2019). Thus, it seems that the conditions for the emergence of a plethora of new smart products and services are excellent.

However, in order to create business value from real smart products and services, these technical and methodological prerequisites alone are not sufficient. Based on our extensive experience with the design and implementation

N. Haefner (✉)
University St. Gallen, St. Gallen, Switzerland
e-mail: naomi.haefner@unisg.ch

P. Morf
Zühlke Group, Zürich, Schweiz
e-mail: Philipp.Morf@zuehlke.com

of AI/ML and smart connected solutions, the perspectives *business* and *humans* must be given due consideration, besides *technology*. This means that if you are trying to develop a connected solution, you must solve a real problem or challenge for your business, and, crucially, you must be able to develop a viable business case. Further, the human factor must not be ignored: Explainability, transparency, and reliability are crucial design factors.

What kind of business value can be generated by data and AI-based solutions? From a business perspective, there are three main reasons for designing, implementing, and applying data and AI:

1. **Better decisions:** data and AI enable fact-based decision-making in all business functions and areas, be it on strategic or operational levels. General objective: be more effective—do the right things.
2. **New products and services:** data, AI, and connection technologies are used as a basis for radically new products and services. General objective: create new sources of revenue.
3. **Optimal processes:** connected, AI-based solutions are used to optimize business and technical processes regarding speed and cost-efficiency. General objective: reduce costs and process lead times.

The present article delves most deeply into the first point—data-based decision-making. From a company's point of view, it is the most fundamental category of use cases and has the highest impact on the company's business performance. As introduced above, we discuss the topic decision-making with a focus on AI and ML technologies in the context of connected businesses. By doing so, we use our holistic viewpoint, i.e., we consider the three mentioned perspectives *technology*, *business*, and *humans*.

We start with a detailed look at the general process of decision-making and bridge the main findings with today's possibilities of AI. Then we outline the status quo of AI-based decision-making in organizations: After a short overview of current use cases, we discuss main challenges and remedies in the implementation of corresponding solutions. Next, we take a deep dive into a crucial topic related to the implementation of AI-based connected solutions—"trust in AI." We conclude by offering a brief summary of the key points elucidated throughout this chapter.

2   The Process of Decision-Making

Decision-making is one of the most fundamental processes that occurs in firms. It involves those "fundamental decisions which shape the course of a firm" (Eisenhardt and Zbaracki 1992). The decision-making process is generally described as consisting of three subprocesses (e.g., Kijkuit and van den Ende 2007; Mintzberg et al. 1976; Simon 1965): (1) Identification: In this subprocess the firm determines which task it will work on. There are different reasons why firms need and want to initiate decision-making processes. Specifically, they may have recognized an opportunity in the market that they want to take advantage of or they may have encountered a problem in the organization that they want to diagnose and ultimately address and solve. (2) Development: In this subprocess firms focus on determining which types of solutions might address the problems or opportunities identified. They, therefore, implement various search routines and design routines to develop possible solutions and approaches to the identified issues and opportunities. (3) Selection: In this subprocess firms screen the various solutions they have developed and designed and evaluate them. Ultimately, they must also make a choice based on which solution is most likely to meet and satisfy their goals. These decision-making subprocesses occur iteratively and should not be considered strictly sequential (Simon 1997).

In the most traditional conceptions of decision-making, the decision-making process was usually described as being rational. However, during the middle of the twentieth century, an important stream of literature pointed out that decision-making is often not a purely rational endeavor: Decision-makers are in fact boundedly rational (Simon 1997). Decision-makers do not have perfect knowledge and must also search for information (Gavetti et al. 2012). Thus, they generally cannot obtain all information relevant to a particular decision or predict all possible consequences of the decision. Similarly, decision-makers also cannot consider all the alternatives before taking a decision. These limitations, which are rooted in human biology, are also referred to as information processing constraints. Since decision-makers are not privy to all possible information, they must search for appropriate information that can be used to determine the possible decision alternatives and to make the best possible decision. However, humans tend to attempt to look for new information and solutions in knowledge domains that are relatively closely related to their existing knowledge base (Posen et al. 2018), i.e., they search what is known as locally.

These human limitations in decision-making can of course lead to suboptimal decisions being taken in organizations. To counteract this, it is quite interesting to consider how artificial intelligence and machine learning systems can support and extend human decision-making in firms. Could there even be situations where AI systems should perhaps replace human decision-making?

From a theoretical perspective it is, therefore, especially interesting to examine the concrete limitations faced by human decision-makers to then examine how AI systems can support humans in these decision processes. Specifically, past research has recognized that humans face two main challenges when making decisions (Eggers and Kaplan 2009; Haefner et al. 2021): (a) Due to biological limitations, humans are challenged by so-called information processing constraints. This refers to the fact that humans can only consider a limited amount of information and possible options at any one point in time. Human brains are not able to consider arbitrarily large amounts of information when examining a decision. (b) Due to humans' tendency to look for possible solutions in knowledge domains that they are already aware of, humans very frequently are only able to consider so-called local solutions to problems or opportunities. Consequently, human decision-makers tend to come up with rather more incremental solutions. That is to say that by primarily looking for solutions that build on knowledge they already possess, humans are often unable to derive more radically different solutions to their problems. When a more disruptive solution should be found, it is usually necessary to consider knowledge and information that is new to the decision-maker. This means that in many instances, human decision-makers must try to access knowledge domains that are beyond those currently accessible within their own firm.

Therefore, AI systems can potentially support, extend, or even replace human decision-making in those instances where the AI system is able to either overcome information processing constraints or allow for the consideration of more exploratory, distant knowledge that would not normally be apparent to human decision-makers. As AI systems increasingly enable managers to process more information and consider more exploratory information, the AI systems will also help managers to make continuously better decisions that are based on a deeper and broader set of knowledge. There is an important caveat to note here: Generally speaking, decision-making support systems that rely on machine learning are limited in that they are built using knowledge derived from available historical training data. As a result, these systems perform best when the environment remains stable—thereby limiting model drift. Conversely, these systems might provide suboptimal results when faced with disruptive technologies or events such as the COVID-19 pandemic.

To gain a better understanding of how and when AI systems can be used in organizations to support and improve human decision-making, we will examine use cases and critical success factors. These considerations will make both the potential application areas and particular challenges regarding implementation clearer.

3   Use Cases and Tools of AI and Data

How do organizations and companies currently use data and AI in order to make better decisions that lead to enhanced value creation? In our data and AI consulting practice, we define the following types of applications, with increasing sophistication regarding technical infrastructure, skills, and implementation effort (Table 1).

Based on our experience, a typical European SME has types 1 and 2 in operation and has made first experiences with types 3 and 4. Common specific use cases of type 4 that have been implemented in connected businesses in the last 2–3 years are:

- **Condition monitoring:** Automated assessment of the condition of infrastructure or manufacturing equipment in order to make maintenance or re-parametrization decisions. This use case often serves as a precursor to the following use cases – product quality control – predictive maintenance. Examples include various applications developed to inspect the structural integrity of bridges or other concrete structures (Karaaslan et al. 2018; Spencer et al. 2019) as well as *Bühler*'s equipment monitoring system (Bühler 2021).
- **Product quality control:** Automated assessment of the quality of created products in real time. This use case is often implemented in two stages: open loop (assessment of quality) and closed loop (in case of decreasing quality, the algorithm automatically adjusts production parameters in order to keep the desired quality level). An example in this area would be the visual inspection platform for manufacturers developed by Landing AI, which is used to detect manufacturing defects in the production line (Miller 2020).
- **Predictive maintenance:** The goal of this use case is to prevent unplanned downtime of a plant or infrastructure components. The algorithm predicts if the supervised system is going to fail in a defined period of time. There is

Table 1 Use cases and tools of AI and data, author's own illustration

Type	Applications and technologies	Explanation	Examples for typical use cases
1	Reporting	Periodically automatically generated reports of defined structure containing statistically prepared, aggregated data	Monthly financial report
2	Self-service business intelligence (BI)	An installed BI platform or tool that can be individually used by a large group of users within an organization to answer questions arising from the business	Research on most demanded products by a specific current customer segment
3	Data analytics	Installed analytics infrastructure and trained staff available that can perform ad-hoc explorative (advanced) analytics on specific data sets	Pre-feasibility check of a specific ML use case with recent acquired data
4	Application of AI-algorithms (rule-based, ML-based, or hybrids)	Decision-supporting algorithms based on rule sets	Condition monitoring, e.g., progress of material wear in infrastructure → Basis for maintenance planning and decisions
	Decision-supporting algorithms based on machine learning	Decision-supporting algorithms based on machine learning	Demand forecasting: What is the expected product demand in function of location and time? → Basis for supply chain decisions

a plethora of examples in this area including systems that can prescribe a maintenance schedule for machines used in automotive manufacturing, systems to provide condition-based maintenance of ship propulsion systems, or systems intended to predict the remaining useful life of machinery (Zonta et al. 2020). Predictive maintenance is especially effective, if unplanned downtime of plants or systems causes high cost (quantifiable as a function of downtime) and/or causes damage to the company's reputation. Concrete examples for companies that are using predictive maintenance include *Mondi*, a global manufacturer of wood and paper, or *Delta Air Lines* (Woodie 2020).

- **Demand forecasting:** Algorithms that forecast the demand of products or materials in function of geographical location, time, or other relevant parameters. This use case's goal is constant optimum supply of sales or production locations with products, materials, and spare parts, respectively. One example in this area would be the purchasing system developed by German e-commerce firm *Otto*. The company's AI system can reliably predict what will be sold within the next month and is tasked to purchase hundreds of thousands of products automatically based on its forecasts (Economist 2017).

In general, we find that companies have not been very keen to experiment with new applications, instead preferring to consider well-known, trendy AI applications. Furthermore, comprehensive AI implementation programs are still rare, and companies tend to implement isolated data and AI use cases only.

4   Implementation Challenges for AI and Data

In addition to the challenges of identifying truly value-adding data and AI use cases, companies are facing several hurdles when implementing these types of projects. The following points have been identified as typical implementation issues in practice:

- **The project pipeline does not get off the ground.** Many companies start with great enthusiasm. They begin to ideate data and AI use cases for their organization. Often, the result is an extensive list of use cases of varying degrees of specifications. The listed use cases usually are too numerous to be implemented and the cost-benefit ratio, the prerequisites for implementation, and feasibility of many items of the list remain unclear. However, since representatives of nearly all business units made an effort to deliver their contributions and ideas, nobody dares to consolidate, evaluate, and prioritize the items on the list and, thus, the list remains unused for a long time.
- **Many proof-of-concepts that do not make the leap into operational business.** Working algorithm prototypes on data scientists' laptops are not productionized. We have seen this so often that we have created a joking expression for this phenomenon: "Pocitis" (from PoC, proof-of-concept). The reasons identified for not putting these prototype algorithms into production are varied: insufficient technical know-how, organizational hurdles, or missing (technical, procedural, resource related) foundations—in

many cases it is a mixture of the mentioned obstacles, which means that the targeted use cases do not generate value for the organizations in which they are pursued.

- **Insufficient adoption of data and AI solutions by the business.** One would think that after the technically and economically successful implementation of an AI use case, nothing should stand in the way of it generating value. But the human factor can be an unexpected hurdle that cannot be ignored. It is not uncommon for technically excellent solutions not to be adopted by targeted users in the business. Fears, professional pride, exaggerated expectations, or unmet personal requirements might lead to the solution not being used and therefore its value potential not being realized.

5   Solution Approaches to AI and Data Implementation

The analysis of real examples of the abovementioned implementation issues has revealed some common, general root causes of suboptimum results from AI and data implementation projects. Strongly simplified and overstated, these causes can be summarized as follows: Single use cases are envisaged and implemented by enthusiasts in isolated units in an unprepared organization, often with a strong technical focus. The following implementation principles are practically proven remedies:

- **Prepare your company:** The intended use of data and AI is a game-changing initiative that is relevant for all areas and units of an organization. Thus, the organization must be prepared for this change. For this purpose, a guiding coalition should be formed, and top management involvement is imperative. A main task of this guiding coalition is to create a strong vision that explains the intended use of data and AI, that appeals to the employees emotionally, and that anticipates and credibly eliminates any fears or resistance.
- **Perform project portfolio management:** Like with other innovation projects, the implementation pipeline must be actively managed. To do so, an effective project portfolio management process must be installed: Created project ideas need to be consolidated and clearly formulated using a standardized scheme. The resulting use cases can then be evaluated regarding

benefit, implementation effort, and risks and eventually must be put into a sensible implementation sequence.

- **Use interdisciplinary implementation teams:** Mastering interdisciplinarity is a key success factor for creating business value by means of data and AI. Thus, your implementation team should reflect the mentioned perspectives business, technology, and humans, i.e., you normally will need data scientists and engineers, IT representatives, domain experts from business, and human/customer experience experts working together in your implementation teams. Involving representatives of the targeted user group of the solution to be created from the beginning is a must.
- **Establish foundations and implement use cases simultaneously:** Many use cases require organization-wide established foundations such as data platforms, data governance processes, established data competencies and skills, and others. Companies often try to establish all these kinds of foundations first and only then begin to implement concrete use cases. We suggest an agile approach to establish the foundations and use cases in parallel, i.e., the foundations are established step by step and always related to a specific use case. This field-proven approach allows for immediate testing and adjusting of the foundations by means of a practical use case.

These principles and measures should be part of a process framework for becoming a data-driven company (Morf 2020). Further selected implementation success factors are described in the subsequent section.

6   A Hidden Success Factor: Trust in AI

Trust in AI is a topic that is currently being discussed throughout society. From our consulting and implementation project experience, we have learned that building trust in data and AI solutions is decisive in determining whether a solution can generate value across the board in a company. For this reason, we discuss the topic in more detail here – first from a theoretical and then from a practical perspective.

Trust is essential for the successful implementation of AI systems on various levels. First, humans who are supposed to use the AI systems need to be sure that the installed AI systems provide reliable information on which business decisions can be made. Second, related to this, humans also need to feel comfortable relying on the recommendations made by the AI systems. Finally, it is critical that humans know when they can trust the AI system recommendations and when they need to collect additional data and information to arrive at a reliable decision.

To address these three points and create the appropriate amount of trust in enterprise AI systems, several aspects should be carefully considered when implementing AI systems. Starting at the most granular level, trust in AI systems is very much contingent on the data quality that flows into the system and largely determines how reliable the predictions made by the system can be. In order to create reliable AI systems, the implementors of the system must both be aware of which data is actually required to create an accurate prediction and then must also either possess this data or have a strategy for acquiring the data (Agrawal et al. 2018). When both conditions can be fulfilled by an implemented AI system, it is much more likely that the system should be able to arrive at reliable predictions. Domain expertise is required to ensure that the AI system implementors are aware of which data is required to build an accurate AI system. Some of the typical challenges associated with data throughout the development process can be summarized as follows:

- **Data selection:** The first challenge when dealing with data comes from needing to select the data most appropriate to the solution you are trying to build. On a theoretical level, it may be difficult to know a priori which features are the most relevant for your problem. Often you may be missing important data (omitted variables in classical statistical terms) or may also be interpreting the direction of relationships incorrectly (reverse causality). On a technical level, it may not always be straightforward to access data, especially when it is distributed across different silos in the organization or perhaps even beyond the boundaries of the firm.
- **Data quality:** The second data-related challenge is related to the quality of the data. At the most basic level, this means having enough high-quality data to implement AI-based decision-making systems. Unfortunately, such data is seldom readily available, and much effort must go into preparing or acquiring it (PwC 2019). Another issue related to data quality is that of biased data, which is the result of social biases including sexism or racism being present in the collected data. This is a particularly tricky type of data quality issue that should be dealt with very carefully whenever person-related data is used in an AI system. Additionally, data quality can also be hampered by response bias (e.g. when only a small share of people contributes user-generated content so that it is not possible to obtain a fully generalizable picture of the population) or feedback loops (e.g., when user responses are influenced by a recommendation system and these responses are used to train the system itself).

- **Data maintenance:** The final challenge occurs once the AI system is implemented. The issue here is related to what is known as model drift, which may occur because the conditions under which the model should make predictions change. These changes can be sudden like the onset of a global pandemic, gradual like customer preferences, or groups changing over time, or they can be recurrent like seasonal changes in buying habits.

A second, very important issue, of course, is the question of which types of systems to build. There is a general decision that businesses can and have to make between building more simple and straightforward systems that are usually easier for humans to understand and trust or building more complex systems that often take advantage of the benefits of deep learning. The technical AI community often speaks of a trade-off between these two types of systems: The general assumption is that more complex neural network-based systems provide more accurate predictions, and they do this at the expense of explainability (e.g., Gunning et al. 2019). To deal with the lack of explainability of these highly complex AI systems, researchers have proposed several approaches. One common method relies on running post-hoc analyses that can offer "local" interpretations of the more complex model. Approaches in this area include Local Interpretable Model-Agnostic Explanations (LIME; Ribeiro et al. 2016) and more recently SHAP (Janzing et al. 2019). The way these approaches work is by being able to identify which features are most relevant in determining why a prediction was made in a specific case. It is important to note that these approaches are not able to explain the functioning of the entire neural network; they explain a *local* excerpt of the entire model. These approaches certainly are a part of increasing human trust in neural network-based AI systems.

However, these models also have certain shortcomings, which indicate that they may not always be the most suitable approach to ensuring explainability and consequently trust in AI systems. Research has shown that these post-hoc explanation techniques may be unstable and unreliable resulting in misleading explanations (Rudin 2019; Lipton 2018; Ghorbani et al. 2018). Further, recent more in-depth analyses of these types of post-hoc explainability methods have shown that LIME and SHAP, for instance, can be fooled with adversarial attacks, thereby manipulating user trust (Lakkaraju and Bastani 2020; Slack et al. 2020). As a result, there is increasing evidence that caution needs to be exercised when trying to use such post-hoc explainability approaches for neural network-based AI systems. In fact, some AI experts argue that in some situations it may be preferable to revert to so-called "interpretable" AI systems where humans are able to understand the model's predictions more easily—these are AI systems that are *not* black boxes—which also means these systems are more trustworthy to human users. Interpretable AI systems include methods such as decision trees or more common regression approaches. Interestingly, for many situations where researchers have compared neural network-based AI systems with more simple machine learning approaches that are interpretable, the performance differences have been negligible (Rudin and Radin 2019). This suggests that the aforementioned prediction accuracy vs. explainability trade-off may not always exist in reality and that one should carefully choose the machine learning approach best suited for the prediction task: A more complicated neural network-based system may not always be the better option.

Finally, once reliable data and the most suitable machine learning approach have been selected, there is a third factor that influences the trustworthiness of the AI system. A recent review of human trust in AI systems notes that there are various aspects in AI system design that can be considered to improve the trustworthiness of AI systems (Glikson and Woolley 2020). In essence, specific design choices influence the level of both cognitive and emotional trust in AI exhibited by humans. Depending on the level of machine intelligence, i.e., the AI system's technical capabilities, and the form of AI representation—whether the system is a robot, appears virtually as in a chatbot, or is embedded—system developers can make different choices to create AI systems that appear trustworthy to humans. Some of the key factors that should be considered by AI system developers are how to demonstrate the tangibility, transparency, reliability, and immediacy of behaviors to users of the AI system. Some of these dimensions, such as reliability, have some surprising characteristics. For example, in the case of physical robots, low reliability decreases trust, but not always: When the robot is perceived as having high machine intelligence, people tend to follow even a faulty robot (e.g. Robinette et al. 2016). Similarly, the task characteristics can also counter-intuitively affect the trustworthiness of AI systems: In tasks that require social intelligence such as recommending and telling jokes, humans generally trust other humans more than they do AI systems, even when these systems are actually superior at task performance (Yeomans et al. 2019). Therefore, when implementing an AI system, the developers should know that different types of trust can be established in varying ways and that recommendations differ based on the nature of the AI system.

7   Designing Trustworthy AI Solutions

Trust in AI solutions should be built on two foundations. The first foundation involves designing the solution, or the system or tool that is to be developed, in such a way that its use generates trust. As a higher-level "design guideline," the Ethics Guidelines for Trustworthy Artificial Intelligence issued by the EU can be used (European Union 2019). It makes general statements on ethical requirements for AI with regard to:

- Human control over AI
- Reliability and security
- Data protection
- Transparency
- Fairness
- Social and ecological well-being
- Accountability

The second foundation for building trust in AI is the actual implementation projects. From our "Best Practices" we now outline the most important points.

Implementation projects should always be coached by an experienced data and AI expert, who is able to bridge the disciplines technology, business, and human experience. This person can act as a "translator" between these disciplines. This "Data Consultant" has broad practical experience in data and AI use cases and therefore is able to pre-evaluate their feasibility and economic viability and knows the critical success factors for concrete implementations.

As previously discussed, a vision is an instrument for building trust in data and AI projects. Its use is especially recommended at the beginning of implementation programs consisting of several implementation items or projects. It should be communicated company-wide at the beginning of the implementation project and should explain the "why": Why does the company want to use AI? In addition to answering this question, the vision can and should anticipate employees' potential resistance and worries.

Another important trust-building element is training: Companies that use AI for the first time should gradually train their employees. The goal is to establish among all employees an understanding of the possibilities—and the limitations—of using AI throughout the company.

An agile, interdisciplinary development team seems to be the most promising setup. However, one of the most important measures is the joint development of the solution with internal "customers"—the users. Involving user representatives as well as the business in the design and development of the solution from the very beginning significantly promotes the acceptance of the solution.

8   Conclusion

In this chapter we have looked at the exciting possibilities presented by the joint opportunities provided by connected devices and increasingly powerful artificial intelligence and machine learning methods. We discussed the potential of these technologies for organizational decision-making and outlined several success factors. We argued that the most important aspect to ensure that any connected solutions based on AI/ML succeed in your company is that it *generates value* for your business. Beyond this, it is essential that the right conditions are created in the company beforehand, i.e., a clear strategy for implementation is communicated. Further, it is best to have an interdisciplinary team with technical, business, and human expertise to implement your use cases. You should have a plan for how to manage building the necessary foundations in your organization while implementing specific use cases in an agile manner. Last but not least, ensure that your AI-based connected solutions adequately consider industry best practices so that your company can implement trustworthy and truly value-adding solution.

Success Factors for AI-Based Decision-Making

- Prepare your company for data-driven business and AI.
- Understand the specific process of decision-making.
- Comprehensively manage your data and AI project portfolio.
- Use interdisciplinary implementation teams.
- Establish foundations and implement use cases simultaneously.
- Emphasize making AI productive – focus on productionizing AI proof-of-concepts, i.e., on transferring AI prototypes to operational solutions.
- Ensure that data and AI solutions are business- and user-driven to avoid the not-invented-here syndrome.
- Create trust in data selection, data quality, and data maintenance.
- Respect ethical requirements for AI by safeguarding human control over AI, reliability and security, data protection, transparency, fairness, social/ecological well-being, and accountability.

References

Agrawal A, Gans J, Goldfarb A (2018) Prediction machines: the simple economics of artificial intelligence. Harvard Business Review Press, Boston

Bühler (2021) Equipment monitoring system: monitoring production: Bühler Group. https://www.buhlergroup.com/content/buhlergroup/global/en/services/Digital-services/Equipment-monitoring-system.html. Accessed 24 Jan 2021

Economist (2017) How Germany's Otto uses artificial intelligence. https://www.economist.com/business/2017/04/12/how-germanys-otto-uses-artificial-intelligence. Accessed 24 Jan 2021

Eggers JP, Kaplan S (2009) Cognition and renewal: comparing CEO and organizational effects on incumbent adaptation to technical change. Organ Sci 20:461–477

Eisenhardt K, Zbaracki MJ (1992) Strategic decision making. Strat Manag J 13:17–37

European Union (2019) EU guidelines on ethics in artificial intelligence: context and implementation. European Parliamentary Research Service (EPRS)

Gavetti G, Greve HR, Levinthal DA, Ocasio W (2012) The behavioral theory of the firm: Assessment and prospects. Acad Manag Ann 6(1):1–40

Ghorbani A, Abid A, Zou J (2018) Interpretation of neural networks is fragile. arXiv:1710.10547v2

Glikson E, Woolley AW (2020) Human trust in artificial intelligence: review of empirical research. Acad Manag Rev 14:627–660

Gunning D, Stefik M, Choi J, Miller T, Stumpf S, Yang G-Z (2019) XAI—Explainable artificial intelligence. Sci Robot 4(37):eaay7120

Haefner N, Wincent J, Parida V, Gassmann O (2021) Artificial intelligence and innovation management: a review, framework, and research agenda. Technol Forecast Soc Chang 162:120392

Janzing D, Minorics L, Blöbaum P (2019) Feature relevance quantification in explainable AI: A causal problem. arXiv: 910.13413v2

Karaaslan E, Bagci U, Catbas FN (2018) Artificial intelligence assisted infrastructure assessment using mixed reality systems. arXiv:1812.05659

Kijkuit B, van den Ende J (2007) The organizational life of an idea: integrating social network, creativity and decision-making perspectives. J Manag Stud 44:863–882

Lakkaraju H, Bastani O (2020) "How do I fool you?": manipulating user trust via misleading black box explanations. In: Proceedings of the AAAI/ACM conference on AI, ethics, and society (AIES '20). Association for Computing Machinery, New York, NY, pp 79–85

Lamarre E, May B (2019) Ten trends shaping the internet of things business landscape. McKinsey Digital Article

Lipton ZC (2018) The mythos of model interpretability. Commun ACM 61(10):36–43

Miller R (2020) Landing AI launches new visual inspection platform for manufacturers. https://techcrunch.com/2020/10/21/landing-ai-launches-new-visual-inspection-platform-for-manufacturers/. Accessed 24 Jan 2021

Mintzberg H, Raisinghani D, Theoret A (1976) The structure of "unstructured" decision processes. Adm Sci Q 21:246–275

Morf P (2020) Insurers on their way to becoming data-driven companies. Zühlke Blog. https://www.zuehlke.com/en/insights/insurers-on-their-way-to-becoming-data-driven-companies. Accessed 4 Oct 2020

Posen HE, Keil T, Kim S, Meissner FD (2018) Renewing research on problemistic search—a review and research agenda. Acad Manag Ann 12:208–251

PwC (2019) Monetizing and trusting data is the year to seize the prize. Data trust pulse survey. Available from https://www.pwc.com/us/en/services/consulting/cybersecurity/data-optimization/pulse-survey.html. Accessed 4 Oct 2020

Ribeiro M T, Singh S, Guestrin C (2016) Why should I trust you? Explaining the predictions of any classifier. arXiv: 1602.04938v1

Robinette P, Li W, Allen R, Howard AM, Wagner AR (2016) Overtrust of robots in emergency evacuation scenarios. ACM/IEEE international conference on human-robot interaction, 2016-April: 101–108.

Rudin C (2019) Stop explaining black box machine learning models for high stakes decisions and use interpretable models instead. Nat Mach Intell 1:206–215

Rudin C, Radin J (2019) Why are we using black box models in AI when we Don't need to? A lesson from an explainable AI competition. Harv Data Sci Rev 1(2)

Russo M, Wang G (2019) The Incumbent's advantage in the internet of things. Boston Consulting Group, BCG Henderson Institute, Boston

Simon H (1965) The shape of automation for men and management. Harper and Row, New York

Simon H (1997) Administrative behavior: a study of decision-making processes in administrative organizations, 4th edn. Free Press, New York

Slack D, Hilgard S, Jia E, Singh S, Lakkaraju H (2020) Fooling LIME and SHAP: adversarial attacks on post hoc explanation methods. In: Proceedings of the AAAI/ACM conference on AI, ethics, and society (AIES '20). Association for Computing Machinery, New York, NY, pp 180–186

Spencer BF Jr, Hoskere V, Narazaki Y (2019) Advances in computer vision-based civil infrastructure inspection and monitoring. Engineering 5(2):199–222

Woodie A (2020) Predictive maintenance drives big gains in real world. Retrieved January 24, 2021, from https://www.datanami.com/2020/01/08/predictive-maintenance-drives-big-gains-in-real-world/. Accessed 5 Oct 2020

Yeomans M, Shah A, Mullainathan S (2019) Making sense of recommendations. J Behav Decis Mak 32(4):403–414

Zonta T, da Costa CA, da Rosa RR, de Lima MJ, da Trindade ES, Li GP (2020) Predictive maintenance in the industry 4.0: a systematic literature review. Comput Ind Eng 150:106889.S

Naomi Haefner, Prof. Dr., is an Assistant Professor of Technology Management at the University of St. Gallen, Switzerland. She is a part of the Global Center for Entrepreneurship and Innovation (GCEI-HSG) and heads the Emerging Technologies Lab at the Institute of Technology Management (ITEM-HSG) at the University of St. Gallen. Her research interests include the impact of artificial intelligence on management and innovation in organizations. Her prior work has been published in *Small Business Economics* and *Technological Forecasting and Social Change*.

Philipp Morf, Dr., holds a doctorate in engineering from the Swiss Federal Institute of Technology (ETH) and holds the position head of the Artificial Intelligence (AI) and Machine Learning (ML) Solutions division at Zühlke since 2015. As Director of the AI Solutions Centre, he designs effective AI/ML applications and is a sought-after speaker on AI topics in the area of applications and application trends. With his many years of experience as a consultant in innovation management, he bridges the gap between business, technology, and the people who use AI.

Cybersecurity: Balancing Efficiency with Long-Term Resilience in Connected Ecosystems

Raphael M. Reischuk

1 Connectivity as Basic Need

Many tasks of our daily life are becoming simpler due to courageous innovators and their brilliant inventions, which often depend on our intriguing new world of interconnected nodes. We can ask *Siri* how long we will need to travel to work today, we can pay our bills within seconds by scanning handy bar codes, and we can get support when choosing political candidates according to how well they represent our political views. The connectivity in our cars improves safety on the road, saves human lives, and might reduce damage to the environment. We also benefit from connected technology for tracing infection chains in a pandemic, for performing surgery at remote locations, and for assisting handicapped people throughout the day. We use digital twins of our society for finding the right partner who, hopefully, steps out of the digital network into our real life—be it for finding diligent hands in the household, for local craftsmen, or for the love of life.

In most of the above examples, the important factor that is necessary for connecting relevant stakeholders is communication. The main purpose of this type of communication, which appears fairly up in Maslow's hierarchy of needs, is to satisfy daily needs that improve the quality of life in a rather stable running society. Communication, however, is even more important during

R. M. Reischuk (✉)
Zühlke Group, Zürich, Schweiz
e-mail: Raphael.Reischuk@zuehlke.com

© The Author(s), under exclusive license to Springer Nature Switzerland AG 2021
O. Gassmann, F. Ferrandina (eds.), *Connected Business*,
https://doi.org/10.1007/978-3-030-76897-3_13

disaster situations; it then becomes absolutely paramount. For example, one of the main concerns of aid relief is how refugees can charge their phones. Or, when Haiti was hit by a devastating earthquake in 2010, all mobile networks went down. Without connectivity, it is almost impossible for relief workers to coordinate where aid is most needed. Luckily, technology has been developed that allows mobile users to communicate directly with each other even where there is no network coverage. Another innovative solution is the mass text messaging program TERA by the *Red Cross*. It allows aid workers to send emergency messages to all smartphones in a certain region containing disaster warnings, health advice, and updates on emergency preparedness and responses.

2   A Network's Value and Cost, Intuitively

While the notion of the *value* of a network is inevitably rather vague, the underlying idea is that a network of connected nodes is becoming more valuable when there are more nodes to interact with, call, or write to. However, this notion of "build it and they will come" is defined precisely for the various kinds of networks, one of the fundamental explanations behind the often-times anticipated growth of a network's value is network effects.

Network effects are said to facilitate scale and are considered the main driver for successful digital businesses such as for *Apple, Facebook, Google, Microsoft, PayPal, Salesforce, Twitter, Uber*, and many more. The US company *NFX* attributes 70% of all value created in technology to network effects (NfX 2017) and lists 15 different kinds in its network effects map: direct network effects (physical, protocol, personal utility, personal, market network), 2-sided effects (2-sided marketplaces, 2-sided platforms, asymptotic marketplaces), data network effects, tech performance effects, and social network effects (language network effects, bandwagon effects, and belief). The less expensive it becomes to connect users on digital platforms, the faster is the growth and thus the rise of the underlying network's value. As more and more users are attracted, the existing users benefit and the network further gains competitive advantages and control due to growing market shares, which affect relationships, data, interaction, and visibility. The value of the network—may it grow exponentially, quadratically, or below following Reed, Metcalfe, or Briscoe et al., respectively—can then be understood as the ability to defend the network and to retain users.

When quantifying the value of a network, it is imperative to also consider the *costs* of running a network. It is easy to see that if all measurable costs lie within the nodes only, then clearly, the costs of the network are linear with the number of participants. But wait, is this assumption meaningful also in adversarial settings?

Metcalfe's Law

Metcalfe's law states that a network's value grows quadratically with the number of nodes, while the costs grow linearly. The intuitive explanation is that all n nodes of a network benefit from the connection to $n-1$ other nodes, which yields $n \times (n-1)$. The connectivity between nodes (or: participants) enables collaboration, which makes the network achieve what individuals cannot achieve on their own. The participants of a network can be computers, servers, pacemakers, industrial control panels, tablets, smartphones, and of course the human users. Simply put, a network with a single node, be it a single telegraph, a single fax machine, a single telephone, or a single user on a dating platform, has no value. With two nodes, interaction is possible and there is value—although limited—for both nodes. With 10 nodes and an assumed value of 100, when joined by 1 additional node, the network's value rises to 121. With the next node joining, the value jumps to 144 and so forth. Metcalfe's considerations, however, do not consider the vulnerability of a network as its cost: the vulnerability of a network grows more than proportionally with the size of nodes, as explained in this chapter.

3   Linear Cost also in an Adversarial Setting?

In the following, we will challenge the assumption of linear cost in light of cybersecurity. By how much is the network's value impacted when a fraction of nodes is poisoned, when malicious and careless players are inside the network? Is the spread between utility and cost in an adversarial setting as it was described by Metcalfe? If not, what are the main reasons and how can the value of a network withstand an adversarial setting?

Adversaries attempt to benefit from the prescribed network effects in the same way as legitimate users. The objectives are different, but relationships, data, and interaction are also important drivers for criminals. Some examples from different kinds of networks are as follows:

- **Platform manipulation attacks** are more effective in larger networks, simply because more targets will consume and then redistribute potentially manipulated content. Social media networks, such as *LinkedIn*, *Facebook*, and *Twitter*, in which one of the value propositions is the reliable distribution of information, rely heavily on a good reputation of not disseminating fake or manipulated content. Manipulated content can lead to mass opinion manipulation, which can undermine democracy and lead to financial and political instability.

- In fact, most platforms do suffer from targeted **spam and botnet activities**: researchers estimate that between 9% and 15% of active Twitter accounts are bots (Varol et al., 2017). Political tweets in the 2016 US election seem to originate from bots in 19% of the cases (Chaffee, 2016). For Covid-19 tweets, it appears that bots account for as much as 45% of all tweets (Allyn, 2020) and that 82% of the top 50 influential retweeters are bots, as well as 62% of the top 1000 influential retweeters (Young, 2020). Around 50 million Twitter accounts are not operated by humans (Newberg, 2017), so "likes," "retweets," and "followers" are totally automated and may serve a potentially criminal intention.

- Attacks based on **social engineering** require trust relationships, which are ideally established between the attacker and as many honest participants as possible. The more connections an attacker has in common with the victim, the more likely will the victim consider an interaction with the attacker legitimate. Moreover, information about the network and its participants can be leveraged by the attacker to make attacks look more authentic and less suspicious. Specific attacks based on **phishing** are best leveraged when proximity (in network parlance: good connectivity) is achievable through the network.

- In **distributed ledger networks**, it is business-critical that the majority of nodes is honest and follows the underlying protocol. The Bitcoin concept paper by Nakamoto describes the consensus mechanism as: "If a majority of CPU power is controlled by honest nodes, the honest chain will grow the fastest and outpace any competing chains" (Nakamo 2009). Consequently, if a subset of malicious nodes manages to control or influence more than 50% of all nodes, the underlying consensus mechanisms become useless. These so-called 51% attacks have been experienced a number of times recently, among others by the Ethereum-based cryptocurrencies in August 2016 and January 2019 and by Bitcoin Gold in May 2018. For cryptocurrencies, the consequences are so-called double-spending attacks, which, in the case of Bitcoin Gold, resulted in theft of more than 18 million USD worth of Bitcoin Gold.

- In IoT networks, nodes typically rely on the **integrity of data** that is passed on to them from other nodes in the network. Reconsidering the examples mentioned above, we see the following anomalies and incidents: the digital piggy bank reports extreme savings making kids feel super rich (in case the amount is positive) or making the bank applications crash (in case the reported amount is negative). Farmers assume wrong prices on the markets and invest in the wrong products, or irrigation systems let the plants dry up. Siri takes us to wrong destinations, possibly through forbidden or dangerous areas. The bills we pay have wrong amounts and wrong payment recipients, yet they look legitimate. Political opinion making and candidate selection yields opposite results of what we would expect; however, we do not notice any anomaly. Cars crash at peak hours because traffic lights all decide to switch to green simultaneously. Contact tracing reports no infections, which renders the approach useless within days. Masses of doctors and ambulances are suddenly absorbed on site to contain the damage from failed remote surgery. Digital twins create false illusions and lead to wrong decisions and disappointments. Disaster communication reports false results and loses its availability, and therefore the trust in its utility is gone.

- In the software economy, in particular in the open-source community, value is generated by sharing source code and therefore by the trust that is placed toward **the correctness and the integrity of the source code.** As software has become the backbone of our society, novel **supply-chain attacks** appear which are deeply nested in the distribution channels of software libraries and applications. One of the most severe attacks in history is the 2020 SolarWinds attack, where the Sunburst trojan hit thousands of organizations globally, such as NATO, the EU parliament, the UK government, many US government organizations, and *Microsoft.* The cyber espionage campaign started in March 2020 with the exploitation of software and credentials from software companies such as *Microsoft, SolarWinds,* and *VMware.* The attackers have planted remote access tool malware into a widely used network monitoring software, which was quickly installed on tens of thousands of systems worldwide. More exploits and attacks were launched as a consequence.

- This supply-chain attack demonstrates the fragility of today's software network: a single infected piece of software can cause damage to thousands of organizations worldwide, at an incredible speed. Due to the complexity, these attacks can go undetected for months.

Put differently, the quality of the experienced network depends on the network's ability to detect and exclude malicious and otherwise unwanted participants. Striving for a high ratio of honest participants has a direct influence on the value of the network. Otherwise, unsolicited email, fake news, and the scenarios described above are a tedious and possibly enduring artifact.

Keeping unwanted attackers at bay is usually a shared responsibility between the network itself (infrastructure and operators) and the participants in the network (devices and users). These efforts clearly pay in on the cost side and must not be neglected when assessing the overall value of the network. Today's networks spend a huge body of resources on that problem and employ entire armies of digital hunters to eliminate the negative influences by human troublemakers and autonomous bots. At the same time, however, some networks invoke self-curing measures such as mutual accreditation of nodes and recommendation-based trust profiles as seen on *Uber* or *Airbnb*.

Long before Covid-19, computer and network engineers started building their architectures around the principle of "zero trust" in order to increase the overall resilience of the architectures. Essentially, this principle states that each node in the network shall assume only little honesty, correctness, and authenticity when exchanging data with other parties. In corporate environments, zero trust means companies should not generally trust their customers, employees, and applications. In particular, no differentiation is made between communication from inside and outside the company boundaries. Instead, everything and everyone who tries to access corporate data must be authenticated and controlled. It is a consistently data-centric approach based on constant monitoring. For example, in authorization decisions, access is granted only after a consequent and reliable identification of the requesting party. As such, the trust boundaries vanish at the expense of a growing cost for scrutinizing devices, humans, and network traffic. Applied correctly, these costs are incurred at every node of a network and thus scale linearly with the number of nodes and data traffic exchanged between the nodes.

Turning back to Metcalfe and Reed: if quadratic or exponential laws were true, there would be overwhelming incentives for all networks of similar technology to merge or at least to interconnect. There is, however, only little evidence for such mergers: in the late 1980s and early 1990s, the commercial online companies such as *CompuServe, Prodigy, AOL,* and *MCI Mail* provided e-mail services to subscribers, but only within their own systems.

Complete networking was not achieved until the mid-1990s. Why has it taken so long? Shouldn't the incentives by the laws of Metcalfe and Reed make isolated networks totally obsolete? The answer is no; still today, plenty of isolated networks exist. A prominent example for non-interconnected networks in the times of Covid-19 is the various national contact-tracing systems, which are not interoperable, mainly due to non-technical reasons.

Isolated networks such as VPNs, closed-user groups, and zero-trust zones serve also a dedicated purpose, inter alia for cybersecurity reasons: isolated networks usually have a high entry barrier, come with minimal trust bases, and offer additional amenities such as free expression of opinion, non-traceability, anonymity, and confidentiality guarantees.

Summarizing the above, in particular when considering aspects of cybersecurity, the value of a network seems far from growing quadratic or exponential. The question we will try to answer in the following is: what does it need to bring the value of connected and distributed systems back to growing beyond linear with the number of nodes?

4   Cyber Resilience Strategies to the Rescue

One of the main differentiating factors compared to early computer networks in the 1970s is the agility and dynamics of today's networks. Hyperscalers spin up containers, virtual machines, and networks in a matter of milliseconds. Messages, posts, media, and other data objects propagate through the nodes of a network with largely varying speeds and densities. Today's software release cycles allow for delivering new functionality and patches to billions of devices within minutes. At the same time, attackers orchestrate entire armies of bots within a blink of an eye and distribute malware to billions of devices at the same pace.

Consequently, protecting the nodes of a network (and therewith preserving the network's value) requires adaptive concepts that are of similar dynamics and agility as today's networks. Any protection concept must adapt quickly to modified circumstances inside the network. Additionally, not only changes of internal network conditions must be considered, but also external threats and attacks that are highly dynamic and often unpredictable must be incorporated in the mitigation concept.

Static approaches such as fixed firewall rules, static network zones, and fixed permission models are no longer adequate. A meaningful analogy to those static measures is a solid rock in the surf. It has a ponderous and unwieldy appearance and would never adapt to changing circumstances. A displacement of the rock by even one millimeter seems infeasible. In other words: no agility.

Cyber resilience is the exact opposite of that rock. Resilience in general describes the ability of a system, an organization, or a network to recover readily from adversity, illness, anomaly, and other unwanted condition. It is the capacity to adapt to disruptive changes in the environment, be it from adversarial input, manipulation, or abuse. Resilient systems are typically characterized by the two features: diversity and redundancy.

A meaningful analogy to illustrate the concept of resilience is a bamboo forest. Bamboo trees have distinguished properties: they are evergreen, they belong to the fastest-growing plants in the world due to their unique rhizome-dependent system (certain species grow up to 1 meter within 24 h), they have a high strength-to-weight ratio making them useful for building structures and withstanding external influence, and they are a source of food and generally constitute a versatile raw product. Being fast-growing and withstanding external changes and being versatile and appearing in large numbers correspond to diversity and redundancy and are thus important key factors for surviving disruptive changes in the environment.

How does the concept of resilience translate to networks and their nodes? As mentioned earlier, most networks carry within them a high degree of dynamics. Nodes come and join, leave, and come back. Networks are very versatile and often unpredictable. This is why most nodes in a network will likely not know all other nodes. In particular, a node might not be able to assess the trustworthiness of other nodes. Nodes can sometimes not even be certain about their direct neighborhood. In order to survive and not become prey of malicious nodes in the network, one promising concept as part of the resilience strategy is the aforementioned concept of zero trust. Despite not always being applicable and sometimes being reduced to "little trust," the concept seeks at benefitting from network effects, but not suffers from typical trust weaknesses as mentioned in the examples above.

Robust Measures for More Network Resilience

Continuous monitoring and anomaly detection: The "zero-trust" paradigm requires probing and scrutinization of all relevant objects on the basis of which business-critical decisions are made. Data sources that are typically fed into machine-learning-based solutions include network traffic between devices, system and application log files, user behavior, dedicated honey pots, and other forms of statistical data.

Incident response and digital forensics: The "assume breach" paradigm, as the name suggests, assumes system compromise and an attacker who is closer and more successful than we think. Consequently, defense expects an incident at any moment and is prepared for various scenarios. Since 100% security is not even true in our dreams, incident response plans should be worked out, trained, and reviewed. A digital forensic team for identifying the root cause and for containing the attack should be quickly accessible upon request.

Regular penetration testing of infrastructure and applications: When constant monitoring of an infrastructure or an application is not possible at runtime, periodic testing of all critical systems should be conducted. The findings should be presented to the executive board and should be addressed with sufficient resources, diligence, and expertise. According to Gartner, CEOs will be held personally accountable for cyber incidents in the future (Moore 2020).

Awareness to defeat social engineering: All kinds of phishing attacks or attempts of illegitimate access to systems where the human nature is exploited can best be prevented by means of education and awareness campaigns. The human weakness has received more attention in recent years: it is reported that between 80% and 90% of all cyberattacks start with the "human factor." It is therefore important to make employees the most effective firewall of an organization. An important insight is to make employees concerned on a personal level about the devastating impact of a small lapse or carelessness.

Blue and red team exercises: To increase the awareness and to actively take on the perspective of an attacker, role plays with two competing teams—red for attack and blue for defense—have proven to be an effective measure. The incentivization for the players is high and the outcome is an improved secure posture.

Network segmentation and security-by-design: System architectures and networks shall be structured in a way that a breach in one component shall affect as few other components as possible. An attacker shall be prevented from moving laterally in a system or network. Firewalls and explicit transitions between network segments and avoiding reuse of credentials across applications and devices constitute examples for a basic cyber hygiene.

Security-by-default: The configuration of all critical components in a network or organization shall be such that no further adaptation is necessary in order to guarantee secure operation. For instance, devices shall only be connectable to a network or ecosystem, *after* an individual strong password is pre-set or chosen by the owner.

5   Why the Quest for Efficiency Proves to Be the Greatest Opponent of Resilience

In contrast to resilience, which we defined above as being adaptable to disruptive changes in the environment, efficiency can be defined as being adaptable to an existing environment. More precisely, in many situations, efficiency translates to a lean way of working in a given environment, in which the essence of a certain goal becomes the focus of our actions. Every detour, no matter how small, should be avoided in favor of an optimized cost-benefit ratio. More precisely, those detours usually provide no benefit, but instead come with a cost. The primary goal when striving for efficiency therefore often consists of reducing cost, not increasing value or benefit.

Reducing cost comes in a number of facets: it means reducing the overhead of managing more than what is utterly necessary and abandoning buffers and additional resources, in particular those that seem superfluous in the here and now. It therefore also means decreasing diversity and redundancy, the two key features of resilience.

From a short-term perspective, this train of thought seems understandable; reducing slack easily finds economic justification in the medium term. However, it excludes from our view all scenarios that are referred to as black swans or the unknown unknowns. These scenarios often come with risks that are intractable in practice. The likelihood is low, but the impact could be devastating. Out of an obsession with such short-term efficiency and growth, humans tend to become blind to such severe scenarios that come with low probability. M. A. Goldberg in his 1975 article "On the Inefficiency of Being Efficient" calls it the narrowness with which problems are defined and the equally narrow range of alternatives sought for solution. Efficiency strives for short-term optimization, whereas resilience seeks long-term optimization.

What if the relentless pursuit of efficiency, which has dominated American business thinking for decades, has made the global economic system more vulnerable to shocks? This thought was brought up by Prof. William Galston in a March 2020 *Wall Street Journal* article on the Corona pandemic. The Corona crisis, which, if understood as a fairly unexpected and unlikely event with devastating consequences, should force us to rethink our security posture. Lean manufacturing and minimal "just-in-time" inventories have demonstrated how Corona has left many organizations unprepared, be it for the weekly shopping or the supply in hospitals.

When efficiency is understood as concentrating all our activities to a single geographic region or to using a single specific tool, all redundancy and slack is designed away. With such single point of failure, the insurance of diversity and redundancy is lost. An extreme local weather phenomenon or a tenacious virus could bring the global economic value creation to a halt. With increased efficiency, we end up with declined resilience.

Martin (2019) gave an illustrative example of declined resilience in monocultures: almonds were once grown in a number of places in America. Today, more than 80% of the world's almonds are produced in California's Central Valley. The high efficiency is a high price at the same time: California's almond blossoms all need to be pollinated in the same narrow window of time, because the trees grow in the same soil and experience the same weather.

This circumstance is exemplary for monocultures: a single factory produces a product, a single company holds sway in an industry, a single piece of software dominates all systems, a single sensor is responsible for two horrific aircraft crashes and years of grounding, and a single state has de facto global sovereignty over certain IT products and services. Diversity declines. Redundancy declines. Resilience declines.

Yet shouldn't resilience be a public good, in particular in the face of unexpected shocks? Shouldn't our society have the ability to recover from difficulties, to spring back into shape after an unexpected shock? Isn't resilience a fundamental societal need? Surprisingly, the seemingly most resilient form of governance, for which also Churchill has not found any better alternative, is highly inefficient: democracy. There are other examples indicating that thousands of years old achievements and circumstances prove either resilient or efficient, but not both. As Livnat and Papadimitriou have illustrated in 2016, sexual reproduction favors genes that work well with a greater diversity of other genes, which makes the species more adaptable to disruptive environmental changes—exactly what we defined as resilience. The efficiency of the selection process, however, is remarkably low when it comes to approximating the optimum solution. Nature prefers long-term over short-term optimization. *Tinder* prefers short-term efficiency over long-term resilience. Its efficiency lowers expectations by both parties, which is why around 32% of the couples who met online had broken up after a year (compared to 23% of those who met offline), according to a 2014 study by Michigan State University.

6   Resilience in Cyberspace, But How?

How then do we achieve more resilience, possibly without having to sacrifice the efficiency we have come to love, the efficiency that serves as a key source of competitive advantage?

Finding the sweet spot between two competing properties, resilience and efficiency, turns out to become a key challenge in the future of designing robust IT systems. For example, in data-driven economies, sorting algorithms play an important role in handling huge amounts of data. These algorithms are often selected solely based on their performance. As David Ackley reported in 2013, the most efficient algorithms known today, *MergeSort* and *Quicksort*, are not resilient against errors in the underlying comparison function. The slightly less efficient *BubbleSort*, however, is robust thanks to its redundancy in the comparison function. This example shows a viable path by accepting minimal losses in efficiency but, at the same time, increasing resilience in return.

Roger L. Martin proposes a number of steps to foster resilience. For example, the increase in efficiency as a justification for mergers in antitrust policy has led to the concentration of powers and market domination by a few powerful players. Such concentration leads to unstable monocultures and should therefore be avoided—in particular if local scopes and policies are dominated by global ones. The philosophy behind entrepreneurial decisions should not be guided not only by the quest for efficiency only but also by considerations of resilience.

Another example is the deliberate introduction of friction. The injection of productive friction can serve as a regular immunotherapy to build up resilience of organizations, societies, and ecosystems. Friction comes in various flavors, for instance as early as in the careful selection of candidates during the hiring process. Investing in a careful recruitment journey proves key to creating sustainable work environments: preserving and developing an organization's culture not only creates resilience but also long-term productivity. In general, labor should not be considered a cost; it is a productive resource that should be treated as such. For example, allowing for slack so that employees have time to serve customers in unanticipated, yet valuable, ways creates enthusiasm and excitement, both for customers and employees.

Coming back to connected ecosystems and distributed networks, a number of principles can help increase resilience. Most important is a mind shift of participants and operators to move away from striving for efficiency. Instead, parts of the resources saved through digitization should be spent on increasing their resilience. Slack and friction should be introduced at every node of the network, well accepting that the increase of the cost per node is unavoidable to preserve the value of a network as described by Metcalfe, Law, and others.

In terms of information security, every node's effort boils down to having strong authentication processes (with more than a single factor) and a zero-trust mindset (with more local checks and skepticism than stupid belief). On the network level, it is important to implement compartmentalization (with more containers than one—possibly efficient—monolith) and redundancy (with more than the absolute minimum necessary). Finally, we should remind ourselves that richness in species (or "biodiversity") is a desirable goal also in the digital space.

Success Factors for Cybersecurity

- Network effects are responsible for 70% of the value created by technology, from which also attacking adversaries benefit. Including the measures necessary for protecting a network's value, the cost of a network grows beyond linear.
- A host of classical cybersecurity measures exist for keeping attackers at bay, e.g., continuous monitoring and anomaly detection, incident response and digital forensics, regular penetration testing, creating awareness, blue and red team exercises, network segmentation and security-by-design, and security-by-default.
- The ubiquitous quest for efficiency is a key reason of why cyber insecurity is on the rise. Consequently, efficiency as a business goal should be rethought and put in comparison with a potential increase in resilience for socio-economical ecosystems.

References

Allyn B (2020) Researchers: nearly half of accounts tweeting about coronavirus are likely bots. https://www.npr.org/sections/coronavirus-live-updates/2020/05/20/859814085/researchers-nearly-half-of-accounts-tweeting-about-coronavirus-are-likely-bots. Accessed 5 Sept 2020

Chaffee I (2016) Real or not? USC study finds many political tweets come from fake accounts. University of Southern California. https://news.usc.edu/110565/rigged-usc-study-finds-many-political-tweets-come-from-fake-accounts/. Accessed 3 Sept 2020

Martin RL (2019) Competitive strategy: the high price of efficiency. https://hbr.org/2019/01/the-high-price-of-efficiency. Accessed 8 Nov 2020

Moore S (2020) Gartner predicts 75% of CEOs will be personally liable for cyber-physical security incidents by 2024. https://www.gartner.com/en/newsroom/press-releases/2020-09-01-gartner-predicts-75%2D%2Dof-ceos-will-be-personally-liabl. Accessed 10 Sept 2020

Nakamo S (2009) Bitcoin: a peer-to-peer electronic cash system. https://bitcoin.org/bitcoin.pdf

Newberg M (2017) As many as 48 million Twitter accounts aren't people, says study. https://www.cnbc.com/2017/03/10/nearly-48-million-twitter-accounts-could-be-bots-says-study.html. Accessed 5 Sept 2020

NfX (2017) 70 percent of value in tech is driven by network effects. https://www.nfx. com/post/70-percent-value-network-effects/. Accessed 5 Nov 2020

Varol O, Ferrara E, Davis CA, Menczer F, Flammini A (2017) Online human-bot interactions: detection, estimation, and characterization. https://arxiv.org/ pdf/1703.03107.pdf

Young VA (2020) Nearly half of the twitter accounts discussing 'reopening America' may be bots. https://www.cmu.edu/news/stories/archives/2020/may/twitter-bot-campaign.html. Accessed 4 Nov 2020

Raphael M. Reischuk, Dr., is distinguished consultant for information security, head of cyber security, and Partner at Zühlke, Vice President of the Cyber Security Committee of Digital Switzerland, and a member of the Cyber Security Advisory Board of the Swiss Academy of Engineering Sciences (SATW). Raphael appears regularly on topics of network, web, and cyber security. He is the author of numerous scientific publications in various fields of information security and cryptography, for which he has received several awards. After studying computer science and mathematics with a focus on information security, Raphael Reischuk received his PhD in web and cloud security at the CISPA Helmholtz Center for Information Security, Germany, and Cornell University, NY, and graduated with distinction. At ETH Zurich, he has done research and teaching on secure Internet protocols and co-developed the new Internet architecture SCION. After a comprehensive research work spanning 12 years, he currently applies his expert knowledge as a distinguished consultant at Zühlke.

Patent Strategies in the Networked Economy

Martin A. Bader and Oliver Gassmann

1 The Rise of a New Patent Value and Enforcement Culture

Many industries are moving toward connected business. The automotive industry considers "connected car" as one of their strategic top topics in 2020 (see also Chapter "Mobility: From Autonomous Driving Towards Mobility-as-a-Service"); the health-care industry has digital health care in diagnostic and intervention as a hot topic for the next decade (see Chapter "Digital Health Interventions"). Also, the whole machinery industry is promoting smart manufacturing and smart services like remote diagnostic, remote parametrization, remote system optimization, and remote maintenance for machines (see chapter "Industry 4.0—Navigating Pathways Towards Smart Manufacturing and Services" and "GF Machining Solutions—Real-Time Manufacturing Process in a Cloud Environment" 6). All these industries are used to have clear innovation protection strategies. However, when these

M. A. Bader (✉)
BGW AG Management Advisory Group, St. Gallen, Switzerland
e-mail: martin.bader@bgw-sg.com

O. Gassmann
Institute of Technology Management, University of St. Gallen,
St. Gallen, Switzerland
e-mail: oliver.gassmann@unisg.ch

© The Author(s), under exclusive license to Springer Nature Switzerland AG 2021
O. Gassmann, F. Ferrandina (eds.), *Connected Business*,
https://doi.org/10.1007/978-3-030-76897-3_14

industries moved toward connectivity, they faced new challenges how to capture value. In the area of connectivity, the aggressive patent culture of the semiconductor and telecommunication industry comes into place. This has a huge impact on the way innovation is protected (Gassmann and Bader 2017; Gassmann et al. 2021).[1]

Every industry which goes into connected business will be confronted with a different patent behavior. Some characteristics are:

- Value-based patent management, where the concrete value created by means of patents is in focus—compared to traditional cost-oriented patent management. *Google*, for example, bought *Motorola* primarily in order to acquire its patents and therefore be able to play in the field of connected business.
- New licensing models are imposed, compared to traditional fee per unit or fee per turnover as such approaches. One game-changing approach by the licensors is to take the value into account a license would have for the licensee in the future. Currently, the automotive industry is confronted with a new patent licensing culture being imposed by the *telecom industry*.
- Aggressive enforcement of patents, frequently processed by patent assertion companies, often also characterized as *patent trolls*. These firms file and/or buy patents which they use for no other reason than suing manufacturing companies which might violate the patent. Various *car manufacturers* pay a two-digit amount of legal fees per year to defend themselves.

In the next years, a lot of new product features and services are expected through 5G technology. These will be all subsequent patent licensing cases for companies like *Ericsson* (2019): enhanced video services, real-time automation, monitoring and tracking, connected vehicle, autonomous robotics, hazard and maintenance sensing, smart surveillance, remote operations, augmented reality.

The 5G patent licensing business is expected to become a multi-billion US$ royalty business again if compared to the so far patent licensing royalty incomes from 3G to 4G (see Fig. 1). In 2016 the top ten of the 3G/4G standard essential patent (SEP) owners took 93% of the total licensing royalty income on mobile phones (Galetovic et al. 2018). Top earner is *Qualcomm* with US$ 7.7 billion, i.e., 54%.

---

[1] Parts of this chapter are excerpts from our book Gassmann et al. (2021) Patent Management – How to successfully protect innovation. Springer: Cham. Used with permission.

Basics on Patents

The most common used intellectual property rights are:
- Patents (technical inventions)
- Design patent (visual arrangements)
- Trademark (brand, acoustic sign, color, scent, 3D shape, business name, origin)
- Copyright (software code—only as such, writing, architecture, art, music)

A patent grants its owner the right to prevent others from:
- Commercially producing, using, offering, storing, importing, or selling the invention
- For a specific jurisdiction
- For a limited period

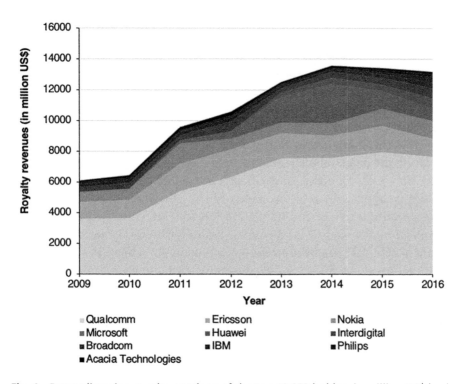

Fig. 1 Patent licensing royalty earnings of the top 10 SEP holders in million US$ business based on 3G and 4G (not limited to), Galetovic et al. (2018) and Pohlmann et al. (2020)

In Europe, an invention in the legal sense solves a technical problem with technology (IPI 2019). However, a granted patent does not necessarily confer on its owner the right of unlimited use for the invention. For example, other industrial property rights or other regulations may prevent the use of the invention by the inventor or the patent holder. Patents are therefore also referred to as exclusionary rights or prohibitive rights. The other types of industrial property rights also have this characteristic.

The *European Patent Office* (EPO), for example, grants patents for inventions which (EPC, Art. 52) are:

- New
- Based on an inventive step
- Commercially applicable

The criteria for novelty and for what is inventive are "absolute" and applicable worldwide, i.e., they are independent of the territorial origin of the knowledge available at the time of the priority date, the so-called state of the art. The priority date is usually the date of the first filing of the invention application at a patent office. The USA is still an exception, since the principle of the invention date (first-to-invent) is used to apply there, rather than the first-to-file principle. Under certain circumstances, in case of doubt, this can be used to substantiate the priority date.

During the patent application procedure, the patent applicant must determine for which countries he needs patent protection. The decision on the subsequent application must be made within 1 year of the priority date. Since there are various official and translation fees for each country/region named, the selection of countries or regions is typically based on the expected economic benefit that patent protection can potentially achieve in that country. The duration of patents is controlled by the patent applicant through the payment of annual fees, which are usually collected by the patent offices on an annual basis (not in the USA). In most countries, the maximum term of a patent is 20 years after the filing date. In the USA, patents filed after 8 June 1995 also have a term of 20 years.

If patent protection is intended in several countries, patent application procedures can be bundled internationally via the Patent Cooperation Treaty (PCT) and grant procedures for numerous European states via the European Patent Convention (EPC). For the area of connected business software becomes more important.

Important to know: Patents are exclusionary rights, not permissive rights—unfortunately a still widespread misconception, which often leads to erroneous investments in the millions. Patents are exclusionary rights which prohibit the imitation of the protected invention by third parties. As a logic consequence, owning patents therefore does not guarantee freedom of action in the patented area, e.g., a product may cover (i.e., "using") two patents, of which only one is owned by the product owner herself but the other patent being owned by a competitor. The latter might bargain on its patent.

When it comes to the question of what is ultimately accessible to patent protection—products, systems, processes, procedures, software, or even business models—regional legal areas play a major role.

2   Patents on Software

Whereas in the past the legal protection of software was mainly covered by copyright in practice, numerous companies now also strive to protect software innovations, also called computer-implemented inventions, by means of patents (see Table 1). It is interesting to note that the *SAP* software group did not start setting up its own patent department until 1998 and only held four software-related patents in May of 2001. The reason for establishing the patent department was the growing international competition in which patents played an increasingly important role.

The trigger for the "software patent boom" was a groundbreaking court decision, which in 1992 led to the so-called Freeman-Walter-Abele Test, which enabled the patenting of algorithms applied in practice and thus of software in the USA. In 1998, this test was replaced by the so-called *State Street Bank* court decision in the USA, which was affirmed in 1999. Mathematical algorithms thus became patentable if the invention led to a concrete and tangible result. This heralded the start of the business method patent era in the USA. As a result, the number of patent applications and granted patents in the software sector skyrocketed internationally at the turn of the millennium (Hall and MacGarvie 2010) to such an extent that there was increasing public criticism of patentability in this sector (Coriat and Orsi 2002). One of the most (in)famous patents was *Amazon's* so-called "1-Click"

Table 1 Four types of protection for software, author's own illustration

Results of software development	Right
– Documentation	– Copyright
– Screen appearance	– Design patents
– Code	– Trade dress
– Processes	– Patents
– Algorithms	
– Branding	– Trademarks

patent, which concerns a technology that makes it possible to make online purchases with a mouse click. *Amazon's* patent was granted in the USA in 1999 and was confirmed with some limitations after a reexamination procedure by the *US Patent and Trademark Office* (USPTO) in March 2010. In Europe, however, the application from the same patent family was not granted by the European Patent Office. While the procedural practice of the European Patent Office in the field of computer-implemented inventions has largely consolidated after some confusion in the mid-1990s, the practice was again confirmed by the Enlarged Board of Appeal of the European Patent Office in mid-2010.

The emerging patenting numbers gained considerable relevance in the software industry after the first patent infringement suits. Initially, mainly large companies were affected that generate large sales volumes and profits with a few product variants, such as *Apple, eBay, Google, Microsoft, SAP*, and *Oracle*. The Internet auction house *eBay* had to pay US$ 29.5 million in damages to *MercExchange* in 2003 after a patent infringement lawsuit, as *MercExchange's* patented proprietary auction technology also covered *eBay's* "buy now" feature. The damages were 30% of *eBay's* goodwill at the time. At the end of 2009, the Walldorf-based software group *SAP* was ordered to pay nearly US$ 140 million in damages to US competitor *Versata* following 2 years of patent infringement proceedings.

In addition to this, it is becoming increasingly clear that software, as a cross-sectional technology, has become a central factor in the convergence of technologies: The Taiwanese smartphone manufacturer *HTC* acquired a license from *Microsoft* after *Microsoft* accused the *Android* operating system, which now belongs to *Google*, of infringing several patents in areas of the user interface and the underlying system. The license agreement between *Microsoft* and *HTC* was concluded against the background that both companies' main competitor *Apple* had also sued *HTC* for infringing the *Linux*-based open-source operating system *Android* from *Google* out of 20 patents at the beginning of 2010. So even users of open-source software are not immune to patent infringement allegations. *Microsoft* in particular accused *Linux* that its operating system core infringes more than 230 of its patents and has already entered into license agreements with *Apple, Hewlett Packard, Novell*, and *Amazon*. In the latter case, *Microsoft* also received licenses to *Amazon* patents in return, which gave the software group easier access to the tablet computer market. This includes e-bookstore solutions that *Amazon*, among others, has at its disposal.

3   Patents on Business Methods in the USA

In 1997, the two applicants, Bernard L. Bilski and Rand A. Warsaw, applied in the USA for patent protection for a business method relating to a method of hedging risks in commodities trading. After the patent application had been rejected twice, first by the Board of Patent Appeals and Interferences and by then the US Court of Appeals for the Federal Circuit (CAFC), the US Supreme Court took up the issue of patentability of business method claims, which in particular also include business methods and software. The Supreme Court upheld the lower court's ruling that "concrete and tangible result" test is not necessarily a sufficient test of business method patentability. The so-called "machine-or-transformation" test introduced by the CAFC was not confirmed by the US Supreme Court as the only test for patentability, but only as a "useful tool for investigation."

Until the *Bilski*, patentability of business methods was based on the *State Street Bank* decision (delivered by the CAFC), where implemented procedures were patentable if they led to an applicable, concrete, and tangible result. As a result, a large number of patents on pure business methods were granted in the USA. With *State Street Bank*, the CAFC now questioned not only these earlier criteria in general but also the Freeman-Walter-Abele Test (delivered by the Court of Customs and Patent Appeals, a predecessor of the CAFC), which had been previously applied to software patents to examine the patentability of mathematical principles and algorithms.

The legal validity of patents of business methods and software-based processes was therefore no longer questioned in principle in the USA—but then came the so-called *Alice* decision that changed everything again. An interesting case is *Alice v. CLS Bank:* the Supreme Court readdressed the patent eligibility of a business method. It held patent ineligible a method of securing intermediated settlement—a form of electronic escrow. In invalidating Alice's patent, the Court announced a two-step test based on the Court's earlier decisions in *Mayo v. Prometheus* and *Funk Bros. Seed Co. v. Kalo Inoculant Co.* This test first determines whether the claimed invention is directed to an abstract idea, law of nature, mathematical formula, or similar abstraction. If it is, the court is to proceed to the second step—determining whether the way the claimed invention implements the abstraction contains an inventive concept, as contrasted with being routine and conventional. Under the Alice test, the claimed invention is patent eligible only if it contains an inventive concept.

The USPTO business method examining work groups responded quickly to the Alice decision. Allowances per month for patents related to finance dropped to 10% of their pre-Alice value. The Patent Trial and Appeal Board has reacted in a similar manner. Only about 20% of the appealed business method rejections by patent examiners are getting reversed by the board.

4   Patenting in the ICT World

Since the 1980s, the *information and communications technology (ICT)* sector has been a highly innovative and rapidly changing area. These technologies include computing and telecommunications and encompass new developments in emerging technologies, e.g. artificial intelligence (AI). More than a third of the 165,000 applications received by the European Patent Office (EPO) in 2017 concerned ICT directly or indirectly. Given this importance, the EPO has even created a specialized ICT department, which brings together several of the EPO's examiners from various other technical sections like computers or semiconductors. This puts EPO examiners in the best position to assess the alleged novelty of inventions described in patent applications (EPO 2018).

In many areas of the electronics, semiconductor, and telecommunications industries, patents are interdependent. Almost no company in these sectors can still develop and sell products independently without being dependent on third-party patents. Accordingly, companies such as *IBM* or *Siemens* are increasingly forced to pursue an open licensing policy and conclude cross-licensing agreements on a broad scale.

Due to market requirements, there are often broad areas of technical overlap. On the other hand, there are usually numerous different technical solution variants that offer the same functionality but can still meet the needed requirements. Since users are demanding ever greater modularization of technical devices, international and cross-company technical standardization initiatives have become unavoidable. These are particularly pronounced in the field of mobile communications. In the standardization committees, however, the companies involved must generally be prepared to sacrifice their patent portfolios in favor of a common standard that is then made available to all participants.

4.1   From GSM to UMTS Standard to 5G

In the late 1980s, when the *European Global System for Mobile communications (GSM)* standard was developed, the American company *Motorola* influenced the standardization process significantly using its own relevant patents, and it pursued a licensing policy that was unusually aggressive at the time (Granstrand 1999). Thus, the GSM standard was kept away from countries in which *Motorola* pursued other interests. In addition, specific licensing conditions could be enforced, such as cross-licensing, which secured *Motorola* access to competitors' patent and technology portfolios and determined the structure of the GSM supplier market (Bekkers et al. 2002): despite a small number of its own relevant patents, Siemens succeeded in joining the GSM standard at a later date. The French-German company Alcatel originally pursued a different technical solution, but this did not become the standard. Once the GSM standard had been defined, the company therefore had to build up a new patent portfolio.

The underlying patent portfolios also played an important role in the worldwide third-generation *Universal Mobile Telecommunications System (UMTS)* standard. There are significant technical dependencies on the *American Code Division Multiple Access (CDMA)* mobile communications standard. This was based on relevant patents of the American company *Qualcomm*, without which the UMTS standard could not be operated. The new race is now about who gets to be part of the new standard for the fifth-generation wireless technology for digital cellular networks "5G" (see Fig. 2).

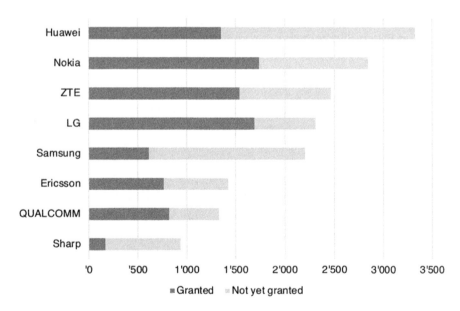

Fig. 2 The 5G patent owners' race: companies which have filed the most 5G SEP patent families as of Nov 2019, Statista, IPlytics (2019)

Patent portfolios are increasingly getting used to keep previously uninvolved newcomers out of the market through raising high barriers to market entry. Technical standards supported by patent portfolios and their licensing regulations force newcomers to disclose their own relevant intellectual property rights and make them available to standard participants. In return, a license to the standard is acquired. Such trade, however, comes up against its limits when standard-relevant patents exist, but their owners themselves have no intention of marketing their own, standard-compliant products, but are instead primarily aimed at licensing revenues.

4.2   The Smartphone Patent Wars

One of the more epic struggles in patenting took place around the so-called smartphone patent wars. As the smartphone was coming into its own, the various players in the industry realized the size and potential of the market. What ensued were dozens of lawsuits between *Apple, Sony Mobile, Google, HTC, Motorola, Microsoft, Nokia, Huawei, LG Electronics, Samsung,* and *ZTE.* This big battle entailed hundreds of thousands of patents ranging from the seemingly simple icon design to sophisticated high-frequency modem chips, and it included everything in between. The iPhone was released mid-2007, marking a new era in connectivity—*Nokia,* a key player in the cell phone industry, kicked the war off by filing suit against *Apple* in late 2009, when the revolutionary device started to gain traction. The Nordic telecommunications equipment provider contended that Apple had not contributed to the patent pool surrounding the GSM, UTMS, and wireless LAN standards and thus owed a royalty of 6–12 dollars per phone. *Apple* promptly countersued, alleging *Nokia* stole some of its technology in 13 patents, the licensing terms of *Nokia* were not *FRAND (fair, reasonable, and non-discriminatory),* and some of the patents in the standards were not enforceable (iam 2015, 2016).

The enmity also brought other players, not even involved in consumer technology, like *Oracle,* to attack *Google* over the use of *Java* in *Android.* It underscores how patent infringement comes out of the woodwork when there is a lot of money at stake; *Java* had become widespread for the very reason that the language was considered an open technology after *Sun Microsystems* had become defunct, and perhaps this is the main reason it had become so popular.

In the ICT sector *standard essential patents (SEPs)* play a key role. SEPs are often subject to compulsory licensing terms under *FRAND* conditions *(fair, reasonable, and non-discriminatory*). The FRAND idea has had to be—and currently still is—interpreted by several courts as having to come up with an operationalizable concept.

4.3   Case: *Apple* vs. *Samsung*

Apple sued *Samsung* in 2011; this case was launched in the broader context of the smartphone war (cf. supra). The lawsuit is a big conflict involving trademarks, patents, designs, trade dress,[2] technology standards, FRAND licensing, anti-trust law, and the patent doctrine of exhaustion.

While the lawsuit was centered around many software elements, trial documents show that these are very complex. The jury had to decide whether *Samsung* had violated rules surrounding "trade dress." It argued that *Samsung* copied its famously minimalistic packaging and design when marketing its devices in violation of its trade dress rights. The jury had to decide whether *Apple's* trade dress was famous and by extension protectable.

Apple also invoked its design rights, alleging *Samsung* had copied its industrial designs filed for the iPhone. In the same suit, *Samsung* had alleged violation of several of its utility patents. The burden of proof in the case was whether it would be "proven by clear and convincing evidence that *Apple's* infringement was willful." *Apple* had even claimed trademark violation under USC §1114 and general trademark law. This intellectual property right was used to cover its icons, design, user interface, and look and feel. On top of those types of rights, *Apple* had claimed various anti-trust violations by *Samsung* for certain Universal Mobile Telecommunications System (UMTS) patents in violation of the US Sherman Anti-Trust Act of 1890. Furthermore, *Apple* claimed that *Samsung* had not offered its standard essential patents at a fair, reasonable, and non-discriminatory royalty (FRAND) rate.

Apple also invoked a more obscure defense against *Samsung's* claims. A doctrine of patent law is the concept of "exhaustion," which means that once the patented product has entered into commercial circulation—the patent right becomes exhausted. The reason for this doctrine is simple—it would be far too complex in an economy to manage a patent royalty right extending beyond the first sale. *Apple* alleged that *Samsung* had granted licenses to baseband chip suppliers, and that once they had done this, *Samsung* had

---

[2] Trade dress deals with the visual presentation of the product, such as colors, shape, markings, fonts, and presentation which shows the consumer the source of the product (see Table 1).

"exhausted" its patent rights on the technology and could not then come after *Apple* for violation of these same patents, even if it incorporated *Samsung's* technology via these chips.

5   Patents in the IoT World

More than 6,700 patent applications for inventions relating to autonomous objects were filed at the European Patent Office (EPO) in 2018 alone, and in the last 3 years, the rate of growth for industrial Internet of things (IoT) patent applications was 54% (see Fig. 3), outstripping the 7.65% overall growth of patent applications over the last 3 years. Connectivity and the application domains personal and enterprise have attracted the largest numbers of such patent applications so far, while the fastest-growing fields are 3D systems, artificial intelligence, and user interfaces.

The rise in IoT inventions has been across all three main subsectors. However, the actual number of inventions varies depending on the subsector to sector. Application domains and core technologies capture a larger share of inventions, with the number of inventions relating to enabling technologies being significantly smaller. In recent years, the number of inventions involving core technologies has been increasing at a faster rate, almost catching up with the application domains.

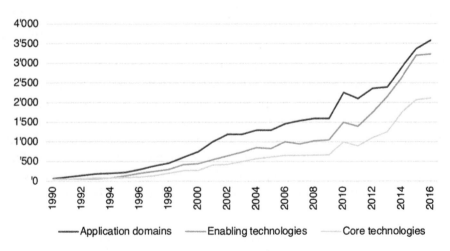

Fig. 3 IoT patent applications at the EPO by technology fields, EPO (2017) and EPO (2020)

The top 20 companies, most of them located in Asia, accounted for 42% of all industrial IoT patent applications recently filed with the EPO. Innovation in core technologies is mainly led by a limited number of large companies focused on *information and communications technologies (ICTs)*. Inventions in enabling technologies and application domains are less concentrated, and the top applicants in these sectors originate from a larger variety of industries (see Fig. 4).

Europe, the USA, and Japan have been the main principle centers of innovation of industrial IoT technologies since the mid-1990s. Large US, European, and Japanese companies from various sectors comprise the dominant applicants in the IoT enabling technologies. IoT innovation started later in China and Korea, which is dominated by a few ICT companies. *LG* and *Samsung* control 90% of the IoT applications in Korea; *Huawei* and *ZTE* control 70% of *"4IR,"* also called as *fourth industrial revolution,* based patents in China.

In Europe, 4IR innovation tends to cluster in Munich and Paris. France and Germany are the dipoles of 4IR technological development. Germany has been the leader since the late 1990s, and it excels in the fields of

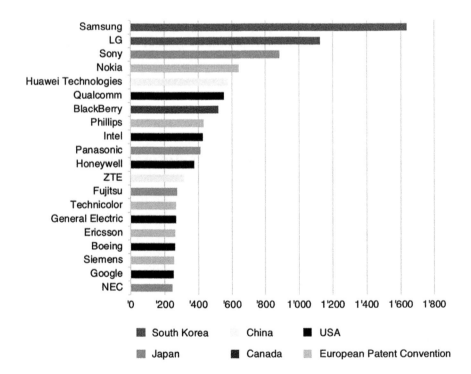

Fig. 4 Top 20 industrial IoT patent applicants at the EPO, EPO (2017) and EPO (2020)

manufacturing, vehicles, and infrastructure. The technological profile of France, along with the Benelux and Nordic countries, is specialized more in AI, user interface, 3D processing, and security. *Philips, Nokia,* and *Ericsson* are key innovation players in those locations. Some forecast project that developments in the IoT will accelerate the advent of the fourth industrial revolution. If anything, the software and social organization to organize the underlying technology have been developing in these regions and organizations. Technology is outstripping the legal paradigm's ability to cope. For example, it has raised what legal and liability changes will be needed in order to allow for self-driving cars, which are arguably statistically safer than human drivers already, but where culpability and liability have not been clarified legally. Taken one step further, society has to consider legally when software and networked devices might allow each one to be its own economic agent using distributed ledger technology, such as the IOTA protocol from the *IOTA Foundation* (EPO 2017, 2020).

6   Patents in the "Connected" Automotive World

As connectivity becomes essential in automotive, so does the strategic pressure increase on patent management for the automotive industry. We want to highlight two interesting phenomena: *patent pools* to license technologies based on the example of *Avanci* and a public commons *patent sharing* approach based on the example of *Tesla*.

6.1   ICT Patent Pool *Avanci* Attacks Automotive

Avanci is a patent pool in the ICT space. *Volvo* along with 14 others, including major automotive brands, has signed patent licensing agreements with *Avanci* to get access to its patent pool. Cars increasingly rely on wireless connectivity.

The *Avanci* patent pool was conceived both to monetize patents and also to eliminate a lot of the legal challenges in the space. Some of the *Avanci* members *(Nokia, Sharp, Conversant)* have sued *Daimler* to coax the company to agree to its licensing terms. The case went into mediation, which eventually failed. *Continental Automotive Systems* argued that *Avanci* in acting for its members violated (fair, reasonable, and non-discriminatory) FRAND principles. *Avanci* would prefer to license to the end-user automotive company, but *Daimler* has resisted this since the royalty rates are then assessed not on the components, which suppliers like *Continental* make, but instead on the end product. To use a concrete case: *Continental* needs a 20-dollar baseband chip, and *Avanci* wants 15 dollars per car—meaning the royalty would be a 75% markup on the cost of that component—the complete connectivity module, which *Continental* sells, is only 75 dollars. *Continental* thus asserts this is not reasonable or fair, considering that patent royalties conventionally have constituted only a 5–15% markup, perhaps US$ 2—so, whether the parties can close the gap remains to be seen (Ropes and Gray 2019; Juve 2020). European case law is still developing in the area of FRAND and standard essential patents (cf. infra "Smartphone Patent Wars").

6.2   *Tesla:* The Pacemaker

One of the most interesting patent strategies of a very high profile and large company is that of *Tesla*. *Tesla* renounced its IP in favor of any open innovation strategy. The following is an ungrammatically titled explanation from Elon Musk himself—it's not that common for a CEO to directly discuss an IP strategy beyond a few platitudes. "All Our Patent Are Belong to You" said *Tesla* CEO Elon Musk (June 12, 2014). Yesterday, there was a wall of Tesla patents in the lobby of our Palo Alto headquarters. That is no longer the case. They have been removed, in the spirit of the open-source movement, for the advancement of electric vehicle technology. *Tesla Motors* was created to accelerate the advent of sustainable transport. If we clear a path to the creation of compelling electric vehicles, but then lay intellectual property landmines behind us to inhibit others, we are acting in a manner contrary to that goal. *Tesla* will not initiate patent lawsuits against anyone who, in good faith, wants to use our technology. When I started out with my first company, *Zip2*, I thought patents were a good thing and worked hard to obtain them. And maybe they were good long ago, but too often these days they serve merely to stifle progress, entrench the positions of giant corporations, and enrich those in the legal profession, rather than the actual inventors. After *Zip2*, when I realized that receiving a patent really just meant that you bought a lottery ticket to a lawsuit, I avoided them whenever possible.

At *Tesla*, however, we felt compelled to create patents out of concern that the big car companies would copy our technology and then use their massive manufacturing, sales, and marketing power to overwhelm *Tesla*. We couldn't have been more wrong. The unfortunate reality is the opposite: electric car programs (or programs for any vehicle that doesn't burn hydrocarbons) at the major manufacturers are small to nonexistent, constituting an average of far less than 1% of their total vehicle sales.

At best, the large automakers are producing electric cars with limited range in limited volume. Some produce no zero emission cars at all.

Given that annual new vehicle production is approaching 100 million per year and the global fleet is approximately 2 billion cars, it is impossible for Tesla to build electric cars fast enough to address the carbon crisis. By the same token, it means the market is enormous. Our true competition is not the small trickle of non-Tesla electric cars being produced, but rather the enormous flood of gasoline cars pouring out of the world's factories every day.

We believe that *Tesla*, other companies making electric cars, and the world would all benefit from a common, rapidly evolving technology platform.

Technology leadership is not defined by patents, which history has repeatedly shown to be small protection indeed against a determined competitor, but rather by the ability of a company to attract and motivate the world's most talented engineers. We believe that will strengthen rather than diminish Tesla's position in this regard (Tesla 2020).

Beyond Elon's high-minded explanation lies actually some very savvy business acumen. By allowing others to use Tesla's technology, he helped roll out the charging stations needed. Moreover, Musk's vision and attitude coincides with the *Tesla* brand. In short, the brand value may be. It's also worth noting that Musk's phrase "initiate patent lawsuits against anyone who, in good faith, wants to use our technology," wouldn't exactly convince legal expert at a major car company to allow cars to go into production. Most of Elon's value added lies not in an ancient motor technology, but rather in the car's software, especially in the sophisticated AI and self-driving features—all of which is trade secret and copyrighted.

Success Factors of Patenting the Connected Business

- Fields like enhanced video services, real-time automation, monitoring and tracking, autonomous robotics and cars, maintenance sensing, smart surveillance, and remote operations are based on connectivity and will import the new patent value, licensing, and enforcement culture.
- Prepare for value-based patent strategies, different licensing practices, and more aggressive enforcement of patents in the area of connectivity. Be ready for patent assertion and patent trolls that do not belong—at least not yet!—to your industry.
- Patents are exclusionary rights, not permissive rights. That means a patent prohibits the imitation of the protected invention by third parties but does not automatically guarantee you freedom of action.
- Software, i.e., the code, as such is legally covered by copyright law; however, software and its applied algorithms may be patented as computer-implemented inventions.

References

Bekkers R, Duysters G, Verspagen B (2002) Intellectual property rights, strategic technology agreements and market structure: the case of GSM. Res Policy 31(7):1141–1161

Coriat B, Orsi F (2002) Establishing a new intellectual property rights regime in the United States: origins, content and problems. Res Policy 31(8–9):1491–1507

EPO (2017) Patents and the fourth industrial revolution. In: The inventions behind digital transformation. European Patent Office, Munich

EPO (2018) Information and communications technology patents at the EPO. European Patent Office, Munich. https://www.epo.org/news-issues/issues/ict/about-ict.html

EPO (2020) Patents and the fourth industrial revolution. In: The global technology trends enabling the data-driven economy. European Patent Office, Munich

Ericsson (2019) The internet of things: challenges for IP and best practices (Dr. C Tapia) Management Circle IP Service World: Munich, November 2019

Galetovic A, Haber S, Zaretzki L (2018) An estimate of the average cumulative royalty yield in the world mobile phone industry: theory, measurement and results. Telecommun Policy 42(3):263–276. https://doi.org/10.1016/j.telpol.2018.02.002

Gassmann O, Bader MA (2017) Patentmanagement – Innovationen erfolgreich nutzen und schützen, 4th edn. Springer, Berlin

Gassmann O, Bader MA, Thompson M (2021) Patent management – protecting intellectual property and innovation. Springer Nature, Cham

Granstrand O (1999) The economics and management of intellectual property. In: Towards intellectual capitalism. Edward Elgar, Northampton, MA

Hall BH, MacGarvie M (2010) The private value of software patents. Res Policy 39(7):994–1009

iam (2015) In search of the next patent war. https://www.iam-media.com/litigation/search-next-patent-war, accessed 2020-04-11

iam (2016) Innovation and survival: lessons from the smartphone wars. https://www.iam-media.com/innovation-and-survival-lessons-smartphone-wars, accessed 2020-04-11

IPI (2019) Gedacht. Gemacht. Geschützt. Marken, Patente und Co. auf den Punkt gebracht, 9th edn. IPI Swiss Federal Institute of Intellectual Property, Bern

Juve (2020) Collision course set for Nokia and Daimler. https://www.juve-patent.com/news-and-stories/cases/collision-course-set-for-nokia-and-daimler/ & Hopes dwindle for peaceful settlement between Nokia and Daimler. https://www.juve-patent.com/news-and-stories/cases/hopes-dwindle-for-peaceful-settlement-between-nokia-and-daimler/, Accessed 2020-03-18

Pohlmann T, Blind K, Heß P (2020) Studie zur Untersuchung und Analyse der Patentsituation bei der Standardisierung von 5G. Study on behalf of the German Bundesministerium für Wirtschaft und Energie, Berlin

Ropes and Gray (2019) Continental Automotive v. Wireless SEP Licensing Presents Challenges for Automotive Industry, Avanci. https://www.lexology.com/library/detail.aspx?g=2e0a83b4-6e78-4faa-8311-9b6e4a0c945f

Statista/IPlytics (2019) Who is Leading the 5G Patent Race? Companies which have filed the most patents for 5G technology as of November 2019. https://www.statista.com/chart/20095/companies-with-most-5g-patent-families-and-patent-families-applications/. Accessed 11 April 2020

Tesla (2020). https://www.tesla.com/about/legal#patent-pledge. Accessed 6 Sept 2020

Martin A. Bader, Prof. Dr., is a European and Swiss Patent Attorney, as well as Partner and Co-Founder of the specialized innovation and intellectual property management advisory group BGW AG St. Gallen. He is Professor for Technology Management and Entrepreneurship at the University of Applied Sciences Ingolstadt (THI). Previously, he was Head of the IP Competence Center at the University of St. Gallen (HSG) and was Vice President and Chief Intellectual Property Officer at Infineon Technologies in Munich until 2002. Further, Martin is a mediator at the Mediation Center for Alternative Dispute Resolution at the World Intellectual Property Organization (WIPO) and has for many years been regarded as being among the top 300 intellectual property strategists worldwide according to the *Intellectual Asset Management* magazine's IAM strategy 300 index.

Oliver Gassmann, Prof. Dr., is Professor for Technology Management at the University of St. Gallen and Director of the Institute of Technology Management since 2002. His research focus lies on patterns and success factors of innovation. He has been visiting faculty at Berkeley (2007), Stanford (2012), and Harvard (2016). Prior to his academic career, Gassmann was the head of corporate research at Schindler. His more than 400 publications are highly cited; his book *The Business Model Navigator* became a global bestseller. He received the Scholarly Impact Award of the Journal of Management in 2014. He founded several spin-offs, is member of several boards of directors, like Zühlke, and is an internationally recognized keynote speaker.

Part III

Case Studies on Connected Business

Bosch IoT Suite: Exploiting the Potential of Smart Connected Products

Sven Jung, Stefan Ferber, Irene Cramer,
Wolfgang Bronner, and Felix Wortmann

1 Towards Smart Connected Products

The Internet of Things (IoT), i.e. the convergence of the physical and digital world, promises enormous business potential and will have a lasting impact on every industry (Iansiti and Lakhani 2014; Porter and Heppelmann 2014, 2015). Specifically, smart, connected products will change the way how manufacturing companies create and capture value in both B2B and B2C (Porter and Heppelmann 2014, 2015). Well-known examples of manufacturing

---

S. Jung (✉)
University of St. Gallen, St. Gallen, Switzerland
e-mail: sven.jung@unisg.ch

S. Ferber • I. Cramer
Robert Bosch GmbH, Stuttgart, Germany
e-mail: stefan.ferber@bosch-si.com; rene.cramer@softwareag.com

W. Bronner
Bosch IoT Lab at University of St. Gallen & ETH Zurich, St. Gallen, Switzerland
e-mail: wolfgang.bronner@bosch.com

F. Wortmann
University of St. Gallen, Institute of Technology Management,
St. Gallen, Switzerland
e-mail: felix.wortmann@unisg.ch

© The Author(s), under exclusive license to Springer Nature Switzerland AG 2021   **267**
O. Gassmann, F. Ferrandina (eds.), *Connected Business*,
https://doi.org/10.1007/978-3-030-76897-3_15

companies that are already successfully using the IoT today are *Tesla* (connected cars) in automotive, *Philips* (connected lighting) and *Sonos* (connected speakers) in smart home as well as *John Deere* (connected tractors) in agriculture and *Trumpf* (connected machines) in the domain of Industry 4.0.

At the same time, many manufacturing companies find it challenging to develop successful IoT offerings. Oftentimes, their expectations in terms of revenue and profit remain unmet (Wortmann et al. 2019). A recent study from 2020 showed that 58% of IoT projects are either mostly or completely unsuccessful (Beecham Research 2020). From a provider perspective, the reasons for failure vary from internal challenges (e.g. lacking capabilities) to external ones (e.g. immature technology). However, one very common challenge is the lack of business focus. Companies concentrate on technology and lose sight of the focal business problem they are trying to solve for their customers. In fact, many companies still search for compelling and financially viable use cases that go beyond 'chasing the cool factor' (Kranz 2017). In light of the depicted challenges, this chapter is focusing on IoT and manufacturing companies and addresses three fundamental questions: What are the recurring and proven IoT use cases across different manufacturing industries? How can they be leveraged by manufacturing companies? And what role do IoT platforms play in enabling these use cases?

2   Internet of Things for Manufacturing Companies

In the context of manufacturing, the term industrial IoT (IIoT) is omnipresent. However, the lines between IIoT and IoT are very blurry and the concepts are often used interchangeably. IIoT refers to the specific application of IoT in an industrial and B2B setting (Boyes et al. 2018). One prominent example is the connected factory (Industry 4.0) where machine-to-machine communication and automation play an important role. Despite different perspectives on IoT, utilizing IoT relies on common fundamental principles across manufacturing companies independent from the domain. Every IoT solution is based on a smart, connected product such as an industrial machine or smart speaker. The objective is to complement a physical product or device (e.g. tractor) with software and sensors (e.g. to track the GPS and engine data of a tractor) to make it 'smart'. Connecting the smart device with the Internet enables different levels of capability: Smart, connected products can be remotely (a) monitored,

(b) controlled or (c) optimized. Depending on the domain, they can also operate (d) autonomously (Porter and Heppelmann 2014).

In the long term, the IoT can enable manufacturing companies to offer their customers a hybrid value proposition that is both physical and digital. This usually includes the analysis of data (gathered through the connected products) to offer value-adding digital services (Fleisch et al. 2014). However, every IoT solution must ultimately solve an unmet need for either the manufacturing company itself or the end customer. Depending on the data source, the literature distinguishes four ways in which IoT data can be used by manufacturing companies (Bilgeri et al. 2019) (Fig. 1).

The first two opportunities relate to smart, connected products, which are not owned by the customer but are in the direct sphere of influence of the respective company. Agricultural service providers that provide harvesting services to farmers, for example, use IoT data from their agricultural machinery to improve the efficiency of their internal processes (domain 1). Telemetry data enables them to monitor the position and operating status of their agricultural machinery and optimize their fleet management. Beyond internal process innovation, the telemetry data can also be used for new products and services. The use of highly specialized, high-performance agricultural machinery has become so expensive that customers require precise minute-by-minute billing. Telemetry data enables such billing, which is perceived as a real value add and thus a differentiating service (domain 2). Connecting agricultural

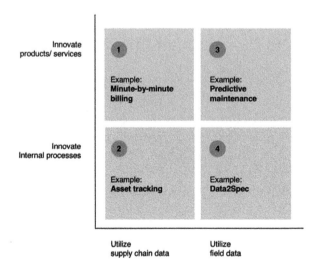

Fig. 1 Four domains to utilize IoT data, Bilgeri et al. (2019)

machinery thereby leads to internal process optimization as well as service innovation for the customer.

The third and fourth opportunity is based on data that is generated by products in the field, i.e. while in use by the customer. *Heidelberger* can serve as an example to illustrate these opportunities. With its connected solutions, the manufacturer of industrial printing systems is in a position to offer innovative services such as predictive maintenance (domain 3). In the event of a malfunction, the system (located at a customer site) automatically sends an electronic error message to *Heidelberger*, enabling service technicians to carry out repair work remotely or to bring the right spare parts directly to the site if necessary. The monetization of this new data-driven service offering, however, covers only part of the IoT potential of connected printing equipment. At the same time, the IoT data is also used to optimize the development processes of *Heidelberger* (domain 4). In the data-to-specification (*Data2Spec*) use case, historic machine data that captures real-world machine usage serves as the basis to prevent costly under- or over-specification of new product generations. Hence, the connectivity of printing machines also leads to service innovation for the customer as well as internal process optimization at *Heidelberger*.

Given the technological possibilities and the increasing number of success stories, there is little doubt that the IoT will transform many industries in the long term. It will alter the way companies design and develop their products and services. At the same time, a new technology stack is emerging, and manufacturing companies need new skills to successfully deliver IoT solutions (Porter and Heppelmann 2015).

3   *Bosch* IoT Suite as an IoT Platform

IoT platforms have become an integral part of IoT projects. Their goal is to provide a manufacturing company with the necessary technology to quickly build and scale an IoT solution. However, the nature of IoT platforms is quite diverse. The value generation of IoT platforms for manufacturing companies can range from very generic (e.g. generic cloud storage) to very specific (e.g. remote update capabilities on the application level) services. Three fundamental IoT platform layers can be distinguished (Fig. 2): infrastructure-as-a-service (IaaS), platform-as-a-service (PaaS) and software-as-a-service (SaaS).

Smart, connected products form the basis for every IoT solution (level 0). The first IoT platform level corresponds to generic cloud services such as cloud storage and computing (storage and computing can also take place on the device itself). This level is often referred to as the infrastructure level (level

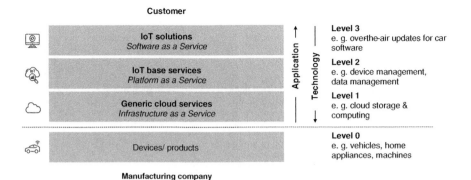

Fig. 2 New IoT technology stack and corresponding IoT platform levels, author's own illustration

1). The next level corresponds to IoT base services (level 2). Offered as PaaS, these services range from the management of devices to the management of data. Applications solving a concrete need for the end-user are built on top of these two levels. The solution level (level 3) is typically very specific to one industry or customer. This could be, for example, a SaaS solution specifically developed for a manufacturer of cars (OEM) to remotely update its large fleet of cars across the globe securely and reliably.

The importance of IoT platforms for developing ready-to-use IoT solutions has led to a strategic buy-or-build question for manufacturing companies. One can either build their own IoT platform or source a third-party platform. Indeed, many large manufacturing companies have developed their own IoT platform to be more independent of third-party providers. In addition, they are also trying to establish themselves as a provider of an IoT platform. For instance, *Bosch* launched its own IoT platform with the *Bosch* IoT Suite in 2013 as one of the first manufacturing companies, alongside *General Electric* with *Predix* and *Siemens* with *MindSphere*. However, over the last years, many IoT platforms have emerged (150+ and counting) creating a very diverse set of IoT platforms (Graf et al. 2018; Hodapp et al. 2019). This diverse competitive landscape makes it increasingly difficult for a manufacturing company to navigate through. Looking at today's market, four main types of IoT platform providers can be distinguished:

1. Companies with a background in manufacturing (e.g. *Bosch, Hitachi*).
2. Companies with a background in Product-Lifecycle Management software (e.g. *PTC, Siemens*).
3. Companies with a pure software background (e.g. *Software AG*).
4. Hyper-scalers with a background in generic cloud services (e.g. *AWS, Microsoft*).

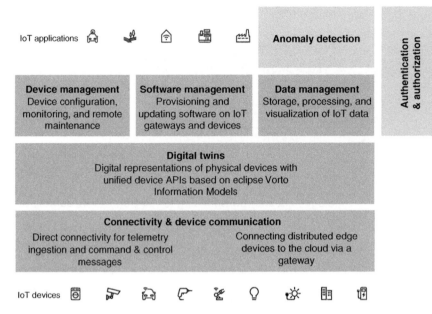

Fig. 3 Bosch IoT Suite services on the PaaS level, Bosch.IO (2020b)

As part of the first group, the *Bosch* IoT Suite, operated by *Bosch.IO*, serves as an IoT platform for *Bosch* internally and external customers. *Bosch.IO* is an independent subsidiary that supports *Bosch* business units and external customers in their digitalization efforts by providing IoT (software) solutions, such as the *Bosch* IoT Suite. Specifically, the *Bosch* IoT Suite focuses on scalable IoT services offered as PaaS, ranging from software for device connectivity and communication to device and data management (Fig. 3). As of today, already more than ten million devices are connected on the basis of the *Bosch* IoT Suite (Bosch.IO 2020a). On the infrastructure level, *Bosch* offers its own cloud service but also enables hybrid cloud set-ups. Hybrid cloud set-ups combine third-party cloud solutions (e.g. *AWS* or *Microsoft Azure*) with IoT services provided by the *Bosch* IoT Suite. Also, industry- and customer-specific use cases are developed. To distinguish itself from other IoT platform providers, the *Bosch* IoT Suite builds on three strategic pillars:

- **Developing open-source software:** Since early on, *Bosch* has been a member of the *Eclipse* IoT working group and has set up several open-source projects. Today, the majority of the *Bosch* IoT Suite is based on open-source software. The decision to provide an open-source IoT platform has several advantages. A strong developer community can lead to better quality in the software benefiting both *Bosch* and its customers. It also provides speed and cost advantages for Bosch as an IoT platform provider. At the same time, *Bosch* customers remain independent (from one provider).

- **Leveraging industry knowledge:** With a long history as a manufacturing company and supplier in various industries, *Bosch.IO* can build on the strong domain know-how of the entire *Bosch Group*. This know-how (e.g. in automotive and household appliances) benefits also customers of the *Bosch* IoT Suite as *Bosch.IO* can develop applications tailored to the needs of a well-known domain.
- **Innovating on proven IoT solutions:** The *Bosch* IoT Suite is used internally by the business units to connect and innovate their products. Today, 92% of all *Bosch* electronic product classes can be connected to the Internet (Denner, 2020). Using the IoT platform internally to become a digital manufacturer has provided *Bosch.IO* with a comprehensive set of proven IoT solutions. These proven solutions are also offered to its customers enabling them to 'manufacture like a *Bosch*'.

4   Six Core IoT Use Cases for Manufacturing Companies

In the last years, IoT base services such as IoT device management have become more and more a commodity. Hence, attractive use cases on the application level—that go beyond the 'cool' factor—became the new source of competitive advantage. In light of this development, we looked at success stories at *Bosch* as well as its customers to identify the most attractive and replicable IoT use cases across industries. In recognition of *Bosch*'s rich history in manufacturing, we focused our analysis on those IoT use cases that provide an added value for manufacturers of discrete products. Through our analysis, we have derived six cross-domain (horizontal) IoT use cases which aim to solve the following needs for a manufacturing company across domains (Fig. 4):

(a) Manufacturers want to provide **better products and services** to their customers.
(b) Manufacturers want to **increase their customers' productivity and experience**.
(c) Manufacturers want to continuously **improve and innovate their portfolio**.

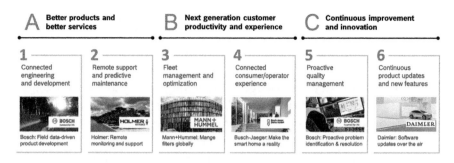

Fig. 4 Framework with six horizontal IoT use cases, author's own illustration

The first two horizontal IoT use cases help manufacturing companies to improve their products and services. This is primarily enabled by remote access to their smart, connected products in the field.

4.1   Connected Engineering and Development

Description

Operational data of devices in the field such as information on device status, usage or failures is used to define future product specifications. Rather than relying on assumptions of how a product might be used in reality, actual field data provides companies with a more accurate picture of the actual use of a particular product in the field. This transparency helps companies to design and develop better products in the long run. For instance, by connecting car brakes to the Internet, *Bosch* was able to measure the actual hydraulic load in a particular car model. This unique insight enabled *Bosch* to use an existing braking system instead of modifying the system as recommended by existing validation models, which were only based on assumed loads. The additional insights prevented Bosch from over-engineering the new generation of brakes. Furthermore, IoT field data and remote access can be used to accelerate and improve product development and validation. Product innovations in the pipeline can be tested, validated and adapted based on models fed with field data—instead of models only based on assumptions.

Business Value

The use case 'connected engineering and development' helps manufacturing companies to reduce cost arising from over-specification of products. As companies typically design products based on a variety of assumptions, products often end up being over-specified, i.e. with features that are not necessarily needed or desired by the end-user. At the same time, this use case helps companies to avoid unsatisfied customers due to under-specification of the respective products. Last but not least, it can shorten time-to-market and development cycles, especially in the validation phase of a new product in the pipeline.

4.2   Remote Support and Predictive Maintenance

Description

While the first use case aims to use IoT technology at an early stage of the value chain (i.e. in product design and development), the second IoT use case aims to improve (after-sales) service. This is based on the condition that not only the customer but also the manufacturer can monitor and access products in the field remotely. This offers the manufacturer many opportunities to make its service efforts more effective and efficient. Products can be monitored and inspected remotely by the manufacturer without the need for an on-site presence. With this, instant support for the customer can be provided if products or machines fail. Also, service technicians can call up data on the condition of the equipment. In this way, the service technicians are kept up to date on which components need to be repaired or which spare parts are required. Furthermore, manufacturing companies can leverage data from the connected products enabling predictive or condition-based maintenance. Instead of repairing a machine, the goal is to service a machine before a potential failure occurs. By analysing historic product failures, patterns indicating a potential failure can be identified. For instance, if analyses show that the temperature just before a machine failure has always exceeded a certain threshold, this pattern can be used to foresee (or prevent) a future failure.

Business Value

The use case 'remote support and predictive maintenance' helps manufacturing companies to avoid long-repair cycles and machine downtimes at the customer site. This is particularly beneficial for the customer as downtimes typically have a direct, negative financial impact on the customer's business. At the same time, this use case eliminates the cost of manual on-site inspections for the manufacturer, as the majority of the service work can be carried out remotely. In the long run, it ensures cost-effective and preventive maintenance, from which both the manufacturer and the customer can benefit greatly. The next category of horizontal IoT use cases aims to benefit the direct user of the machine or product. The goal of both use cases is to create a better experience for the end-user and increase the customer's productivity.

4.3   Fleet Management and Optimization

Description

The first use case of this category provides value to the particular user group that is not using a single device but managing an entire fleet of devices. This could be, for example, a dispatcher in the context of logistics, who manages a fleet of

(continued)

(continued)

trucks, or a manager in the context of a factory, who manages a fleet of machines. By connecting an entire fleet of devices, fleet managers can remotely check the status of the devices (e.g. location, health, usage) or benchmark the performance of individual devices and machines. Typically, a dashboard or desktop application is provided which enables intuitive use by the customer. The objective is to enable simple monitoring of devices and machine states. This, in turn, enables easy benchmarking across the fleet to identify best practices and well-/bad-performing machines. Typically, integrated into the existing IT systems, fleet managers can seamlessly order spare parts and consumables as part of this use case.

Business Value

With the use case 'fleet management and optimization', manufacturing companies can increase their customers' productivity. It primarily increases transparency for the customer's fleet manager. In particular, it allows fleet managers to optimize the performance of individual devices or increase asset utilization across the entire fleet as well as decrease administrative costs.

4.4   Connected Consumer/Operator Experience

Description

The second use case of this category provides value to the individual user of a product or machine. In a B2C context, this could be a homeowner, but in a B2B context, this can also be a machine operator on the shop floor. The objective for a manufacturer is to complement the smart, connected products with a digital experience for the end-user. In comparison to use case 3, this use case is about the individual device and not a fleet of devices. Moreover, the focus is not on a central fleet manager but on a local operator. This is why this use case typically includes a user interface with functionality to monitor and control single devices (e.g. kitchen appliances, lighting or sound in the smart home). Thereby, consumers (B2C), as well as operators (B2B), are being empowered to optimize their device usage and they profit from increased convenience. This can be supported by offering data-driven advice or a remote assistant (see IoT use case 2). For instance, *Daimler* offers a smartphone application that is connected with the car. With the app, users can remotely review the status of the car (e.g. location, driven mileage, petrol left, warranty) and perform both simple actions like closing or opening the car and more complex actions such as remote car parking via the smartphone (Mercedes 2020).

Business Value

With the use case 'connected customer/operator experience', manufacturing companies can open up new revenue streams or secure the existing ones. Given the increasing demand for digital product experiences, this use case ensures that consumer expectations are met and enables manufacturing companies to stay competitive. Also, it helps consumers and operators to become more efficient and productive in their product usage.

The third category of horizontal IoT use cases aims at improving and innovating a company's product portfolio—both the products that are currently in the field and the new product generation that is still under development.

4.5 Proactive Quality Management

Description

Without the use of IoT, manufacturing companies have to collect information on individual product failures or warranty issues from their distributors or repair shops. This is a very costly approach and relevant information can get easily lost in the long process of consolidation. Due to device connectivity, manufacturing companies can now collect this same data remotely and investigate product problems much faster and more reliably. This allows for a much better problem and quality management (Quality 4.0). The objective is to identify potential, systematic problems across the entire value chain, from sourcing, design, to manufacturing and sales. By automatically collecting failure information from connected devices in the field, the manufacturing company can respond to systematic failures and possibly find the root cause in the value chain much earlier. This, in turn, allows for fast adjustments of the product specification and early customer communication (e.g. to prevent dissatisfied customers and public recalls). In the long run, it can also help set up service-level agreements between customer and manufacturer without the need for a middleman.

Business Value

The use case 'proactive quality management' can significantly increase customer satisfaction. By detecting systematic problems earlier than before, potential recalls including penalties as well as warranty costs can be avoided. In the long run, this helps to increase the quality of the products across the entire value chain.

4.6   Continuous Product Updates and New Features

Description

Originally, to be updated, products had to be brought into a dealership which was a cumbersome and lengthy process for the customer. Due to device connectivity, manufacturers can now remotely update embedded firm and software of devices in the field (and even while being in use by the customer). Besides updating the existing firm and software, this also allows manufacturing companies to remotely upload new applications or functionalities to a device. This 'smartphone-like' approach becomes more and more important for traditional product manufacturers. For example, the *Bosch* IoT Suite enables *Daimler* to remotely update the firmware of roughly four million *Mercedes* cars worldwide (Bosch.IO n.d.). Via the cellular network, the infotainment system (e.g. navigation maps) or even security and safety-relevant components of the cars can be updated ensuring consistent customer experience. In turn, this means that car owners no longer have to visit their car dealer to receive an update for their car.

Business Value

With the use case 'continuous product updates and new features', manufacturing companies can sustain (and even increase) the product lifetime and value for the customer. It can assure device security by updating to the newest software and even increase revenue by adding new functionalities after the product has been sold to the customer. In addition, updating products and devices that are already deployed in the field is often considered the foundation for many of the other mentioned IoT use cases. As part of remote services, it can support managing product failure as the firmware can be updated to fix a bug. Overall, this horizontal IoT use case can lead to new revenue opportunities for the manufacturer while increasing customer satisfaction at the same time.

5   Managerial Implications

The six IoT use cases have showcased the great potential for manufacturing companies across domains. By leveraging IoT, manufacturing companies can make their products and services better, increase customers' productivity and innovate their product portfolio in the long run. Many recent studies, however, also suggest that most IoT projects and initiative still fail. We, therefore, want to highlight seven takeaways for manufacturing companies that want to embark on an IoT journey:

1. **Systematically assess your IoT opportunities:** In a first step, screen your own as well as adjacent industries for successful IoT solutions and identify the most important trends. Companies often focus too much on their own industry while overlooking competitors from adjacent markets building cross-industry IoT solutions. Understanding the potential of IoT for your business also requires you to look closely at your own hardware portfolio. Based on this internal and external analysis, evaluate systematically the chances and risks for your IoT endeavour.

2. **Define your own role and think about partnerships:** Doing IoT alone becomes increasingly difficult due to the complex technology stack needed. In fact, most IoT solutions require close collaboration among several companies. It is therefore important for you to define early on what role you want to play in this ecosystem. Based on this, analyse what you can develop in-house, where you need a supplier and where you want to strategically partner up with other leading companies (e.g. IoT cloud or software providers).

3. **Stay true to your core:** Most companies follow mainstream and focus on 'catchy' IoT use cases that are heavily discussed in news or marketing. Because they are hyped, they initially seem promising, but often do not end up as successful as expected. Manufacturing companies should always start by selecting those IoT use cases that are close to their core business. In addition, they should focus on proven IoT use cases that have the potential to generate short-term profits.

4. **Customer value first, technology second:** Many IoT products result in low adoption when the manufacturing companies focus on technology improvements instead of building compelling use cases for their customers. Therefore, start with addressing a concrete customer or business problem. Only then think about how the use of IoT technology can help to solve this problem. Our set of six horizontal IoT use cases can help to embrace such use-case focus.

5. **Have a holistic IoT strategy in mind but prioritize:** Despite the potential, don't try to boil the ocean with a large number of IoT use cases. It is important to focus only on a few, selected IoT use cases, in the beginning, to build up momentum and scale. Nevertheless, to become an IoT company, in the long run, you need to transform your entire business and build up IoT-specific capabilities. In the end, designing and manufacturing pure physical products differs significantly from developing software and IoT-enabled products.

6. **Start small with a prototype:** Building a successful IoT solution comes with many challenges, from simply connecting the devices, managing them

to monetizing them. Therefore, every IoT endeavour should start with a prototype to validate an idea and to not get lost in potentially unscalable ideas. This is especially true for traditional product companies that are new to agile product development.

7. **Develop a long-term roadmap:** Oftentimes, companies invest a lot into their digitization efforts (e.g. IoT) but their expectations do not meet their actual returns (Wortmann et al. 2019). This digitalization paradox needs to be kept in mind when dealing with stakeholders. Once kicking off your IoT journey, it is important to develop a set of relevant KPIs (beyond return on investment). In the beginning, the adoption and number of connected devices can serve as good proxies for tracking and managing success. In addition, a long-term strategy for the monetization of the IoT products and services needs to be outlined already at the very beginning.

Lessons Learned for the IoT Journey

- Systematically assess your IoT opportunities.
- Define your own role and think about partnerships.
- Stay true to your core.
- Customer value first, technology second.
- Have a holistic IoT strategy in mind but prioritize.
- Start small with a prototype.
- Develop a long-term roadmap.

References

Beecham Research (2020) Why IoT projects fail. Retrieved from https://www.why-iotprojectsfail.com/?cs=br2. Accessed 4 Sept 2020

Bilgeri D, Gebauer H, Fleisch E, Wortmann F (2019) Driving process innovation with IoT field data. MIS Q Exec, 18(3):191–207. https://doi.org/Bosch IoT suite capabilities

Bosch.IO (2020a) Bosch IoT suite. https://www.bosch-iot-suite.com. Accessed 20 Sept 2020

Bosch.IO (2020b) Bosch IoT Suite capabilities. https://www.bosch-iot-suite.com/capabilities-bosch-iot-suite/. Accessed 20 Sept 2020

Bosch.IO (n.d.) Bosch IoT Suite connects cars, mobile machinery, and baby buggies. https://blog.bosch-si.com/bosch-iot-suite/bosch-iot-suite-connects-cars-mobile-machinery-and-baby-buggies/. Accessed 2 Oct 2020

Boyes H, Hallaq B, Cunningham J, Watson T (2018) The industrial internet of things (IIoT): an analysis framework. Comput Ind 101(June):1–12. https://doi.org/10.1016/j.compind.2018.04.015

Denner V (2020) Driving change in challenging times. Retrieved from https://bosch-connected-world.com/wp-content/uploads/BCW20_Denner_Volkmar.pdf

Fleisch E, Weinberger M, Wortmann F (2014) Business models and the internet of things. Bosch IoT Lab White Paper

Graf J, Krenz W, Kronenwett D (2018) IIot platforms: Source of profit or inflated hype? How machinery companies should target their investments to maximize benefits. https://www.oliverwyman.com/content/dam/oliver-wyman/v2/publications/2018/november/perspectives-on-manufacturing-industries-cover-story.pdf. Accessed 19 Sept 2020

Hodapp D, Remane G, Hanelt A, Kolbe L M (2019) Business models for internet of things platforms: empirical development of a taxonomy and archetypes business models for internet of things platforms. In 14th International Conference on Wirtschaftsinformatik

Iansiti M, Lakhani KR (2014) Digital ubiquity how connections, sensors, and data are revolutionizing business. Harv Bus Rev 92(11):90–99

Kranz M (2017) Success with the internet of things requires more than chasing the cool factor. Harv Bus Rev

Mercedes (2020) Mercedes me connect. https://www.me.mercedes-benz.com/passengercars/mercedes-benz-cars/mercedes-me/my-mercedes-me.module.html. Accessed 2 Oct 2020

Porter ME, Heppelmann JE (2014) Smart, connected products are transforming competition. Harv Bus Rev 92(11):64–88

Porter ME, Heppelmann JE (2015) How smart, connected products are transforming companies. Harv Bus Rev 93(10):96–114

Wortmann F, Bilgeri D, Gebauer H, Lamprecht C, Fleisch E (2019) Geld verdienen im IoT – aber wie? HMD Praxis Der Wirtschaftsinformatik 56(6):1094–1112

Sven Jung is a PhD candidate at the Institute of Technology Management at the University of St. Gallen. He is part of the Bosch IoT Lab, a cooperation between the Bosch Group, University of St. Gallen and ETH Zurich, where he investigates (IoT) platform strategies and platform business models. Sven holds a Master's degree in Finance and Strategic Management from Copenhagen Business School and a Bachelor's degree in Business Administration from the University of St. Gallen. During his studies, he worked for a leading management consultancy, a biotech start-up and an investment bank advising technology start-ups.

Stefan Ferber, has been Co-CEO and CTO of Bosch.IO (formerly Bosch Software Innovations GmbH) since January 2020. Before that, he was CEO of Bosch Software Innovations GmbH and served in several leadership roles at Bosch, including the development of the Bosch IoT Suite and leading a research department. He also represents Bosch on the Board of Directors of the Eclipse Foundation and is a member of the European Internet of Things Council. Stefan Ferber has more than 35 years experience in software development, software processes, software product lines, and software architectures for embedded systems, computer vision, and IT domains. Stefan Ferber holds an undergraduate degree and a PhD in computer science from the University of Karlsruhe, Germany and an MSc in computer science from the University of Massachusetts Dartmouth, USA. He is a certified ATAM lead evaluator by the Software Engineering Institute of Carnegie Mellon University, Pittsburgh, USA.

Irene Cramer, Dr., is a Director of Business Development at Software AG. Irene Cramer has worked as a Chief Product Owner and Business Development Manager at Bosch.IO GmbH and is an expert in IoT and industrial applications of Artificial Intelligence and Machine Learning methods. She holds a PhD in Computational Linguistics.

Wolfgang Bronner, Dr., is managing director of the Bosch IoT Lab, a cooperation between the Bosch Group, University of St. Gallen, and ETH Zurich. This lab is particularly dedicated on the Internet of Things, Data Science, and Business Model Innovation. Wolfgang Bronner had his first insight into the high-tech industry as a student at IBM in Silicon Valley. He has been working as an expert and manager in various industries and functions at Bosch in Germany and the USA since 2002. In his last position, he analyzed the impact of the most significant future technologies such as AI on Bosch, derived strategic recommendations, and discussed them with the executive management. He received his PhD in physics from the University of Stuttgart in 2003.

Felix Wortmann, Prof. Dr., is Assistant Professor of Technology Management at the University of St. Gallen. He is also the Scientific Director of the Bosch IoT Lab, a cooperation between the Bosch Group, University of St. Gallen, and ETH Zurich. Felix Wortmann has published more than 100 publications and is among the top 5% of all scientists in business administration in the German-speaking countries (Wirtschaftswoche 2019). His research interests include the Internet of Things, machine learning, blockchain, and business model innovation in manufacturing, mobility, healthcare, and energy. From 2006 to 2009 he worked as an assistant to the executive board of SAP. After studying information systems, Felix Wortmann received his PhD in Management from the University of St. Gallen in 2006.

GF Machining Solutions: Real-Time Manufacturing Process in a Cloud Environment

Andreas Rauch

1 *GF* Addressing the Market Trends in Manufacturing

GF Machining Solutions is a world leading manufacturer of milling, electric discharge machining, laser texturing and cutting and additive manufacturing and automation systems and devices, servicing a wide spectrum of industries ranging from specialized aerospace, automotive, medtech, ICT and electric connectors to traditional mould and die segments. One of the new key strategic developments supporting this wide portfolio is an industrial IoT infrastructure, delivering solution applications, based on edge processed and OPC UA standardized machine data, from a cloud environment: the Digital HUB. This infrastructure focuses on real-time, remote service delivery and advanced process optimization, augmenting machine capabilities and simplifying the use of the technologies by the customers. The main driver for such a transformative development has been the increasing pressure on those customers regarding productivity, costs and resource efficiency, at a varying degree for the market segments of attention.

Mould and die manufacturing has been historically the major target for *GF Machining Solutions*, and the company has provided dedicated innovations for improving the corresponding process performance, in particular with

A. Rauch (✉)
Georg Fischer AG, Schaffhausen, Switzerland
e-mail: andreas.rauch@georgfischer.com

© The Author(s), under exclusive license to Springer Nature Switzerland AG 2021
O. Gassmann, F. Ferrandina (eds.), *Connected Business*,
https://doi.org/10.1007/978-3-030-76897-3_16

Electric Discharge Machining, which enables a high-precision profile and cavity shaping independently of material hardness. More recently, conventional and advanced manufacturing devices have been integrated in the portfolio, which, together with automation systems, provide the most efficient framework for modern demanding applications extending to production markets.

The high-precision capabilities of those technologies have been pulled, on one side, by the miniaturization trend of the various products manufactured out of moulds and dies: ICT devices, sensors, connectors, IC circuits, etc. On the other hand, performances have been pushed by the growing capacity of numeric controllers in terms of digital data handling and real-time feedback loops adapting to changing process dynamics. These advances implied a quantum leap in terms of stability at higher productivity rates independently of part complexities (Suh et al. 2008).

For production markets like aerospace and medtech, additional requirements for surface quality and traceability are met thanks to the development of appropriate advanced sensor networks and post-processing data analytics, which results in optimum machining strategies. These require, however, external machine learning or AI processing capabilities, and offline adjustments, often performed by domain experts, who converge only gradually to the desired operational efficiencies (Caggiano et al. 2015).

2   Production Efficiency Through 5G Process Manufacturing

The current context makes necessary a new framework for sustaining the improvements required by industries, as end-product's lifetime becomes shorter and functionalities demand increasingly diverse features and new materials. 5G manufacturing in a cloud environment presents here a great potential for delivering high-performing process stability and productivity as it responds to the quest of real-time transfer of multiple sensor data at high rates, amplified processing capabilities and low latency-secure feedback to machine controllers and automated systems for monitoring and optimization at new levels. Table 1 summarizes the different new features and advantages of the 5G framework with respect to traditional CNC frameworks.

Eventually such capabilities will lead to the implementation of full Digital Twins, where prediction capabilities incorporate all the relevant asset information for the most accurate control of manufacturing towards any required, possible KPI for the real system.

Table 1 Comparison between traditional CNC and 5G IoT augmented process manu-facturing, author's own illustration

Feature	Traditional CNC	5G IoT augmented CNC
Sensors	– Fixed	– Wireless, mobile and secure
Data process and aggregation	– Bounded to local computer capacity	– Expandable through cloud infrastructure
Process control	– Real time: limited to single sensor data and relatively linear domains	– Possible sensor fusion and non-linear machine learning modelling in real time
	– Pre-processing needed for high-frequency sensors	– Raw data process able even for high-frequency sources
Knowledge management	– Information silos, bounded to machine or personnel	– Open, shared between machines and personnel
Flexibility	– Static, dependent on redesign or offline re-programming	– Dynamic, smoothly adaptive and customizable online
Business model	– Product oriented	– Service oriented

3   *GF* New Digital-5G-Enabled Industrial IoT Infrastructure

The new *GF* digital foundation infrastructure, Digital HUB, has been built up around GFMS devices following a dedicated industrial IoT architecture, based on OPC UA standards for machine-to-machine communication and a common EDGE environment collecting and structuring machine data for delivering business applications with different solution targets. The vision of the corresponding, future, 5G-enabled infrastructure is represented in Fig. 1. Based on new features from Table 1, the advantages of such a framework are the following:

- Remote services and real-time information from machines: 5G brings unlimited capacity for data transfer and processing so that full fleet information is available for condition monitoring of all the machine functional components, providing live remote assistance, readily enhanced with augmented/virtual reality.
- Process monitoring from multiple sensors which can be arbitrarily located inside the machine or cell, close or attached to process parts for maximum sensitivity and aggregated for sensor fusion and holistic regulation of manufacturing processes, this in order to deliver the highest accuracy and productivity framework.
- Process and service analytics using machine learning and artificial intelligence at cloud level, using modern data science approaches, with distributed and high-speed computing which are necessary for new real-time control of current complex systems (multi-axes cutting, laser machining and additive manufacturing).

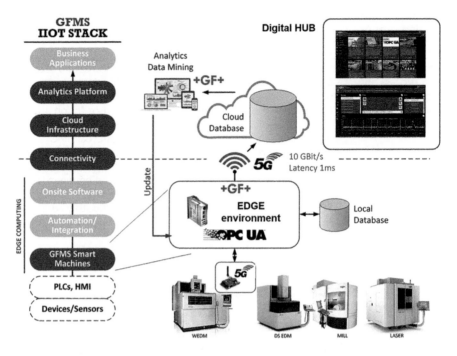

Fig. 1 GF Machining Solutions—5G industrial IoT infrastructure vision, author's own illustration

• Manufacturing process and services control: able to reach loop time dynamics of the order of 1 ms thanks to new 5G latency possibilities in an industrially secure environment, either on private or encrypted public networks.

Finally, in aggregate, those advantages around a cloud environment allow to envision a real-time, seamless available, delocalized manufacturing, with remote monitoring, service and control of all components of the manufacturing processes along their lifecycle, as they clearly establish the virtual teleportation capability of those manufacturing assets in complete information systems.

4   Creating Value in Manufacturing with a New 5G IoT Infrastructure

The new 5G framework offers different opportunities against current challenges in manufacturing for critical aerospace and automotive components, medical implants and instruments as well as high-precision moulds and dies, at single machine or automated robotized cell level, along the full lifecycle of the process.

5   A Use Case for 5G Manufacturing: Real-Time Process Monitoring

In collaboration with *Fraunhofer IPT* and *Ericsson*, *GF Machining Solutions* has implemented the first pilot for 5G-enhanced manufacturing of high-quality components, by integrating real-time wireless sensors attached to the part, during a 5-axis machining process, into the IoT framework, for seamless visualization and real-time analytics. This innovative approach allows simultaneous quality control and optimizes the efficiency of the full process. The system and results are represented in Fig. 2.

An analysis of benefits of such a system is presented by *Fraunhofer* and *Ericsson* (Fraunhofer IPT 2018), for the particular case of aerospace component manufacturing. The production of such components involves high-strength Ni and Ti alloys; complex geometries requiring multi-axes, high-speed milling, resulting in special manufacturing strategies from the point of view of parameter design; long machining times and dedicated quality control; and high costs parts and relatively high level of rework and scrap rates. Defected part levels can be as high as 25% for some critical components as turbine blades and disks, as they require achieving the highest surface quality standards for ensuring secure turbomachinery performances.

Thereby vibration analysis is with wireless sensor data integrated into the *GF* industrial IoT Digital HUB infrastructure. Vibration spectra can be correlated with surface quality on the part 3D model, allowing real-time follow-up of process quality, defining a new business model with simultaneous online analytics capabilities of the system.

The 5G industrial IoT-enabled manufacturing allows in this case to first reduce the development time of the machining strategies as extended trial times can be shortened when parameters appear to create chatter phenomena putting at risk the surface quality. Secondly, the system can provide real-time warnings during the production process so this can be managed in a way to reduce resource waste or accelerate the quality control process in a final stage. Eventually, the framework will allow the real-time control of manufacturing so that control parameters are adjusted online for constraining vibration values to required tolerance bands while keeping the process stable and performing.

6   IoT Infrastructure Benefits and Business Models

While the previous methodology and system can be conceived in a traditional CNC environment, it will be far from efficient in terms of costs and performances. Only a 5G industrial IoT infrastructure will allow such a solution by

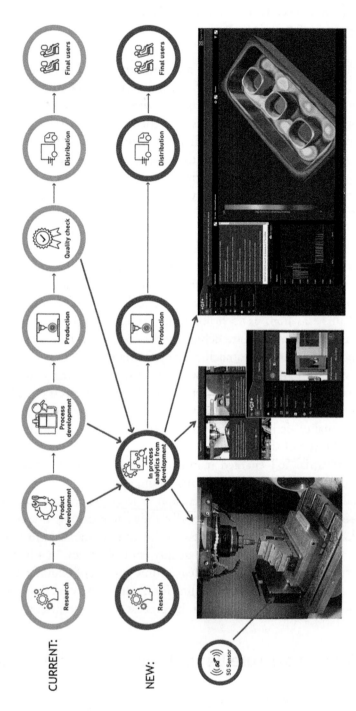

Fig. 2 5G real-time process monitoring system and test use case for part, author's own illustration

delivering a high-fidelity Digital Twin of the process dynamics, by integrating various data sources at high frequency in a cloud environment, able to aggregate and process it with analytic tools in real time. Additionally, the framework provides unlimited, low-cost capacity for storing this information in data lakes or warehouses, which, with appropriate information models and ontologies, will enable to integrate learnings from other similar systems and update particular ones in automated way (Cho et al. 2018). This as long as data can be shared between stakeholders by taking into account their concerns for data protection and legal regulations.

Finally, such dynamic framework will enable switching to new business models by lowering barriers for PaaS and SaaS in manufacturing, as it will convey the implementation of Digital Twins, through which costs can be under the full control of machine tool manufacturers. These can thus provide advantageous contracts including continuous improvement packages as well as maintenance and quality guarantees, and OEMs can further lower investments by enabling data sharing within the new network. For instance, it is estimated that up to 70% of costs during machine tool lifecycle arise in the maintenance area (Mourtzis et al. 2016). As most of these costs are due to unexpected failures and quality issues, implementing 5G industrial IoT-enhanced control will therefore eliminate those risks and provide a unique tool for a sustainable, economic manufacturing. *GF* will use the industrial IoT infrastructure to implement the strategic ESG (environmental, social and governance) goals.

7   Conclusion

As the leading provider of complex manufacturing systems involving diversity of technologies and manufacturing applications, *GF Machining Solutions* can provide unique advantages for dealing with current manufacturing challenges in mould and die and production industries. A new 5G industrial IoT infrastructure in place provides the best framework for implementing those solutions by extending the capabilities of traditional numeric controls in such a way that they can delegate the pre-processing, post-processing and data analytics of multiple, appropriate data sources to a cloud environment. The new framework opens the door to Industry 4.0 integration of smart sensors, machines and human expertise into a common, seamless available, source of optimization of processes and services as quality monitoring and predictive maintenance, and to new advantageous business models for all involved stakeholders and the global sustainable environment.

Lessons Learned for Implementing Real-Time Manufacturing via Cloud

- Assess and document your manufacturing process chain in terms of data, information flow and functional objectives.
- Map your costs and related relevant business and technical KPIs.
- Design a Digital Twin for your process delivering the previous information needs.
- Identify sensor gaps in order to enable process data collection automation for your Digital Twin.
- Assess data network needs in terms of data velocity, veracity and variety in order to specify the best transmission channels and protocols.
- Design or adjust requirements for cloud infrastructure architecture, from connectivity to process analytics and business application availability levels.
- Implement pilot data collection and the required, secured Digital Twin monitoring applications.
- Collect insights and deploy analytics applications.
- Launch large data collection and deploy digital twin intelligent solution.
- Learn and improve.

References

Caggiano A et al (2015) Wire EDM monitoring for zero-defect manufacturing based on advanced sensor signal processing. Procedia CIRP 33:315–332

Fraunhofer (2018) Fraunhofer IPT, Ericsson and GF to present 5G manufacturing solution for the first time in the US Press release Fraunhofer IPT, September 11

Mourtzis D et al (2016) A cloud-based approach for maintenance of machine tools and equipment based on shop-floor monitoring. Procedia CIRP 41(2016):655–660

Andreas Rauch is Head of Digital Business at GF Machining Solutions and is responsible for digital strategy, the development of digital business models, and sales. He fosters the implementation of IoT with a focus on standardization, machine-to-machine communication, big data management, analytics platforms, legal frameworks, and customer experience. Born in Zürich, Switzerland, he graduated in Mechanical Engineering and postgraduate studies in business administration and software development. Andreas founded his own company in 1998, specialized in Design to Manufacturing processes, and sold it in 2010 to a leading company in the turbomachinery environment. Before joining GF Machining solutions, he was GEs Head of Advanced Works in Europe and responsible for Digital Twin implementation projects and Brilliant Factory Systems.

Linde: Business Value with Connected Cylinders in Hospitals

Wolfgang Emmerich and Mike Hogg

1 Medical Grade Gas as Commodity Product

Hospitals rely heavily on a stable supply of medical grade gases—oxygen, medical air and nitrous oxide to name those most required. Patients who have been prescribed a gas treatment have it delivered through gas networks plumbed into the hospital and accessed via wall-mounted valves. Further, healthcare providers require gas on the move, for instance, when transferring patients within emergency care. In such cases, medical gas cylinders are used. The supply of medical gas cylinders, a business revolving around cylinder rentals and gas refills, is a commodity business with the product subject to common standards. For customers it is a straightforward procedure to change a vendor, and purchasing decisions are purely price driven.

How can a gas supplier provide more value to their customers, not only those responsible for maintaining supply but also those who use the cylinders, arrange their movements and manage costs? This precisely is the challenge *Linde Healthcare* is facing. *Linde* is a multinational chemical Fortune 500 company, the largest industrial gas company worldwide. The company's

W. Emmerich (✉) • M. Hogg
Zühlke Group, Zürich, Switzerland

Mike Hogg, Isotropic Systems, London, UK
e-mail: Wolfgang.Emmerich@zuhlke.com; mike@mountdrive.com

primary business is the manufacturing and distribution of atmospheric gases for many different industries like the healthcare sector. As they hold a market leading position in various markets worldwide, they remain under constant competitive pressure.

2   The Current Environment for Gas Cylinders

Gas cylinders have not developed much over the past 50 years. A pressurised cylinder chamber is topped by a valve assembly with a gas tap to regulate supply. The valve has an analogue pressure dial to provide an indication on how much gas is left in the cylinder. This gauge includes a visual tragic light indication, green down to 50% pressure, amber to 25% and red below these measures. *Linde* realised from examining the cylinders arriving back at fill plants that many hospitals were sending cylinders back to be refilled as soon as the gauge entered the amber zone, and hence were often being sent back half-full. This paved the way for an opportunity: finding a way to increase customers' confidence in continuing to use each cylinder until it was deep into the red zone. This, in turn, would enable hospitals to reduce their refill costs and eventually build trust with their gas supplier.

Linde Healthcare determined that the issue was one of both perception (yellow and red spell danger in most usage) and uncertainty of how long the gas remaining in a cylinder would last. Prescriptions for gas are usually based on time and flow rate, which was hard to relate to a pressure indication. To address this particular need, *Linde* developed a next-generation digital gas valve that displays simultaneously the traditional green-yellow-red pressure gauge and a countdown timer. This is rendered digitally on an LCD panel on the valve. It uses the selected flow rate and the remaining pressure to calculate the remaining time of supply. Now a cylinder can confidently be used up until the pressure is depleted, as long as the countdown timer indicates that there is sufficient gas left to complete the prescribed dosage. This new digital valve was designed by *Linde*, named LIV IQ, and eventually launched on the market (Fig. 1).

The final results were mixed. Those charged with administering gas treatments found the new valve of value; however, those in the hospital responsible for purchasing the cylinder supply did not consider that this value justified the higher rental cost of the new LIV IQ cylinders. *Linde* was definitely onto something interesting, but further innovation was required.

While the new digital valve was under development, *Linde* determined that the microprocessor required to calculate the remaining time of supply could

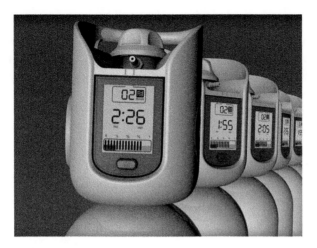

Fig. 1 The cylinder valve, indicating the remaining time of supply, author's own illustration

also perform as a data logger, recording the cylinder pressure over time. This would not add to the cost of the valve but would yield *Linde* valuable data in understanding how the cylinders were being used. Extracting this logged data from the valve was challenging; cylinders only return briefly to *Linde* when they arrive at the fill plant batched on lorries, are quickly evacuated and filled, then shipped again. It was determined that a wireless data transfer solution would be beneficial, and a Bluetooth network interface was added to the cylinders. By installing Bluetooth-enabled data interrogation systems within the fill plants, the cylinders could have their data downloaded and reset while being refilled. The fact that these new cylinders were Bluetooth equipped for this purpose raised the question of whether Bluetooth could enable further purposes and innovations.

3   The INETIQ Project Created a Lot of Business Value

The initial motivation for the new cylinder was driven through clinician need and helping them to optimize the use of the cylinders. Which other stakeholders within a hospital had problems or opportunities that the new Bluetooth-enabled cylinder could help with?

- Porters are responsible for logistics within a hospital, which for cylinder means collecting used cylinders as well as distributing full cylinders. Many hospitals organise these activities via paper-based systems, for instance, faxing cylinder request forms to the porters managing the cylinder stores. A system that could assist this logistics process, not only bringing the ordering process onto a digital system but also automating large parts of it, was found to be a compelling proposition when tested within hospitals.
- Then there are the hospital personnel responsible for overseeing consumption, managing costs and driving efficiencies. If they could be provided with data to help them in these tasks and better still be offered specific cost-saving suggestions, that would be another valuable enhancement to these cylinders.

Bluetooth is cleared for use in clinical environments, and Bluetooth devices can be programmed to send out periodic signals, known as advertisements, that can be detected by any listening device. Data can be embedded in the advertisement signal to indicate the status of the cylinder. This data can include its identifying code, its current fill level and any error conditions such as running empty. If *Linde* provided hub devices for installation at key points within a hospital, the hubs could detect Bluetooth advertisements from cylinders located nearby and send them to a central system for further processing. If that central system was hosted in a globally available cloud, then any of *Linde's* clients worldwide could install the system and be provided with their own private tenancy within a common *Linde Healthcare* cloud system (Fig. 2).

Once this platform opportunity was understood, the routes to business value could be explored. With respect to *porter logistics*, the system knew the cylinder locations and their state. Once the system is informed which hubs are installed at which location (a process achieved using a mobile app to configure the hubs), then web dashboards could be provided that inform the porter of the stock levels at each location. This enables them to track in real time the empty cylinders that need collecting and replacing, cylinders in use that might need collecting soon and any cylinders that are in an error state. In addition, automatic orders can be raised for the collection of empties and delivery of new cylinders. And the effectiveness and efficiency of the logistics operation could be measured by how long it took for orders to be met (Fig. 3).

For *hospital management* the value was found to lay in higher-level metrics. One key concern was cost allocation, understanding which hospital departments were consuming cylinder gas, and how long the rented cylinders were stored by each department. Furthermore, the aspect of usage efficiency was important. A primary metric was the gas pressure in cylinders which were sent

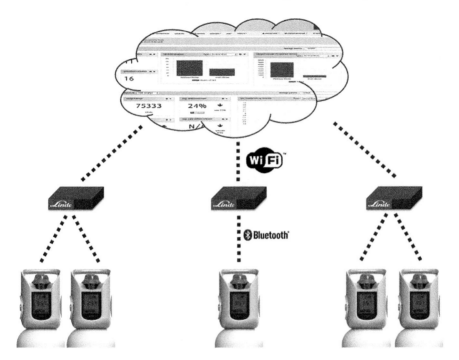

Fig. 2 INTEIQ solution: with hospital-installed hubs detecting Bluetooth advertisements from cylinders and forwarding them over Wi-Fi to the cloud, author's own illustration

back to be refilled: the higher the pressure, the greater the missed opportunity to use that residual gas. By following cylinders on their journey from central store to a department for usage and then back to central store, the manager dashboard can present department-level statistics on how well each team is leveraging the resources to consume the gas within a cylinder before refilling. Other efficiency measures were considered of value, such as how long a cylinder is stored in a department before being in use (a key indicator of departmental over-stocking) and how long it takes for empty cylinders to be collected. Measures such as the total oxygen storage at a location are important for fire regulations (Fig. 4).

The INETIQ system was developed using lean innovation mechanisms, taking small steps and reacting to the feedback gained. It was initially tested by customers using simple prototypes to test the value hypothesis. As this was well received a pilot implementation was deployed in a hospital in Hong Kong and trialled for a few weeks. Important lessons were learnt about hospital connectivity options, the pathways that cylinders take within a hospital and most importantly which features were recognized to be of value by

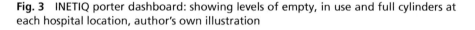

INETIQ™ Henry Ford Allegiance Health

&Smoke Test User (smoketest@iqhospital.io) ← Back to Admin ☞ Sign Out

Linde

⊞ Dashboard   ⚙ Settings   Role: Porter ▾   🌐 English (United Kingdom) ▾

Locations		Cylinders							Items per page: 25 ▾ ⌕
Name ⇕	Total Cylinders: 278	Cylinder Name ⇕	Type ⇕	Location ⇕	Fill Level ▲	Operating Mode ⇕	Advice ⇕	Last seen ⇕	
search by Name		search by Cy...	search by Ty...	search by Locati...		search by ...	search by...	search by ⌕	
3rd Floor Storage		201606IH06040	Oxygen, LIV IQ E	Respiratory Therapy 6T		OFF		2 mins ago	
LIV IQs 6		201606IH06079	Oxygen, LIV IQ E	Respiratory Therapy 6T		OFF		2 mins ago	
IQ E 0 0 6 6 0 0		201509IH00176	Oxygen, LIV IQ E	Respiratory Therapy 6T		OFF		2 mins ago	
IQ E' 0 0 0 0 0 0		201510IH00845	Oxygen, LIV IQ E	Cath Lab 1T		OFF		3 mins ago	
4th Floor Storage		201510IH00776	Oxygen, LIV IQ E	Warehouse Storage		OFF		2 mins ago	
LIV IQs 6		201509IH00367	Oxygen, LIV IQ E	Respiratory Therapy 6T		OFF		2 mins ago	
IQ E 0 0 6 6 0 1		201510IH01282	Oxygen, LIV IQ E	Emergency Department		OFF		a min ago	
IQ E' 0 0 0 0 0 0		201510IH01063	Oxygen, LIV IQ E	Respiratory Therapy 6T		OFF		5 mins ago	
5th Floor Storage		201606IH06192	Oxygen, LIV IQ E	Emergency Department		OFF		a min ago	
LIV IQs 7		201606IH05591	Oxygen, LIV IQ E	Emergency Department		OFF		4 mins ago	
IQ E 0 0 0 7 0 0		201606IH05779	Oxygen, LIV IQ E	Warehouse Storage		OFF		8 mins ago	
IQ E' 0 0 0 0 0 0		201606IH07751	Oxygen, LIV IQ E	Cath Lab 1T		OFF		6 mins ago	
6th Floor Storage		201510IH01408	Oxygen, LIV IQ E	Emergency Department		OFF		13 mins ago	
LIV IQs 7		201510IH00926	Oxygen, LIV IQ E	Geriatric Unit		OFF		a min ago	
IQ E 0 1 6 6 0 1		201511IH01914	Oxygen, LIV IQ E	6th Floor Storage		OFF		a few secs ago	
IQ E' 0 0 0 0 0 0		201509IH00276	Oxygen, LIV IQ E	7th Floor Storage		OFF		5 mins ago	
7th Floor Storage		201510IH00833	Oxygen, LIV IQ E	Respiratory Therapy 7T		OFF		a min ago	
LIV IQs 11		201607IH08062	Oxygen, LIV IQ E	Respiratory Therapy 7T		OFF		4 mins ago	
IQ E 0 1 0 9 0 1		201606IH06158	Oxygen, LIV IQ E	PACU		OFF		5 mins ago	
IQ E' 0 0 0 0 0 0		201607IH08064	Oxygen, LIV IQ E	7th Floor Storage		OFF		2 mins ago	
Cath Lab 1T									
LIV IQs 5									
IQ E 0 2 0 3 0 0									
IQ E' 0 0 0 0 0 0									

Fig. 3 INETIQ porter dashboard: showing levels of empty, in use and full cylinders at each hospital location, author's own illustration

hospital staff. Word of the pilot spread quickly, leading to the development of a production system and deployment to the first major customer in the USA. The system, a hospital-wide cylinder monitoring platform, is now deployed to systems across the USA, Europe and Asia, and both LIV IQ and INETIQ are popular in the market.

Lessons Learnt

- Innovation is iterative: Making a delivery mechanism digital opens new opportunities that do not end after the first deployment. Make and test hypothesis, gather feedback, learn and iterate.
- Customer-centricity is key: Innovation must be driven through business value and with technology as an enabler rather than a driving force. Customer value comes first.
- It's all about information: Many IoT solutions collect and display all the raw data that they possibly can. Data is valuable only when used to derive information and insight. Only visualize data that users need to make decisions.

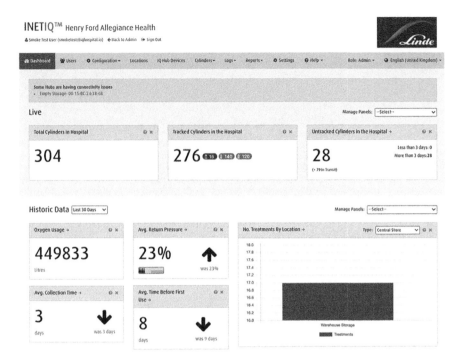

Fig. 4 INETIQ management dashboard: showing stock levels, breakdowns of usage by department, time before cylinders are first used and importantly how much gas pressure remains on average when the cylinders are returned, author's own illustration

Wolfgang Emmerich, Prof. Dr rer-nat, is the CEO of Zühlke UK and a co-founder of the Zühlke Group, where he serves on the Group Executive Committee. Wolfgang is Professor of Distributed Computing at UCL, where he led the Software Systems Engineering Research Group prior to his appointment at Zühlke UK. Wolfgang is internationally most well known for his work on software engineering techniques for distributed systems. He is Chartered Engineer and Member of the IET. Wolfgang holds a Doctor of Science from the University of Paderborn, Germany, and a Diploma in Informatics from University of Dortmund.

Mike Hogg holds a Masters in Engineering from Cambridge University and is a software engineer by trade. He has been fortunate to be involved in the development of software solutions across a wide range of domains, including network appliances, medical devices, industrial systems, government online services, and financial trading platforms. His career has involved leading the delivery of many elements that make up the Internet of Things, from the connected devices, the infrastructure, the cloud services, and web and mobile interfaces. He is a Chartered Engineer and Member of the IET.

ABB: Creating Value with Open Smart Home Automation Systems

Thorsten Müller and Alexander Grams

1   Smart Home Automation Systems

ABB is a B2B global leader in electrical products and solutions and a front runner in the smart home market. Building its digital business offering step by step means aligning with the increasing and diversified demands of customers, while following the trends towards adding value services and simplifying solutions. Smart homes as we know them today came of age in the early 1990s, gaining more mainstream popularity at the start of the twenty-first century when supporting technologies and internet connectivity emerged. Following the introduction of iPhones in 2007 and tablets in 2010, increased acceptance and understanding of user interfaces began.

Shortly thereafter in 2014, *ABB* launched its free@home smart home automation system that enabled the control of lights, blinds, heating and cooling. While other smart home systems progressed with technical user interfaces, the *ABB* smart home automation system offered a graphical user interface, which

T. Müller
ABB, Heidelberg, Germany
e-mail: thorsten.mueller1@de.abb.com

A. Grams (✉)
ABB, Lüdenscheid, Germany
e-mail: alexander.grams@de.abb.com

could be set up and controlled with little to no training. The system made it simple for the user—via personal computer, tablet or mobile phone—to manage multiple functions and create the desired home environment.

2   Pitfalls of the Early Versions

However, it soon became apparent there were some pitfalls. One of these was that the system required hard wiring between all components, which made it suitable only for newly constructed homes. This reduced the flexibility of the system. Another disadvantage was that the system, although connected to the Internet, was not connected to the cloud. As a result, it has been necessary to bring in an outside technician for installation, any changes or maintenance tasks.

Other challenges, like the unwillingness of customers to pay for remote access and fear of lack of security, became additional barriers to the success of the early solution. These barriers, of course, were addressed in the next generation of free@home, along with broad improvements on the digital front.

3   Implementing the Learnings

In 2016 *ABB* launched an updated free@home automation solution, expanding the system capabilities to include devices that connect to each other wirelessly. It also added Geo-fencing capabilities, where the house knows when its inhabitants are arriving based on the proximity of their mobile phone and prepares the home atmosphere accordingly. A key enabler for the digital evolution of the updated free@home automation solution is its connection to the cloud, which opened vast new possibilities, allowing suppliers to expand services with less hardware interaction and only software updates. Upgraded remote control via the cloud is another value-added benefit of the solution, allowing you to connect when out of range of the home Wi-Fi from virtually anywhere in the world. The system also includes an upgraded central access point, which is the "brain" of the smart home system. The central access point connects to the web and to the user interface and allows connectivity to other systems, providing easy programming and control of the system via the web interface.

Behind the central access point is MyBuildings portal, powered by *ABB*'s cloud-enabled digital platform, *ABB* Ability. MyBuildings portal is a key differentiator offered only by *ABB*, allowing users to choose from a wide range of products and value-added services to add to their smart home application. It also ensures a secure connection, which had been an issue in the past.

4   Partnering Strategy Supported Growth

In 2019 *ABB* continued to unlock further potential for the new era of smart home automation by widening the ecosystem with the addition of API (application programming interface) to its free@home offering. The open API provides full open access to *ABB* technology for third-party applications, including the integration of partners and their partners and their applications and customers. This continues to enable exponential growth for *ABB* based on the laws of the platform economy, with current partners like *Google*, *Amazon*, *Signify* and *Sonos*.

White goods, or full electric appliance integration with partners like *Philips Hue*, *Miele* and *Bosch*, opened the opportunity for multiple new use cases for more digital services and increased functionality for end-users. While white goods are a good example of how *ABB* integrates third parties by utilizing their API, other partners like *Olisto* integrate *ABB* with their partners utilizing their API. This brings together numerous IOT products that can all talk to each other and work together, providing the potential for rapid growth for all parties. Additional upgrades to the new platform continue, like enabling push notifications to be sent to your mobile phone with a simple app and enabling users to set up and control their smart home systems. And the newest addition expected to become a main driver of success is the "installer portal", where an installer can program and change the system from afar. This negates the need for house visits, which has become critically important since the onset of the Covid-19 pandemic.

As home automation continues to become more mainstream, adding new digital services in a step-by-step manner in response to customer demand and willingness to pay will provide endless possibilities for functionality and personalization of smart home systems. And, continual improvement in the areas of ease of use and exceptional user experience is key. Currently *ABB* is leading the acceleration of smart home technology and is well-poised to fully leverage the IoT, cloud analytics, Wi-Fi and mobile devices for the future. The *ABB*-free@home system has nearly 5 million of its connected components installed in over 40 countries worldwide. Figure 1 summarizes the business model along the framework of Gassmann et al. (2020). With over 70,000 using the smart automation platform, the product is considered a big success.

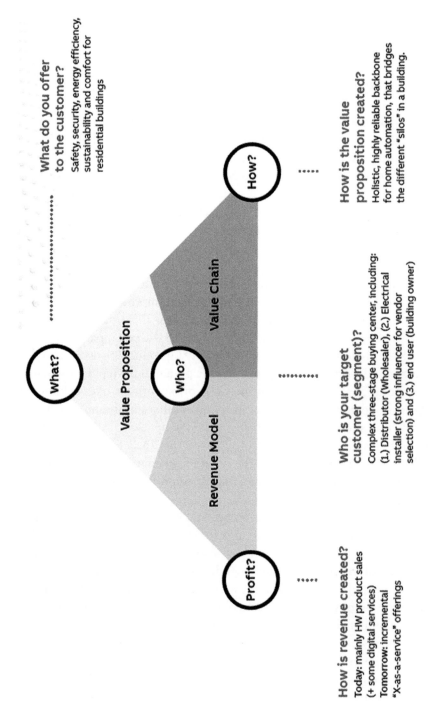

What do you offer to the customer?
Safety, security, energy efficiency, sustainability and comfort for residential buildings

How is the value proposition created?
Holistic, highly reliable backbone for home automation, that bridges the different "silos" in a building.

Who is your target customer (segment)?
Complex three-stage buying center, including: (1.) Distributor (wholesaler), (2.) Electrical installer (strong influencer for vendor selection) and (3.) end user (building owner)

How is revenue created?
Today: mainly HW product sales (+ some digital services)
Tomorrow: incremental "X-as-a-service" offerings

What?   Who?   How?   Profit?

Value Proposition   Value Chain   Revenue Model

Fig. 1 The business model of ABB-free@home, Gassmann et al. (2020)

5   Challenges of the Solution

However, to keep up with the lightning speed of the ever-changing digital world and the increasing demand of customers for better and improved offerings, several challenges must be met.

One such challenge is being a B2B2B2C business selling through wholesalers via installers to end-users, because currently *ABB* doesn't deal directly with the consumer. This will eventually need to change. Updates to the smart home system will be offered through an online community, where end-users can learn more about the ecosystem and how to program it themselves, and *ABB* can communicate directly with them.

Another challenge for determining future success will depend on understanding what services end-users want and are willing to pay for, then creating new products and service combinations that add value and customers will buy. Currently firmware updates, new functions, improvements and bug fixes are provided free of charge to all customers via *ABB*'s constantly evolving auto update system. *ABB* charges for hardware devices, but in most instances not for digital services for smart homes, which could have compelling upside potential. So, although successful by most measures, the *ABB*-free@home® automation system has not created a significant recurring revenue software-as-a-service business model, at least not yet.

New KPI's will bring additional value when integrated step by step. Selling more platform hardware systems, finding more users through organically growing the business through partnerships and continually making the platforms better are critical to success.

A key factor in becoming a fully viable digital business model and further developing the business will be re-thinking how revenue can be derived from the value created and figuring out how to monetize the different types of services and functionalities when it comes to partner integration. While there is no doubt that the *ABB*-free@home automation system has achieved digital success, with continued flexibility, scalability and experimentation, even more financial success with digital services will surely follow.

Lessons Learnt

- Create solutions with less hardware interaction and software over-the-air.
- Cloud-based solutions allow flexibility in installation, changes and maintenance.
- Address the end-users' fear of lack of security and create trust.
- Get partners committed to collaborate on the customer journey as an ecosystem.
- Think in clear business models, including addressing B2B2B2C business selling.
- Adapt KPIs to address the specific challenges of the business model.

Reference

Gassmann O, Frankenberger K, Choudury M (2020) The business model navigator: the strategies behind the most successful companies. FT Pearson, Upper Saddle River, NJ

Thorsten Müller, Dr., received his PhD in physics from the University of Duisburg-Essen. He began his professional career at the Bosch Group in the corporate sector research and advance engineering, where he developed innovative sensor systems for new applications. Further he held various management positions within the Bosch Group for around 11 years, including strategy, M&A, R&D, and operations. In his last role at Bosch as CEO of Bosch Connected Devices and Solutions, he was responsible for strategic connectivity projects for the entire group and successfully implemented new IoT business models. This was followed by his position as Group SVP Innovation & Innoventures at Osram, where he led the transformation from a lightbulb toward a high-tech company before he took over the leadership of the global building automation business at ABB in 2019.

Alexander Grams joined Busch-Jaeger Elektro GmbH, a member of the ABB group, in 2001, and has held several managerial positions in Marketing and Sales within ABB's Smart Buildings Division. He is currently Head of Marketing, Communication and Product Design for the Smart Buildings Division. Alexander holds a degree in economical engineering as a Diploma Engineer at the University of Applied Science in Meschede, Germany.

Covestro: Digital Technical Services as New Business Model for the Polymer Processing Industry

Sairam Potaraju, Hans Kespohl, and Hermann Bach

1   Polymer Industry Under Pressure

Polymers are ubiquitous in our world today and the success story of this material class continues. From 2009 to 2019 the global plastic production volume increased by nearly 50% from 250 to 368 million tons. This growth is mainly driven by China, while European volumes remained more or less at the same level. At the same time, many polymers have increasingly become commodities where polymer processing knowledge is well established and many customer needs can be met with existing formulas that only require minor adaptation. Over the last couple of decades, we have thus observed an increasingly fierce supplier competition with volatile margins largely determined by supply-demand balances and supplier cost structures. As a result, the traditional polymer industry business model comprising making and selling of products along with comprehensive (technical) customer services has come under pressure—*Covestro* is here no exception. This article describes a new business model approach to render digital technical services to the polymer processing industry.

S. Potaraju (✉) • H. Kespohl • H. Bach
Covestro Deutschland AG, Leverkusen, Germany
e-mail: sairam.potaraju1@covestro.com; hans.kespohl@covestro.com;
hermann.bach@covestro.com

© The Author(s), under exclusive license to Springer Nature Switzerland AG 2021
O. Gassmann, F. Ferrandina (eds.), *Connected Business*,
https://doi.org/10.1007/978-3-030-76897-3_19

305

2   Start with a Customer Problem and Work Backwards

Covestro's customers use PUR raw materials (MDI, TDI, polyether, polyester) to manufacture foam used in building envelopes (sandwich metal panels), refrigerator insulation, automotive seating, upholstery, or mattresses just to name a few of the biggest applications. Customers purchase polyurethane raw materials from *Covestro* and its competitors and additives from other suppliers and formulate recipes based on supplier recommendation and/or their own know-how, and process them using complex machines into the respective parts like insulation or mattress. Chemical suppliers like *Covestro* as well as additive suppliers support customers with starting recipes, initial product testing, and process optimization to establish and fine-tune processing conditions. In case of quality issues, customers approach the raw material suppliers for support as needed; otherwise customers manage the operations themselves.

A holistic, design thinking-based analysis jointly with several *Covestro* customers revealed some real pain points that exist in day-to-day usage of PUR raw materials. These are scrap, higher material usage than potentially needed, relatively high manual effort by experienced operators, at times claims from varying product quality. These pain points have their cause in the operating manner primarily dependent on operator knowledge and experience, iterative trial-and-error approach, and mostly reactive management of occurring issues during production. The process is fully run and controlled by *Covestro*'s customers and comprises several processing steps with multiple variables affecting the outcome in each step. At times customers could be using perfectly in-spec raw materials only to produce scrap or in other instances experience occasional but costly failures of the final product after several months in usage.

How might we create customer value in new ways by assisting operators reducing scrap, optimizing raw material usage, and helping to create a consistent product quality? The solution concept—called "Digital Production Assistant"—is a new digital business model, i.e., Digital technical Services (DtS; see Fig. 1). But is it desirable? Is it feasible? Is it viable?

Covestro can create new value for its customers by creating and implementing a new digital business model, where raw material, formulation, processing, and quality data from customers' plants are analyzed for patterns and trends. The insights can be deployed in real time to reach optimal processing and formulation settings for customers resulting in lower scrap rates, no product quality issues, and higher efficiency and utilization.

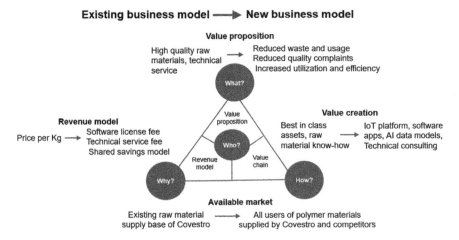

Fig. 1 Initial ideation using St. Gallen's business model innovation approach, Gassmann et al. (2014)

After internal assessment with marketing and technical experts, we decided to start with PUR metal panel products as a pilot but envisioned the concept to be applicable for the other businesses of polymer processing as well. To drive this experiment and to test problem-solution fit were the first tasks of the newly created internal venture, called "DtS."

3   Minimum Viable Product: Build, Test, Learn!

In customer workshops, the venture team evaluated the complete "raw material to end product" journey (see Fig. 2) to understand critical steps, key personas involved, jobs-to-be-done, and desired outcomes/failure modes. It became apparent to all participants esp. our customer leadership that several jobs-to-be-done and interdependencies were not clearly defined, critical data was not being collected in several steps, and—if available—the data was not leveraged for generating and deploying insights. There was immediately a high desirability for a solution that enables proper collection and use of data to automate jobs, eliminate operational errors, and create savings for the customer business.

We also discovered during technical deep dive discussions that the existing data infrastructure at our customers manufacturing facilities is not sufficient for building and deploying advanced digital tools which are needed for IoT in

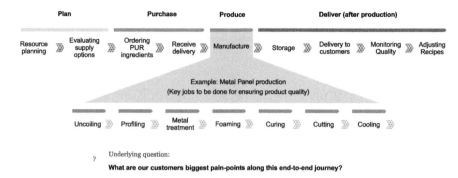

Fig. 2 Customer discovery of PUR metal panel production, author's own illustration

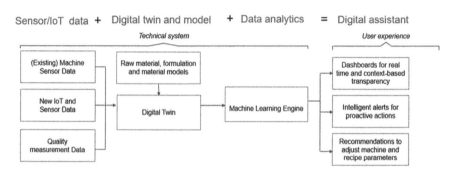

Fig. 3 Technical solution outlining the digital product concept of DtS, author's own illustration

PUR application segments. Therefore, to develop and test our digital solution, we would have to overcome this hurdle and include a robust data infrastructure (e.g., industrial IoT platform) as a part of our solution.

Based on these findings specific technical use cases were formulated together with customers for testing the core idea behind DtS and to evaluate customer value. The general setup is shown in Fig. 3.

The technical use cases required installation of new sensors and hardware (data infrastructure) to collect the "right" data which is critical for real-time product quality monitoring. *Covestro* knowledge of polymer processing was essential here to design and deploy this technical setup. It was also important to scope the technical use cases such that the implementation would be agile and the core hypothesis could be tested and validated quickly.

Once the technical setup was functional, DtS applications (apps) were released to the customer step by step for testing and validation. Basic apps for monitoring and tracking of parts created immediate visibility and transparency which was very much liked by customers. However, these tools only created awareness around existing problems and its impact. We still needed advanced apps—intelligent tools based on algorithms (AI models) and data analytics—for solving (at best avoiding) the problems and creating a real business impact. To build these apps we entered an extensive data collection phase where a sufficient number of data sets were generated to train and test AI models for prediction and classification of quality parameters.

As customers were familiar with our solution, this resulted in high usage rate and they started asking for more technical improvements, features, and possibilities to extract maximum benefit. During this phase of product development, the Minimum Viable Product (MVP) was elevated to the level of a Minimum Desirable Product (MDP) for maximum user impact. The willingness to improve and expand the product stack with new functionalities based on customer feedback was given. This substantially increased the overall value creation of our solution especially compared to existing solutions available in the market. This made our product not only unique and desirable but also tailor-made for the specific PUR application segment. We learned that for our solution to be viable, it must address several tasks (core, non-core, spread over several personas) and automate (or eliminate) several jobs-to-be-done from the customer standpoint.

4   What Do We Offer to Customers, and Can We Scale It Profitably?

During the MVP co-creation phase with customers, significant effort was needed by DtS team in building and operating the pilot setup and supervising data collection for developing and testing algorithms. This experience clearly indicated that the DtS concept cannot be offered as a plug-and-play solution or as a standalone software tool. DtS needs to be deployed as an onsite fully supported, turnkey solution (Fig. 4).

Another observation was related to the nature of the supply chain of the applications where customers source raw materials from several suppliers including Covestro competitors. For commercial scalability of DtS over several customers and manufacturing lines, DtS solution must ensure data governance and protect customers' internal information (e.g., supply share). To make our offer credible and realistic, we decided to go "vendor agnostic" independent of our existing raw material business, thus the offering to customers required to set up the venture team separately from the core business.

* DtS is available for use with all raw material suppliers and machines

Fig. 4 Customer offer to deploy the digital product concept of digital technical service, author's own illustration

5   How Can We Deliver Our Solution at Scale?

Having defined key components and activities needed to deliver the solution, we had to identify key resources needed to build and scale this offer profitably. Technical scalability addressed "make-or-buy" choices of DtS technical components (sensors, IoT platform, software applications, algorithms, etc.) and services (deployment, maintenance, consulting) including partnership vs. "go in alone."

Our main focus was to balance the overall quality of our digital solution with cost, efficiency, and speed of implementation. On one hand we leveraged existing established suppliers in the market (e.g., IoT platform providers, system integrators, etc.), and on the other hand we entered into joint development partnerships with startups and/or research institutes depending on the technology (e.g., image analytics) and competencies needed to deliver the best customer value based on a lean cost structure.

Covestro would ensure ownership and responsibility of frontend applications, data analytics modules for real-time process control and optimization, and onsite deployment including customer training and support. To ensure frictionless implementation, it was agreed by all DtS partners (and suppliers) that *Covestro* would be the "face-to-the-customer" and responsible for overall contract management. In addition to external partners, further *Covestro* internal resources are needed for building, delivering, and scaling the DtS solution. These are primarily Covestro PUR experts in polymer chemistry with several years of experience in the application areas in dealing with final product quality aspects.

The next step was to evaluate the best go-to-market option for DtS specifically defining the pricing strategy and the revenue model that would best fit customer and *Covestro* expectations (Fig. 5). We accomplished this by conducting interview sessions with participation of key customer stakeholders. This survey was conducted with several customers (both DtS pilot and non-pilot customers, SMEs, and global players) within each segment to develop a sound basis. During these sessions the solution concept of DtS and context was presented, customer response/feedback on value and desirability validated, perceptions on core DtS product vs. features understood, and finally, their willingness to buy/pay and decision criteria and constraints identified.

Customers liked the overall value story and preferred using a professional version to ensure the value creation and overall benefits are justified. Customers would like to evaluate the solution and benchmark own benefits before making a commitment for a multi-line and multi-year license contract for DtS. The findings indicate that DtS is a fairly new solution in our value chain and customers prefer a traditional software buying approach (e.g., install and deploy with perpetual license and services as needed). This also fits within the existing software buying and budgeting/controlling approach of companies. The willingness-to-pay is within a very broad range based on specific customer experience with digital tools, perception of cost savings possible by DtS, and understanding of the offer in terms of effort needed by DtS team to maintain and service the solution. DtS offer needs to be clearly differentiated with a standard software (e.g., deploy and run type solution for supply chain or inventory management).

Buying preference	**Install & Deploy** One-time investment into solution with minimal adaptions, no ongoing development	**Software plus service** One-time investment into core solution; ongoing support & new features on a fee-based model	**Solution as a service** Licensing/ subscription based on an annual fee-based model (all inclusive)
Product bundles	**Basic** Basic features and services included	**Advanced** Basic as well as advanced features and services included but partially limited in terms of usage	**Professional** Full-scale solution including unlimited access (to all product features and services)
Value and ROI	**Evaluation phase** Evaluation phase required to prove RoI for customers (at discounted prices)	**Business case** Reference data like value calculators or customer references sufficient to prove RoI	
Solution approach	**All applications and segments** Target all applications and segments with one holistic solution	**Application focus** Application specific adaption and targeting (PUR foaming application)	**Segment focus** Application and segment specific adaptions (e.g. PUR Metal panel and PUR mattress manufacturing)
Pricing	**Land & expand pricing strategy** Rapid market penetration with low customer lock-in and relatively low revenue per customer	**High entry pricing strategy** Rather slow market penetration with high customer lock-in and relatively high revenue per customer	

Fig. 5 Possible options for the go-to-market approach for DtS, author's own illustration

To ensure that DtS creates maximum sustainable benefit for customers and is a viable solution for *Covestro*, we decided to deploy this as **solution-as-a-service** with renewable yearly fees. The revenue model would comprise a one-time deployment fee followed by a yearly subscription fee for licenses, maintenance, and model/application upkeep and technical consulting. Any modifications or extensions to new use cases would be delivered as an extra one-time development service. We have identified a few lead customers and are currently in the process of negotiating commercial contracts which are the basis for a commercial product launch.

6   What Are the Key Learnings so Far?

- Data access and ownership of intellectual property: One of the areas where the team spend quite some time was in identifying, defining, and implementing data and legal requirements for this new situation. Before starting co-creation with customers, clearly defined agreements for sharing of data (on-premise vs. cloud) and ownership and IP aspects of work results (algorithms, process insights) must be in place to avoid misinterpretation at a later stage. *Covestro* as a raw material supplier needed extra caution to ensure that only Covestro supply-relevant (and not competitor relevant) data is accessed.
- Product development and time-to-fit: Our learning is that the time and effort needed to set up hardware, shop floor configuration, iteratively test, and improve/validate a IIoT solution is significantly higher (almost double) as compared to software only digital products. On top of this, the availability of key customer experts for workshops, product testing/approval, and feedback can be speed-limiting factor. Our product development was dependent on the availability of labeled quality data from destructive testing of parts in customer labs which took several months to generate. These challenges led to extended period of time for MVP building as compared to the initial plan.
- MVP vs. MDP (beyond core competencies): We learned that to create a great user experience, high usage and willingness-to-buy the MVP usually need to be extended with tech stack, features that were not initially planned or foreseen. This means going beyond existing core competencies and partnering with external suppliers to extend the desirability of our product. Ventures and startups need to operate with this open mindset and listen/adjust to customer feedback. In the long run it pays off to invest time and effort to build a MDP.

- Customer willingness-to-pay (WtP) and sales cycle: Customer WtP is primarily driven by value creation and available alternatives; however, with a new solution like DtS there is a wide range of customer perceptions in value of the solution and best pricing approach. Marketing and selling DtS solution will take long sales cycles typical of enterprise IoT solutions. Companies invest in DtS-type solutions as part of their digital transformation with a long-term perspective. This leads to extensive stakeholder management on customer side, participating in yearly budget approval (CAPEX), and several negotiations with different customer functions.

At the time of publishing this article, DtS has successfully demonstrated a product-market fit in the polyurethane (PUR) foaming application of sandwich metal panels used in the construction industry. Business model fit is currently being tested in this segment in preparation of a commercial market launch. At the same time the DtS approach is being piloted in other *Covestro*-relevant polymer processing applications to leverage *Covestro*'s market reach and to maximize the potential of this idea.

As a next step, DtS must be offered as a vendor-agnostic (raw materials, machines, etc.) standalone digital service. We are currently in the process of evaluating possible setups in preparation for launch. Toward building and growing DtS into a scalable, sustainable, and thus viable business, several hypotheses remain to be tested. In this context, *Covestro* is currently evaluating funding needs to reach key milestones and the risk-reward profile of DtS (as an early stage venture) compared to other available investment opportunities and priorities.

Lessons Learned

- Think in terms of business model innovation during the complete process and check/validate critical assumptions regularly.
- Include all customer personas and stakeholders upfront in developing a complete understanding of the "problem" to be solved.
- Address issues around data access and ownership of intellectual property early as this is crucial for scaling a digital product developed with several collaborators.
- Plan for a realistic product development timeline as IoT software development takes more time (than expected). Invest in building an MDP (minimum desirable product) which may go beyond your core competencies instead of only doing a minimum viable product (MVP) and proof of concept.
- Customer willingness-to-pay (WtP) is largely driven by overall perceived value created for the customer and this should be reflected in the pricing model.
- Ensure different stakeholder's interests at customer buying center are managed/addressed.
- Ensure that your investors as funding sources fully understand and share the purpose and vision of your venture.

Reference

Gassmann O, Frankenberger K, Csik M (2014) The business model navigator. 55 models that will revolutionise your business. Harlow: Pearson.

Sairam Potaraju is responsible for Digital Technical Services (DtS) a Business Model Innovation venture of Covestro, a leading supplier of high-tech polymer materials. Sairam previously held positions in technology consulting, operations management, product strategy functions, and in general management roles for Bayer MaterialScience/Covestro. Sairam holds a MS in Systems Engineering and a PhD in Chemical Engineering from Washington University in St. Louis, USA. Born in India and educated in the USA, he has gathered work experience in the USA, Germany, and India.

Hans Kespohl is heading Business Model Innovation and Digital Solutions Labs for Covestro. In this role, he is enabling Covestro to develop and test new business models and new digital solutions. Prior to this, he was partner of the innovation management consultancy UNITY AG. Hans studied industrial engineering, receiving a Diploma from the University of Paderborn, and a PhD in mechanical engineering at the Heinz Nixdorf Institute where he was 3 years team leader for computer-aided product innovation. At the same time, he collected his first experiences being an entrepreneur in the context of e-commerce.

Hermann Bach is heading Innovation Management and Commercial Services for Covestro. Hermann and his team help Covestro to drive innovation everywhere in the company. His particular focus lies on digitalization, business model innovation, sustainable materials, and innovation culture. Hermann holds a MS in chemistry from Marburg University and a PhD in physical chemistry from ETH Zurich and has completed several executive education programs at leading business schools. Born in Germany, he has gained international experience in the UK, in Switzerland, and in the USA.

BASF: Precision Farming with Lark Bread Initiative

Christoph Wecht, Matthias Nachtmann,
and Frank Koppenhagen

1   Agriculture and the Need for Digital Farming

BASF SE is a global leader in the field of industrial chemicals with companies in more than 90 countries, 6 production networks, and around 355 additional production sites. The group develops and produces main and intermediate products in six segments: chemicals, materials, industrial solutions, surface technologies, nutrition and care, as well as agricultural solutions. As competitive pressure is constantly growing and new competitors for the standard products appear, business model innovations are becoming increasingly important for the global market leader *BASF*.

In principle, the chemical industry is in a relatively safe position due to its characteristics: large network locations as well as very high investment costs

C. Wecht (✉)
New Design University, Wien, Austria
e-mail: christoph.wecht@bgw-sg.com

M. Nachtmann
BASF, SE, Limburgerhof, Germany
e-mail: matthias.nachtmann@basf.com

F. Koppenhagen
Hochschule für angewandte Wissenschaften, Hamburg, Germany
e-mail: frank.koppenhagen@haw-hamburg.de

© The Author(s), under exclusive license to Springer Nature Switzerland AG 2021   **315**
O. Gassmann, F. Ferrandina (eds.), *Connected Business*,
https://doi.org/10.1007/978-3-030-76897-3_20

and specialization in complex processes that have been tried and tested for decades and are often still protected by patents. In the past this very solid market entry barrier preserved the existing competitive industry structure. This security was very pronounced in the past, but the increasing digitalization creates new opportunities and challenges. New business models and start-ups with disruptive approaches can now be seen more and more in the conservative chemical industry which harbors both opportunities and threats. Innovation is therefore recognized as the essential ability in order to remain competitive and to maintain the leadership claim for *BASF*.

In the following, agriculture, a central market for the *BASF* division agricultural solution, will be used to show how digitization of products and processes brings new possibilities for innovative customer-oriented solutions. Agriculture is becoming a key industry of the twenty-first century. Climate change, water scarcity, eroding soils, and population growth make it increasingly difficult to feed the world population. Pest and weed control, fluctuating market prices, and increasing drought are omnipresent issues with a world population of almost eight billion people.

These challenges require constant readiness for innovative solutions in the sense of new technologies to increase efficiency. *BASF* is traditionally represented in the agricultural market with a broad portfolio. Active ingredients, seed varieties, biological crop protection, and services enable users to increase plant quality and yields. The agricultural market and *BASF*'s position in it to date can be summarized as follows:

- Traditional industry with established markets
- Innovations mainly in classic crop protection and seed variety portfolio
- Traditional business models with billing per quantity or number of items sold
- Increasing pressure on margins and thus on costs and efficiency
- Strong consolidation among market participants
- Start of digitization by equipment manufacturers and new entrants

In the last 150 years, great increases in yields per hectare were made possible by the technological leaps in fertilizers, machines, and crop protection. At the beginning of the twenty-first century, further increases in productivity are made possible via biotechnology as well as data and information technology. New approaches to digitization bring the next big and necessary boost to food value chain productivity. Agriculture is a typical example of the need to digitize an established, conservative industry. There is a growing understanding that something has to change in agriculture. One out of many drivers is the waste we produce with the current system. Another driver is the EU's green deal, including its farm to fork strategy which targets a significant decrease in crop protection usage combined with an increase in the share of organic farming.

BASF has a lot of activities going on to create value in a connected agriculture and food economy. Solutions for a more sustainable, more productive agriculture are developed together with farmers. In this context, digital technologies are an essential part of the solution. The innovation goes beyond the actual plant protection:

1. On the one hand, processes and channels to sell traditional products are now digitized, i.e., the existing business models are digitally enhanced.
2. On the other hand, some physical products are enriched with additional data in order to obtain relevant knowledge for increasing customer benefit and productivity. In combination with the core product, this adds value for the customer, around which new digital business models are possible.

2   Digital Farming Solutions from *BASF*

BASF's digital solutions for farmers are marketed under the xarvio™ brand. They support farmers with digital solutions to optimize crop production and crop protection. This includes that farmers always know what is happening in their fields, providing more planning and decision security.

By monitoring soil and crop conditions xarvio™ SCOUTING helps farmers and advisors to identify field stress caused by weeds, diseases, or pests. The xarvio™ FIELD MANAGER recommends treatments based on in-field conditions. It supports farmers with a spray timer, as well as variable rate application maps for seeds, fertilizers, and crop protection. The xarvio™ HEALTHY FIELDS product features the first outcome-based pricing model for fungus-free fields. Farmers no longer pay by volume of crop protection any more but for healthy fields (Fig. 1).

One of the key features for field-specific crop management are power zones. These zones show high- or low-performing field zones based on up to 15 years of historic satellite data. They are using historical biomass information and can be used for more effective seeding and field preparation. High-yielding zones can be used to optimize yield performance. Low-yielding zones can be excluded from farming crops and used for biodiversity management. Therefore, farmers can define biodiversity zones and exclude these zones from their seeding maps.

Fig. 1 Digital farming solution xarvio™ FIELD MANAGER, showing field specific power zones, author's own illustration

3   The Lark Bread Project as a Connected Business Model in Digital Farming

The Lark Bread Initiative supports farmers in a community pilot project to promote biodiversity while at the same time to work productively. It runs as follows: participating farmers make at least two "nonproductive" areas per hectare on their wheat fields available for skylarks. Those lark windows are open spaces of about 20 m² serving the skylarks as "runways" while they breed in the fields and search for food. Farmers with the latest seeding machinery can use the abovementioned seeding maps showing excluded biodiversity management zones (i.e., lark windows). The wheat obtained from those fields is processed into flour in a local mill and baked into Lark Bread by a regional bakery chain. This bread is then sold at the counter at a surcharge of EUR 0.10 per leaf. This surcharge is passed on to the farmers as compensation for their effort for setting up lark windows and accompanying biodiversity measures (Fig. 2).

The demonstrable decline in biodiversity poses the challenge of modern agriculture to strike a balance between high productivity and the protection of biodiversity. However, the implementation of appropriate measures is often associated with a loss of earnings or high costs. In a pilot project with farmers from the southern Palatinate, *Walter Mühle*, a regional mill in Böhl-Iggelheim, and the local bakery *Görtz*, *BASF* is showing how biodiversity measures become business-relevant for farmers for the first time. The project is about the protection of the skylark, the population of which is considered an

Fig. 2 Lark window in the wheat field, author's own illustration

indicator of biodiversity. For this purpose, four farmers from the *BASF* Farm Network Sustainability, with the support of the digital seed maps from xarvio Digital Farming Solutions, created the so-called lark windows on a total of 40 hectares of wheat area—at least 2 per hectare (Fig. 3).

The farmers involved receive this surcharge as compensation for the creation of further biodiversity measures, such as perennial flowering areas and hedges, and the associated loss of yield. "With this Lark Bread, we want to specifically promote biodiversity," says Peter Görtz, owner of the *Görtz* bakery. "But it also shows that there is regional craft behind all this—the wheat comes from farmers in the region, is ground separately and processed into Lark Bread in the bakery. With lark flour from these fields." In this project his regional bakery takes on everything that has to be done around Lark Bread, naming it, selling it, and ensuring direct consumer contact.

The specific commercials of the pilot project made another key factor very transparent, the crop value share of the end product. Considering the 40 hectares of wheat, around 240 t of bread grain are harvested at an average of 6 t/ha, which yields around 200 t of lark flour. If 1 kg of flour is enough for three loaves of bread, about 600,000 can be baked. The EUR 0.10 per bread would correspond to around EUR 600/ha, which could be achieved in additional added value. Considering principle winter wheat revenue of EUR 1.400–1.700/ha, this business model provides tangible additional value for farmers.

Fig. 3 The entire value chain is involved in the Lark Bread Initiative—from the farmer to the mill to the baker, author's own illustration

In order to scale this idea, *BASF* is planning to create skylark windows in 10,000 hectares of winter wheat and to market the Lark Bread throughout Germany. Furthermore, they are working intensively with farmers and partners along the entire food value chain on similar projects in other crops such as rapeseeds, potatoes, and hops. Further projects are already being planned promoting digital field manager to combine productivity and biodiversity more easily.

4   Conclusions for a Connected Agriculture Business

The project introduces a completely new logic of thinking. In addition to the traditional business models, a completely new customer benefit is created that is based on a level of expertise that has not yet been widely developed. The success of such a project was anything but guaranteed. The following experiences were made within the Lark Bread project:

- **Ensure strategic anchoring:** Support from top management is essential. Only then can the necessary decisions, which are often associated with high risks, be made. Resistance has to be overcome; this is all the more relevant as existing silos have to be broken open and completely new paths have to be explored.

- **Bundling activities:** The responsibility must be clearly regulated. In addition to a committed "driver" who is passionate about the topic, a small, powerful core team is required as the nucleus of change. The bundling leads to the fact that the momentum in the team remains and the various interfaces, also organizational ones, are managed well.
- **Plan implementation time:** In a traditional company with a conservative, traditional culture, new business models are not introduced overnight. Patience is necessary—project planning times that are too short lead to false expectations, which can endanger the entire project.
- **Use active communication:** Since these are change processes, the associated challenges and cultural changes must be approached proactively. Targeted communication both internally and externally is of great importance. It is advisable to develop an overarching brand strategy and to regularly and consistently inform all stakeholders.
- **Increase specific knowledge level:** A broad awareness of the topic of business model innovation is required. Employees must be made aware that new products and technologies are not enough. The more fertile the ground for such business model and digitization initiatives, the easier to overcome the hurdles. Tailor-made training courses should be developed and offered for those involved.

It can make sense to approach markets with a high degree of openness and a lower regulatory environment first. There are also two other specific success factors:

1. Standardization and involvement in standardization organizations: Standards already play an essential role in the physical world (e.g., track width of tractors); in the digital world their importance will continue to increase. The Internet of things (IoT) will only become a successful basis for new business models if the scalability, flexibility, and security that come with standards are ensured. The use of openly available information in particular requires such uniform formats and interfaces.
2. Data security: The security and protection of data have top priority. The rights of the data owner (producer or collector) are respected. Country-specific rules and laws must be taken into account. The latest technologies to ensure IT security are used. Transparency is key here.

5   Conclusion

Projects like Lark Bread show that digital farming solutions can enable farmers to make fact-based, improved decisions. It is based on integrated data solutions and mobile access. The analysis of the data that is collected via mobile devices and sensors plays an important role. In addition to this partner data, freely available data, i.e., open data, knowledge, and expertise from *BASF*, are also integrated. The local customer experience flows into such precision farming projects. Smart farming is therefore no longer limited to the high-tech niche. This is a typical lesson for traditional industries: The solutions for digitization and new business models are already in place if you analyze them in sufficient detail. It is important to understand digitization as opportunity and not as threat. Then long-term potential for success can also be secured in other traditional industries.

> **Lessons Learned from the *BASF* Digital Business Model**
> – Ensure strategic anchoring of the new initiative.
> – Bundle activities for concentration on your core competencies.
> – Schedule implementation time.
> – Use active communication inside and outside the company.
> – Increase specific knowledge level, especially business-relevant knowledge and implementation on business models.

Christoph Wecht, Prof. Dr., is a full Professor of Management at the New Design University (NDU) in St. Pölten, Austria, where he also heads the Bachelor's degree program Management by Design. Prior to joining the New Design University, Professor Wecht headed the Competence Center for Open Innovation at the Institute of Technology Management (ITEM-HSG) at the University of St. Gallen. He has authored or co-authored more than 80 scholarly and practitioner articles, conference papers, and book chapters. From June to September 2019, Prof. Christoph H. Wecht continued his research as visiting professor at the Center for Design Research (CDR) at Stanford University, California.

Matthias Nachtmann, Dr., holds a degree in agricultural sciences from the University of Gießen and a doctorate with distinction in business administration from the University of Oldenburg. His main experience lies in the development of business models in the areas of agricultural technology, plant breeding, and protection and digital farming. He has worked in the Digital Farming division of BASF SE since 2012 and is in charge of Data Business Development. Further he is chairman of the Förderverein Digital Farming e.V. and holds various supervisory board mandates in science and start-ups.

Frank Koppenhagen, Prof. Dr., has been Professor of Product Development and Engineering Design at the Hamburg University of Applied Sciences since 2009. His research focuses on engineering design methodology and modular product architectures. He has authored and coauthored several publications in these fields. In 2012, he received the Hamburg award for excellence in academic teaching. He was invited as a visiting professor at the Center for Design Research at Stanford University in 2019. Prior to his academic career, Koppenhagen worked in different capacities in the Mercedes-Benz Car Group's development department.

AgriCircle: Innovating Agricultural Ecosystems

Florian Huber and Daniel Markward

1 Innovation in Agriculture Today Is a Connected Rather than an Individual Endeavour

For 10,000 years agriculture has been the most important industry for humans. Its increasing productivity has been a major determinant of population growth in recent centuries. This success is reflected by the fact that in principle, there is enough food for 7 billion people today. In some regions hunger is still a scourge, but the challenges are distribution problems rather than production problems (Smil 2017). This is remarkable, because forecasts only a few decades ago would never have thought this amount of food production is possible. In 2050 agriculture will have to feed 10 billion people (United Nations 2019). The odds are high that this will also be feasible and sufficient innovation will lead to the required rates of food productivity. However, the logic of agricultural innovation is changing a lot.

F. Huber (✉)
Helvetia Insurance, St. Gallen, Switzerland
e-mail: florian.huber@helvetia.ch

D. Markward
AgriCircle AG, Zurich, Switzerland
e-mail: daniel.markward@agricircle.com

For thousands of years there has been innovation in agriculture (Diamond and Ordunio 1999). Naturally, innovation was initially primarily related to process technologies such as irrigation systems or the three-field economy, but from the nineteenth century onwards it was increasingly machinery and fertilizer. In the 1960s, new methods of genetic modification played a significant role in further increasing the productivity of agricultural land. In absolute terms, the number of people that each farmer could feed rose from 26 in the 1930s to 155 (EY 2017). Today, a large part of agriculture is highly industrialized, at least in the highly developed parts of the world. Current and prospective developments suggest that today, innovations in agriculture are driven primarily by two other megatrends: biotechnology and information technology.

2   New Digital Orchestrators Enter the Market

This poses challenges for established players. No company has the necessary know-how in all areas. For example, *John Deere*'s core competence is the construction of sophisticated agricultural machinery, and *Syngenta*'s core competence is biological and chemical crop protection. These companies do not have outstanding IT competencies. IT companies such as *Google* or *Microsoft* on the other hand lack the technical and market knowledge in the agricultural sector to develop innovative solutions on their own. This is why companies are increasingly turning to another solution: cooperation and joint development. By connecting their various core competencies, new innovation opportunities arise (Huber et al. 2018).

The public projects of large corporations, such as the open platform of *John Deere*, are the primary focus of the press (Gustafson 2014). However, the majority of innovation projects are below the radar of the public. Small, agile start-ups can act as a neutral authority and work together with various companies to develop targeted solutions. They often develop small ecosystems and orchestrate their partners to develop an innovative value proposition.

One example of one of the most active and networked start-ups is *AgriCircle*. Based in Switzerland, the start-up operates throughout Europe. *AgriCircle* is a leading company in the field of digital modelling and data processing and the development of decision support for agriculture. Together with its partners, the small company develops digital solutions to increase productivity and sustainability. *AgriCircle* works closely with research and industry partners on an interdisciplinary basis to bring innovative applications quickly to market. Its core competence lies in the modelling and processing of complex data structures and the development of decision-making aids based on them. Due to the professional background of the two founders—a farmer who worked as a manager for a chemical company and a former manager of an IT consulting firm—*AgriCircle* also has know-how in both agriculture and technology. The networking with the partners and the common use of know-how is indispensable for the start-up, which itself has only limited resources at its disposal. With its team of about 15 persons, it is involved in several major collaborative initiatives in Europe that focus on the digital transformation of agriculture. Two examples of such cooperation show the possibilities of connected solutions in agriculture. Data collected via satellites, drones, in-field sensors and soil samples are used to optimize agricultural practices. The collected information is passed on to the food industry to improve sustainability, safety and traceability of food along the supply chain (Fig. 1).

3   The *Höcklistein* Project to Detect Disease in Vineyards

This project was concerned with the detection of disease in the vineyard. Using innovative data analysis methods, the partners wanted to gain new insights that complemented the physical expertise of the oenologists. To develop this new value proposition, the partners had to contribute their

Fig. 1 Data collected via satellites, drones, in-field sensors and soil samples are used to optimize agricultural practices, author's own illustration

specific core competencies. The vineyard *Höcklistein* provided know-how in the area of oenology and crop assessment as well as testing grounds. *AgriCircle* had expertise in data processing and digital modelling. Another key player was a project team from the *Fraunhofer Institute*, which specialized in sensor technology and data processing. This knowledge was complemented by the scientific perspective of several viticulture and technology institutes in Europe. In addition to these ecosystem partners, there were a number of suppliers who specifically supplied or assembled hardware such as drones or a hyperspectral camera.

Several high-tech data sources were needed to phenotype each individual plant: The laser scanning system developed by the *Fraunhofer* team was built on a small tractor that created a 3D model of the *Höcklistein* vineyard as it passed through. This 3D model was used to determine the area of the vines. The hyperspectral camera mounted on the drone acquired complex hyperspectral data at the molecular level during the flight. Thus, the chemical properties of each individual object, in this case of the vine, can be recorded. This way the drone enables the chemical phenotyping of the individual vines and can quickly reveal changes. Physical phenotyping was also carried out by experts in the field. These were both internal and external experts of the *Höcklistein* winery.

The combination and analysis of these data allowed more precise insights into the condition of the vineyard than ever before. This was made obvious by an interesting case: a pandemic. Spreading from another region, an infestation of the phytoplasma bacterium destroyed 20% of the harvest in 2019. Without countermeasures, this bacterium could spread to the entire vineyard, so that the entire stand might have to be cleared. The solution is to detect infested plants early and cut them back by hand. With this knowledge, the vineyard data could now be examined retrospectively and the infestation could be traced back to 2 years ago. In other words: the innovative data analysis had a lead of 2 years over the human discovery.

The advantages of the value proposition were now also comprehensible in monetary terms for all stakeholders. In autumn 2019 the management of the *Höcklistein* vineyard therefore decided to expand the cooperation and to lobby in the canton, since several smaller vineyards suffer from the same infestation. Some public research institutions should also be involved. For instance, the national centre of excellence for agricultural research should provide expertise with regard to the disease and support the communication with the smaller wineries. With the extension to other vineyards and the broad application of the tool, the project will enter new dimensions.

4   The Atlas Project for Interoperability in Connected Agriculture Applications

A much larger and more visible project is currently developed at EU level. Specifically, some core partners such as *AgriCircle* and the *Fraunhofer* project team, who knew each other from the *Höcklistein* project, had applied for an innovative Atlas project. A basic problem with many connectivity applications in agriculture is the lack of inter-operability between the systems of manufacturers and users. The partners now want to bring together agricultural machinery, sensors and algorithms. This should be made possible in a way that allows a farmer to flexibly decide which machine is combined with which sensor and which data analysis platform.

The around 30 project partners can be divided into different categories, each of which contributes different core competencies. First, there are data service providers with expertise in the analysis and processing of agricultural data. These include several research institutes as well as *AgriCircle* and the Fraunhofer team in charge of the project. Fraunhofer is coordinating the project, and *AgriCircle* is responsible for the software architecture of the overall system and the interfaces with the farmers. Secondly, there are drone and sensor technology operators and sensor providers. Thirdly, there are machine manufacturers, and fourthly, there are farmers as end users.

This diversity of partners opens up a wide range of possibilities for applications. The simplest objective is for a farmer to be able to select sensors for his agricultural machinery on a modular basis and use the data. In concrete terms, however, the diversity of farmers, agricultural machinery and sensors means that there are several applications that need to be taken into account. For instance, a wheat farmer wants to have an automated irrigation for monitoring plant stress. For this he needs a tractor equipped with soil moisture sensors. The corresponding data should be linked with satellite data on the weather. The software could also automatically make recommendations on sowing or the use of plant protection products.

Another example is a dairy farmer. This farmer can set up sensors on milk robots, for example, as well as a laser scan analysis in the barn. The AI systems for image analysis of video surveillance data help to determine the nervousness level of the animals. The farmer can thus track the health and even the well-being of each individual cow in real time and follow the software recommendations for optimized milk production.The project is still ongoing. It is expected to significantly enhance connectivity in the agricultural sector across Europe and create a wide range of innovative applications.

5   Conclusion

Both cases show that in agriculture, major digital innovations can hardly be pursued by individual corporates anymore. Instead, it requires a joint effort to connect services and develop common value propositions. Small and agile companies such as *AgriCircle* point the way to advance such digital innovation: joint developments and connected services.

Agriculture and to an even larger extent the agricultural industry are characterized by the heterogeneity of players that are required to work together. While the big players lack the cloud to do things on their own, industry associations lack the dynamic to drive innovation fast enough. To build new ecosystems in a digital environment, connectors such as *AgriCircle* are therefore essential in these industries.

Further it requires a certain degree of independence to drive good ideas that might be unpopular from the perspective of a single stakeholder. An owner-managed company with a long-term vision is often better positioned here than a company driven by internal politics and short-term thinking.

Lessons Learnt
- Agricultural innovation becomes increasingly data-based.
- Ecosystem thinking helps to combine complementary assets and allows specialization.
- Research-based approaches to business innovation will change traditional agricultural processes.

References

Diamond JM, Ordunio D (1999) Guns, germs, and steel. Norton, New York

EY (2017) Digital agriculture: helping to feed a growing world

Gustafson M (2014) Big data and agriculture. Agri Marketing 52(2):24–25,27

Huber F, Miehé L, Lingens B (2018) Helvetia: Neue Customer Journey im Ecosystem "HOME". In: Gassmann O, Sutter P (eds) Digitale Transformation gestalten. Hanser, München, pp 225–232

Smil V (2017) Energy and civilization: a history. The MIT Press, Cambridge, Massachusetts, London

United Nations, Department of Economic and Social Affairs, Population Division (2019) World population prospects 2019: highlights (ST/ESA/SER.A/423)

Florian Huber, studied Business Administration and Accounting and Finance at the University of St. Gallen (M.A. HSG), supplemented by stays in Singapore and the USA. From 2018–2020 he was a research assistant and doctoral candidate at the Institute of Technology Management at the University of St. Gallen. As a member of the Helvetia Innovation Labs, the Bavarian-born researcher was involved in the practical implementation of an ecosystem in the home. In his research, he is particularly dedicated to inter-firm collaboration in ecosystems. Since 2021, he has been working as a strategy manager for Helvetia Insurance.

Daniel Markward, is chairman of AgriCircle, a HSG-spin-off that connects farm data for better decision support along the food value chain. He co-founded the company in 2013 after finishing his MBA at the University of St. Gallen and has won several innovation prizes with AgriCircle since then. Before becoming an entrepreneur, he worked for seven years as a management and technology consultant for KPMG in Zurich and Los Angeles across industries.

AGL Energy: Moving to the Connected and Orchestrated Customers

Jonas Böhm and John Chambers

1   Innovating the Energy Sector

For over 180 years, *AGL Energy* has been at the forefront of energy innovation in Australia. From lighting the first gas streetlamp in Sydney in 1841 to helping shape a sustainable energy future for Australia. *AGL* operates the country's largest electricity generation portfolio, is its largest private investor in renewable energy and provides 4.2 million electricity (which reflects 30% market share in Australia), gas and telecommunications services to residential, small and large business and wholesale customers. *AGL's* traditional business model is that of a classical gentailer: a company that is operating at both ends of the electrical value chain by owning energy generation assets and selling retail energy to customers in a competitive market.

AGL—as most players in this industry around the world—must navigate non-trivial large-scale transformations on many ends. Decarbonization, digitization and decentralization are accelerating the countdown to a new energy world. The accelerating shift towards small and utility-scale renewables,

J. Böhm (✉)
AGL Energy, Crows Nest, Australia
e-mail: jonas.e.boehm@gmail.com

J. Chambers
AGL Energy, Docklands, Australia
e-mail: jchambers3@agl.com.au

complemented by declines in the cost of decentralized generation-plus-storage solutions, reduces the competitive advantage of owning large generation assets. For example, in 2010, 1 in 100 households in Australia had rooftop solar. Today one in four households have solar on their rooftop. There is more rooftop solar in Australia than all of the United States. Additionally, other complementing digital energy technologies such as battery storage, electric vehicles, artificial intelligence and machine learning are moving quickly from being emerging trends to integral parts of the energy system and reshape the business model of the gentailer: from a pipeline business model producing energy to platform business models orchestrating energy and the connected customer. Some of these strategic trends are already materialized.

In 2017, *AGL* entered the Top 50 Most Innovative Companies list in Australia and New Zealand at number 13 and won the Business Model Innovation Award for the Powering Australian Renewables Fund (PARF). PARF is a landmark financing initiative. The US\$ 2–3 billion fund aims to develop and own approximately 1000 Megawatt in large-scale renewable generation projects, providing opportunity for investors to finance a portfolio of renewable assets, to diversify risk and reduce costs. Other emerging examples of value proposition and complete business model redefinition include personalized energy voice services for the *Google* Assistant and *Amazon* Alexa, an app that goes beyond account management, a virtual power plant connecting 1,500 residential batteries and orchestrating them in the wholesale market to share value back to customers and an electric vehicle subscription service. Moving *AGL* from business models that rely mostly on analogue value creation to business models that rely on digitally connecting customers and orchestrating their energy assets required (and still requires) the transformation of the organizations technological core, customer interaction channels and data capabilities and business innovation capabilities. To put things into context—still 5 years ago, the main interaction point of *AGL* with its customers was a paper-based energy bill, billing for energy produced in large power plants far away from its consumption. Moving from this analogue and transactional relationship to start digital value creation with the long-tail of customers required several concurring changes for *AGL*.

2   Transforming the Technological Core: Getting the Fundamentals Right

Creating customer value in a digitally enabled energy world required *AGL* to transform its technological core. *AGL* needed to move from pure systems of record keeping (to just bill customers correctly), to provide a technological core that additionally enables systems of differentiation and innovation.

AGL invested 300 million Australian dollars into a technological uplift. This included the decision to move almost all workloads to the public cloud (by 2022). In this, *AGL* will become the largest energy company and one of the first ASX top 50 companies with virtually all its technology applications in the public cloud. This move promises to change the technological capabilities from mostly record keeping to systems of innovation.

For example, it used to take 3 to 4 weeks to get a development environment at *AGL* for software engineers to start working. Using public cloud services, it now takes minutes. Another example of the more rapid time frames possible from using the cloud is in *AGL*'s modelling of cost scenarios in the energy marketplace. It used to take 35 minutes to model 150 different simulations, and now it can process more than 10,500 scenarios in 2.5 minutes. Also, in terms of output, 3 years ago *AGL* could deliver about 8 to 12 projects to improve customer experience per month, but that has now increased to around 80. This investment presents a technological precondition to enable digital business models.

With the initiative regarded as a big success internally, a lot of the good results and longer-term potential benefits to a decision taken are ascribed to the decision not to rely too much on external consultants to get the job done. This enables that once the transition project is finished, the capabilities to understand the systems and to keep them alive are in-house.

Renewing the technological core reduced the cost to serve customers significantly, enabling business models that build on segments-of-one and addressing the long-tail of customers. Serving thousands of virtual power plants customers where the shareable value pool per customer lies in the hundreds of dollars is only possible with significantly lower costs to serve.

3   Creating a Digital Infrastructure Through Digital Customer Transformation

Next to a technological core, business models that build on data and the digital connection of cyber-physical systems require a digital connection with the customer. Often, these business models rely on real-time information sharing and interaction with the customer. Latency times of 3 months in non-interoperable systems (paper bills) makes it impossible to create value for customers through connected devices.

Only 3 years ago, *AGL* could have been largely described as contact centre business from the customer's point of view. *AGL* had a website, but it was very limited in traffic. It had a mobile app but had only about 15,000 users/customers on the app, and touchpoints with the customer were very bill driven—which gave customers also limited value in the app. To achieve a digital connection with the customer, *AGL* took the decision to go Mobile First and beyond transactional value (bill and account management). This decision enabled to build a digital relationship with customers that is fundamental for digital value creation. The digital connection with customers presents a core digital infrastructure where additional business models can be built on top of. Use cases that require real-time interaction or use cases that profit from data network effects only become feasible and viable through this direct digital infrastructure with customers. Additionally, the digital connection with customers might account for demand-side economies of scale and support strategies such as multi-product retailing.

One of the examples where the digital connection with customers serves as the digital infrastructure for new business models is the virtual power plant, where customers have a battery (e.g. a *Tesla* Powerwall) and typically rooftop solar. Customers agree that *AGL* can monitor and orchestrate (remote charge/discharge the battery to share value with the electricity market). The first level of value creation happens through digitally connecting the physical assets, but the second important level of value creation is sharing information and actionable insights back with the customer.

Establishing a standing digital channel is required to move away from a bill and account-centred value of the application, to provide much more ongoing value to customers. Customers, for example, can get real-time energy consumption details through Energy Insights, 'trade sunshine' with Solar Exchange or customize push notifications.

Engaging customers beyond account management features resulted in an app rating of 4.6/5, almost 8 app launches per month on average for customers and more than double engagement for battery customers.

4   Data Revolution

First of all, for many unfamiliar with the energy sector, the amount of data that is available to *AGL* might be surprising. A few snapshots highlight the breadth and depth of data available. *AGL* runs a virtual power plant with residential batteries, currently connecting around 1,500 batteries (think of Tesla Powerwalls). Just from these relatively small number (in Australia it is expected that this number grows by a factor of a thousand by 2025), *AGL* has the following:

* Currently 150 billion rows of raw telemetry data in the database
* Adding 800 million rows per day
* Total of ~25 terabytes of data

In *AGL*'s owned asset base, *AGL* has 800,000 sensor reads every second and 700,000 customers with smart meters in the state of Victoria alone. These smart meters measure and record how much electricity a household or business is using at 30-minute intervals.

To leverage this data for both operational efficiency and value creation in new business models, *AGL* established a Data and Analytics Center of Excellence. Setting up this centre helps to move from one-off data projects to templatized workspaces for initiatives. This Center of Excellence is paired with an internal Data Council—made up of leaders from across the business—to align investments in data projects and initiatives. Moreover, the council aims to bring a data-driven lens to everything to the whole business.

For example, using *AGL*'s analytic platform, *AGL* can identify if customers' batteries have an operational issue or if the customers' battery was not installed properly. *AGL* knows if something is wrong, which might not actually be apparent to the customer and might not even be apparent to the battery vendor installer themselves. If it is not operating as it should, we can help customers to rectify it by providing them a baseline performance of what they should expect.

Generally, creating business models based on data collected requires a delicate trade-off: costs of storing and handling data approximately scales linearly; hence, whenever there is an opportunity to increase the volume of data in use, we must be convinced that we can identify customer value that scales super-linear. For example, the settlement period for the electricity market spot price in Australia will move from 30 min intervals to 5 min intervals in 2021. Simplified, this increases the amount of available data by six times. Hence, the question is whether we can identify value pools that are six times the size of today's data. *AGL* uses the following (simplified) graph to work with data and find the right management technique (Fig. 1):

1. Costs of data and value have a perfect positive correlation. Can we move to curve 2 or 3? Bring the right business expertise into the picture, e.g. at the Data Council, or move to templatized versions to achieve more scale or lower costs.
2. We have data network effects! A product's value increases with more data, and additional usage of that product yields data. Central success factors: getting the flywheel spinning and convincing management of the worthiness of the idea for the time the value lies below the cost curve.
3. Data has decreasing marginal returns. Smart handling of the data increases margins. Knowing enough about the data to know what matters and understanding which parts of the data is the trick. Storing too much data can destroy the business case. Which parts of the data are essential to create the value?

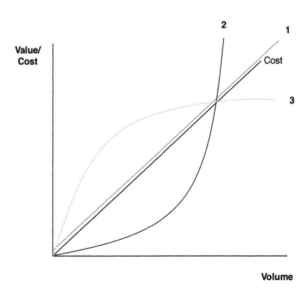

Fig. 1 Managing data for customer, author's own illustration

5   Business Innovation: Making the Elephant Dance

Building on an improved technological core, a standing digital channel with customers and data capabilities, *AGL* in 2019 established the Future Business function. The role of Future Business is to identify and incubate growth opportunities for *AGL* in collaboration with the broader business. It combines the corporate venture capital, innovation strategy and innovation execution function. Future Business forms ideas for new growth businesses using the insight gathered from internal and external sources. In a lean start-up approach, the ideas and hypothesis are then tested through market tests and early customer feedback, thus triggering a process known as the 'build-measure-learn' loop (Blank 2013; Ries 2011). Through a structured process of exploration, validation, incubation and scale, these ideas are progressed. The Future Business pipeline is governed by an internal Tech Council consisting of senior leaders across the business that guides and decides on funding for initiatives—similar to a venture capital investors board.

6   Making the Business Model Switch

As outlined above, the first steps towards business model change for *AGL* was to get the foundations right: laying the technological foundations, digitally connect with the customer and combining the two to continuously improve customer value. The next important step to make a business model switch is for the company to understand the new mechanics of the digital business model. *AGL* recognized that many opportunity areas in the new energy world will follow platform architectures. The electric vehicle and virtual power plants opportunities—to name the two most prominent ones—follow platform architectures (see chapter "Groupon: Managing a Rapidly Growing Platform with Scale Up Metrics"; for a detailed analysis of these mechanics in the electric vehicle sector, see Boehm, Bhargava and Parker (2020), for virtual power plants Palmié et al. 2021). In both cases, the product offered increasingly depends upon external actors to provide the necessary complements to create a complete system that delivers value to end users, and the value to a platform's user is dependent upon the number of other users who also affiliate with the system. The implication of this network effect is that, unlike traditional goods, a user's utility is not a constant and increases as more buyers adopt the good. The overall value creation of a product or service is a combination of an independent product/service value and network value. Managing both, the independent product value and the network value, is the next critical success factor to make the business model switch. *AGL* took strategic steps in this direction. For example, *AGL* is the first retailer in the world to orchestrate multi-asset vendor batteries through cloud technology to open the complementor base. This opens up the network of batteries. From initially selling and integrating batteries into the virtual power plant, *AGL* then opened up the business model to allow bring-your-battery into the system.

Lessons Learnt

- Do the homework: Moving to a connected business requires doing the required homework in technological and organizational uplift first. It's not 'fake it until you make it'.
- Rethink the customer relationship on both ends: The customer is not just a billing account and the utility is not just someone sending bills. The change in relationship needs to happen on both ends.
- Find the assets and capabilities: There are more than you think in places where you don't expect them. It requires a re-evaluation of assets and capabilities in light of new business models. Things that haven't been identified as strategic advantage previously can become core in new business models.
- Understand the new game you play in depth and learn to play: New business models—such as platform business models—follow fundamentally different business logics. Understanding them in depth requires deep work across the organization; playing the game requires closing the 'say-do' gap.
- Be open. Find novel ways of partnering across industry borders.

References

Blank S (2013) Why the lean start-up changes everything. Harv Bus Rev 91(5):63–72

Boehm J, Bhargava H, Parker G (2020) The business of electric vehicles: a platform perspective. Found Trends in Tech Inf Oper Manag 14(3):203–323

Palmié M, Boehm J, Lekkas CK, Parida V, Wincent J, Gassmann O (2021) Circular business model implementation: design choices, orchestration strategies, and transition pathways for resource-sharing solutions. J Clean Prod 280:124399

Ries E (2011) The lean startup: how today's entrepreneurs use continuous innovation to create radically successful businesses. Currency

Jonas Böhm, Dr., is a Venture Strategist in AGL's Future Business division and leads platform opportunities across AGL. He serves as a Fellow at the World Economic Forum to provide thought leadership on digital platforms and shape the Forum's agenda. Jonas previously held positions in Innovation, Product Management, and Inhouse Consulting at SAP, BMW, and Credit Suisse, as well as in his own venture Bridge17. He holds a PhD from the University of St. Gallen, a Master in Business Innovation, and CEMS Master in International Management and is a Visiting Scholar at Dartmouth College.

John Chambers leads AGL's technology, data, and business innovation teams. He completed a Bachelor of Economics at Macquarie University in 1994 and has enjoyed an executive career in product, technology, and innovation across the telco and energy sectors. John started Fresh Ventures, an innovation consultancy, in 2018 and sold it and its IP to a larger digital consultancy IE only 12 months later. John also founded Moorup, a circular economy platform business, which is currently experiencing 100%+ ARR growth.

EnBW SMIGHT: Addressing the Energy and Mobility Transition as Electricity Grid Operator

Oliver Deuschle, Mirijam Hübner, and Anja Martin

1 Addressing the e-Mobility Challenge

The energy and mobility transition is presenting energy network operators with big challenges. Since the advent of electrification over 100 years ago, electricity grids have been designed solely for easily foreseeable supply tasks and for distributing electrical energy from large power plants to the electricity consumer. The task of supplying power changed massively following the start of funding for renewable energies and the associated growth in wind and photovoltaic feeders. In 2020, around 50% of the total quantity of power supplied in Germany was attributable to renewable energy sources. This is associated with a significantly fluctuating amount of energy being fed into the electricity grid—depending on the levels of wind and sunshine. Furthermore, these new systems are primarily found on the medium- and low-voltage grids. This is precisely why there has so far been no need for any measurement or control—and where there is neither a full connection to central control centers nor any transparency from the grid operator about the influence of renewable feeders. Due to the solid planning of electricity grids in the past, the new feeders had no noteworthy impact on the security of supply. At present, however, a second wave of dynamic change to the medium- and especially low-voltage grids is in the offing. The mobility transition and the considerable

O. Deuschle • M. Hübner • A. Martin (✉)
EnBW Energie Baden-Württemberg AG, Karlsruhe, Germany
e-mail: O.Deuschle@enbw.com; M.Huebner@enbw.com; a.martin@enbw.com

© The Author(s), under exclusive license to Springer Nature Switzerland AG 2021 **343**
O. Gassmann, F. Ferrandina (eds.), *Connected Business*,
https://doi.org/10.1007/978-3-030-76897-3_23

increase in electric vehicles (e-vehicles), as well as the associated expansion of the charging infrastructure, will place even more strain on the electricity grids. Over the coming years, the number of e-vehicles in Germany is expected to rise from today's figure of almost 200,000 to 5 million by 2025 and 10 million by 2030.

If the load situation changes—for example, as a result of local hotspots caused by several electric vehicles being charged at once—this generally remains undiscovered until the grid is overloaded, and the cable's overload fuse is triggered. Local measurements to ascertain the actual load situation are subsequently necessary. These are followed by grid planning and expansion processes and ultimately the laying of a new, larger cable. All German electricity grid operators are required to get to grips with the impact of the energy and mobility transition for the as yet unmonitored grid facilities at local supply level. Here, it is necessary to gradually turn the roughly 600,000 local transformer stations into intelligent hubs with the aid of technically advanced and economically viable solutions.

Extending the established measuring technology used for the high- and extra-high-voltage grids to the lower voltage levels is not an option. That is because an inexpensive and comprehensive rollout is not possible due to the high safety and quality requirements and the very complex processes. *EnBW* identified this challenge and founded a corporate start-up that addresses this market: *SMIGHT.*

As a corporate start-up belonging to *EnBW*, *SMIGHT* had the necessary freedom to devise the business model for *SMIGHT* Grid quickly, flexibly, and in a way that is geared toward the needs of the market. At the same time, *SMIGHT* (now an independent *EnBW* business unit) has full access to the resources of a large company and the in-depth expertise in all areas of the energy sector. The team was quickly able to verify the findings with internal (friendly) customers and adapt the product to the needs of the users. Based on this customer feedback, the team was able to work with in-house embedded developers to create a new kind of technology specifically for the measuring technology not yet available on the market and elaborate the solution as a full service—from hardware, over installation process, to data management.

2   Sensor and IoT Technology Create Transparency Within the Distribution Grid

SMIGHT has been working on the development of IoT solutions for 6 years. Together with *Netze BW*, one of the biggest German distribution grid operators, a solution was developed that provides greater transparency within the grid and is not only capable of being rolled out on a mass scale but also optimized in terms of procurement and operation costs. The solution has primarily been designed for the distribution grid operators that possess very little IT expertise due to their operating structures and are therefore reliant on highly integrated plug and play solutions. Of the roughly 850 distribution grid operators in Germany, small and medium-sized grid operators in particular require such solutions.

As a full-service provider, *SMIGHT* is adopting a unique position in the competitive sphere. That is because existing providers are either currently concentrating on precise measuring technology with no process connection or on generic IoT platforms with no measuring devices. *SMIGHT* is combining these areas in its holistic approach and focusing on data management. Besides the one-off revenue generated by the sale of hardware, the underlying business model is based on fixed monthly earnings for operating the hardware and the infrastructure needed for the entire process. SMIGHT Grid combines both elements. Neither the hardware nor the service is offered separately. Since the energy transition is a subject of international relevance, there is greater potential than just the German market. A foreign grid architecture could also adopt the concept.

The developed SMIGHT Grid solution is characterized by its integrated approach, which connects the local transformer stations to the Internet of Things (IoT). The focus here is on the connection of sensor technology (SMIGHT Grid Sensor), decentralized data and device management (SMIGHT Grid Gateway), and an IoT platform (SMIGHT IQ).

A sensor has been specially developed for the process requirements of the operating personnel. It can be installed in the local transformer station without the need for wiring and measures the load (current) of the individual cable outlets that run to the various home connections. The sensor sends the readings via radio to a gateway, which is also installed in the local transformer station. The readings are taken from the cable's magnetic field. An inductive measuring transformer attached to the cable sheath in a contactless process serves as the sensing device. This prevents the engineers from having to touch the voltage-carrying components, avoiding the need for complex occupational health and safety processes associated with live-line work. The key here is that the power is supplied to the sensor by means of energy harvesting (obtaining energy from the environment). It therefore only takes a matter of minutes to install the sensor technology for a cable outlet. It is no longer necessary to document the process in the local transformer station's installation plan. From a technological perspective, the sensor is an edge computing device that can be used with algorithmics for data analysis directly at the measurement source by means of over-the-air communication via the gateway.

As a central data concentrator, the gateway receives the readings via radio from all installed outlets (usually around seven to ten low-voltage cables per local transformer station). It buffers them and can be used for data analysis purposes in addition to the sensor. The gateway sends the readings via the integrated mobile radio modem to the SMIGHT IQ back end. Both the gateway and the sensors are specially designed for retrofitting in existing local transformer stations. In the case of small and medium-sized grid operators, the local transformer station is managed by their own grid fitters. The measuring system requirements in terms of installation and operation were therefore based on the skills profile of this user group. In order to make sure that no additional strain is placed on the scarce resources of the operating teams, it takes less than an hour to complete the installation at a local transformer station. The fitter is assisted during the installation by an app, which registers the hardware and establishes a connection with the IoT platform. As a result of the retrofit approach of SMIGHT Grid, the renewal of the local transformer station is not determined by the need for measuring technology but can instead be done based on the condition of the equipment (transformer or switchgear).

Besides the hardware solution, covering the entire process—from data acquisition to visualization and evaluation—is a second important element of SMIGHT Grid. The data will be collected, aggregated with the gateway, and sent securely in an encrypted form via mobile radio to the back end. It is therefore not necessary to set up any additional infrastructure for transferring data. The data is kept secure on an IoT platform hosted in Germany and made available for direct use. Due to the high precision of the recorded readings (approx. 1000 measuring points per second), several million data sets per measuring point are produced every day, which must be stored and managed. Being able to manage this amount of data requires an IT architecture that guarantees efficient data management.

Customers can configure their devices themselves via the front end of the IoT platform as well as manage user rights and set values for individual notifications. These alert the grid operator if any values have been exceeded. Thus, they are made aware of hotspots proactively without having to monitor the stations at the front end. The data can be accessed at any time in real time. It is available in graphic form and can be exported in CSV format for individual analysis. Access to the platform is password protected and is possible from any device with Internet access and a browser. Using open interfaces and formats makes it possible to connect to analysis tools or grid planning tools from other software providers at any time.

Operating services are also part of the solution along with other services. Machine learning-based algorithms monitor the operational status of the sensors and report or predict faults, enabling the system's maintenance processes to be optimally integrated into the grid operator's existing workflows. The engineer is also given assistance via a hotline and the app in the event of the sensors being changed or migration to another local transformer station.

With SMIGHT Grid, operators can generate real-time data from the low-voltage grid and use it immediately. The grid operator can manage the installation quickly with no interruption to operations, which makes a comprehensive rollout possible within a short space of time. The data can be used to identify grid bottlenecks and overloading in good time and prevent power outages. This enables the grid operators to save a considerable amount of money (according to the Hamburg Institute of International Economics, a 1-hour midday blackout in Berlin would cost 22.74 million €). Furthermore, the ability to identify consumer hotspots allows a needs-based expansion of the grid, which is essential in terms of the security of supply. *SMIGHT's* value proposition is implemented alone. The customer receives hardware and services from one single source and does not have to worry about data communication or device management.

3   Digitalization Enables Automated Data Analysis and Grid Management

On the basis of the acquired data, the distribution grid operator's various departments can organize their processes and take appropriate measures. For instance, the asset management department can identify the real load on the equipment and draw up a highly precise renewal and maintenance strategy. Accordingly, investment in the distribution grid is made precisely where it is needed, and unnecessary maintenance work is avoided. When dealing with grid connection inquiries—relating to the connection of wall boxes for e-vehicles, for example—the data on a cable's current load situation gives grid planners the basis for providing reliable statements. One look at the front end is enough to be able to make a quick decision as to whether additional grid connections are possible using this cable. In the event of a power outage, the data can help to make a needs-based decision about which emergency generator is needed to temporarily restore the power supply for customers.

Digitalization of the distribution grid will continue to increase, right through to the establishment of self-regulating grids. Being able to regulate

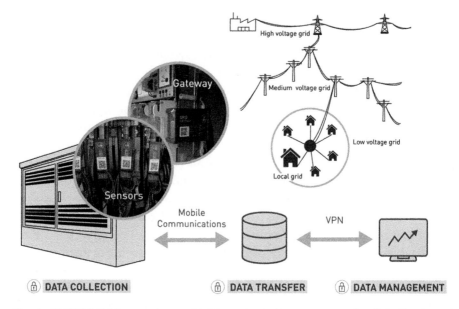

Fig. 1 SMIGHT Grid, a sensor- and IoT-based solution, supports the digitalization of the distribution grid, author's own illustration

and manage consumers and feeders on a needs basis or offer customers discounted electricity usage slots at certain times is a use case for which the grid operators must prepare. If cables are overloaded, it will be possible to partially limit the energy needed by electricity consumers that are capable of using power at a later time, such as heat pumps and e-vehicles. The regulation is based on measurement and prediction data as well as the connection of the grid customer's measuring technology, prediction tools, and control equipment. Entry into this digital, automated world of the electricity grid begins for distribution grid operators with the installation of measuring technology such as SMIGHT Grid, enabling them to react flexibly to future demands (Fig. 1).

Lessons Learned

- Use of *EnBW*'s strength, while maintaining the flexibility of a start-up.
- Entrepreneurship combined with in-depth industry expertise.
- In-house development of embedded IoT components and systems.
- Fast verification of the development stages using internal (friendly) customers creates a high degree of market relevance.
- Go with the business model toward a full-service solution: hardware and device management and data management.

Oliver Deuschle studied electrical engineering at the Baden-Wuerttemberg Cooperative State University Stuttgart (Dipl.-Ing.). In 1996, he started his professional career at EnBW AG as a planning engineer for the high voltage grid. Since then, he took on various roles, e.g., as a project manager responsible for design and implementation of workforce management at EnBW and a department manager for network operations at high voltage and extra high voltage networks. In 2014, Deuschle was appointed program manager for corporate innovations. Three years later, he became the CEO of SMIGHT (a corporate start-up of EnBW).

Mirijam Hübner studied Industrial Engineering at the Baden-Wuerttemberg Cooperative State University Stuttgart (B.Eng.). During her studies, she specialized in product and innovation management. Since then, she gained more than 6 years of experience in the energy industry in various corporate roles. In 2018, she joined SMIGHT (a corporate start-up of EnBW) and started developing the business model for the IoT solution SMIGHT Grid. Now, as a product owner, she is responsible for the further development of SMIGHT Grid and its digital services.

Dr. Anja Martin studied Biotechnology and did her PhD in the field of Plant Biotechnology at the University of Freiburg. As a product manager for molecular biology products, she started her professional career at Thermo Fisher Scientific. During her 6 years with the company, she specialized in marketing and took over roles as a marketing manager. Subsequently, she worked for medicine and IT companies. At SMIGHT (a corporate start-up of EnBW), she is responsible for marketing and communication.

Siemens: UK's First Fully Converted Electric Avenue "W9"

Irina Penzo Feliu de Cabrera and
Mariana Porley Cavallero

1 Toward a Growing Market of Electric Vehicles

Climate change and environmental concerns dominate the majority of today's governmental, societal, business, and even individual's agenda. For this reason, the use of renewable energies has become one of the key elements to minder our societies negative environmental impact. If we look at the evolution of the top five global risks unfolded through the *World Economic Forum*, we can observe a clear transition over the past years, proceeding from economical risks to a scenario in which environmental, biodiversity, and climate change seize a prevailing matter and hence have become the center of discussions. It does therefore not a surprise that the top five global risks for 2020, in their core, all can be tracked back to environmental issues (WEF 2020). In addition, current consumers show increasing awareness toward their carbon footprint as well as a deeper concern about air quality. This boost in environmental consciousness leads to an increasing demand for electric vehicles (EV), which are cleaner, more efficient, and less noisy and help to reduce greenhouse gas emissions.

I. Penzo Feliu de Cabrera (✉) • M. Porley Cavallero
Siemens, Zug, Switzerland
e-mail: irina.penzo_feliu_de_cabrera@siemens.com; mariana.porley@siemens.com

© The Author(s), under exclusive license to Springer Nature Switzerland AG 2021
O. Gassmann, F. Ferrandina (eds.), *Connected Business*,
https://doi.org/10.1007/978-3-030-76897-3_24

According to the latest research conducted by *Siemens* in Great Britain (generation EV), over half of respondents (53%) believe that EVs and hybrids are the future of personal transportation. Thus, it may be of no surprise that Gen Y showed the highest concern for their carbon footprint when it comes to driving. Furthermore, around half (51%) of those aged between 18 and 24 years revealed that they are concerned about the impact their driving has on the environment, compared to just a third (33%) of Gen X and just 8% for boomers. Hence, it could be concluded that mostly Gen Y are accelerating their efforts to reduce their carbon footprint—with 38% of those aged 25 up to 34 years revealing they have paid additional travel costs to follow an eco-friendlier route, and a further 37% opted for a staycation rather than flying abroad. In comparison with those surveyed aged 55 years and above, just 2% paid additional travel costs to follow an eco-friendlier route and 22% chose a staycation.

The combination of renewable energy and EV is a key element to address some of the most critical environmental issues of the cities today. However, there are still some challenges to overcome, such as the limited availability of EV chargers and the slow charging speed, as well as the high investment in infrastructure and the space that the EV chargers occupy in public areas.

This chapter elaborates an example of the city of London, including how technology together with an innovative business model can accelerate the transformation needed to improve environmental conditions.

2   Today's Dominant Business Logic for EV Chargers

In the city of London, as in major cities, the EV-charging systems are very similar and share the same limitations to support the change in the demand of electric vehicles. *Siemens* analyzed today's business with the Business Model Navigator (see Gassmann et al. 2020) that allows us to define any type of business model through considering the following four dimensions: who, what, how, and value. These four dimensions help us to identify the value proposition of the business model, the value chain, as well as its revenue model. Now, let us identify the four dimensions of the business model for the EV charging hubs that we have in the market today.

Who are our target customers today? In most cases, we have B2C (business to customer) models, where the final customer remains the end user, the drivers that charge their cars at home or at any EV-charging hub. The utility companies provide the electricity and thereupon directly bill the consumption upon the driver. What do we offer to customers today? There are two types of EV chargers: the EV charging hubs in limited number of locations and the chargers that consumers may have in their homes. How do we produce our offerings today? In general, the utility companies or other enterprises build the EV charging hubs very similar to the traditional petrol stations. These hubs are very limited in the number of locations, they do not always provide renewable energy, and they are not very efficient in terms of speed of charging.

How does it generate value today? The revenue model is based on the energy consumption of the customer. A relevant topic is that the prices that are charged at rapid charging hubs can be ten times higher than the flexible home energy tariff.

In conclusion, the current model contains certain characteristics that constrain the scalability of the usage of electric cars and the big potential to improve the environment. The high prices and the low availability of EV chargers reduce the adoption rate of electric cars. In addition, the environmental impact when the electricity does not come from renewable energies is substantially higher. Finally, the substantial investment needed in the infrastructure will also hinder the faster adoption of electric vehicles by car drivers.

3   *Siemens* and *Ubitricity*: A Revolutionary Business Model for London

Data shows that 80% of motorists in central London believe it is "very important" that air quality is improved. The area of Westminster has seen a 40% growth in EVs charged during 2019. A research conducted by *Siemens* shows that over a third (36%) of British motorists planned to buy a hybrid or electric vehicle as their next car, and 40% say that a lack of charging points stopped them from doing so earlier.

Siemens has unveiled the UK's first avenue, which measures over half a mile, that has been fully converted to cater for electric vehicle (EV) charging, coined "Electric Avenue, W9." The project, in collaboration with *Ubitricity* and the *Westminster City Council*, has successfully converted 24 lampposts into EV charge points using existing city infrastructure. There are plans to reach a thousand charging stations across the *Westminster City Council* within the next year.

The St. Gallen framework considers it as a rule of thumb that business model innovation differs from product or process innovation when it significantly affects at least two of the four components of the model (who-what-how-value). If we analyze the *Siemens* Smart Infrastructure and the *Ubitricity* new business model for EV chargers using this framework, we observe that all four dimensions have changed with respect to the standard business model existing in the market today. Hence, we consider it as an innovative way of doing business within the electric vehicle ecosystem.

Who Are Our Target Customers? We can identify a different business model, a B2G2C (business-to-government-to-consumer), where the end consumer is still the driver and user of the electric car. However, *Ubitricity* and *Siemens* are new players. They sell the infrastructure (hardware and installation) to local government municipalities or councils with an agreement covering operation and maintenance over a defined period of time. As can be extracted from Fig. 1 (*), Transport for London (TfL) is a functional body of the greater London authority. Its primary role thereby is to implement the Mayor of London's transport strategy and manage transport services to, from, and within London. The TfL contract is managed by *Siemens* with *Ubitricity's* support.

Councils have the responsibility for local air quality targets, and they take local actions to improve the environment. Electric vehicles represent an immediate opportunity to drastically reduce CO_2 pollution from road transportation which would be otherwise difficult to control. The faster these councils can support their residents to switch from combustion to electric cars, the faster they can achieve these pollution reductions and make associated savings in healthcare costs and improve the general well-being of local residents. In this new business model, the dimension "who" has been changed and innovated with the introduction of two additional players: *Siemens* and

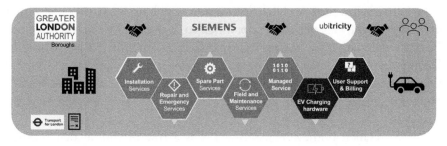

Fig. 1 Representation of the new business model with the new key players, Siemens and Ubitricity, author's own illustration

Ubitricity. Their partnership with councils and municipalities supports the strategic environmental targets of the city.

What Do We Offer to Customers? What is the value proposition? There is not one single customer; instead it is the council of London and the electric car driver. What do we offer to the council? The value proposition of lamppost charging vs hubs or freestanding chargers provides the council the possibility to increase the impact of their investment due to the lower installation and running costs of the charge points. Using the streetlight's power supply and, in most of the cases, the lamppost as the housing for the charging stations reduces costs to roughly one third of a freestanding charging point. This means they can provide a much wider spread of charging stations in urban areas. The utilization of the existing infrastructure (lampposts) derives in a small footprint and minimal extra street furniture, reducing clutter on pavements and complaints from residents. Minimal civil works mean the charge points can be relocated at low cost. This provides councils flexibility of the streetscape by, for example, redeveloping parking spaces, car accesses, traffic-reducing measures, and so forth. *Ubitricity* provides monthly reports on how their charging points are performing and how they are used by residents. This information is relevant for the councils to track the impact on air quality. It also helps them to understand which areas ought to be prioritized for future investments. What do we offer to the end customer, the electric car driver? The value proposition for drivers is lower cost and higher convenience. A large proportion of the city residents are not enabled to enjoy the convenience and cost benefits of home charging fully because they park in the streets. Therefore, they spend time while charging the car, or they go to rapid chargers that are more expensive. In the London area, prices are 30p per kWh + connection fees + penalties for overstays. Consumers utilize rapid charging only when the car is low on charge and/or when they need to drive for long distances.

The *Ubitricity* solution reduces the cost to 24p/kWh versus an average price of 30–35p/kWh for hubs and freestanding chargers and increases convenience for the drivers due to lampposts being located in a place where residents park. So they can charge overnight. An additional value comes from encouraging low power overnight charging that supports a more renewable friendly grid. Longer charging times, usually at times of lower demand on the grid, align well with renewable energy generation patterns. Charging at high speed or during times of high demand increases the use of fossil fuel electricity production (Fig. 2).

4   How Do We Produce Our Offerings?

The solution uses the existing streetlight infrastructure and shared electricity supply. *Ubitricity* charging "SimpleSocket" solution is installed within each street lamppost. The installation typically takes less than an hour per lamppost, reducing cost of deployment and disruption to residents. The sockets blend into their environment and do not take much space as a standard charging unit. Drivers can park at a converted lamppost and can be connected to the *Ubitricity* "SimpleSocket." The socket is an Internet-of-things device that allows the identification of the end user (car driver) using the charging point and communicates its status and charging event data with *Ubitricity's* backend systems. This remains regardless how drivers connect with "Smart Cable" or "Standard Cable." Eventually users can monitor the charging remotely and in real time by using *Ubitricity's* online portal or smartphone app (Fig. 3).

Eighty percent of drivers connect using their standard cable and use their smartphone to control their charge session and use the pay-as-you-go tariff. In turn, 20% of drivers purchase *Ubitricity's* Smart Cable, which has a mobile meter built in. This allows them to benefit from a simpler connection process

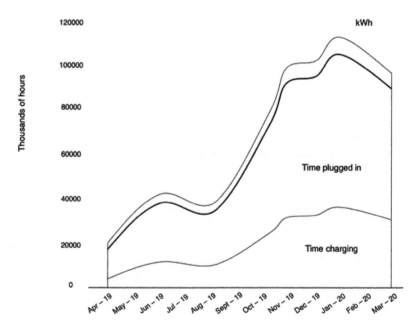

Fig. 2 On average, cars are plugged in more than the needed charging time, author's own illustration

The SimpleSocket   The SmartCable   The ConnectivityManager

Fig. 3 The three key hardware and software elements of the new business model, author's own illustration

(plug in and walk away), monthly billing, and a subscription tariff, which can work out cheaper for high mileage drivers.

5 Why Does It Generate Value?

The revenue model is critical. Through this new partnership between *Siemens*, *Ubitricity*, and the councils, *Siemens* provides the necessary infrastructure to convert the lampposts into charging points and takes care of the maintenance of the installations. *Ubitricity* provides the hardware (SmartSocket and SmartCable), and it is also responsible for the energy supply, billing, and user hotline. Two pricing models have been generated: pay-as-you-go and subscription tariffs.

Multiple benefits can already be expressed through numbers; 100% renewable energy can be generated through the *Ubitricity* charging stations. Further, based on the UK's average electricity emissions, EV drivers cut emissions by 75% per mile compared to a typical new combustion car sold today. In addition, lamppost-based charging points are 38% cheaper than rapid chargers. Thus, the most popular plug in and out times are from 8:30 pm to 9:00 am, meaning most drivers are charging while they sleep. And finally, Westminster has seen a 40% growth in plug-in electric vehicles during the year of 2019.

6 Conclusion

The collaborative *Siemens-Ubitricity* business model is a creative and sustainable approach to provide the cities with the necessary infrastructure to fulfil the demands of the increasing number of electric vehicles. And this, without placing additional stress on the local electricity grid and further enabling lower carbon electricity production.

We know that half of London's air pollution is caused by road transport and Westminster is a particularly busy area. While we cannot solve the challenge of air quality overnight, the "Electric Avenue, W9" is an important showcase of what is possible using existing city infrastructure. It illustrates how residential streets will look in the near future and accelerates the shift to zero-emission vehicles. Cedrik Neike, member of the Managing Board of *Siemens* AG.

The dominant factor leading the London project toward success is the powerful partnership between *Siemens* and *Ubitricity,* as it has enabled the creation of an innovative new business model. The combination of different technologies (smart grid and smart devices) is a game changer providing a significant benefit for both end users and governments by decreasing charging costs and pollution and through enhancing the availability and convenience of electric vehicle chargers.

A key learning is the importance of thinking outside one's own dominant logic. Conventional wisdom and habits are a major obstacle for electric vehicles achieving their full potential. People are used to the petrol station model, and additionally they do not believe that a streetlight can deliver enough power to charge an electric vehicle. Therefore, lamppost-based charging point operators need to promote the benefits of this new model. In conclusion, the combination of creativity and the selection of the right partners enables the transformation of a traditional infrastructure into a smart solution that creates value for the customers, the society, and the environment. Finally, it allows a sustainable model for *Siemens* and *Ubitricity* to support the long-term targets of the city.

Lessons Learned

- The power of the right partnership enables the creation of innovative and successful new business models.
- There is not one customer but the public side and the end user to be considered.
- A key learning is the importance of thinking outside one's own dominant logic.
- Smart infrastructure results in the merging of the physical infrastructure and the digital world, providing huge data to enable better performance at lower cost and increase the utilization of existing assets.

References

Gassmann O, Frankenberger K, Choudury M (2020) The business model navigator: the strategies behind the most successful companies. FT Pearson, Upper Saddle River, NJ

WEF (2020) The global risks report 2020. World Economic Forum, Davos. https://www.weforum.org/reports/the-global-risks-report-2020. Accessed 8 Sept 2020

Irina Penzo Feliu de Cabrera is the head of Strategy and Quality Management at Siemens Smart Infrastructure—Fire Safety. She holds an engineering master's degree in Management, Technology, and Economics from the Polytechnic University of Catalonia with a master thesis in Open Innovation done at ETH Zurich. Before, she graduated in Electrical Engineering and Information Technology, supplemented by studies at RWTH Aachen University. Through her experience in large corporations like ABB, Schindler, and Siemens, she developed a strong passion for disruptive innovation.

Mariana Porley Cavallero is the global CFO of Siemens Smart Infrastructure—Building Products. As an Uruguayan with a master's degree in applied economics from American University in the USA, she worked for more than 20 years internationally across diverse business sectors, inspiring change in the face of disruptive market forces, innovating business models, and devising new organizational setups. She has driven the implementation of platforms to enable XaaS models to position the company in the future economy of subscriptions. She is a strong believer in the impact of new technologies such as AI, cloud computing, IoT, and blockchain on the future of businesses.

Groupon: Managing a Rapidly Growing Platform with Scale-Up Metrics

Philipp Engelhardt and Klaus Möller

1 Groupon's Innovative Business Model Created a Significant Blue Ocean Market

The digital era with its connected business is characterized by the emergence of hyper growth companies. It used to take decades to build an international corporation before the digitalization. Yet digital business models—and especially platform models—can achieve global reach within just a few years. Founded in 2009, the social commerce platform *Groupon* wrote such an extraordinary growth story. According to the *Forbes* Magazine, it took *Groupon* less than 24 months to grow to almost 50 international markets and earn its first one billion dollars in revenue (Steiner 2010). To compare: *Amazon* and *Google* needed more than 5 years for their first billion dollars in revenue. According to our analysis (Engelhardt et al. 2019), *Groupon*'s extraordinary growth was the result of an innovative platform business model executed through a strictly metrics-centred scaling strategy.

P. Engelhardt (✉)
scaleon GmbH, Berlin, Germany
e-mail: philipp.engelhardt@gmail.com

K. Möller
Institute for Accounting, Control and Auditing, University of St.Gallen, St.Gallen, Switzerland
e-mail: klaus.moeller@unisg.ch

Groupon was one of the first digital companies to address a burning question of small, local businesses: How can small businesses—such as restaurants, beauty salons and cinemas—leverage the Internet to acquire new customers beyond a website and some social media? To answer this question, *Groupon* invented the 'deal': Small businesses can offer a deal at a significant discount to potential customers who subscribed to *Groupon's* daily deal newsletter. The revenue generated by a deal is shared between the small business and *Groupon*. The price point of the voucher and hence the payout to the small business are calculated so that the payout at least covers the deal's variable costs basically resulting in zero customer acquisition costs.

Groupon's innovative two-sided platform business model created a completely new and very large market—a 'blue ocean market'—for millions of small businesses and their marketing campaigns. However, this business model is easily copyable. Soon start-ups as well as several tech giants such as *Amazon*, *Google* and *Facebook* started their own offerings. The only substantial entry barrier for this 'winner-takes-it-all' business appeared to be scale—thus, *Groupon* was pressed to develop strategies to grow particularly fast all over the world.

2   *Groupon's* Business Model Translates into Integrated Scale-Up Metrics

Groupon's platform business model creates value by connecting and transacting the needs of sellers and buyers. On the one side of the platform, small businesses offer daily deals to acquire new customers. On the other side, *Groupon's* subscribers receive a newsletter with daily deals specifically for their city. If a subscriber likes a deal, she buys a 'deal voucher' and becomes a customer. A threshold number of vouchers must be sold to make a deal happen. This mechanism was designed to incentivize referrals and create another growth engine. The deal transaction is facilitated through the platform, and Groupon takes a commission.

The clarity of this innovative idea allows to translate the four dimensions of *Groupon's* business model (Gassmann et al. 2013) into four core *scale-up metrics*. Number of small businesses and number of subscribers as well as number of customers on the platform describe the business model's customer dimension. Number of deals describes the value proposition dimension as well as the revenue mechanism. As outlined in the next chapter, these scale-up metrics translate into an organizational setup and hence cover the business model's value chain dimension.

The growth potential of *Groupon*'s business model is created through the tight integration of its scale-up metrics. All four scale-up metrics work into each other and create a *reinforcing growth cycle* in each city. The more subscribers receive *Groupon*'s daily deal newsletter, the higher the likelihood that more of them turn into paying customers. The more paying customers, the more effective are the marketing campaigns and the easier is it for *Groupon* to acquire more small businesses. The higher the number of small businesses participating on the platform, the more deals and the more diverse deals are being offered. The more deals and the higher their variety, the more attractive is the *Groupon* platform for further deal newsletter subscribers. This growth cycle is fuelled by subscribers and small businesses—which makes the strategic focus particularly clear for *Groupon*'s organization.

3   Scale-Up Metrics Translate into Organizational Functions

Groupon's four core scale-up metrics describe the organizational setup that creates the value propositions for both sides of the platform. Put differently, scale-up metrics are a particularly precise, measurable form of descriptions of the performance, which organizational functions must deliver in the context of *Groupon*'s business model. Therefore, the translation of the business model into metrics also allows to structure *Groupon*'s primary value chain (Fig. 1).

The online marketing function increases the number of subscribers by advertising deals and acquiring additional subscribers to the newsletter. Existing subscribers are activated by the daily deal newsletter. The editorial

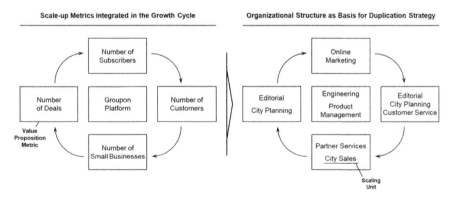

Fig. 1 Scale-up metrics in Groupon's growth cycle and their translation into organizational functions, author's own illustration

function writes attractive descriptions for the deals, and the city planning function schedules the right combination of daily deals in each city. These two functions drive two scale-up metrics: They convert subscribers into paying customers, thus increasing the number of customers; and they ensure that deals are scheduled and put online, thus increasing the number of deals. The customer service function supports these metrics by answering to customer requests. Sales teams in each city acquire new small businesses, and the partner service function maintains the relationship with existing small business partners. Both increase the number of small businesses that can be featured on the platform. The engineering and the product management functions develop and maintain *Groupon*'s online platform. These two functions thus provide the tech infrastructure on which all transactions are administrated.

4   *Groupon* Applied an Effective Duplication Strategy

The precise understanding of *Groupon*'s business model through scale-up metrics as well as its translation into a clear organizational setup was the basis for *Groupon*'s scaling strategy. Von Krogh and Cusumano (2001) conclude that 'companies must combine strategies for growth with explicit strategies for learning'. In this sense, scale-up metrics are the object of learning efforts, and organizational functions are those who must learn about how to drive them (Engelhardt 2020). To foster learning, *Groupon*'s organization was structured according to the criterion of where information can be processed most effective. The performance required by the growth cycle's four scale-up metrics (subscribers, customers, small businesses and deals) was delivered by a combination of central and decentral functions—as well as by the *scaling unit*.

Engineering, product management and online marketing provided the same core business processes for all countries with just small adjustments; they were thus centralized in *Groupon*'s international headquarters in Berlin. In contrast, city planning, editorial, customer service and partner service require to understand the local context and speak the local language; thus, they were decentralized functions in each country's headquarters. The sales teams were even more decentralized and operated in each individual city to acquire small businesses.

As soon as the central platform was up and running, decentral country headquarters with respective functions could be opened. And as soon as country headquarters were operational, sales representatives could be hired in each city. In order to grow into almost 50 countries and more than 500 cities as of

2013 (Bhatnagar and Thadamalla 2013), *Groupon* developed a playbook of how to set base in a new country and—most importantly—of how to enter into a new city. *Groupon* founder Andrew Mason (2014) stated: 'We identified a *Groupon* unit, which was each city. Then we came up with a playbook that we could just repeat over and over again.' The city was *Groupon*'s scaling unit: Equipped with particularly strong financial value propositions, *Groupon* could simply duplicate their constantly evolving sales playbook from one city to the next in order to realize extraordinary growth rates.

5 The Performance Management System Needs to Fit to the Duplication Strategy

Business-model-orientated scale-up metrics and associated organizational setup were the basis for *Groupon*'s duplication strategy. They are the strategic framework for business processes and managers' and employees' activities. Yet scale-up metrics need to be managed continuously and rigorously. To drive scale-up metrics, *Groupon* applied a specific design of their *performance management system* with a focus on performance measurement, goal setting, recruiting and rewarding.

First, key performance indicators (KPIs) were defined that worked into scale-up metrics, for instance, the classical KPIs of a sales funnel, which were used to acquire additional small business partners. Second, scale-up metrics as well as associated KPIs were driven by a particular intense design of the operative goal setting process. Goal setting took place in remarkable short frequencies. Employees in sales and operations typically received weekly and sometimes daily stretch goals. These goals could be formulated with high precision due to their centricity on KPIs. These both precise and aggressive goals exercised strong performance pressure. Third, hiring was done particularly fast and without much investigation into candidates to grow the organization fast. This recruiting approach was possible as stretch goals allowed to let go 'under-performers' early. The socialization of new employees was intense and thoughtfully executed by regional managing directors and other role models. Fourth, so that managers and employees would accept such a demanding performance management approach, the system of KPI focus, high frequency goal setting, stretch goals as well as fast hiring and firing was complemented by particularly high-powered financial rewards in the form of salaries, bonuses and stock options.

The design of *Groupon*'s performance management system was well calibrated. Its individual management practices were complementary and reinforced one another. Yet as with the scaling strategy, at the system's core was the clear understanding of scale-up metrics: Its design was only possible due to the profound, quantitative understanding of *Groupon*'s business model.

6   Value Proposition Metrics Have a Particularly Important Role

Subscribers, customers and small businesses are essential metrics of *Groupon*'s business model. However, the most central metric for success is the number of deals that actually take the minimum threshold as well as the vouchers sold through these deals. In fact, the entire growth cycle is directed towards these *value proposition metrics* (Engelhardt 2020) of number of deals and number of vouchers sold. The number of deals is the aggregated and combined value proposition metric to both sides of the *Groupon* platform.

The scale-up metric of number of deals is driven by further value proposition metrics. *Groupon* reports on these metrics in detail. For the small business side, the number of subscribers reached, the number of new customers to their respective business and especially the payout they generate through the *Groupon* platform are further, more fine-grain value proposition metrics. For the subscriber and customer side, the number of new experiences and the monetary discount they realize are additional value proposition metrics. It was particularly relevant for *Groupon*'s hyper growth that their set of value proposition metrics is grounded in financial value propositions to both sides of its platform, i.e. pay-outs to small business and discounts to customers.

Many successful, fast scaling companies report those central value proposition metrics that integrate both sides of their platform. *Uber* highlights that they facilitate 21 million rides per day. *Delivery Hero* advertises that they receive up to 4 million orders a day. *Airbnb* points out that they broker more than 2 million bookings per night. Even the food waste fighting platform *Too Good To Go* emphasizes that they "saved" more than 50 million meals to date. Value proposition metrics have a special role in platform business models. We suggest that only when a venture is able to translate its business idea into scale-up metrics and especially identify their value proposition metrics, then the business model is clearly understood and ready to be scaled (Engelhardt 2020; Engelhardt et al. 2019).

7 The Strategic Focus on Scale-Up Metrics Needs to Be Staged Over Time

Groupon's knowledge about their core scale-up metrics also helped them to overcome the 'chicken-and-egg problem', which is often associated with two-sided platforms. *Groupon* solved this problem by focusing on the number of subscribers to initiate the growth cycle. Their strong financial value proposition—getting an entertaining deal at a significant discount—enabled *Groupon* to convince subscribers to sign up for the free newsletter even without a substantial amount of actual deals in the respective city. Subscribers are potential customers and hence an asset that *Groupon* could leverage to acquire small business partners. It is thus a particular relevant insight that *Groupon's* growth cycle includes subscribers and does not simply start with paying customers.

As soon as the growth cycle is running in a city, however, the strategic focus changed to small businesses. The intention was to offer more daily deals, since as outlined in the growth cycle a greater variety of deals increases the attractiveness for additional subscribers and thereby reduces the online marketing investments required. Hence, the acquisition of small businesses became the *strategic bottleneck*, and efforts increased to drive the number of small businesses. *Groupon's* duplication strategy was thus supported by the understanding of a necessary temporal staging of strategic focus and concentration of organizational resources between the scale-up metrics in each city.

7.1 What Can We Learn from *Groupon*?

Groupon's business model innovation created a completely new market for small business online marketing. This large, attractive market was highly competitive. Size and market leadership provided the most relevant entry barriers. *Groupon* needed rapid growth and put exploitative, metric-based learning in the centre of their scaling strategy. Business models in general and platform businesses specifically can learn from *Groupon's* scale-up metrics approach.

We analyse a five-step process. First, the four business model dimensions are described qualitatively. Second, qualitative business model dimensions are translated into quantitative scale-up metrics. These metrics are integrated into a self-reinforcing growth cycle. Value proposition metrics should be defined most clearly: If their definition is difficult, the business idea might still be blurry. Third, necessary organizational functions as well as a central-decentral organization structure can be derived from scale-up metrics. In this process, the scaling unit is identified as that organizational unit that delivers the value proposition to at least one side of the platform and addresses the strategic bottleneck. Fourth, scale-up metrics and associated central-decentral organizational functions allow to play out a duplication strategy, which means to basically copy and paste a blueprint for the scaling unit from one market to the other. Fifth, further practices of the performance management system—performance measurement, goal setting, performance evaluation and incentive structures—should be designed so that they fit to this scaling approach.

Rapid scaling causes 'growing pains'. *Groupon* focused one-sidedly on metrics, organizational hierarchy, fast-paced, aggressive goal setting cycles as well as high-powered financial incentives. Scale-up metrics were used in an exploitative way. Founders and managers neglected cultural practices, which might have allowed for more exploration-related organizational activities. *Groupon's* unbalanced management system brought fast growth in the short run. However, *Groupon's* approach did lack innovative power in the long run. Scale-up metrics are an essential element in rapid scaling. However, they should be balanced with cultural management practices as well as an evolving performance management system in order to ensure sustainable growth (Engelhardt 2020; Möller 2017).

> **Lessons Learned**
>
> - Groupon's business model innovation created a completely new market by connecting small businesses and customers around the "deal".
> - Rapid growth requires metrics-based learning.
> - In the case of platform business models, the integration of scale-up metrics leads to a self-enforcing growth cycle.
> - Scale-up metrics should be translated into an organizational structure with clear responsibilities for each metric.
> - The scaling unit delivers the value proposition to all sides of the platform.
> - The scaling unit can be managed by knowing and driving the value proposition metrics.
> - The performance management approach must fit the scaling strategy.

References

Bhatnagar M, Thadamalla J S (2013) Leadership turmoil at Groupon—challenges for the new CEO, Fallstudie, Reference No. 413-093-1. Amity Research Centers, Bangalore

Engelhardt P (2020) Growth performance management: the design and use of performance management systems in entrepreneurial growth companies. Difo-Druck GmbH, Untersiemau

Engelhardt P, Gassmann O, Möller K (2019) Innovative Geschäftsmodelle steuern und skalieren. Control Manag Rev 2(2019):16–25

Gassmann O, Frankenberger K, Csik M (2013) Geschäftsmodelle entwickeln—55 innovative Konzepte mit dem St. Galler Business Model Navigator, 1. Auflage, München

Mason A (2014) Andrew Mason at Startup School SV 2014. www.youtube.com/watch?v=uX9ldi32Xnc. Accessed 1 Nov 2020

Möller K (2017) Wirksame finanzielle Führung—Vom Abweichungs-Controlling zum Integrated Performance Management. Expert Focus 91(10):689–693

Steiner C (2010) Meet the fastest growing company ever. Forbes 12.08.2010. https://tinyurl.com/entrepreneurs-groupon. Accessed 2 Nov 2020

Von Krogh G, Cusumano MA (2001) Three strategies for managing fast growth. MIT Sloan Manag Rev 42(2):53–61

Dr. Philipp Engelhardt is the founder and managing director of the strategy consultancy scaleon in Berlin. He has served as Head of Controlling Europe and Chief Financial Officer in Central Europe during Groupon's hyper growth phase. In these roles, he was part of the team that prepared and executed Groupon's initial public offering to Nasdaq. Philipp Engelhardt's academic research focuses on the management of the rapid growth of tech ventures as well as the formal design of performance management systems in particularly dynamic business environments. He received his PhD from the University of St. Gallen and studied Economics and Philosophy at the London School of Economics and the University of Bayreuth.

Prof. Dr. Klaus Möller is a professor of controlling/performance management at the University of St. Gallen and the director of the Institute of Accounting, Controlling and Auditing since 2011. His research focuses on performance management system design and business analytics. He founded and serves as the director at the Hilti Lab for Integrated Performance Management and the Performance Management Network, a research initiative of multi-nationals with ABB, Bayer, Infineon and others. He is the co-editor of *Controlling*, the leading management accounting journal in German-speaking countries, is a board member of the International Group of Controlling and was in 2016 awarded with the title "IMA Honorary Professor in Management Accounting" from the US-based Institute of Management Accountants (IMA). As founder, partner and board member, he actively transfers his knowledge into practice.

Marquard Media: 4Player's Learning DNA to Survive Disruptions

Bijan Khezri and Phillip Schuster

1 *4Players* to Serve Gamers and Game Publishers

Disruption and shocks leading to environmental scarcity (Schmitt et al. 2016) such as a gradual erosion or a sudden contraction within a sector or market segment are the source of strategic renewal opportunities. Whether those discontinuities are embraced as threat or opportunity is largely dependent upon the simplicity of the firm's purpose guiding sensing and sensemaking as the basis for renewal initiatives. Business model innovation in the form of the Business Model Navigator (Gassmann et al. 2020) rather than product innovation is eventually the trigger for renewed scalability. Essentially, as *Intel* founder Andy Grove is quoted: "Disruptive technologies is a misnomer. What it is, is trivial technology that screws up your business model" (Chesbrough 2010).

We introduce *4Players*, a Hamburg-based gaming solutions provider, as a case study of continuous strategic renewal. First, value creation in the networked economy is defined as purpose-directed environmental engagement,

B. Khezri (✉)
Marquard-Media Group AG, Zug, Switzerland
e-mail: bk@marquard-media.ch

P. Schuster
4Players GmbH, Hamburg, Germany
e-mail: phillip.schuster@4playershq.com

© The Author(s), under exclusive license to Springer Nature Switzerland AG 2021
O. Gassmann, F. Ferrandina (eds.), *Connected Business*,
https://doi.org/10.1007/978-3-030-76897-3_26

business model innovation, and organizational learning. Second, we apply the framework to select and study five key events in the firm's 20-year history. Third, we distill five key lessons.

When *4Players* was founded by passionate gamers in early 2000, the firm's purpose was timeless and simple: *serve the needs of gamers and game publishers.* Originally, *4Players* was opportunistically experimenting with hosting servers, programming and building webpages before launching in August 2000 the gaming news portal, *4Players.de.* Shortly after a formative period, *4Players* was capitalized for growth as part of a controlling shareholding by acquisitive freenet, Germany's leading reseller of communication services that was then in the process of building a diversified "dot-com"- inspired conglomerate.

The euphoria did not last for too long. Five events—some external, some self-inflicted—have challenged *4Players'* purpose, business models, and over-all relevance. By default, organizational learning became integral to *4Players'* DNA, successively building core competencies that position the firm for exceptional value creation today.

2   Dot-Com Bubble in 2000

The infamous "dot-com bubble" started bursting in October 2000, resulting in a sudden contraction of online advertisement spending. Overnight, *4Players'* survival was at stake, as had been true for most start-ups at the time. *4Players* had to abandon its dependency on third-party ad spend or otherwise surrender. What next? The founding team connected two dots: (1) As part of the *4Players.de* launch-promotion, the founders experienced that gamers increasingly attended so-called LAN Parties, i.e., gamers meeting up at desig-nated space to competitively game. At the time, *Counter-Strike* was one of the very first games available for online gaming in Germany, but with very limited server capacity. (2) Prior to launching the news portal, the founders gained experience in hosting technologies. Combining both dots, an obvious market opportunity crystalized: hosting online game servers.

Transitioning *4Players* from a B-B ad-dependent to a B-C subscription-centric business model on the back of developing a game-server (hosting) business was a critical strategic choice. Controlling shareholder Freenet empowered *4Players* to acquire *TNX*, a company that developed "LAN Party" software. In September 2001, the game server business *4NetPlayers* was launched with an intuitive (industry-first) and user-friendly web-based inter-face to flexibly configure and manage game servers. Today, *4NetPlayers* is one of Germany's leading publisher-independent game-server hosting providers strongly expanding internationally.

- **Who**: PC gamers in need of an online gaming infrastructure solution
- **Why**: Empowering gamers by substantially reducing server-related costs and eliminating (hardcore) IT-knowledge bottlenecks
- **What**: Intuitively configurable and easy to manage game servers, seamlessly combined with value-added services based on third-party technologies such as *TeamSpeak*'s online voice communication
- **How**: Monthly subscription; since September 2002 processed on proprietary *4Players Payment* system with fully automated online payments and subscription management to support automated growth

New competencies and knowledge developed in online payments, fraud prevention, B-C marketing and sales, automated e-commerce funnels, customer support, and game-server and hosting technologies.

3   Amok Run in German School in 2002

In April 2002, a German teenager killed 19 people in a horrific school shooting. When it became apparent that the teenager was "addictively" playing *Counter-Strike*, online shooter gaming and parental intervention became a stormily debated topic. Within weeks of the shooting, *4NetPlayers* lost 60% of its subscription business. This sudden contraction required an immediate "renewal" response. *TeamSpeak*'s online voice communication tool—a then global market leader in enabling gamers to communicate "inside the game"—had to be unbundled from the game server offering as a stand-alone. In 2020, *TeamSpeak* still represents 80% of *4Players* revenues, making *4Players* *TeamSpeak*'s largest global distribution partner.

- **Who**: PC gamers playing Massively Online Role Player Games (hosted by the game publishers) that did not need our game servers but were looking for communication solutions.
- **Why**: Setting up *TeamSpeak* servers was not user-friendly. An easy-to-use solution was needed.
- **What**: Intuitively configurable and always-on *TeamSpeak* servers with automatically installed software updates.
- **How**: Monthly subscription.

New competencies and knowledge developed in real-time voice communication systems, real-time handling of massive databases, and crisis PR as *4Players* had to publicly defend its position as Germanys' largest *Counter-Strike* server provider and owner of the website counterstrike.de.

4   *4Players eSports* in 2012

Long before *eSports* became a hyped buzzword—for either something that most people still do not understand or based on a value chain that certainly remains rather diffuse to this day—in the years 2009–2010, *4Players* "secretly" built and then launched one of the first eSports platforms—*4Players eSports (4PL)*. At the heart of *eSports* is gamers' innate passion for competitive and prize-awarding gaming. Simply put, *eSports* is a sort of professionalization of competitive gaming where individual games represent a "team sport" in their own right. *4Players* innovatively leveraged its established game-server know-how and portal-related sponsor relationships to tap as a first mover into this emerging and promising market space.

4Players eSports democratized (de-professionalized) *eSports* by setting up sponsored tournaments for all player levels, integrating livestreams, and automatically paying out prize money on a daily basis. The user-friendly intuitiveness and accessibility defined early periods of success. By then, *4Players'* "signature trademark" was to take the infrastructure-tech complexity out of gaming and empower gamers to have the most seamless gaming experience.

However, the success did not last for too long. The larger game publishers spotted the opportunity and started steadily ring-fencing their proprietary "sport" (i.e., game). By 2010–2011, events started to scale in both the online and offline worlds drawing massive audiences. Marketing and infrastructure investment requirements exploded. By April 2013, *4Players* could not compete investing, losing promotion partners and market reach, eventually forcing a shutdown of all *eSports* activities.

- **Who**: Competitive gamers and promotion/sponsorship partners.
- **Why**: Programmatic approach to prize-winning tournaments was an obviously massive but untapped market opportunity serving the innately competitive gamer mindset.
- **What**: Intuitively engaging, open, and prize-awarding daily tournaments
- **How**: Sponsorships and advertisement.

New competencies and knowledge developed in *eSports* business and competitive gaming/gamers, B2B sales (promotion partners), and community management.

5   *Selfbet* in 2018

By the summer of 2017, *4Players* had a slowly declining but still EBITDA-positive business (roughly 10% EBITDA margin on revenues of approximately EUR6M). Following the acquisition of *4Players* by *Marquard Media Group's Computec* in 2012, it now became apparent that a long-standing profit-insisting lack of R&D investment has relegated an originally innovative "gaming company" in a fast-growing market segment to a third-rate cocktail consisting of (1) a loss-making but highly respected gaming news portal and (2) a hosting business that became overly dependent on reselling TeamSpeak servers. Discord, now the global leader in online voice communication for gaming, entered Germany with its free-to-use offering, further accelerating erosion of *TeamSpeak's* market position.

Again, *4Players* was challenged to urgently reinterpret its purpose and relevance in the explosively growing online gaming space. By now, *4Players* had amassed a rich portfolio of experiences, competencies, and knowledge in the online gaming space, awaiting to finally ignite a super-growth model. Bijan Khezri, appointed as CEO of *Marquard Media Group* in July 2017, embraced the opportunity: leveraging past experiences, expanding *4Players'* exploration ecosystem, institutionalizing ideation and fast-track prototyping processes, and, above all, building upon Founder-CEO Schuster's pioneering drive for innovation.

Leveraging *4Players eSports'* relevant capabilities and experiences, *Selfbet*, a B-C mobile app, was eventually created as a next-level democratization of eSports. Gamers were empowered to design the game experience in the form of betting in real time on their very ability to accomplish self-determined challenges. The technology hurdles were high. Roadblocks after roadblocks in a highly complex IT setting were successfully resolved.

- **Who**: Gamers striving for a more thrilling, engaging, and self-determined game experience.
- **Why**: Need for continuously enhancing gamers' engagement level for monetization.
- **What**: Gamers are able to bet in real time on their very success of self-selected challenges.
- **How**: In-app purchases via proprietary *Selfbet* coins to be used for betting as well as in-store product purchases.

New competencies and knowledge developed in betting technologies and regulations and blockchain-inspired token economics.

Unfortunately, it became apparent that the notion of betting alone was not met with equal euphoria by gamers and game publishers. *4Players* had to rapidly change course without abandoning a product philosophy and technology that, at their core, appeared to be too appealing and valuable.

6   *SCILL* Gamification-as-a-Service (GaaS) Since 2018

Selfbet was eventually rebranded to *SCILL Play*. The product was recalibrated away from betting to gamer's "skilled" ability to beat a predetermined challenge. The market and regulatory hurdles of the betting space were instantly eliminated. The only challenge now, it appeared, was growth execution. *SCILL* was positioned as a B2B "gamification-as-a-service" (GaaS), empowering game publishers to customize in-game challenges (such as battlepasses) on a SaaS model.

- **Who**: Game publishers determined to engage users through continuously reinvigorated game experience.
- **Why**: Developing gamer-engaging gamification features requires deep knowledge of server infrastructure technologies, GDPR (European online data protection regulations), and other related services (such as online voice communication). More than 60% of mobile games are freemium based. Add-on engagement-driven monetization models are key to generating revenues.
- **What**: SCILL offers tools to seamlessly integrate an agile gamification layer into any game.
- **How**: SCILL provides a user interface for desktop/mobile users as both second screen and layover app. SDK (software development kit) empowers game developers to send game events to SCILL. Game developers share revenues generated through items sold in the proprietary SCILL store.

4Players' deep knowledge around game-server technologies combined a natural ecosystem resulting from its sister companies *Computec* and *Golem* in Germany provides a natural basis to succeed with GaaS. However, the integration of *SCILL* with game publishers, turned out to be too time-consuming and laborious an undertaking, increasingly representing an insurmountable bottleneck to automated "scalability"—the ultimate driver of value creation in the networked economy. Creating challenges and battlepasses requires deep knowledge of a specific game. Sending game events to *SCILL* was wrongheaded. Game developers should be empowered to self-service.

Eventually in the autumn of 2020, *SCILL* GaaS was released in the form of a fully automated and "game-agnostic self-service station". SDKs and an "Admin Panel" to manage all aspects of GaaS empower developers to leverage *SCILL* as a driver of revenue generation on the back of enhanced gamer engagement and retention. Further, sectors beyond gaming in need of engaging users and sales conversion such as an insurance company selling insurance online should equally benefit from the GaaS self-servicing station. Finally, the business model changed from a revenue-sharing to a tier-structured subscription model based on the number of active users as well as events. *4Players* is now positioned for fully automated high scalability growth.

Lessons for Value Creation in the Networked Economy

- **Build the foundation for success upon a simple and timeless purpose.** Successful organizations do not change their purpose but continuously reinterpret purpose within the context of time and a correspondingly evolving vision for the future. *4Players* did just this: *serve the needs of gamers and game publishers* was relentlessly reinterpreted.
- **Leverage past learnings and failures to steer toward future success.** As painful as failure is, it is a potent beholder of future relevant competencies. *4Players* could have hardly recovered from the slump in ad spend back in 2000 if it had not revitalized previously retained competencies in hosting technology combined with acquiring software specialist *TNX*. To this day, in-depth game-server technology expertise defines *4Players'* future growth potential. This is equally true for its pioneering venturing into *eSports*. In the face of a sudden market contraction, acquiring capabilities and market access by way of M&A may be absolutely essential.
- **Be bold and prepared to forgo profitability and be patient.** The more increasingly fast paced our experience of the "networked economy" may be, nonetheless, we must remind ourselves that great (sustainable) success stories are a hockey stick with a rather extended flat front end. More importantly, ownership governance is essential to funding and facilitating sustainable breakthrough growth. The change in leadership at *Marquard Media Group* was critical to *4Players'* reinvigorated growth path, recombining existing resources with new capabilities.
- **Eliminate third-party bottlenecks compromising automated scalability.** Empower the marketplace to self-service and avoid turning your firm's limitations into the offering's growth bottleneck. As intuitive as "gamification-as-a-service" (GaaS) is, it could never take off unless the business model changed from a revenue-share to a tier-based subscription-based model where wholesale clients (e.g., game publishers) are empowered to customize according to their very needs.
- **De-mystify technology.** As important as tech expertise is in the networked economy, the real challenge is business model innovation. It is a dynamic, data-driven, and experimental process. Nonetheless, the importance of a tech- and product-minded business leader cannot be underestimated as a foundation for business model innovation and market success. *4Players* proves the point.

References

Chesbrough H (2010) Business model innovation: opportunities and barriers. Long Range Plann 43:354–363; p 358

Gassmann O, Frankenberger K, Choudury M (2020) The business model navigator. the strategies behind the most successful companies, 2nd edn. Pearson, Harlow, UK

Schmitt A, Barker VL, Raisch S, Whetten D (2016) Strategic renewal in times of environmental scarcity. Long Range Plann 49:361–376

Dr. Bijan Khezri is the Group CEO and part owner of Swiss-based Marquard Media Group AG, a media-tech solutions provider. He is a board of director of Zühlke AG, a Zurich-headquartered global leader in innovation consultancy; the chairman of the Board of EEM World; and the owner and operator of five-star equestrian sports competitions in Europe and Asia. Bijan has been serving as chairman, CEO, and non-executive director of leading public and PE-sponsored companies in Germany, Switzerland, the UK, and the USA. He is an approved individual of the Financial Conduct Authority in the UK. For more than 20 years, he has extensively published in the *Financial Times*, the *Wall Street Journal*, and others. Bijan is completing his PhD on "Free-Energy Governance" at the University of St. Gallen, Switzerland.

Phillip Schuster is the founder and CEO of 4Players since 2000. Before founding 4Players, Phillip created various large-scale software applications for companies like freenet and Nintendo. Phillip has been programming since he was 10 years old and is "speaking" all major development languages. Combining product development and technology with business models has always been his passion and focus. As a member of the Group Management Board of Marquard Media, his experience in digital business models and technology is an important part to drive innovation and transformation at both 4Players and the Group level.

Vontobel: Rethinking Wealth Management

Christian Gmünder and Markus Reding

1   Pressure on Traditional Wealth Management

For many years wealth management was an extremely stable industry with appealing profit margins and very solid business models. However, since the financial crisis in 2008, the wealth management industry has faced extraordinary challenges. The industry had to deal not only with increasingly restrictive regulations, a historically low interest rate environment and rapidly changing client behaviour but also got confronted with fast-growing competitive pressure through new entrants. Driven by rapid technological change, new challengers are entering the market, targeting individual elements of the wealth management value chain and disrupting them through new technological capabilities. Thus, such players enter the market with a distinct customer-centric view and are often less focused on high-end investment expertise. In doing so, they are consistently focusing on new needs of clients who want a similar user experience for their financial transactions, as they have learned from companies like *Google*, *Amazon* and *Facebook*.

C. Gmünder
Vontobel, Zürich, Switzerland
e-mail: christian.gmuender@vontobel.com

M. Reding (✉)
Zühlke Group, Zürich, Switzerland
e-mail: Markus.Reding@zuehlke.com

Certainly, in wealth management, values such as personal advice, emotional human interaction and trust will remain crucial elements for the client experience. However, these aspects alone will not be enough in the future. Equally important will be the user-friendliness of solutions, contact with clients across many channels and new forms of client interactions in general. In the future, clients will choose how and when they interact with their bank, simply because they are used to doing so in other industries. Additionally, clients seek for journeys, which are seamlessly embedded in larger life event journeys, in an ecosystem view between wealth managers and other players.

Good news is that the increasing regulatory complexity and today's remaining of high level of personal interaction with clients act as a shield against emerging competition. Shifting millions of one's wealth is a highly emotional matter, where in today's time most clients still prefer talking to a trusted human being. Moreover, business with wealthier clients grows with individual contacts and trust; hence, easily automatable mass journeys are often not sufficient.

Nevertheless, this shield is deceptive. Today, for example, the account opening process for a more complex client is often so cumbersome and time-consuming due to the ever-increasing regulatory demands that it is a real hassle for the client. Not surprisingly, surveys show that some clients would rather go to the dentist than to their bank. Hence, clients highly appreciate any improvement of the onboarding process.

Increasing complexity of the business model, decreasing margins, dissatisfied clients with high expectations and new competitors entering the value chain result in an uncomfortable situation or—as some say—an almost perfect storm. Like always, such uncertain situation bears not only risks but also opportunities.

How can wealth managers navigate this storm, which is likely to last longer? They need to reinvent themselves and this within several aspects of their business. The client needs to shift towards the centre of all efforts, even more so than in the past. Complexity must be reduced into an excellent client experience. The wealth manager should meet the client where and how the client wants, physically and digitally via all conceivable channels. After all, every client is individual, and that is how they want to be served in high-end banking, exactly according to their needs and emotions.

Traditional wealth managers who want to take on this challenge will have to change fundamentally. This change affects everything: organisation, work methodology, culture and, above all, technology. Technology is already, and this will further accelerate, a decisive factor for future change. However, technology alone is not enough; successful players must learn to be fast, stay flexible and focused, adapt quickly and learn to listen to the client. Moreover, they must collaborate with others even more than in the past.

Vontobel (wealth management) embarked exactly on this path some time ago to respond to the 'new challenges' the organisation is facing.

Let us now look at a particular example of *Vontobel*'s journey: the development of its 'Digital Hub'. The Digital Hub enabled *Vontobel*'s wealth management unit to solve the complexity of the cross-border advisory process, to launch *Vontobel* Volt, the first digital investment app of a Swiss wealth manager, and finally to develop a similar digital offering for a large retail banking—all this within just 2 years.

VOLT: A Platform-Based Opportunity

Digital wealth managers are well established in Switzerland and currently manage more than CHF 600 million. Rather than building yet another robo advisor, *Vontobel* set out to build a flexible platform for digital wealth management and digital client onboarding.

The underlying API-based wealth management platform provided *Vontobel* with a basis for developing digital solutions in investment advisory and discretionary portfolio management. Triggered by the MiFID requirements and based on this newly created advisory platform, *Vontobel* Volt, digital investment solution, was the first experimental project that emerged. *Vontobel* Volt allows for digital onboarding from CHF 10,000 and enables clients to invest in actively managed funds and tailor their personal portfolio. It is currently the only product that allows clients to jointly manage free investments and assets of a personal pension plan (pillar 3a) in a combined and active way. The Volt app informs clients about market events, new investment themes and portfolio changes and is thereby enabling them to profit from the same active investment know-how that *Vontobel* also makes available to all other clients.

Initially conceived as a mere functionality of the *Vontobel* platform, the Volt app today offers a wide range of possible opportunities for clients to explore. It is not merely a solution for one concrete business problem; rather, it can be seen as an incubator and an infrastructure on the basis of which the client interface can be taken to a whole new level. The arising opportunities are manifold. What's more, Volt allows *Vontobel* to enter second-tier and cross-border markets. B2B *Vontobel* clients benefit from a low-investment, ready-to-use, integrable and customisable solution that enables them to defend their business against new competitors. Raiffeisen, for example, successfully uses the Volt platform as basis for Raiffeisen RIO, its own digital solution for 3.5 million retail clients.

2   Embracing Change by Experimenting in the Unknown

The *Vontobel* Digital Hub was launched in January 2018, when *Vontobel* wealth management had just implemented the strict MiFID II regulation (European Securities and Markets Authority 2021). The investment advisory process—one of the most important and complex processes of a wealth manager—was updated through the existing IT platform and could be carried out in a regulatory compliant manner. However, it became so complex that a simple trade at the client's request, which used to take 1 min, now took 10–15 min due to the comprehensive disclosure and documentation requirements that the new regulation entailed. In addition, the old way of calculating portfolio risks—an important component of the investment advisory process—only just met the new requirements. All of this led to a frustrating advisory experience for clients as well as relationship managers.

Vontobel decided to solve this problem fundamentally by completely reengineering the advisory process and—as an additional element—to launch a digital wealth management solution as a response to the various robo advisors that were increasingly emerging in the market. The time schedule was ambitiously set, and the necessary financial resources were made available. A new risk engine, a fully digitised investment process, a new digital investment experience for a new client group—which also required a fully digital onboarding process—and all this in an extremely short timeframe were the expectations in 2018.

It rapidly became clear that these goals could not be achieved through a traditional way of doing projects. *Vontobel*'s change team would not have been large enough, traditional project setups would never have been able to meet the ambitious goals, and the existing IT architecture was simply not designed for such rapid developments.

To succeed, *Vontobel* decided to bring all stakeholders from different units together, to combine different skills, internal and external specialists as well as relationship managers in a separate building called the *Vontobel* Digital Hub. In the Digital Hub, all stakeholders worked towards one goal: to develop a platform that would enable *Vontobel* to develop and operate the various planned functions quickly and comprehensively. The team was guided by the notion that in order to be best prepared to overcome new challenges, *Vontobel* had to gain traction not only in terms of its digital offering but also on a methodological and technological level. Agile working methods such as SCRUM were chosen by the teams and adapted to their specific needs.

However, this demanding schedule could only be met with the help of experienced external specialists. *Vontobel*, therefore, established a strategic partnership with the German software provider *aixigo* and *Zühlke*. The aim was to lay together the foundations for *Vontobel* to be able to react more flexibly to changing market needs within the future. A key aspect was that despite uncertainties regarding the vision or scope of the endeavour, *Vontobel* adopted a mind-set of experimentation as a learning strategy.

As stated earlier, one of the main projects was the creation of a digital wealth management journey. Starting with the basic idea of developing a product or service that would give *Vontobel* access to new client segments, a digital investment platform was built. Using an application programming interface (API)-first approach, the team sought to make the platform as open and future oriented as possible. The aim while building the platform was to develop a mind-set that would help the collaborating partners to each perform at their best and seize opportunities along the way. The team was driven by the purpose of not only transferring the *Vontobel* investment philosophy into the digital world but also making it accessible to new client segments. The four decisive factors were the desire to move faster than the peers; the need to fundamentally change the way of working; the freedom to try something and change it, if needed; and, finally, the ability to seize opportunities when they arise.

3   Collaboration Is Key

The development team maintained a strict focus on the client journey, developing the flow early on during the project and refining it step by step from a client's perspective. Zühlke took strong responsibility, challenging ideas and approaching any issues openly, objectively and constructively from the outset. It brought extensive experience in the banking and finance sector and in highly regulated markets and interdisciplinary work to the table, simplifying the collaboration for all involved disciplines and partners. Further success factors were a high level of engineering competence, vast methodological know-how as well as flexible and short notice staffing. Starting with a concrete business case might be detrimental in the long run, and it certainly would have been in the case of *Vontobel* Volt. Instead of charging the team with building Volt, *Vontobel* merely had a rough vision of where its Digital Hub investment should lead towards. It is imperative that investments are made even though one cannot know for sure if it will be a success.

Lessons Learned

- Wealth managers must apply a client-centric view rather than one focused on assets.
- Adopting an experimentation mind-set rather than starting with a concrete business case makes it possible to seize any unforeseen opportunities that arise—this requires courage and foresight.
- Seizing opportunities requires three key ingredients: a top performing team, agile working and planning methods as well as technological capabilities.
- Vital digital capabilities such as agility can only be learned and adopted internally and bottom-up through personal experience when jointly tackling an actual challenge.
- Successful innovation initiatives require management leadership and an environment that recognises the fundamental need for transformation in order to tackle current market challenges.
- To be successful in today's fast-changing world, traditional companies must undergo fundamental cultural changes.
- Sustainable change requires going the tough way by not building a 'bank within the bank' in a garage but by remaining fully integrated in the main organisation. Today's organisations must learn to operate two operating systems: for the existing business and for innovation.

Reference

European Securities and Markets Authority (2021) MiFID II/MiFIR. https://www. esma.europa.eu/policy-rules/mifid-ii-and-mifir. Accessed 6 Jan 2021

Christian Gmünder is COO for Private Clients at Vontobel. He is responsible for the operation and digital development of the platforms on which the processes for Wealt Management, Platform and Services and Digital Investing clients are handled. In 2018, he initiated the Vontobel Digital Hub in order to increase customer orientation and shorten development times. There, more than 60 specialists are working on Vontobel's digital future in an interdisciplinary team. The Digital Hub received the Digital Economy award for business transformation in 2019. Christian Gmünder holds a master's degree in Business Administration from the Goizueta Business School at Emory University in Atlanta, GA. He studied law in Freiburg i.Üe and is a member of the bar. Before joining Vontobel in 2016, he held similar positions at Julius Baer, J. Safra Sarasin and Raiffeisen.

Markus Reding is Partner and Director Solution Center at Zühlke. He is responsible for the offerings for the financial services sector. In this role, he assists banks and insurance companies in the development of individual solutions and supports companies on the path to digitalisation. Markus Reding holds a Bachelor of Science in Computer Science and an MAS in Business Administration. His career path took him from hardware engineer to software engineer, enterprise architect and IT project manager. Before joining Zühlke in 2010, he worked for 7 years at the health insurer CCS, where he was responsible for the software development process and the development of the basic ECM systems.

Cambridge Analytica: Magical Rise, Disastrous Fall

Raphael Bömelburg and Oliver Gassmann

1   Microtargeting Revolutionized Advertisement

While traditional marketing communication of companies and organizations is still based on the principles of mass communication, widely available data sets on social media create the opportunity of microtargeting. Based on the knowledge of individual preferences and characteristics of people, the technique is used to influence voters and identify potential supporters. Connectivity is a new source of increasing influence on people. One of the most controversial discussed companies that totally changed the way advertisement is done has been *Cambridge Analytica*.[1]

Cambridge Analytica captured huge value out of connectivity in social media but completely overstretched the ethical and legal boundaries. With

---

[1] This chapter is based on Gassmann, O., Boemelburg, R. (2018) Cambridge Analytica: Rise and Fall, case study of European Case Clearing House (ECCH).

R. Bömelburg (✉)
University of St. Gallen, St. Gallen, Switzerland
e-mail: raphael.boemelburg@unisg.ch

O. Gassmann
Institute of Technology Management, University of St. Gallen,
St. Gallen, Switzerland
e-mail: oliver.gassmann@unisg.ch

O. Gassmann, F. Ferrandina (eds.), *Connected Business*,
https://doi.org/10.1007/978-3-030-76897-3_28

the surprising presidential election of Donald Trump, the fame of the company reached its peak and started with its decline. In 2016, the firm seemed to stand to revolutionize political consulting. *Wired* (2016) named then-CEO Alex Nix one of "25 geniuses who are creating the future of business," and *Cambridge Analytica* was widely featured in national and international news as the company behind the poll-defying success of Donald Trump in the 2016 presidential election and Brexit referendum in the UK to leave the European Union (Politico 2018). Armed with an innovative, data-driven approach to political campaigning that heavily relied on social media, as well as the support of conservative influencers, such as the billionaire Robert Mercer and former White House Chief Strategist Steve Bannon, *Cambridge Analytica* all but took over the political campaigning for the Republican Party in the USA and for right-wing causes around the globe.

To personally meet Alex Nix, the former CEO of *Cambridge Analytica*, has been impressive for the author. He has been a mix of smart, highly analytical, charming, direct-confronting, and—above all—extremely self-confident. At that time, *Cambridge Analytica* was the magic company which seemed to change the whole advertising industry.

Only 2 years later, in 2018, the company brought the following press release: "Despite *Cambridge Analytica*'s unwavering confidence that its employees have acted ethically and lawfully, the siege of media coverage has driven away virtually all of the Company's customers and suppliers. As a result, it has been determined that it is no longer viable to continue operating the business, which left *Cambridge Analytica* with no realistic alternative to placing the company into administration."

In early May 2018, *Cambridge Analytica* started insolvency proceedings in the USA and the UK. The scandal surrounding its acquisition and usage of *Facebook* data of up to 87 million users for political campaigning in the USA led Mark Zuckerberg, CEO of *Facebook*, to testify in front of the Congress. From the time the scandal broke on March 17, 2018, with articles in *The Guardian* and *The New York Times*, to the end of March, *Facebook*'s share price fell by 14%, thereby erasing US$ 50 billion in market value as fear of regulatory action against the company rose. Alex Nix, then-CEO of *Cambridge Analytica*, was laid off in March 2018 after having to testify himself on the role of *Cambridge Analytica* in the Brexit referendum before the British Parliament and (voluntarily) on its role in the 2016 presidential election before the US House Intelligence Committee.

How did it come so far so fast? What are the origins of this company that rose to prominence and international coverage just 3 years after being formed? What was the secret behind its success? Was it possible to save the company, and if so, would it have been the right thing to do?

2 Building *Cambridge Analytica*

In the summer of 2013, Christopher Wylie, a PhD student from Canada, was introduced to Alex Nix by politicians from Britain's Liberal Democratic Party. Wylie had impressed them with his ideas on how personality can be used to predict and influence voting. He was inspired by research from Michal Kosinski, a Cambridge scholar who had shown how *Facebook* data could be used to automatically assess personality with a huge degree of precision. After unsuccessful negotiations with Cambridge scholar Michal Kosinski, *Cambridge Analytica* entered an agreement with Aleksandr Kogan, a fellow psychologist at *Cambridge University* who offered to replicate the research of Mr. Kosinski. Through his newly founded entity Global Science Research (GSR), Mr. Kogan gathered personality data and *Facebook* profiles of 320,000 participants in a matter of weeks. However, *Facebook* allowed researchers at that time to not only access the profiles of study participants but also the profiles of friends of study participants. Mr. Kogan capitalized on this access to additional data and obtained information on additional 160 profiles on average for each participant. *Facebook* changed these terms in 2014 to be considerably more restrictive, but it did not retroactively impose them, so Mr. Kogan was able to keep his massive data collection. Mr. Kogan then sold these data to *Cambridge Analytica*, which violated *Facebook*'s terms and conditions at that time, since his access to data was limited to purely academic use. This dataset, which contained reportedly up to 87 million *Facebook* accounts, was the foundation for everything *Cambridge Analytica* would achieve in the coming years, including the 2016 presidential election.

3 The Secret Sauce of *Cambridge Analytica*: How Did Its Method Work?

Cambridge Analytica's strategy relied heavily on its methodology of microtargeting prospective voters with messages targeted to their respective personality. For this approach to work, the company had to solve two challenges: How to reliably infer the personality of a person from his or her *Facebook* profile and how to use this personality assessment in a scalable way to influence voting behavior.

3.1   You Are What You Like: Using *Facebook* for Personality Assessment

The methodology *Cambridge Analytica* used to link *Facebook* profiles to personality relied heavily on research conducted by Michal Kosinski and as such is well documented in scientific publications. The main challenge in building such a model lied in gathering a large enough dataset of people about whom the company knew both the personality and the *Facebook* profile. These data could then be used to build a statistical model on the aspects of the *Facebook* profile that predict various aspects of personality. As soon as the model was able to predict the personality of a person based on his or her *Facebook* profile with a sufficient degree of precision, it could be used to predict the personality of new *Facebook* users.

To build this dataset, Mr. Kogan recruited 320,000 people on *Amazon Mechanical Turk*, an online service where people can complete "micro-tasks" such as taking surveys or transcribing interviews for payment. These people would become the so-called seeders who were asked to provide their *Facebook* profile information and that of their friends, as well as to fill out a classical personality test. Accordingly, *Cambridge Analytica* had the *Facebook* profile information and personality assessment for the seeders, but only the *Facebook* profile information for their friends. However, with the statistical model from the seeders for which both personality and *Facebook* profile were known, it would be possible to predict their friends' personality so that *Cambridge Analytica* would end up with a large dataset of *Facebook* profiles and their respective personalities.

The most common method in psychology to assess an individual's personality is the so-called OCEAN model or big five model. The OCEAN model differentiates people according to five different personality dimensions, where each individual has a higher or lower score on each dimension. The dimensions are openness to experience (Are you curious about new input, or do you prefer the comfort of familiar routines?); conscientiousness (Are you disciplined in getting the details right, or are you more focused on the bigger picture?); extraversion (Are you easily sociable and do you enjoy making new acquaintances, or do you prefer to be alone or with people you are very familiar with?); agreeableness (Are you very socially aware and do you care what others think about you, or are you more focused on your own perspectives?); and finally neuroticism (Are you easily stressed by negative things, or are you emotionally stable?).

These dimensions are extremely well established in psychology because they allow for accurate differentiation between people, are stable over time, and predict various other differences between people. Accordingly, a wide variety of validated psychological tests exist for them. This model and such psychological tests were used by Mr. Kogan to assess the personality of the seeders on these five dimensions. While the exact statistical procedure he used to link these personality assessments with their *Facebook* profile data is not publicly known, one can reasonably believe that it was fairly similar to the one successfully used by Michal Kosinski in his research. Kosinski built lasso regression coefficients between *Facebook* likes and personality scores on these five dimensions, which automatically select the most predictive features as inputs into the statistical model. The procedure can be seen in Fig. 1:

As shown in Fig. 1, the majority of the dataset is used to establish the statistical relationship between individuals' *Facebook* likes and their personality scores. The likes are then used as an input to predict the personality score of the rest of the study participants, which were not included in the training data to establish the relationship. If these predictions are valid, i.e., if they align with the assessment from the psychological test, then the model is also assumed to be valid for people not in the dataset and can be used to predict personality in "unknown" cases. This procedure is then iterated across the sample to provide predictions for all cases to build the most generalizable model out of the sample data.

However, this procedure relies on an important assumption, which is that people's *Facebook* profiles have sufficient information for their personality to be predicted. As Mr. Kosinski's research and the success of *Cambridge Analytica* show, profiles do have sufficient information.

> With only 70 likes, the algorithm can assess personality better than a friend of the person would be able to; with 150 likes to feed it, the algorithm is better than the parents; and with 300 likes, it is even better than the spouse.

Based on this knowledge, *Cambridge Analytica* built both a library of up to 87 million *Facebook* users and their personalities and a statistical model that would predict the personality of a new *Facebook* profile with a high degree of accuracy. These insights were in turn combined with addressable ad tech to provide a scalable solution for targeted messaging.

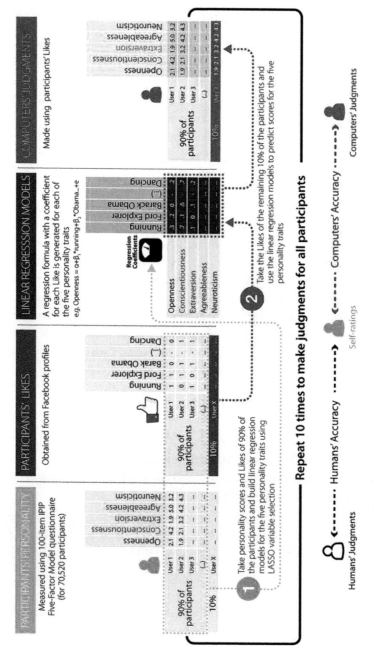

Fig. 1 Analytical procedure for linking personality scores and *Facebook* likes, Youyou et al. (2015)

4   Knowing Which Buttons to Push: Using Personality Assessment for Political Messaging

"My Children will certainly never, ever understand the concept of mass communication," said Alex Nix in 2016. Knowing individual personality profiles does not help much in regard to influencing prospective voters if all or a very diverse group of voters must be targeted with the same influence vector. However, advances in addressable ad tech such as sponsored *Facebook* posts that only show up in the newsfeeds of people in a certain location, such as a swing state, and with a certain set of profile features, such as a set that corresponds to a given personality type, allow the targeting of voters in a very precise way: Each voter receives the type of message that is most likely to have the intended impact on him or her. Broadly speaking, political messaging can have two goals: persuasion, i.e., influencing attitudes, and (dis-)activation, i.e., making people more or less likely to act on their attitudes. Microtargeting can be used for both.

For example, in the Republican Iowa Caucus, it was important for the campaign of Ted Cruz to influence a segment of voters that was very likely to vote by addressing an issue they cared about—Second Amendment rights, i.e., the right to bear arms. Based on a personality assessment using *Facebook* likes, *Cambridge Analytica* could differentiate between two clusters of people who cared about Second Amendment rights as a crucial political issue: one being high in neuroticism and conscientiousness and the other one being low in openness and high in agreeableness.

Facebook provides an ideal infrastructure to have each cluster receive only the image that is tailored to its profile, since advertisers can specify criteria for the persons who should receive a given advertisement. Possible criteria include *Facebook* likes, which *Cambridge Analytica* could link to the personality cluster via its dataset and algorithms that connect these data points. Accordingly, filters for the advertisement can be specified in such a way that they specifically filter for the targeted personality profile.

This approach can be extended beyond *Facebook* postings in practice, for example, by having an app that allows door-to-door campaigners to only knock on doors of prospective voters who are likely to be persuaded and activated and showing them conversation guidelines for how to engage the personality of the voter.

Cambridge Analytica's services (The Guardian 2018) went beyond this personality-powered microtargeting, however, and included more classical political advertising strategies such as native advertising, i.e., sponsoring articles on news websites that are not clearly indicated to be sponsored content, optimizing video ads based on geographical data of the viewer, *using Google AdWords*, and placing conversational ads on *Twitter* to drive certain hashtags. These approaches were woven together by a comprehensive strategy of audience segmentation.

Cambridge Analytica summarizes its approach as follows: "CA Political will equip you with the data and insights necessary to drive your voters to the polls and win your campaign. We offer a proven combination of predictive analytics, behavioral sciences, and data-driven ad tech. With up to 5000 data points on over 230 million American voters, we build your custom target audience, then use this crucial information to engage, persuade, and motivate them to act. Our team of PhD data scientists, expert researchers, and seasoned political operatives have produced decisive results for campaigns and initiatives throughout the world. In the US, CA Political has successfully worked on projects for all three branches of government and at local, state, and national levels."

5   The Climb to the Top

In the Trump campaign, *Cambridge Analytica* employed several ways to capitalize on its methodology of microtargeting political ads and messaging adapted to the personality of recipients. First, it optimized donation services, raising US$ 27 million in its first month of work (TechCrunch 2017). Second, it optimized outreach efficiency by focusing exclusively on the battleground swing states, such as Michigan, Pennsylvania, Wisconsin, and Florida, and within these states focusing on potential voters whom they predicted would be most influenced by messaging. Finally, according to a former employee, the company ran a disengagement campaign and targeted African-American voters with messages designed to suppress their presumably Democratic leaning turnout. Donald Trump won the 2016 presidential election counter to a strong consensus of pollsters who predicted Hillary Clinton would win. Shortly before the 2016 presidential election, *Cambridge Analytica* had been asked by *Facebook* to delete the data obtained by Aleksandr Kogan. Though the company states it complied, former employees disagreed.

6   The Tides Have Been Turning

While *Cambridge Analytica* seemed to be at the height of its success in early 2017, with then-CEO Alex Nix being a sought-after keynote speaker around the globe, controversy regarding its methods was also gathering pace. In early 2017, two articles published in *The Guardian* (2017) critically examined the role *Cambridge Analytica* played in the Brexit referendum, alleging that it had been part of the defense establishment and called the decision to allow the referendum result to stand in light of *Cambridge Analytica*'s activities "the first step into a brave, new, increasingly undemocratic world." CEO Alex Nix has been questioned at the British Parliament about his role at the Brexit referendum. Whistleblower at *Cambridge Analytica* brought a full set of doubtful and illegal practices of the company into the global newspapers. The wave caught *Facebook* only a few weeks later. On April 4, 2018, Mark Zuckerberg admitted that data of up to 87 million users may have been improperly shared with *Cambridge Analytica*. A week later, he was called to testify before the Congress. A group of lawyers launched a class action lawsuit against *Facebook*, *Cambridge Analytica*, *SCL Group*, and *Global Science Research* for misusing personal data. On May 2, 2018, *Cambridge Analytica* and *SCL Elections* closed and began insolvency proceedings.

The impact of the *Cambridge Analytica* case has been enormous. Over the course of several short weeks, *Cambridge Analytica* went bankrupt, Facebook lost several hundred million dollars, CEO Mark Zuckerberg was interrogated before the US Congress and the EU parliament, and society's trust in social media was challenged. In early 2020, a release of more than 100,000 documents showed that *Cambridge Analytica* has been working in 68 countries with a global infrastructure to manipulate voters on an industrial scale. As a result, the complex interplay between data-driven technology business and politics is in the process of being fundamentally rewritten.

Lessons Learned

- Advertisement in the social media world is changing from mass communication toward addressing individuals.
- The analysis of social media activities creates deep relevant knowledge: With only 300 likes of a Facebook user, the Kosinski algorithm can assess the personality better than the spouse of the person.
- If data is highly sensitive. Obeying ethical and legal boundaries is crucial and should be as a matter of course.
- Never misuse trust.

References

Politico (2018) Cambridge Analytica helped 'cheat' Brexit vote and US election, claims whistleblower. https://www.politico.eu/article/cambridge-analytica-chris-wylie-brexit-trump-britain-data-protection-privacy-facebook/. Accessed 6 Sept 2020

TechCrunch (2017) Cambridge Analytica CEO talks to TechCrunch about Trump, Hillary and the future. https://techcrunch.com/2017/11/06/cambridge-analytica-ceo-talks-to-techcrunch-about-trump-hilary-and-the-future/. Accessed 6 Sept 2020

The Guardian (2017) The great British Brexit robbery: how our democracy was hijacked. https://www.theguardian.com/technology/2017/may/07/the-great-british-brexit-robbery-hijacked-democracy. Accessed 6 Sept 2020

The Guardian (2018) Leaked: Cambridge Analytica's blueprint for Trump victory. https://www.theguardian.com/uk-news/2018/mar/23/leaked-cambridge-analyticas-blueprint-for-trump-victory. Accessed 5 Sept 2020

Wired (2016) 25 Geniuses who are creating the future of business. https://www.wired.com/2016/04/wired-nextlist-2016/. Accessed 8 Oct 2020

Youyou W, Kosinski M, Stilwell D (2015) Computer-based personality judgements are more accurate than those made by humans. Proc Natl Acad Sci USA 112(4):1036–1040

Dr. Raphael Bömelburg holds a PhD in Management and a master's degree in Psychology and has international work experience in the technology sector. Building on this multidisciplinary background, he is interested in emerging business opportunities in the intersection of Psychology and Technology. He advises multinational companies on data-driven business models and relational analytics. He is currently a visiting researcher at Rotterdam School of Management.

Prof. Dr. Oliver Gassmann is a professor of technology management at the University of St. Gallen and the director of the Institute of Technology Management since 2002. His research focus lies on patterns and success factors of innovation. He has been a visiting faculty at Berkeley (2007), Stanford (2012), and Harvard (2016). Prior to his academic career, Gassmann was the head of corporate research at Schindler. His more than 400 publications are highly cited. His book *Business Model Navigator* became a global bestseller. He received the Scholarly Impact Award of the *Journal of Management* in 2014. He founded several spin-offs; is a member of several boards of directors, like Zühlke; and is an internationally recognized keynote speaker.

About Zühlke

1 Empowering Ideas: That Is Our Mission

Zühlke is a global innovation service provider. We believe that innovation and technology are a positive force of change for business and society. Therefore, we support our clients to envision and create a sustainable future.

Innovation requires entrepreneurial vision and the courage to push boundaries and break new ground. This is something of which we as an innovation provider are convinced. And this conviction applies particularly to connected business, seeing as the network economy is putting long-standing business models to the test. To remain competitive, companies have to take an active part in this process and make the most of the opportunities it offers. This transformation means questioning the familiar, learning from other industries and market participants, and using agile methods to move forward. For many established companies, this is easier said than done. Their own histories weigh too heavily, and their mature organizational structures are too restrictive. Collaboration with innovation service providers like *Zühlke* can provide new impetus for developing future-oriented solutions together.

Zühlke helps businesses turn their digital vision in a network economy into a reality—from an ingenious idea to implementation and market success. Along the way, the company covers all the phases of the business innovation process. *Zühlke* has over 1200 experts who help to find, develop, and evaluate new ideas. They support customers so that they can advance rapidly yet securely beyond their familiar patterns of thinking and acting. *Zühlke* draws on its extensive, cross-sectoral expertise of over 50 years and more than 10,000 projects in this.

Zühlke consciously combines expertise in both business and technology. That's because a purely technological mindset isn't enough these days. The changes in the digital and network economy are too comprehensive, too radical. Customers find out what they need to know at any time of day, make purchases through their chosen channel, and expect personalized services. This means that companies have to develop new concepts in production, distribution, communication, and service. And they need integrated, interdisciplinary expertise to do this.

Coming up with ideas is one thing; implementing them is quite another. *Zühlke* is a partner that does both to help companies turn visions and ideas into reality. The company counts on the skills and expertise of its own employees. The *Zühlke Group* continuously invests in training and development. This ensures that the specialist skills relevant to success can seamlessly interact in interdisciplinary teams. In an increasingly networked world where people, machines, and the Internet are moving closer together, this interaction will only become more important.

Zühlke was founded in Switzerland in 1968 and is owned by its partners. *Zühlke Group* is present in Bulgaria, Germany, the UK, Hong Kong, Austria, Portugal, Switzerland, Serbia, Singapore, and Vietnam and supports customers from a broad range of sectors. On top of this, *Zühlke*'s venture capital service offers financing for start-ups in the high-tech field.

www.zuehlke.com

Index

© The Author(s), under exclusive license to Springer Nature Switzerland AG 2021
O. Gassmann, F. Ferrandina (eds.), *Connected Business*,
https://doi.org/10.1007/978-3-030-76897-3

Printed by Printforce, the Netherlands